HISTORIC PHOTOS OF
ALBUQUERQUE

TEXT AND CAPTIONS BY SANDRA FYE

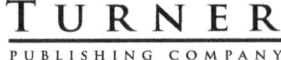

TURNER
PUBLISHING COMPANY

This was how Albuquerque looked in 1916. This aerial view was taken looking east on Central Avenue. Albuquerque High School is in the left background and the University of New Mexico is near the horizon. The Alvarado Hotel is on the right side of the photograph; the YMCA was built to match its architecture.

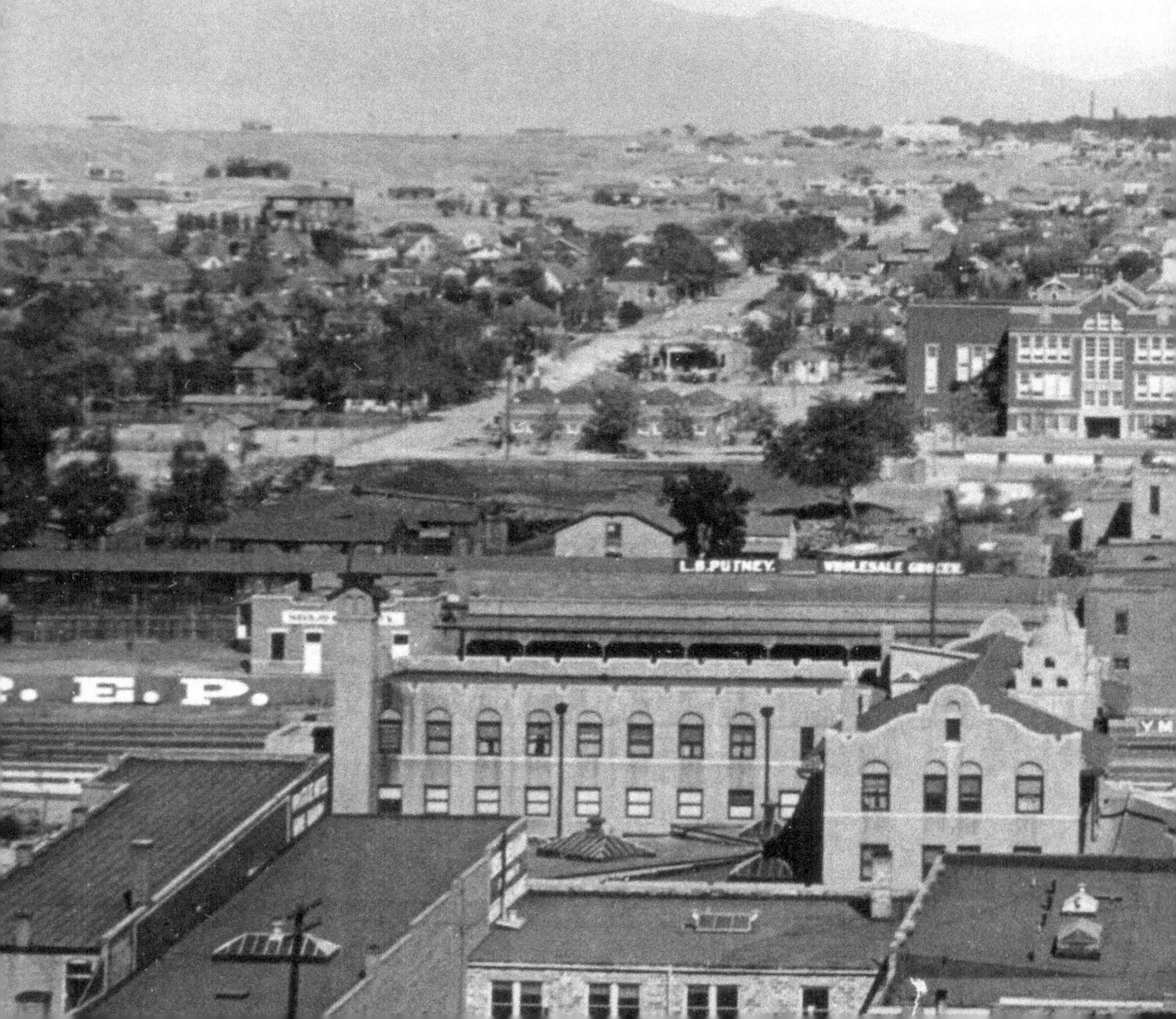

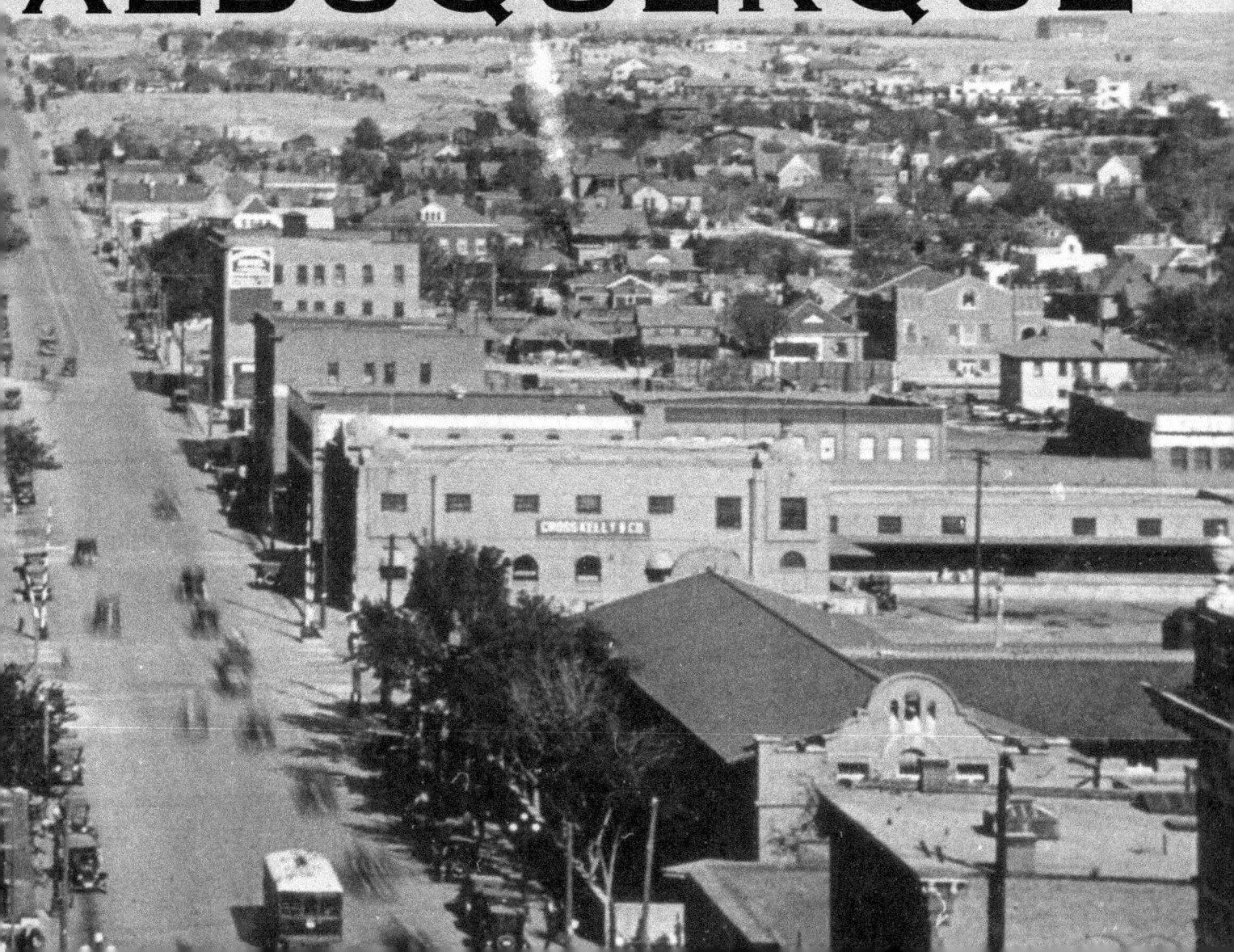

HISTORIC PHOTOS OF
ALBUQUERQUE

Turner Publishing Company
www.turnerpublishing.com

Historic Photos of Albuquerque

Copyright © 2007 Turner Publishing Company

Library of Congress Control Number: 2007923676

ISBN: 978-1-59652-376-0

Printed in the United States of America

ISBN 978-1-68336-963-9 (hc)

CONTENTS

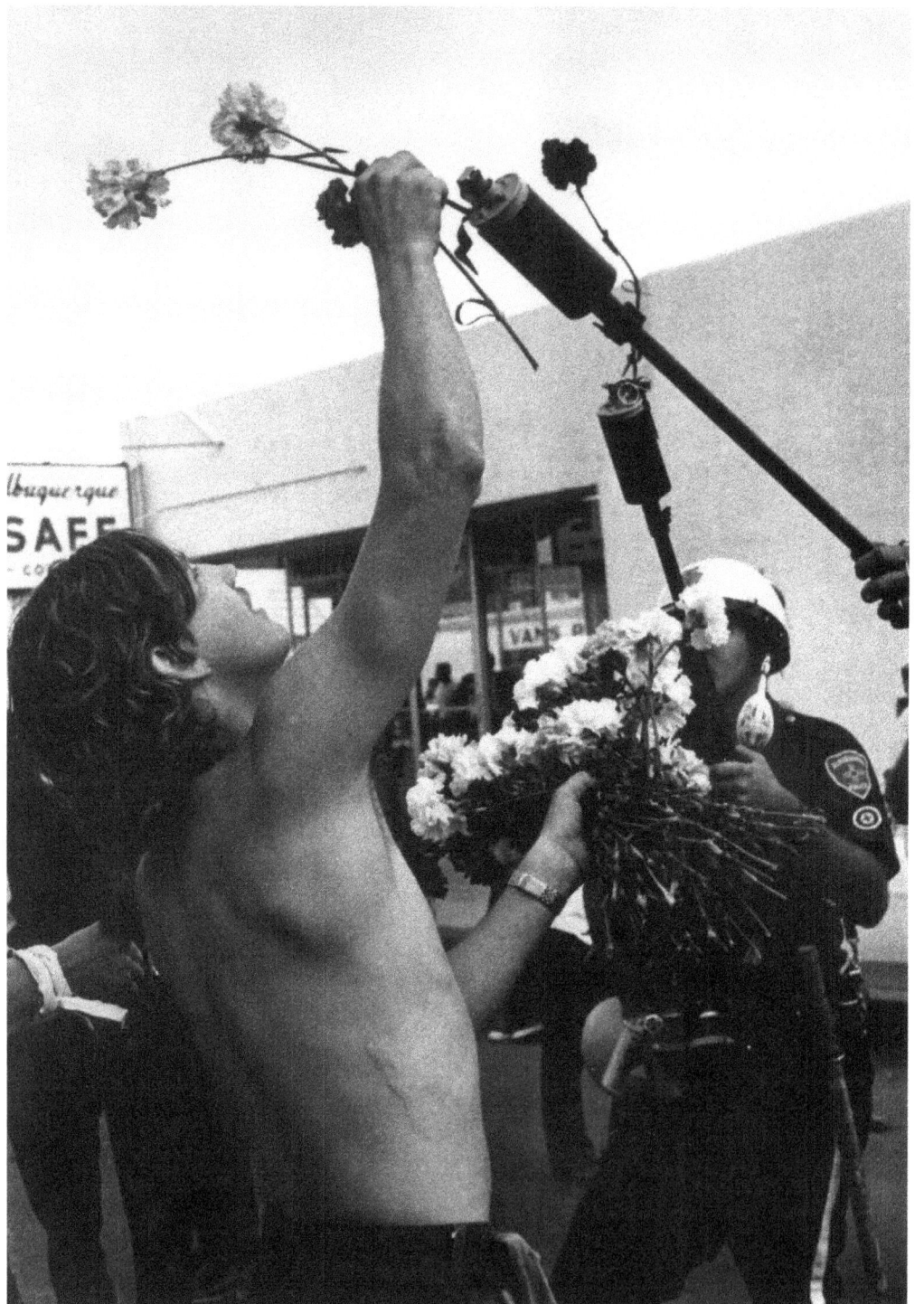

University of New Mexico
student protests the war in
Vietnam in 1972.

ACKNOWLEDGMENTS

This volume, *Historic Photos of Albuquerque* is the result of the cooperation and efforts of many individuals and organizations. It is with great thanks that we acknowledge the valuable contribution of the following for their generous support: the Albuquerque Museum, the University of New Mexico, and the Library of Congress.

A special thanks to the Albuquerque Museum Photoarchive's employees and volunteers, past and present. The University of New Mexico Center for Southwest Research and the Albuquerque Museum have preserved these wonderful photographs for the future. Thank you to the friends who provided encouragement and assistance.

—*Sandra Fye, Author*

This project represents countless hours of review and research. The researchers and writer have reviewed thousands of photographs. We greatly appreciate the generous assistance of the archives listed here, without whom this project could not have been completed.

The goal in publishing the work is to provide broader access to a set of extraordinary photographs. The aim is to inspire, provide perspective, and evoke insight that might assist officials and citizens, who together are responsible for determining Albuquerque's future. In addition, the book seeks to preserve the past with respect and reverence.

With the exception of touching up imperfections caused by the vicissitudes of time and cropping where necessary, no other changes have been made. The focus and clarity of many images is limited to the technology of the day and the skill of the photographer who captured them.

We encourage readers to reflect as they explore Albuquerque, stroll along its streets, or wander its neighborhoods. It is the publisher's hope that in making use of this work, longtime residents will learn something new and that new residents will gain a perspective on where Albuquerque has been, so that each can contribute to its future.

—*Todd Bottorff, Publisher*

PREFACE

Albuquerque just celebrated its 300th birthday, but the Petroglyph National Monument has iconography from prehistoric times. Pueblo villages were in the area by about 1300. The Villa de Alburquerque was founded in 1706, when New Mexico was one of Spain's colonies. The acting governor of New Mexico, Don Francisco Cuervo y Valdes, named it after the Viceroy of New Spain, the Duke of Alburquerque (note the additional "r"), and made San Francisco de Xavier its patron saint, but Cuervo y Valdes had created the villa without authority and was ordered to change the patron saint to San Felipe. Under Spanish administration, Albuquerque's status as a villa made it a center of defense and government.

The first San Felipe de Neri Church was built at this time, of adobe, and was on the west side of the plaza. It collapsed, and today's church was built in 1793. The *acequia madre* (mother ditch) was about fifty yards east of the plaza and diverted water from the Rio Grande. Most of the early structures were one-story adobes with small windows and doors. Life along the Rio Grande centered around family, religion, and agriculture. All the families shared common grazing land.

In 1821, Mexico declared independence from Spain and opened trade with the United States. Albuquerque developed as a commercial trade center with the opening of the Santa Fe Trail. Merchants arrived with cloth, books, china, and other items. Craftsmen moved to the area.

General Stephen Watts Kearny and his forces marched into Albuquerque in September 1846, during the war between the United States and Mexico, and raised the American flag in the plaza. He had a civilian government set up within a month. A regiment of soldiers was stationed in Albuquerque, which brought a cash economy to the area. Hotels and saloons opened, merchants opened stores, and soldiers stayed after they were discharged.

News of the railroad coming brought growth in 1879. When the railroad arrived in 1880, the track was laid more than a mile east of Old Town. Growth started around the depot. The buildings were brick and frame. Professional photographers living in Albuquerque recorded the early building boom.

The main photographers of the time were Emma Albright, W. Calvin Brown, William Walton, Ben Wittick, William Henry Jackson, William Henry Cobb and his wife, Eddie Ross Cobb. William Henry Cobb bought W. Calvin Brown's photo studio in 1889. He married Eddie Ross, the daughter of U.S. Senator Edmund G. Ross, in 1891 and she helped in the business. After Cobb died in 1909, she ran the studio until her retirement, at 80 years old, in 1942. The Cobb Studio Collection of historic photographs of Albuquerque includes pictures from four other pre-1900 photographic studios.

Alabama Milner came to Albuquerque in 1918 and worked with William Walton at his studio. She bought Walton's studio in 1919 and moved to the Barnett Building, where she remained until she sold her business in 1958. Alabama Milner's brother, Algernon Milner, worked at the studio and did photography for the University of New Mexico yearbook. These early photographers left a wonderful visual record of a unique city of the Southwest and its multicultural residents.

The C. W. Lewis Building in Old Town, with an ox cart and driver in front of the Territorial style building. The 1897 city directory says Charles W. Lewis owned the Western Homestead and Irrigation Company and lived in Old Town Albuquerque.

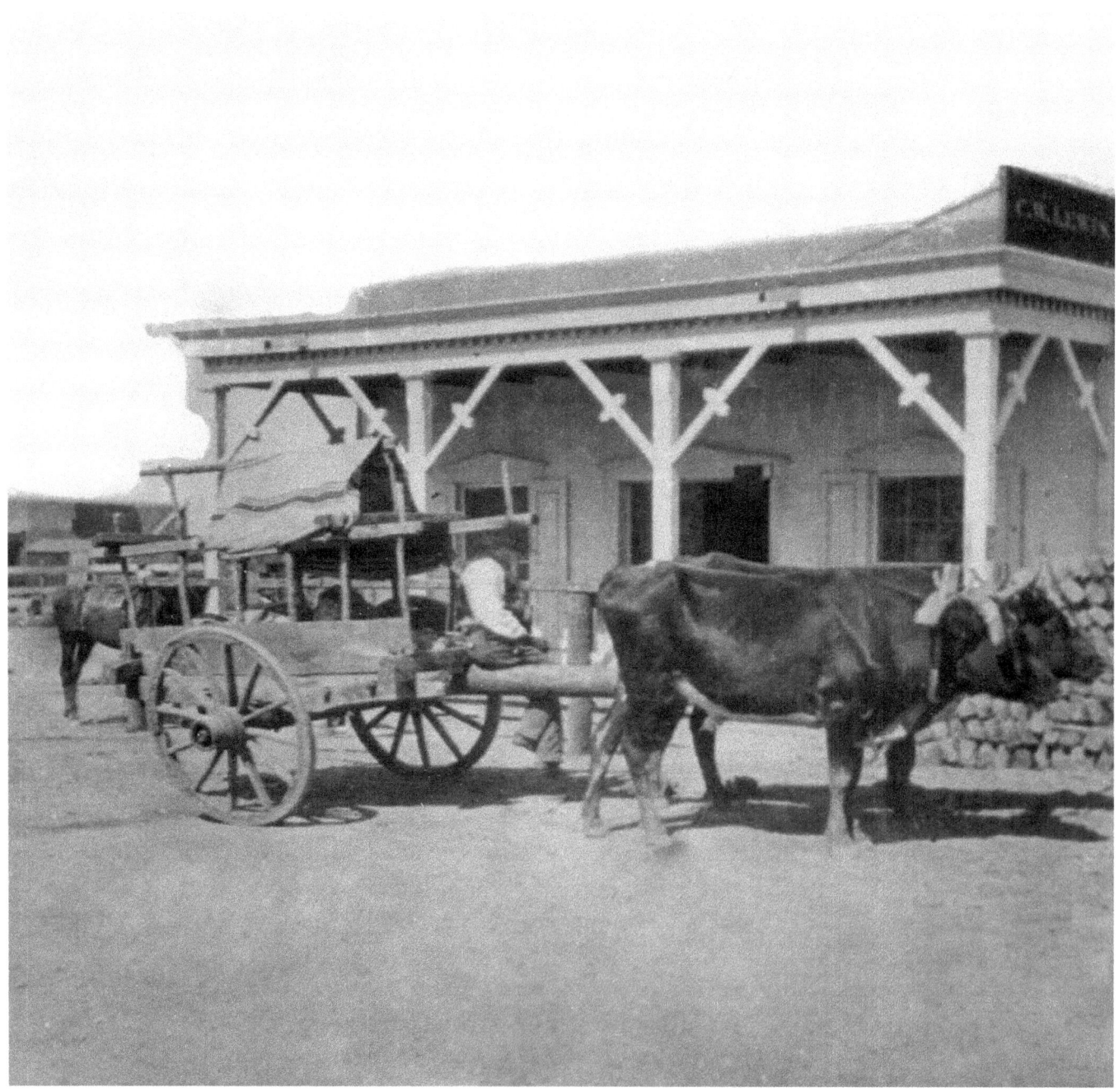

The Railroad Boom Years

(1880–1899)

In 1880, Albuquerque was about to be transformed. The arrival of the Atlantic and Pacific Railroad, a subsidiary of the Atchison, Topeka and Santa Fe (AT&SF) Railway, brought people of many different cultures and changed the economy. The town became a shipping center for livestock, wool, and lumber. The rails were laid a mile and a half from the town plaza. Most new businesses opened near the railway, and even some existing ones moved closer to the tracks. The two areas became known as Old Town and New Town. Some new businesses were opened near Old Town Plaza, such as saloons and Herman Blueher's Market Garden.

The Bernalillo County Courthouse and Jail were also erected near the plaza. The Territorial Fair was held in Old Town, starting in 1881. Wagon freighters came to the area to move the goods from the railroad to other communities. The Armijo House and the San Felipe Hotel opened to house travelers. Banks and Wells Fargo and Company opened, and the Albuquerque Street Railroad operated between Old Town and New Town. Offices opened for doctors, lawyers, newspapers, real estate, insurance, apothecaries, and builders.

The Commercial Club formed to promote Albuquerque, sponsoring social events and dances. Booster booklets were printed to lure businesses and travelers. Mercantile shops opened and wholesale businesses developed. Some men moved entire prefabricated buildings on the railroad to set up businesses; these were called "perhaps houses." Education became a priority as more people from the East and Midwest moved in. Fire and police departments were started, and the Albuquerque Public Library was formed. The Catholic Church was the first church in the area, but after 1880 other faiths started congregations. Public education facilities were set up, first by the churches, then by the city.

The AT&SF set up major repair and administration facilities; the railroad business office reported receipts of over a million dollars in 1882. A foundry and machine works opened to do work for the railroad. The Southwestern Brewery and Ice Company manufactured beer and ice for saloons and homes. Utility companies were set up. The historic town of Albuquerque was becoming a city.

Looking north on Romero Street in Old Town in the 1880s. The building
on the right is the Sister Blandina Convent. The brick building is the
Florencio Zamora Grocery Store and Post Office. In 1913 Charles Mann
bought the store. It is now the Old Town Basket and Rug Shop.

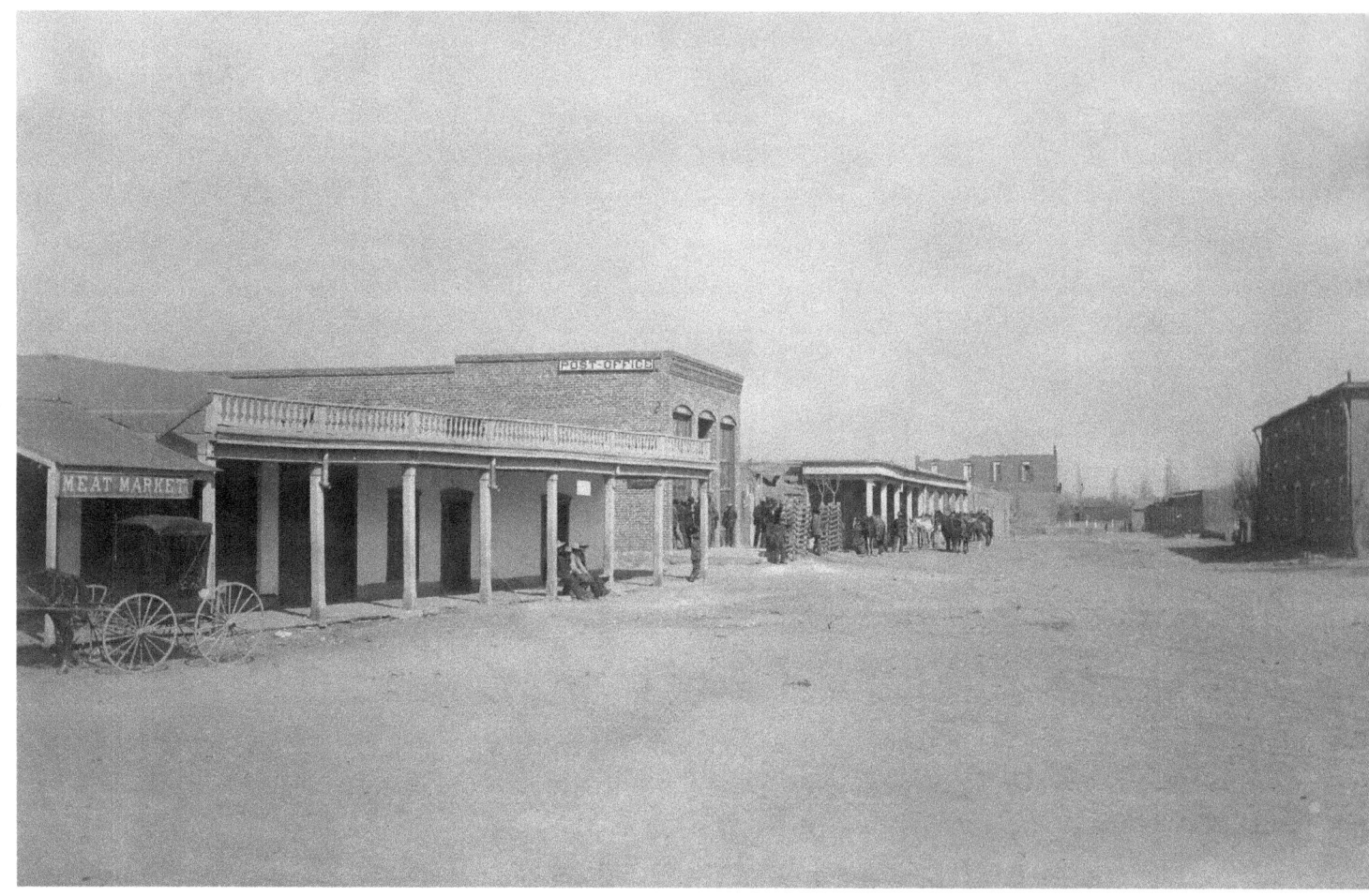

An early view of the San Felipe de Neri Church, with a fiesta in progress. The church has been in Old Town since 1706, but this building was constructed in 1793. The first baptism recorded was June 21, 1706. The San Felipe de Neri Church still has fiestas.

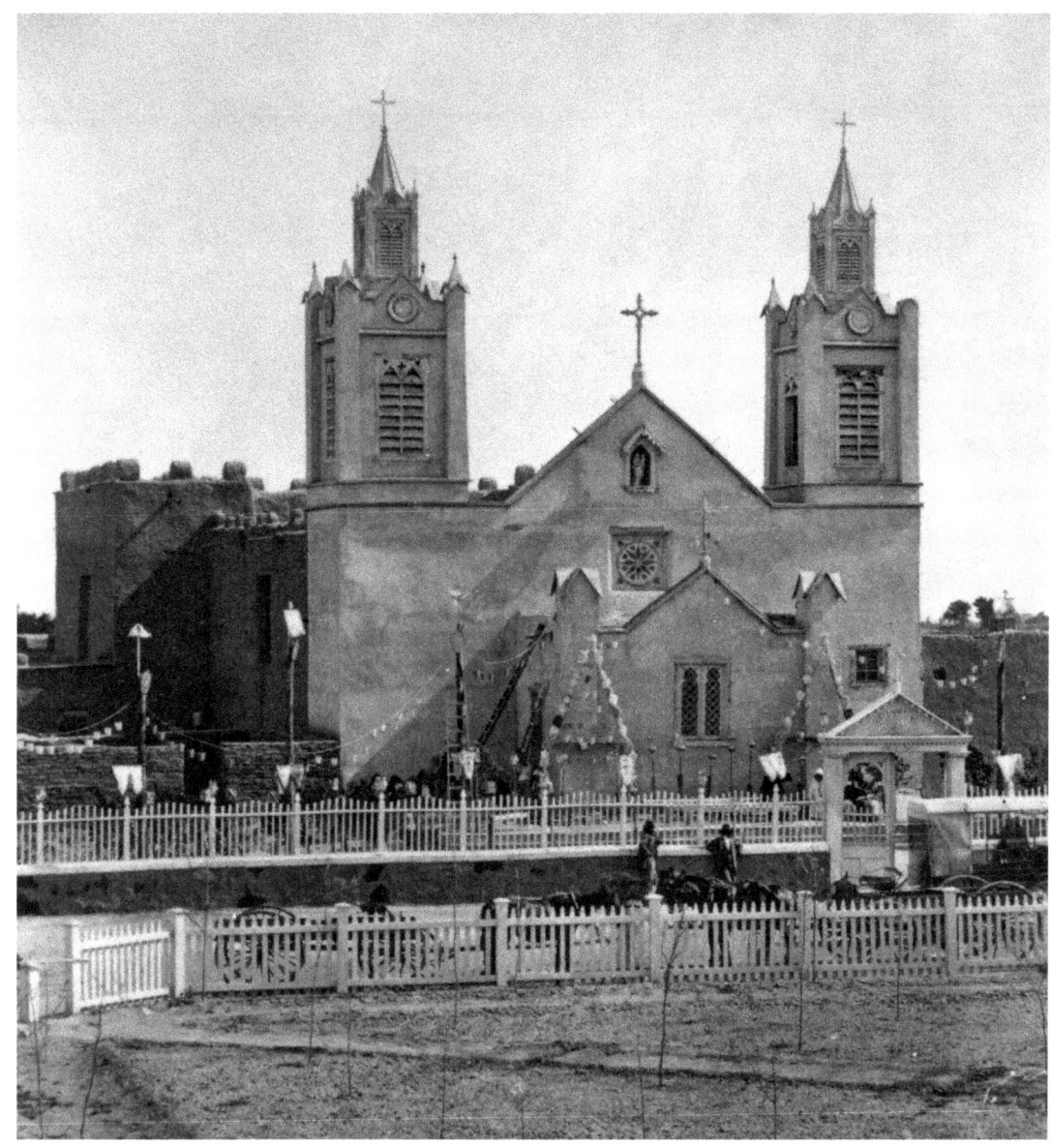

The Armijo House was the first luxury hotel in Albuquerque. It opened in 1881 on the corner of Railroad Avenue and South Third Street. It was built with wood and adobe for $25,000. Wyatt Earp, Doc Holliday and Pat Garrett stayed there. It was destroyed by fire on February 10, 1897.

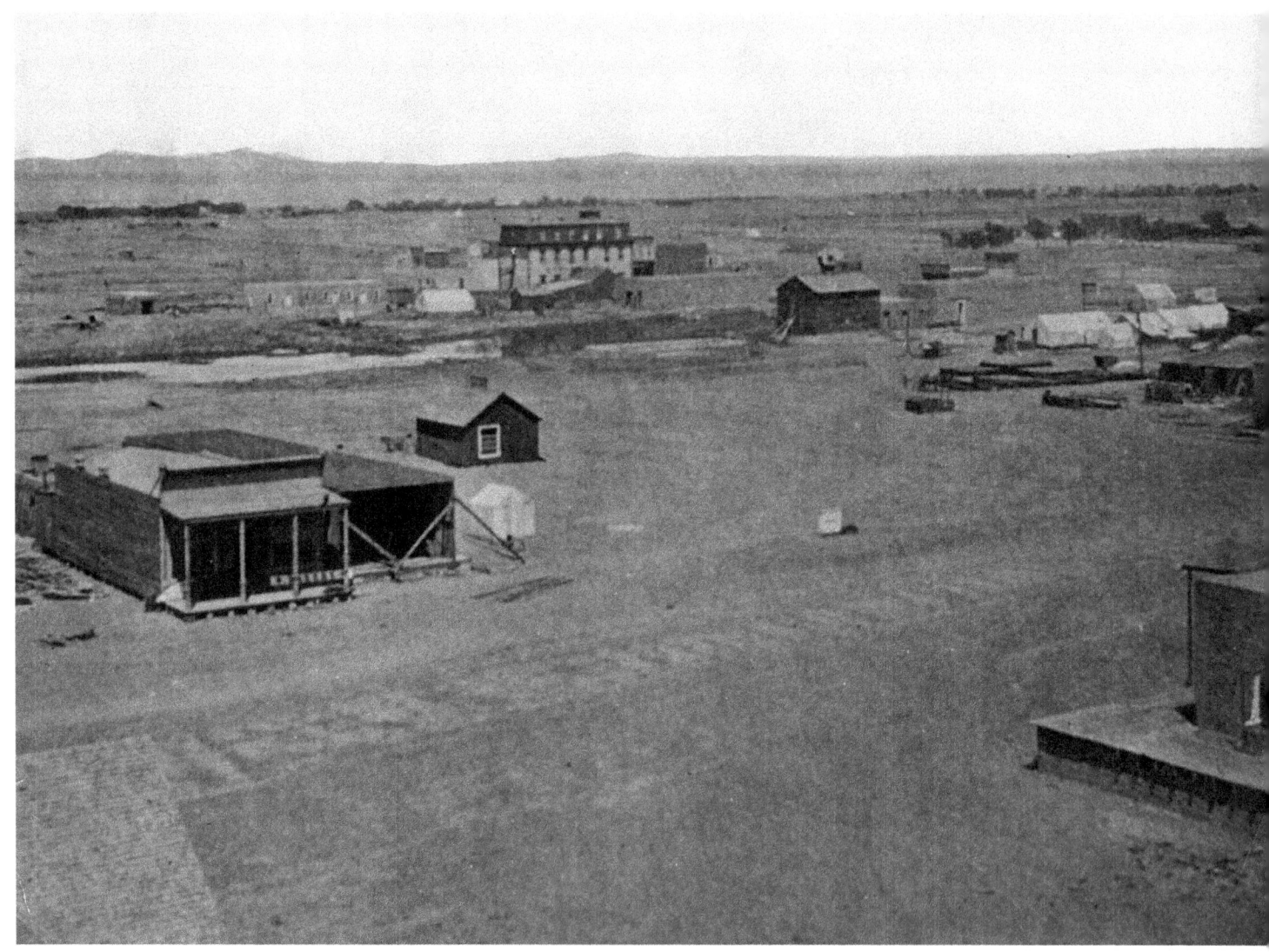

The bridge across the Rio Grande connected Albuquerque and Atrisco. It was completed in 1882 and had a span of 600 feet. A tollhouse was in the middle of it. Passage cost five cents per person. The bridge was washed away by floodwaters in 1891.

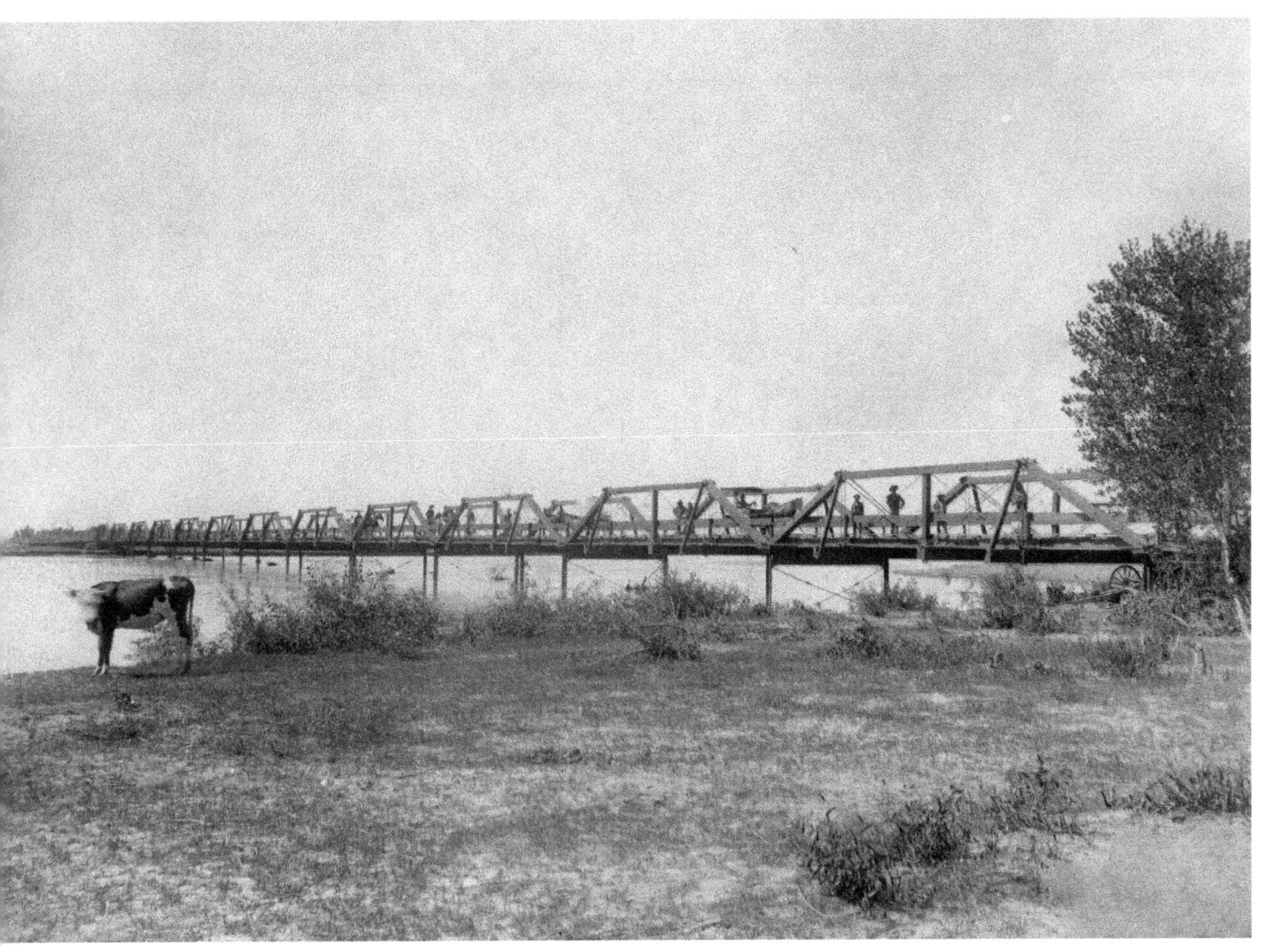

The Atlantic and Pacific Railroad Company received a charter from Congress in 1866 to build the railroad from Springfield, Missouri, to San Francisco, California. After many complications, the Atlantic and Pacific became a subsidiary of the Atchison, Topeka and Santa Fe Railway and finally reached Albuquerque in April 1880.

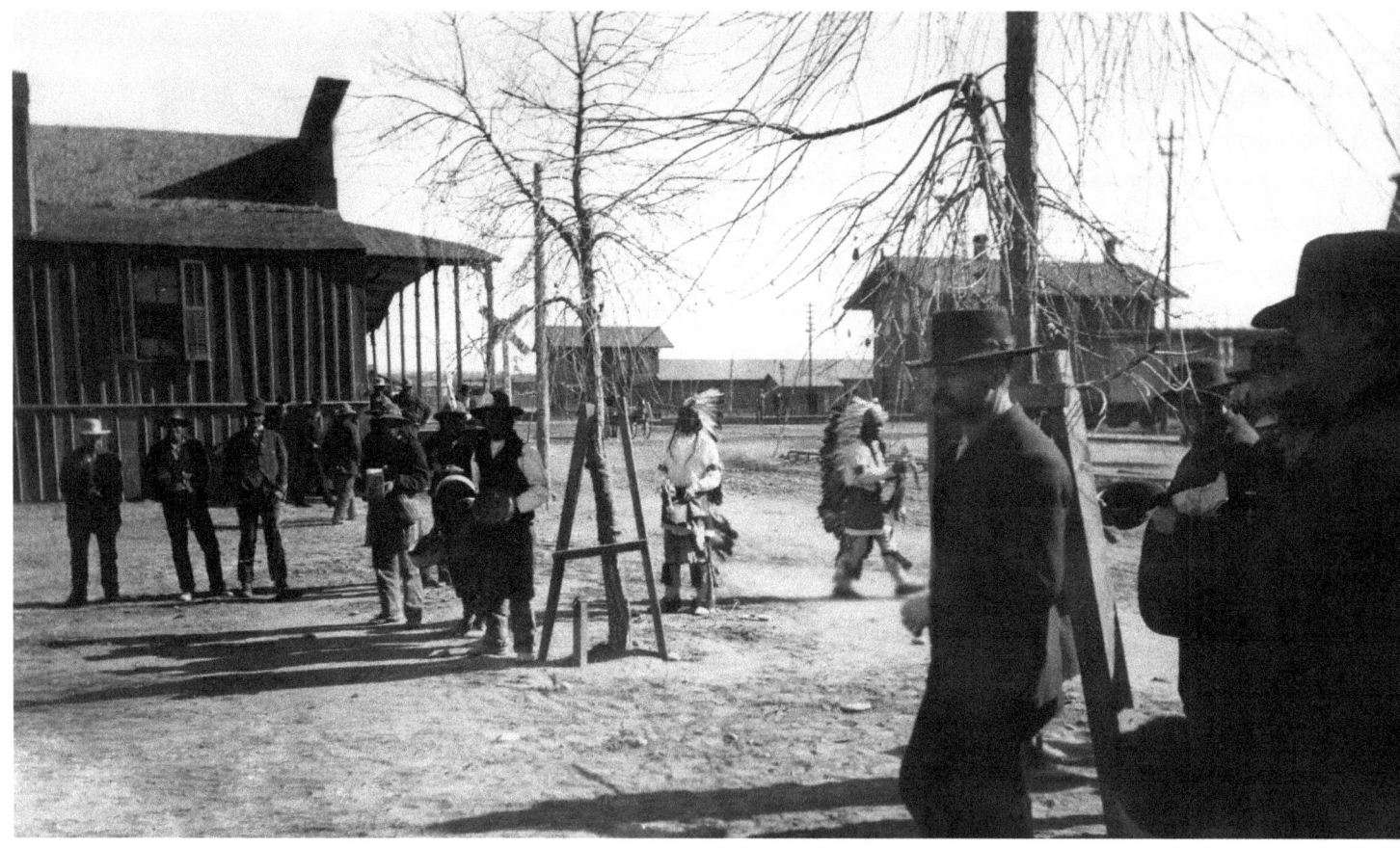

The Metropolitan Hotel and Saloon was at Railroad Avenue and First Street. The horse-drawn and mule-drawn streetcars operated in Albuquerque from 1881 until 1904. Butt's Drugs took over the location after Prohibition was enacted. Railroad Avenue, which became Central Avenue, was a main thoroughfare for shoppers and business people.

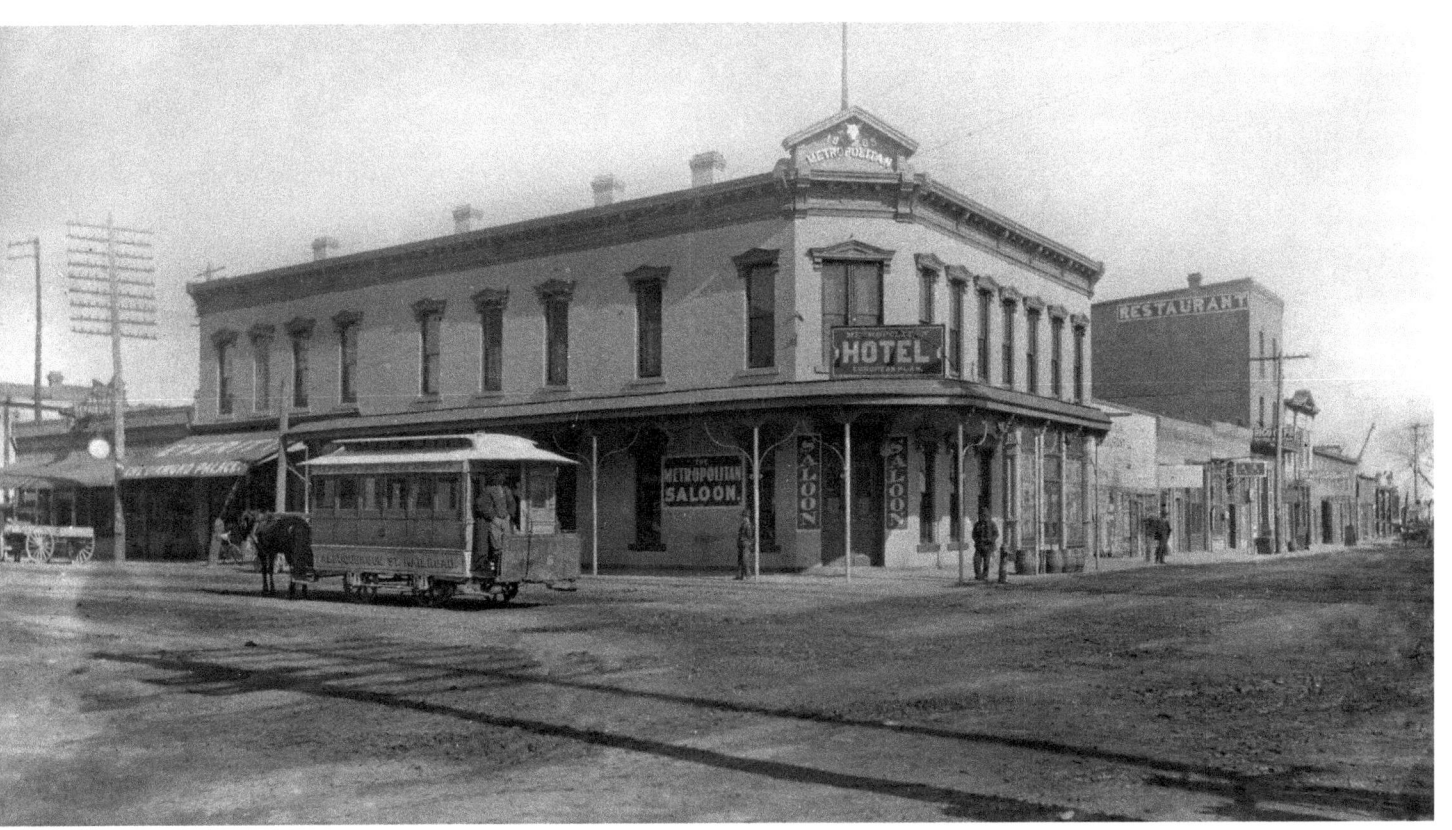

This is thought to be the old Barelas schoolhouse. Barelas was an early Hispanic community settled around the acequia madre (mother ditch) and was a farming area. The Sisters of Charity opened day schools in Barelas, Old Town, and Los Duranes, under the guidance of Sister Blandina Segale.

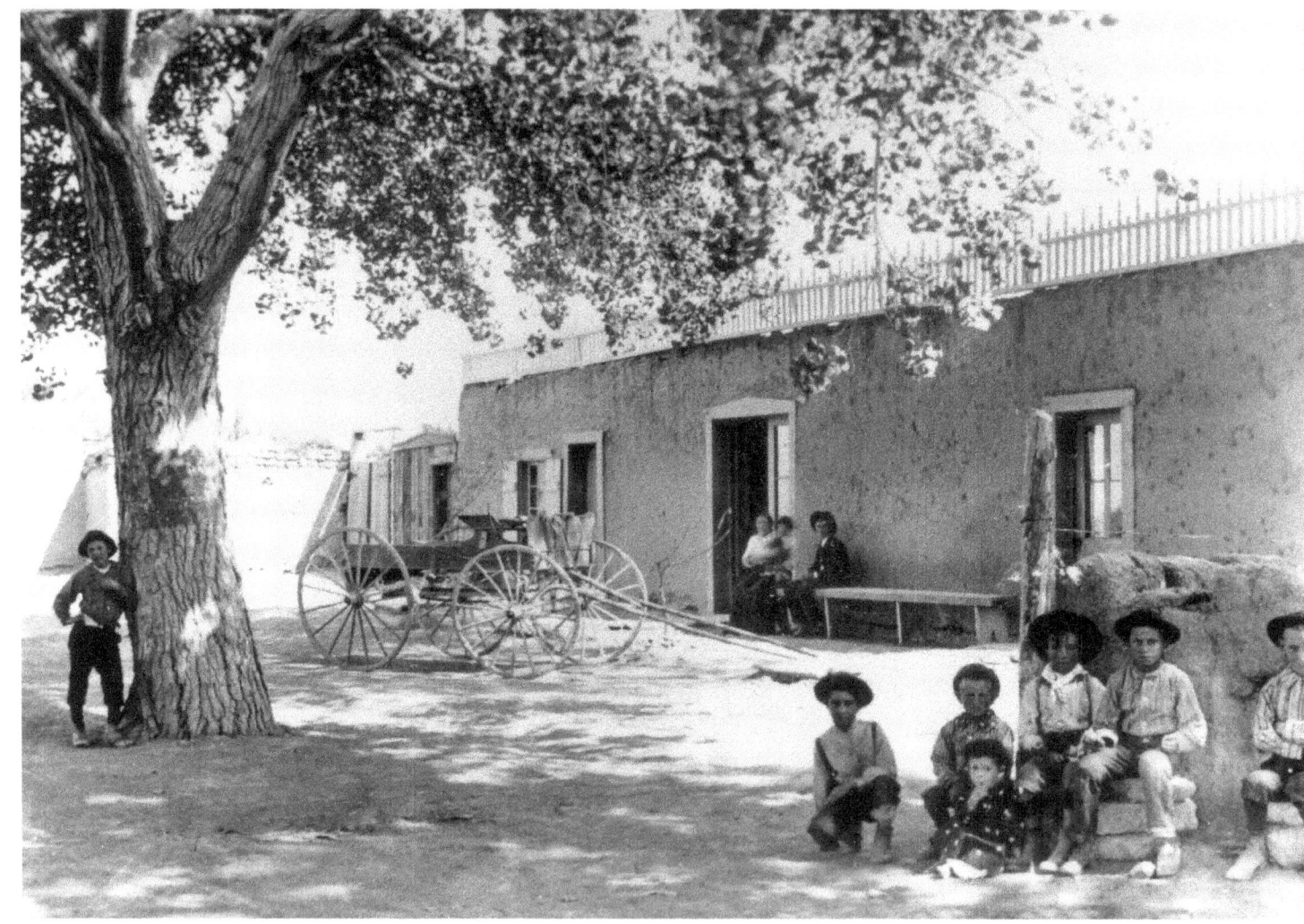

Looking southwest along First Street and Railroad Avenue. The building on the left is Harsch's Coyote Bottling Works, which bottled mineral water, the favorite whiskey chaser in local saloons. Harsch also opened the first New Town bakery. The horse-drawn trolley is going between Old Town and New Town. The Albuquerque Museum owns one of these trolleys.

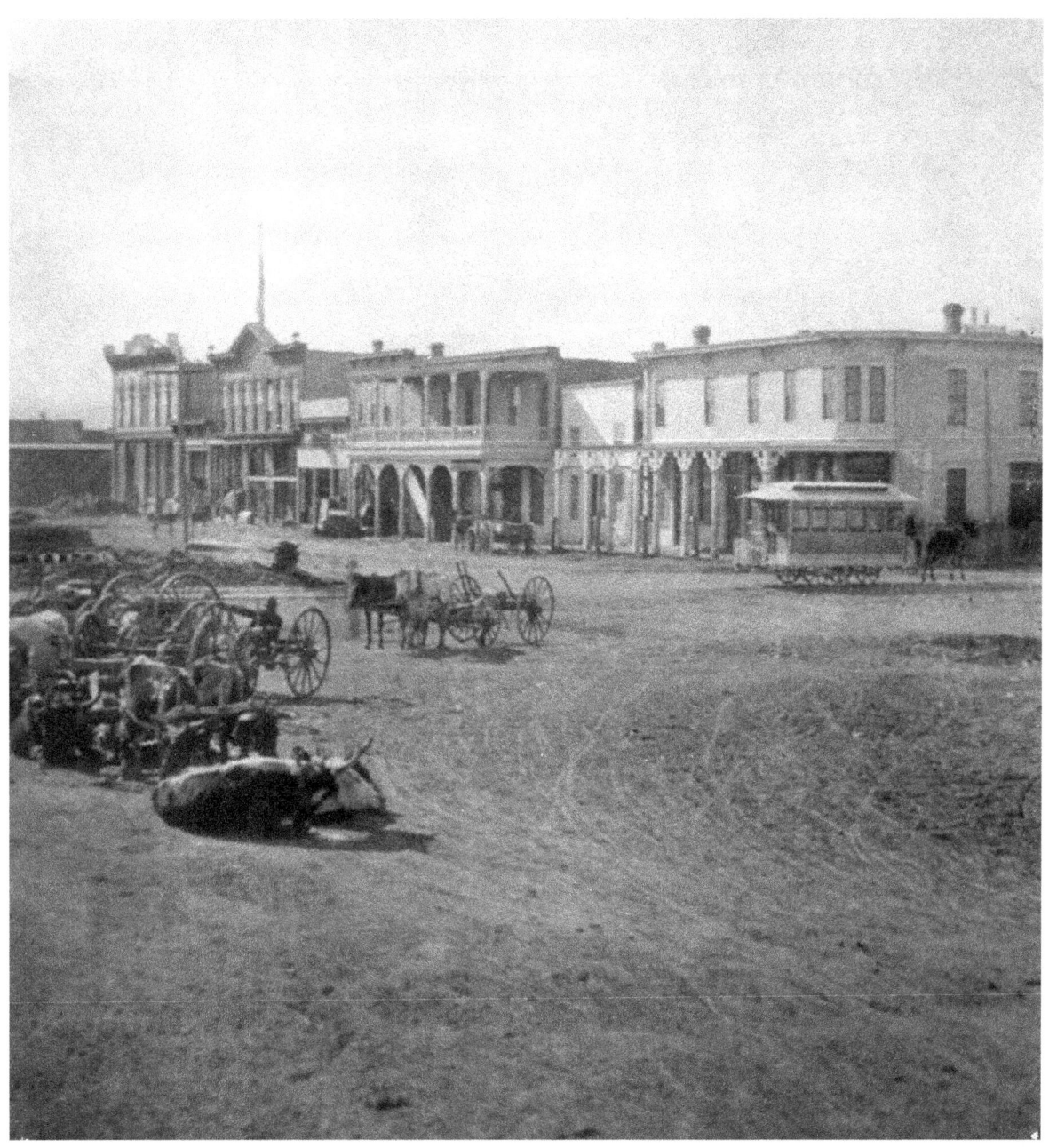

The Central Bank opened in 1878, on the southwest corner of the Old Town Plaza.
In 1881 construction was started on this building at Second Street and Gold Avenue.
The president of the bank was Jefferson Raynolds, who with his brother bought out the
First National Bank of Albuquerque and changed the name of the Central Bank to First
National. The bank was at Second and Gold until 1922.

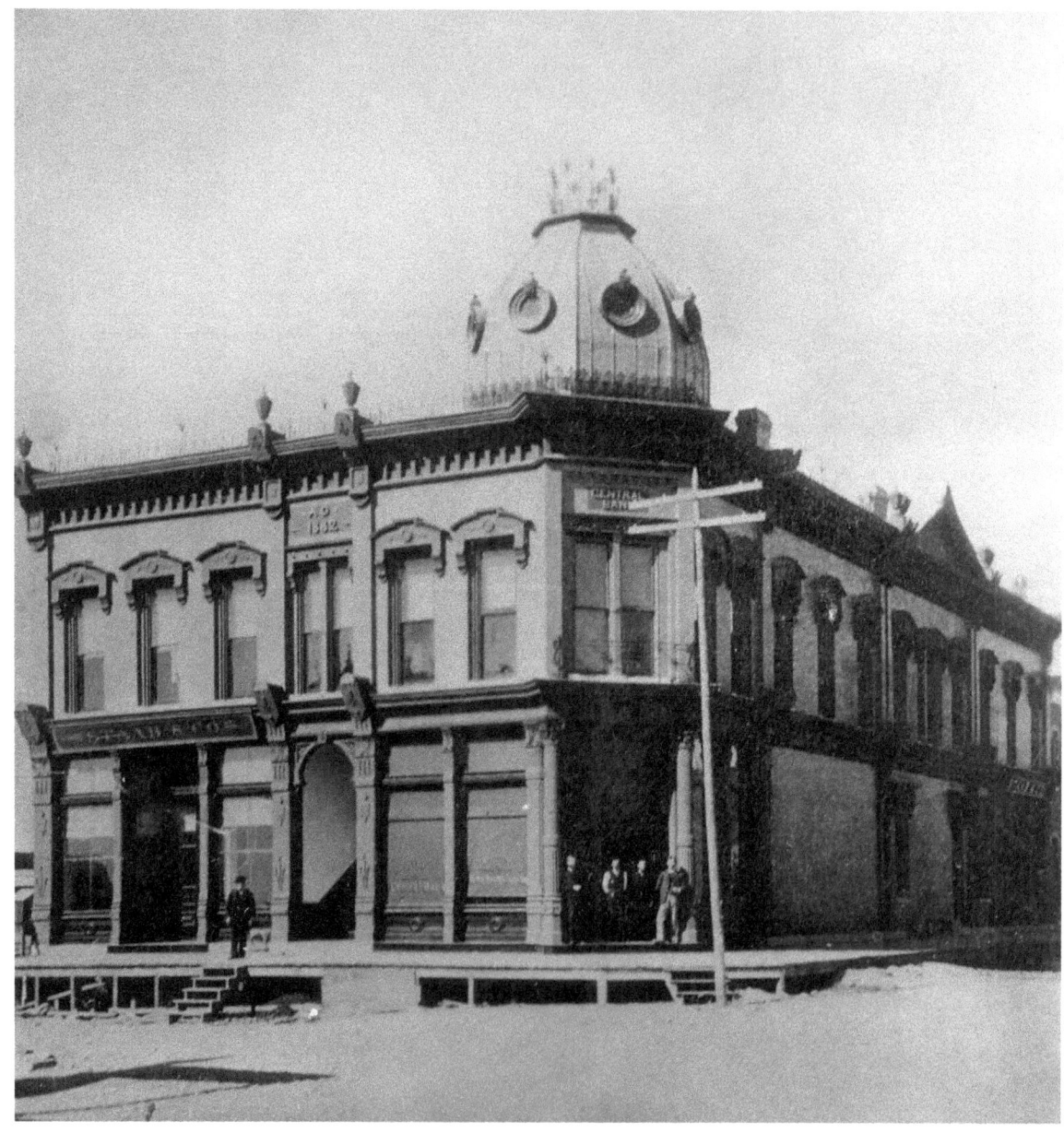

Albuquerque's first balloon flight was during the Territorial Fair of 1882. On July 4, the Elite Saloon owner, "Professor" Park Van Tassel, ascended from a vacant lot. He reached an altitude of 14,207 feet and landed in an Old Town cornfield. The balloon was named "City of Albuquerque" and took two days to inflate.

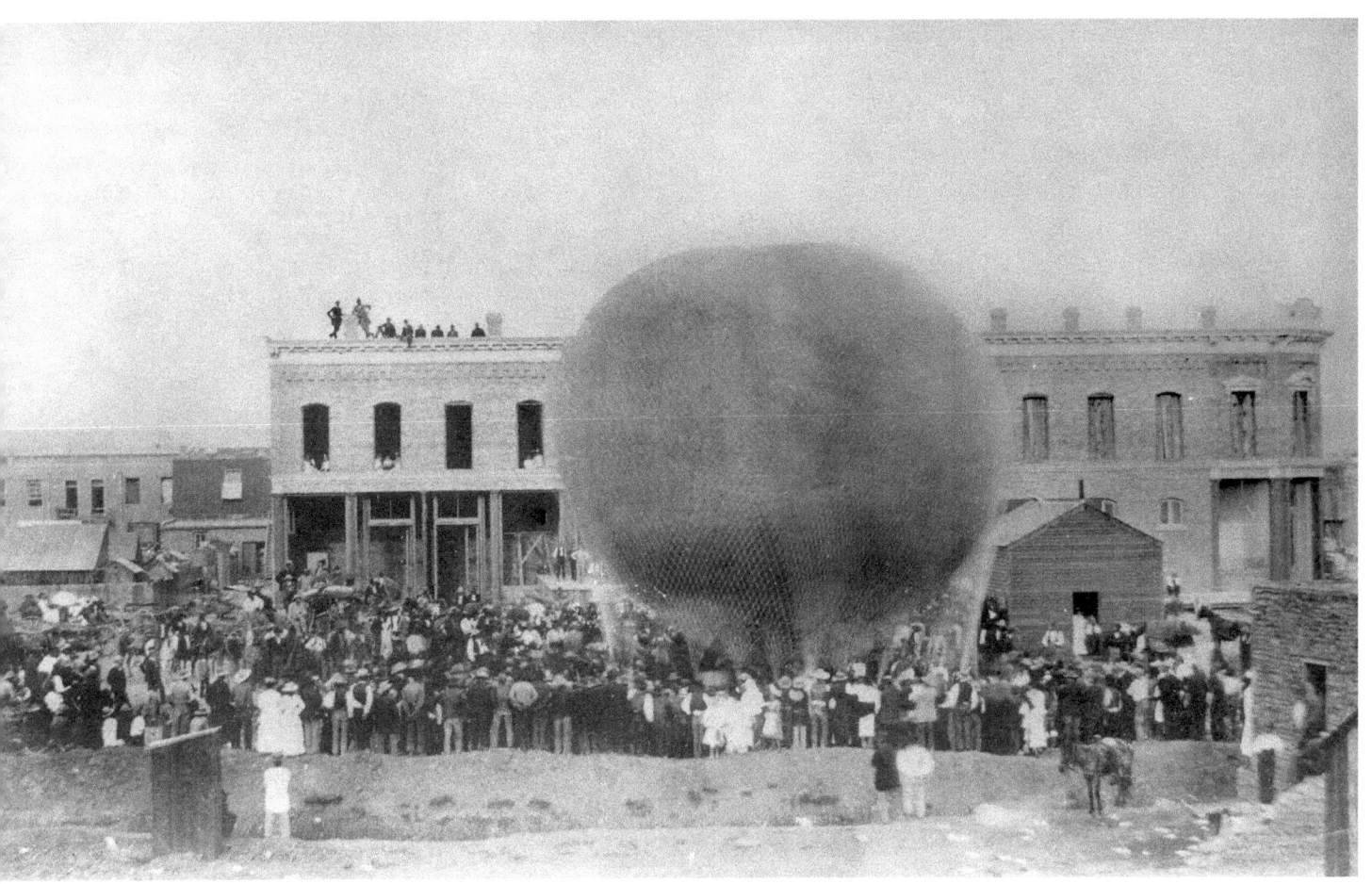

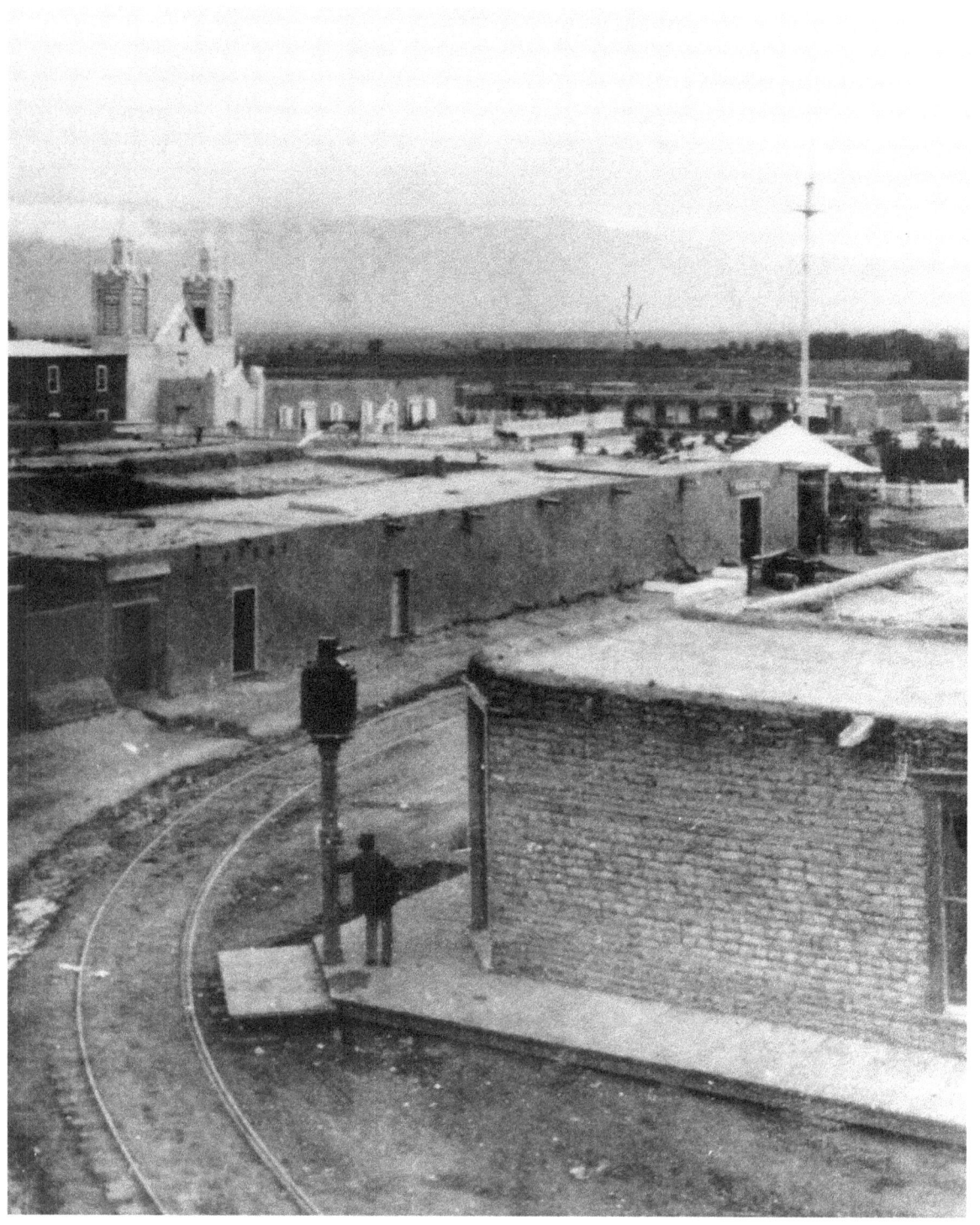

This man is waiting at Main and James streets for the streetcar to New Town. Albuquerque Street Railroad, the horse-drawn streetcar, took passengers between Old Town and New Town for ten cents. It was a big success. San Felipe de Neri Church can be seen in the background.

The Albuquerque Indian School was started in 1881, by the Presbyterian Church, in a rented adobe house in Los Duranes. It was there from January 1, 1881, to October 1882, when a new school was built at Twelfth Street and Indian School Road. The U. S. government took over the school in 1886. The children were taught agricultural methods and domestic skills such as tailoring.

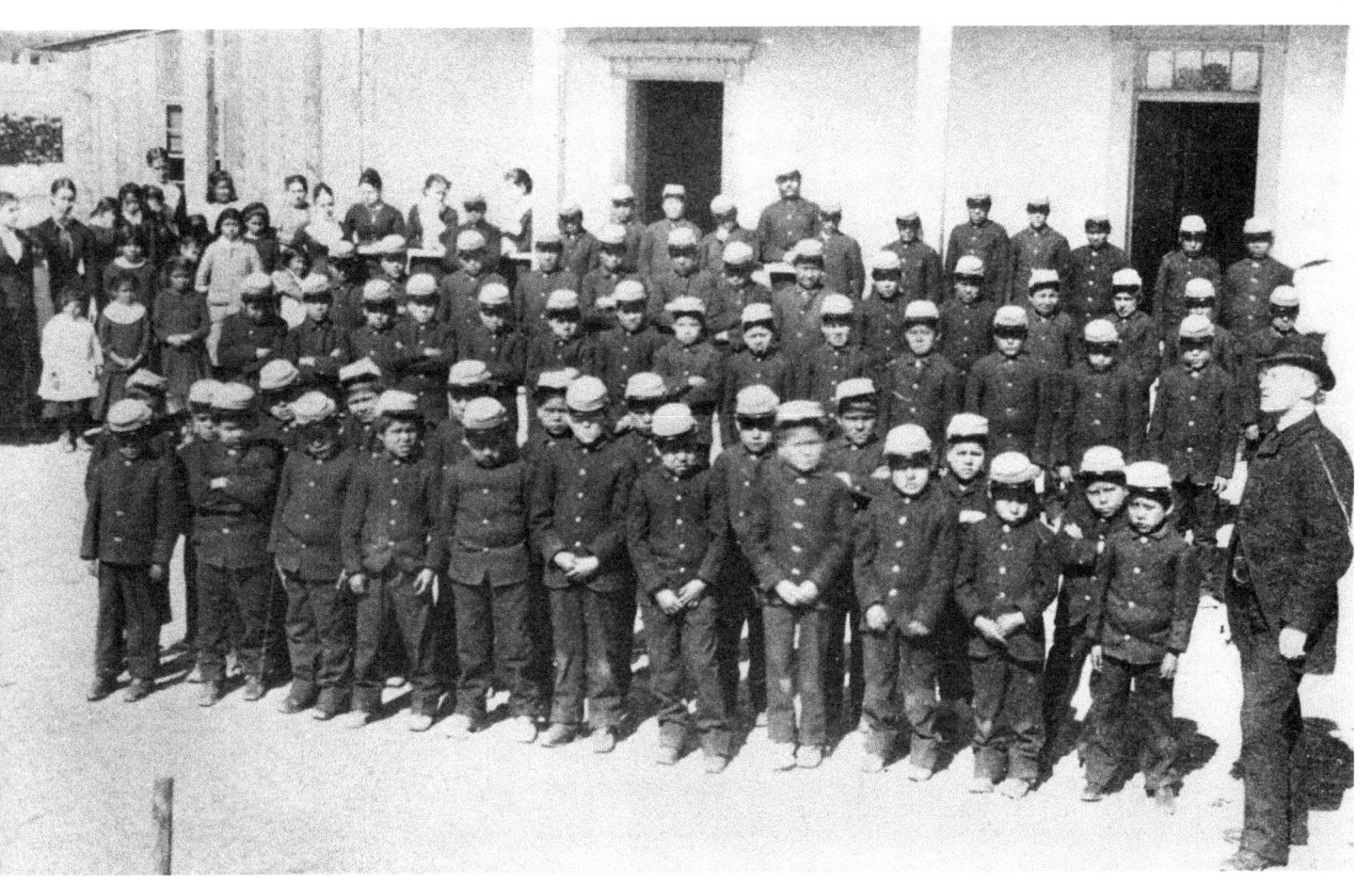

Looking north on First Street from Gold Avenue. From the left are Spiegelberg's Dry Goods Store, the First National Bank, and Whitney Hardware. Beyond the carriage is the European Hotel, one of the "perhaps houses." If the business was not successful, the prefabricated building could be dismantled and moved.

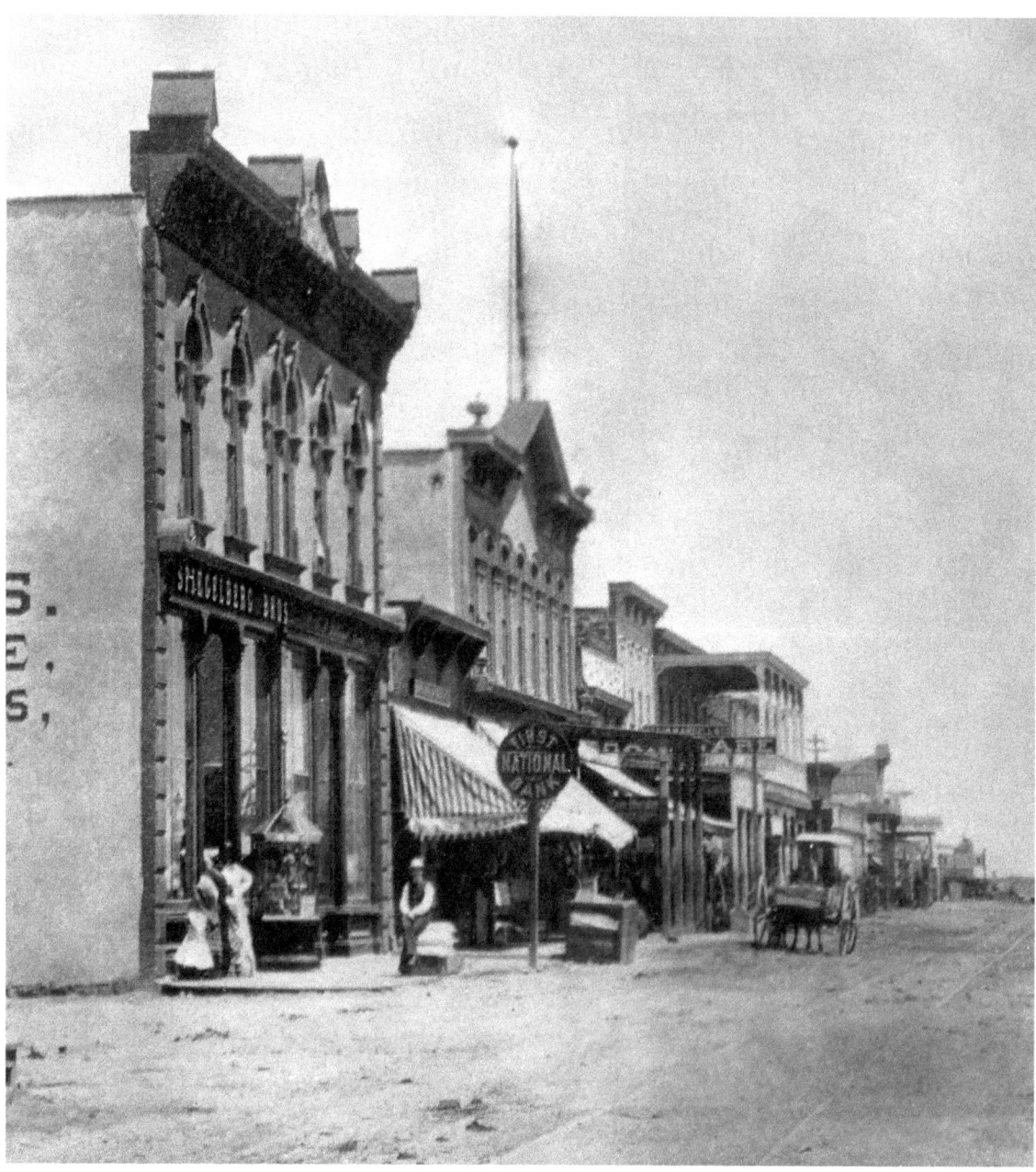

Looking west across Huning's Highland Addition, which was east of the railroad tracks, facing the depot. It was a prestigious area. Franz Huning was the main backer. By 1888, 63 percent of the lots were sold. The houses were mainly Victorian in style, and middle-class professionals lived there.

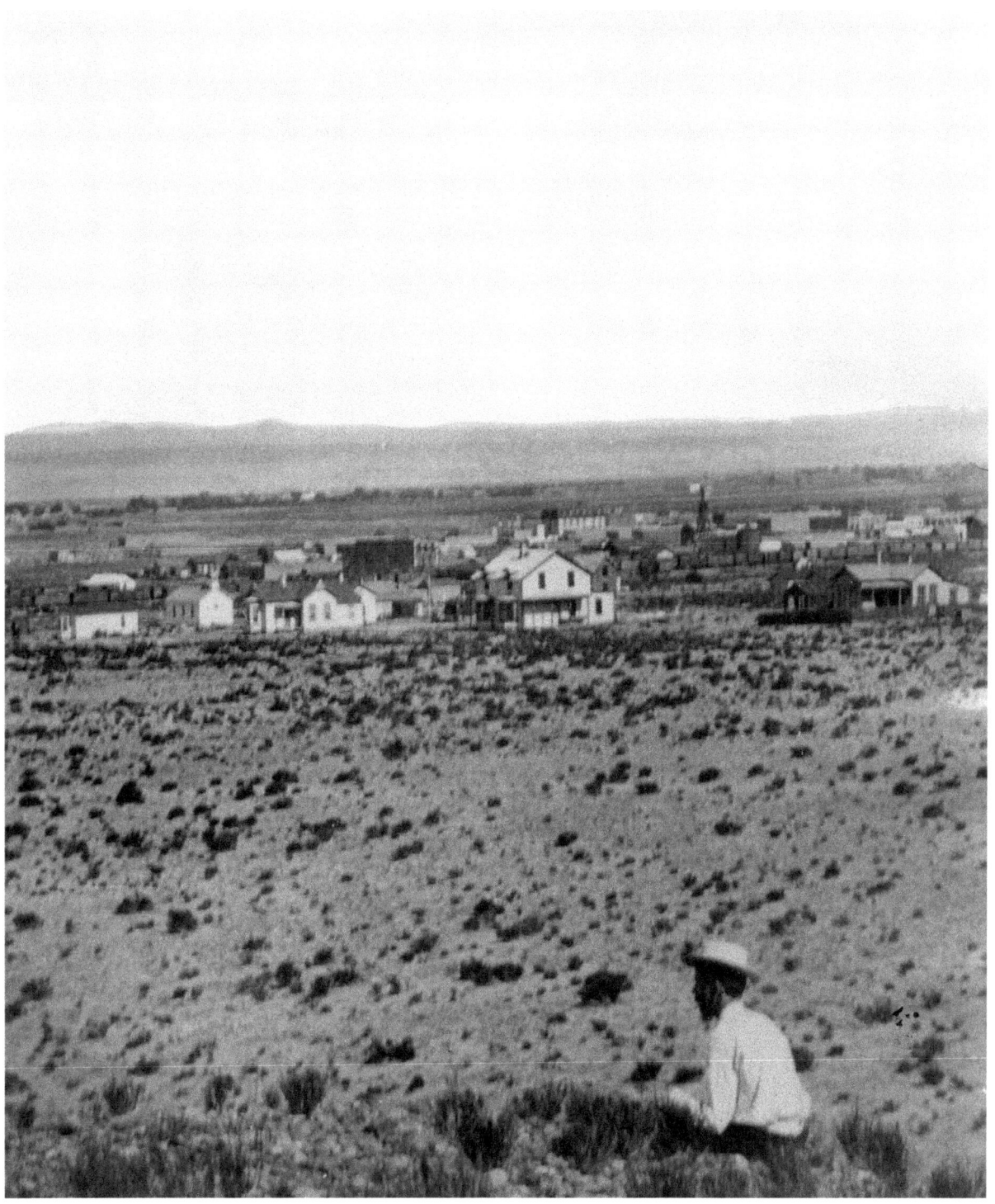

The Cromwell Building was built in 1882 and housed the Albuquerque National Bank downstairs and the Jesse M. Wheelock Real Estate and Insurance office upstairs. Oliver Cromwell moved to Albuquerque in 1879 and invested in real estate. He was the president of the Albuquerque Street Railway Company, which operated cars pulled by mules and horses.

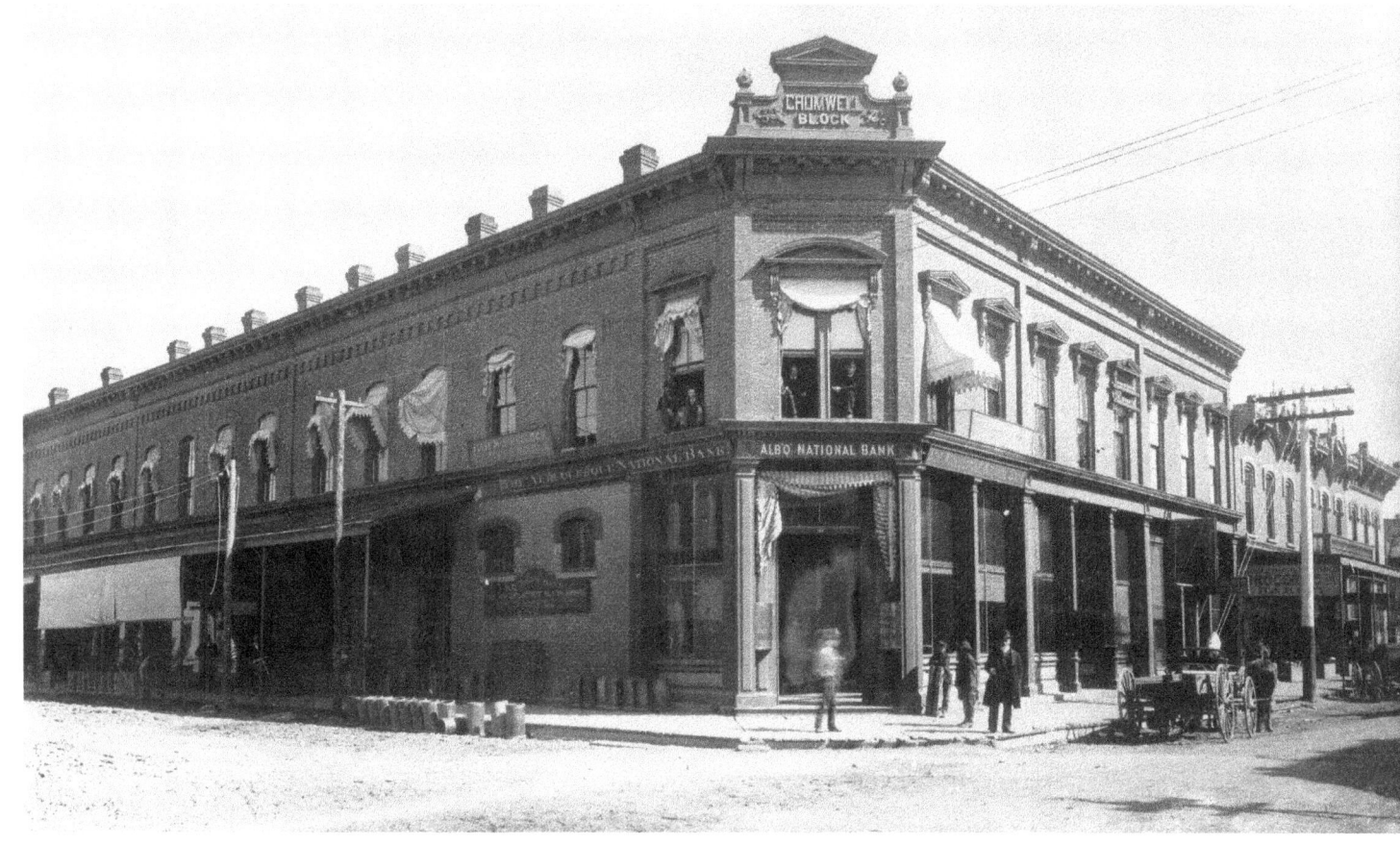

Looking north at sewer construction on Second Street in 1891. The Central Bank is on the left center and the Cromwell Building is across the street, near the *Daily Democrat*. The newspaper was started by J. G. Albright in 1882, when he moved his press from Santa Fe.

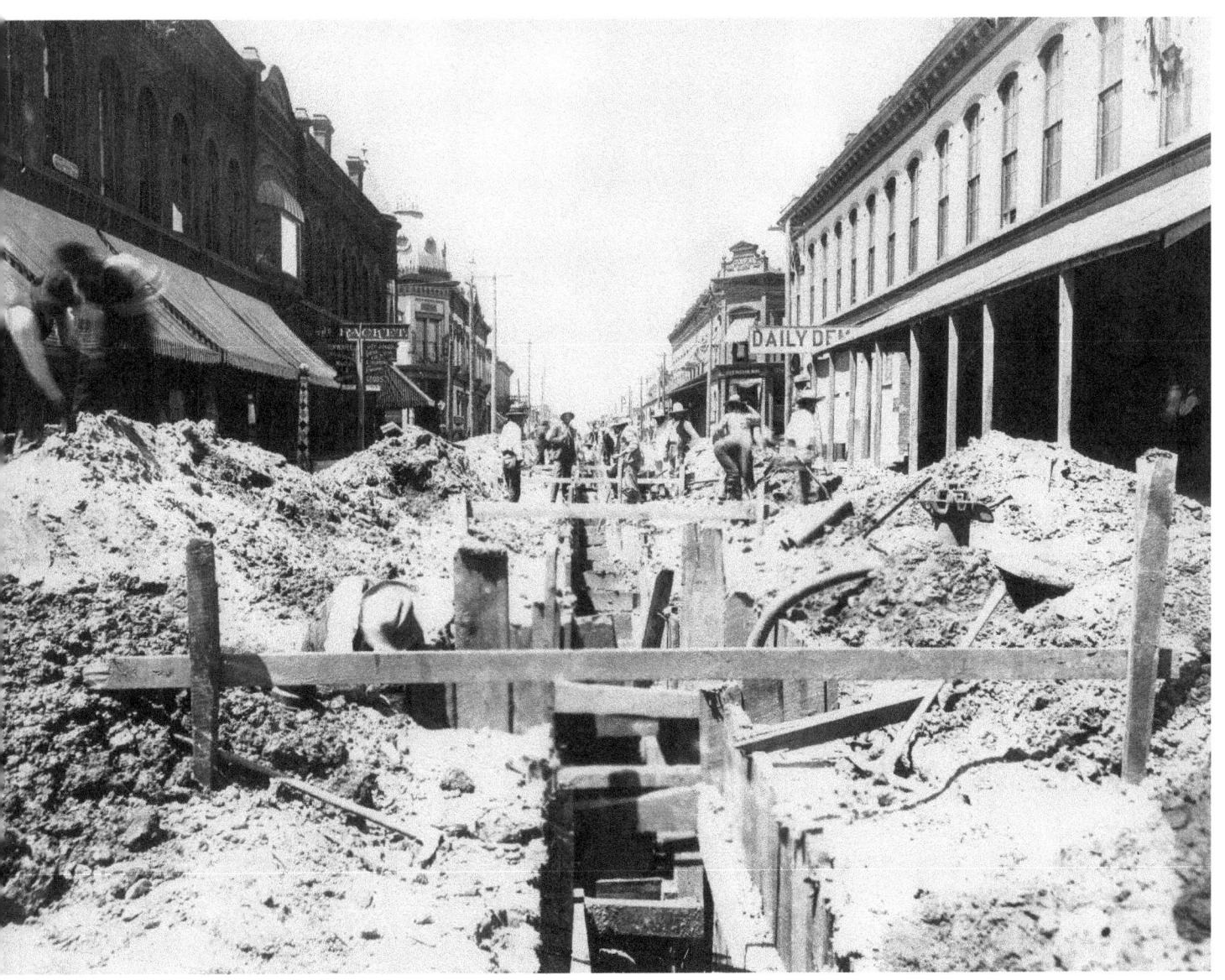

A. E. Walker Lumber Company, at First Street and Marquette. This was one of the first lumber companies in Albuquerque.

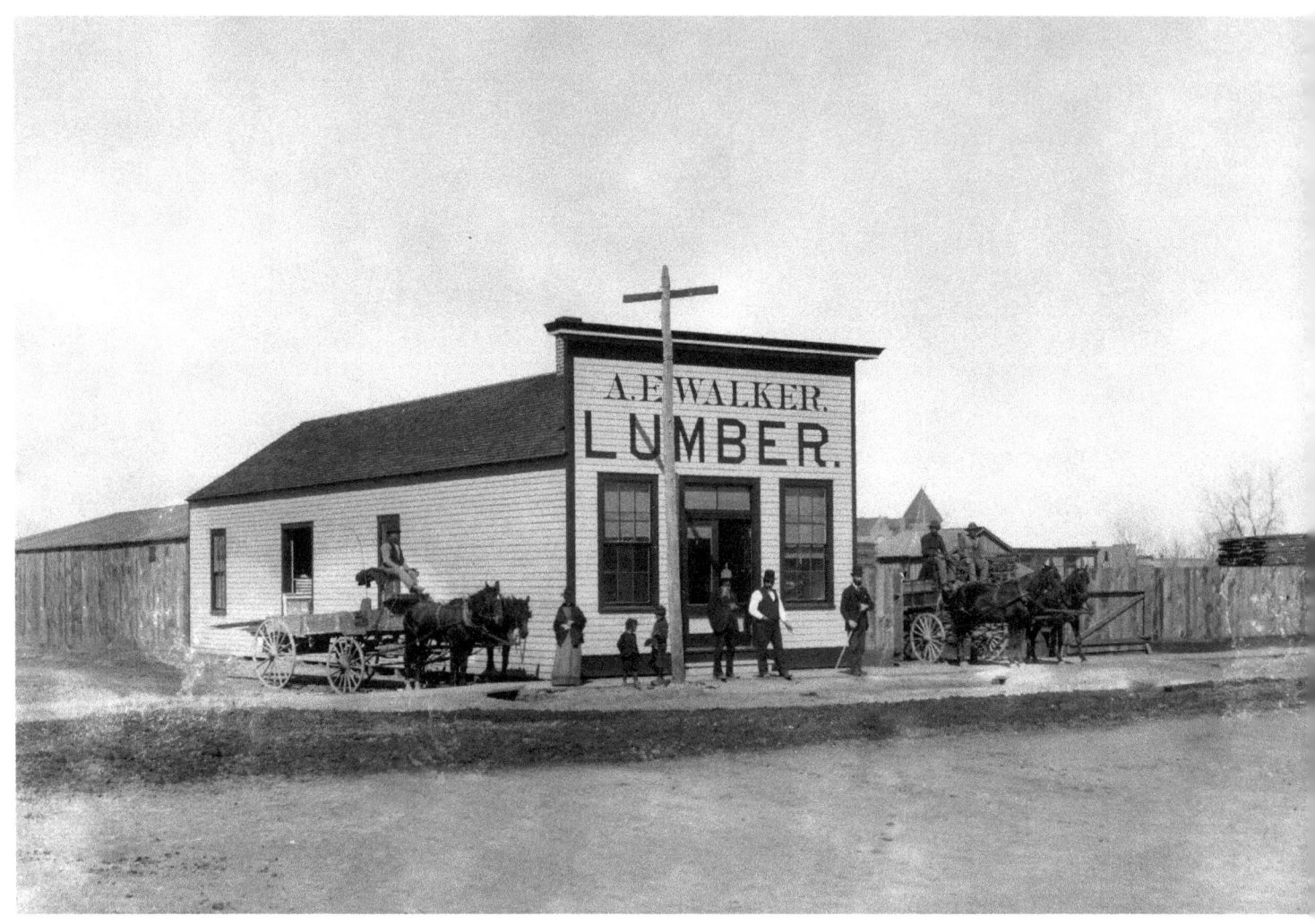

This was the depot before the Alvarado complex was built. The Albuquerque train station had separate entrances for ladies and gentlemen. The Atlantic and Pacific Railroad had shops and offices in Albuquerque and was the largest employer at the time.

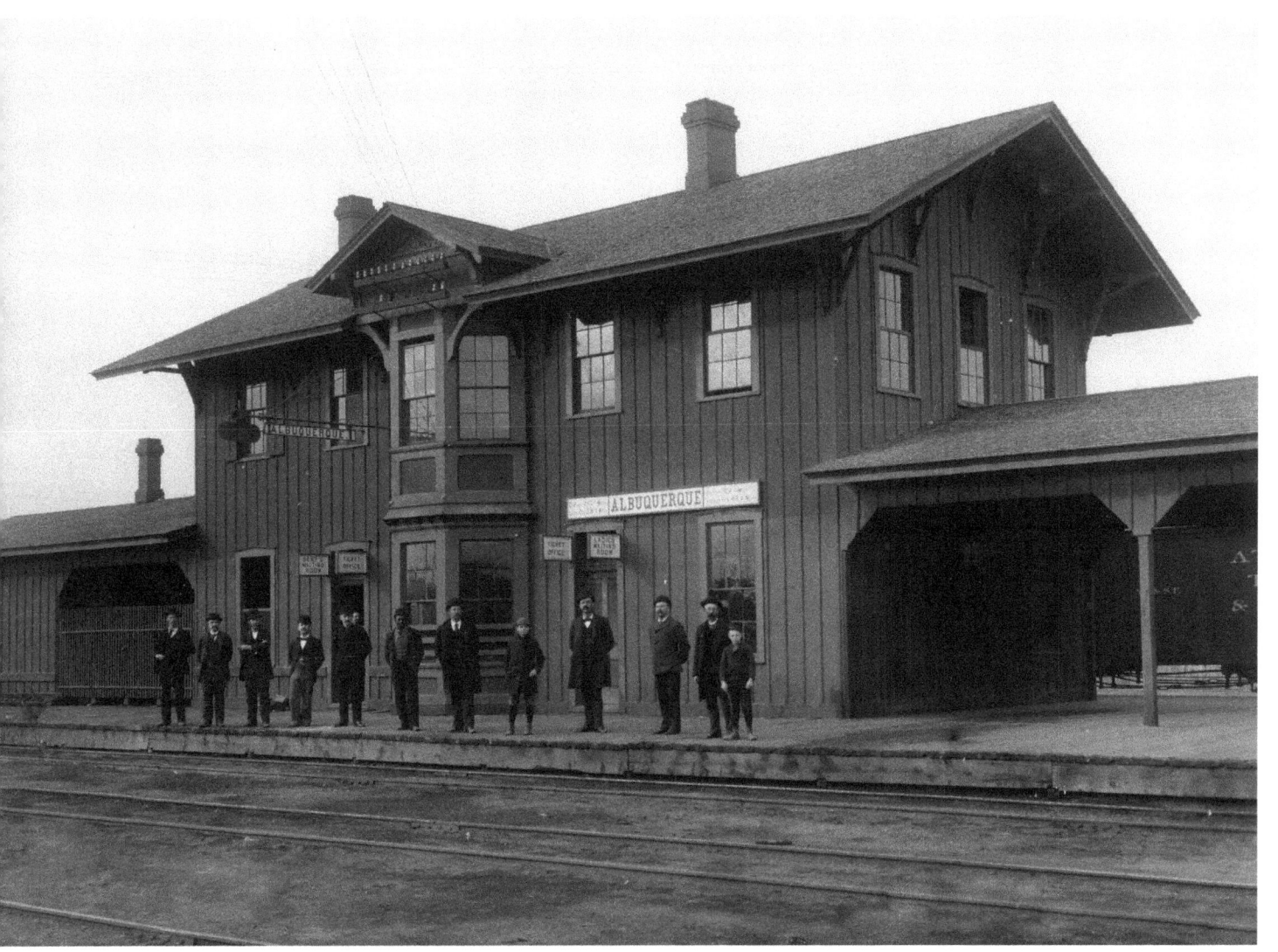

During the election of November 4, 1890, the polls were at A. F. Overman Tailor Shop, 212 W. Gold Avenue. William Henry Cobb took the picture looking east on Gold Avenue.

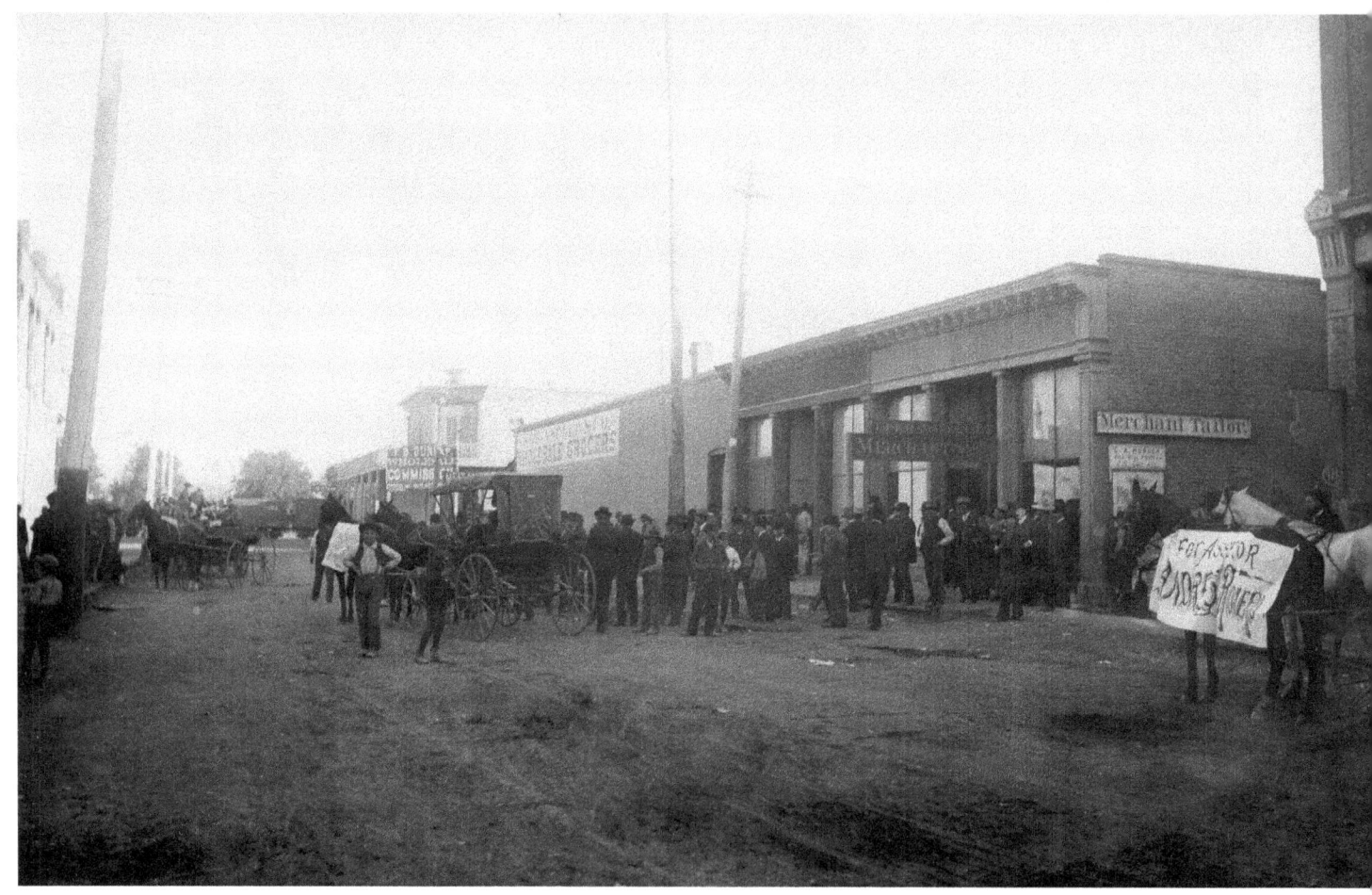

Perkins Hall, at Railroad and Edith, was the home of the Albuquerque Academy in 1890. In 1891, the Territorial Legislature mandated public education, so the city rented Perkins Hall for the Albuquerque High School. Joshua and Sarah Raynolds deeded the building and adjacent land to the city for the Albuquerque Public Library in 1900.

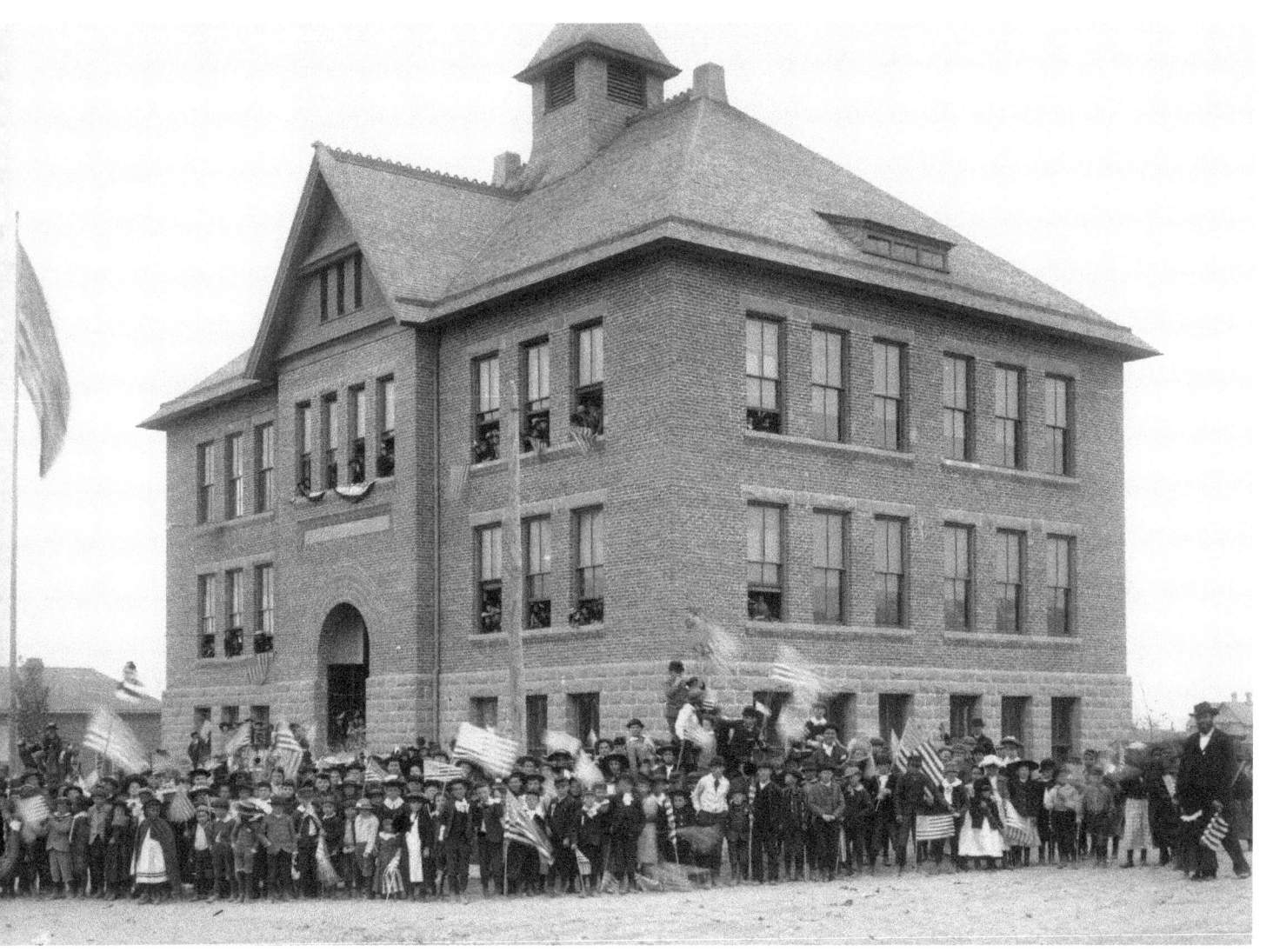

Looking southwest on Morris Street, in Old Town about 1892. One sign reads Ribera's Groceries, Dry Goods, Grass, and Hay. The other sign reads Restaurant, Native Wine.

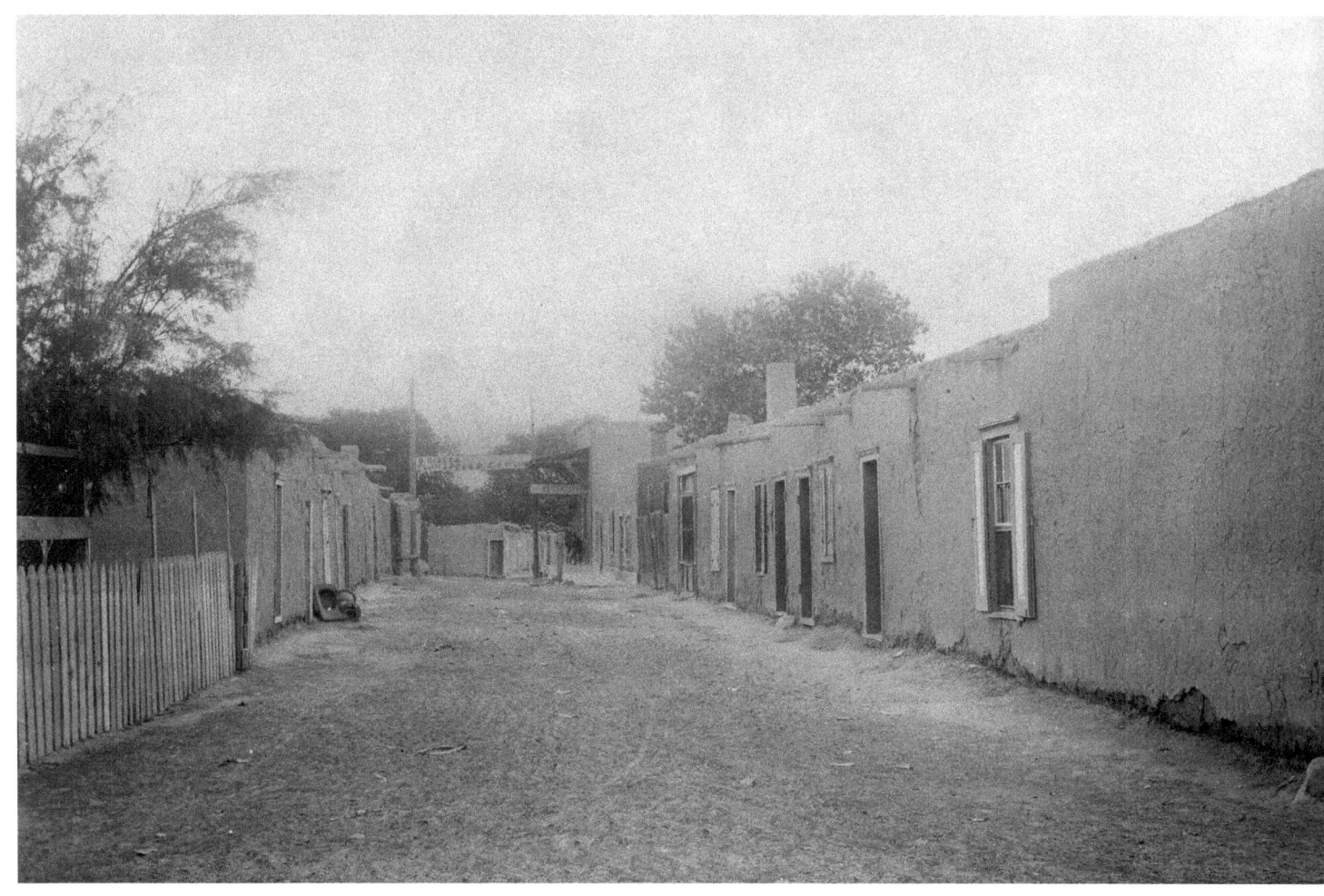

The Southwestern Brewery and Ice Company, on Fruit Avenue, east of the railroad tracks, started operations in 1883. In 1898, a five-story brick stock house was constructed and was the largest structure in the area. In 1900, eighteen men were employed and beer was being shipped throughout the southwest. Prohibition put the brewery out of business, but distilled water and ice production continued. The building is still standing.

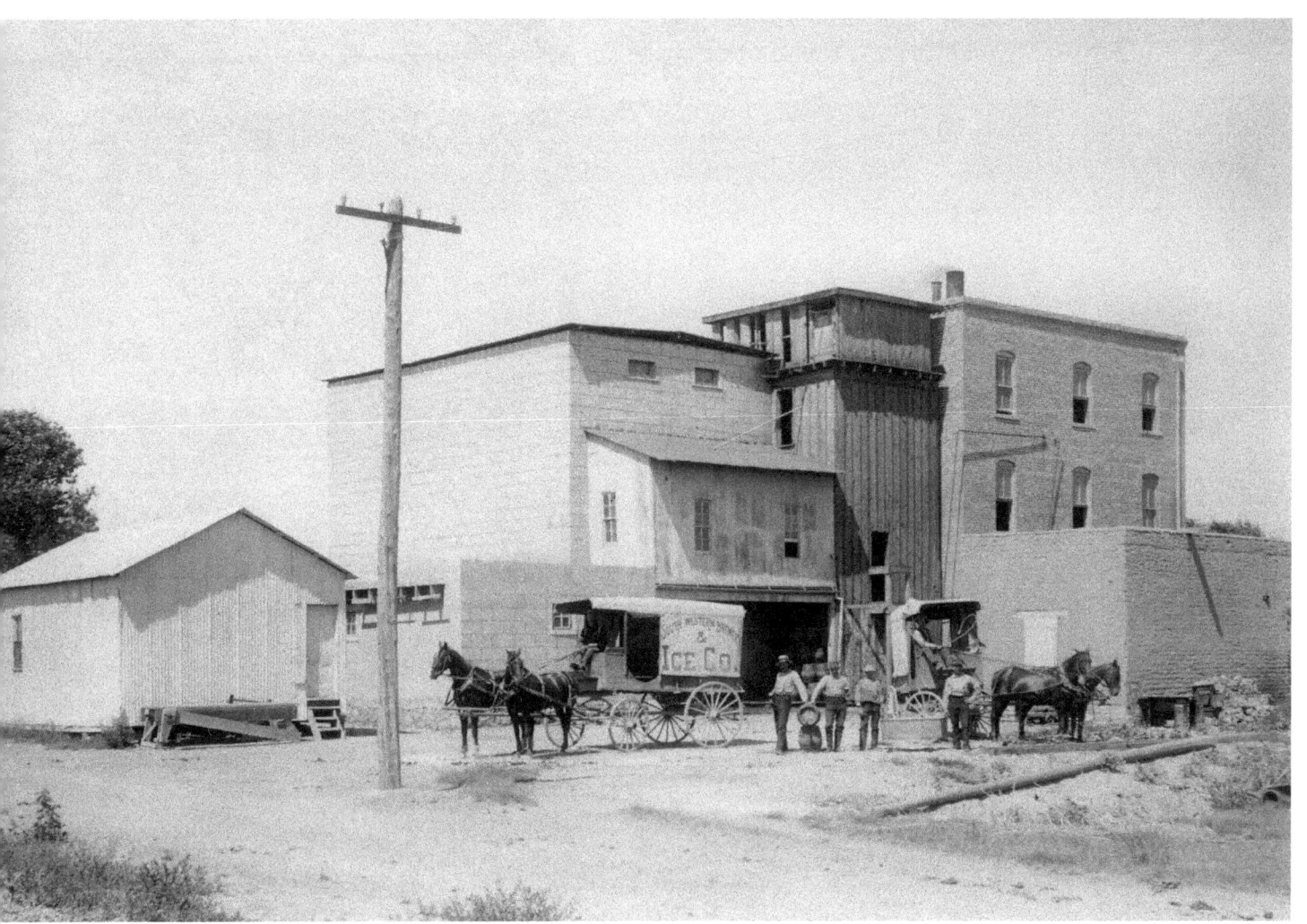

H. M. Hosick and Company on Railroad Avenue in the 1890s, with loaded wool wagons in front. The wool trade was important and sheep were grazed in many areas. The Albuquerque Wool Scouring Mills and the Rio Grande Woolen Mills employed about forty people.

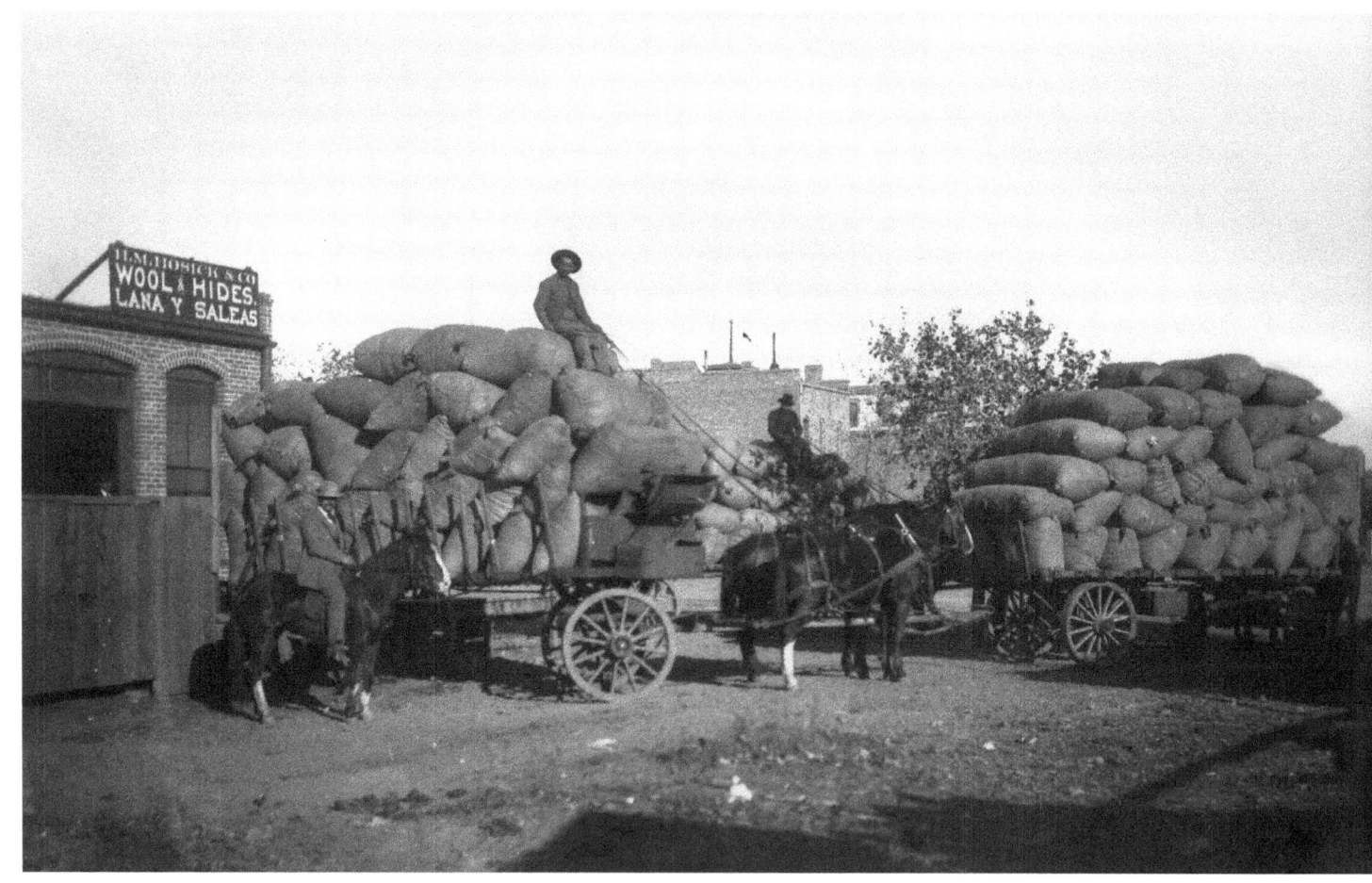

Charles Mausard's Flour Mill was near the railroad track and Fruit Avenue. The Atchison, Topeka and Santa Fe Railway was the stimulus behind the growth of Albuquerque.

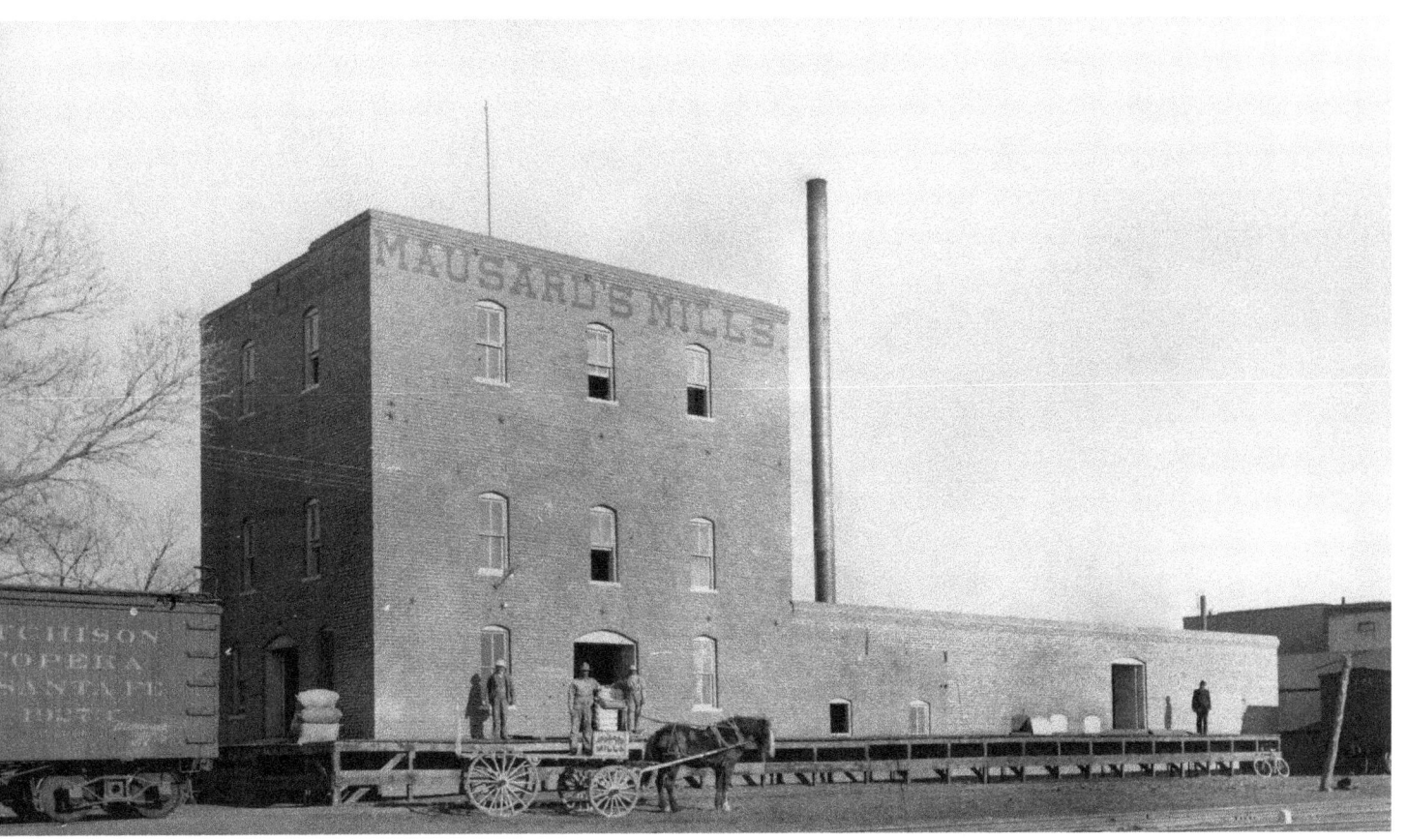

The Atlantic and Pacific Railroad Company Office was a busy place. Albuquerque was chosen for the railroad offices and shops due to geography and the availability of land for commercial facilities. The railroad chose the straightest route and New Town was born.

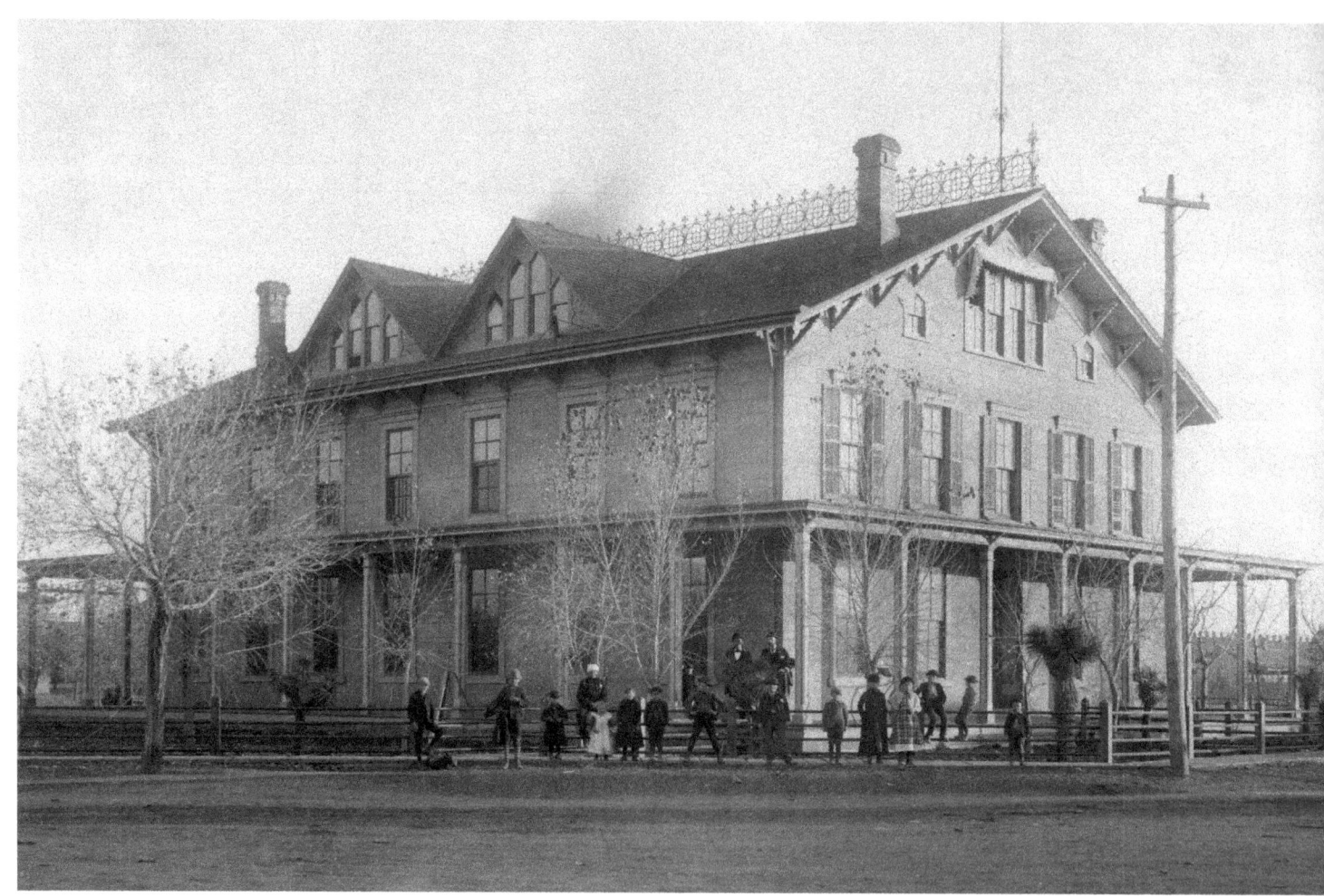

The first Territorial Fair was held October 3-8, 1881, and was called the New Mexico Agricultural, Mineral, and Industrial Exposition. It was held west of Old Town, on Main Street (Rio Grande) where Railroad Avenue dead-ended. Volunteer Fire Companies came from all over to participate in wet and dry hose contests, horse cart races, foot races, and team trials.

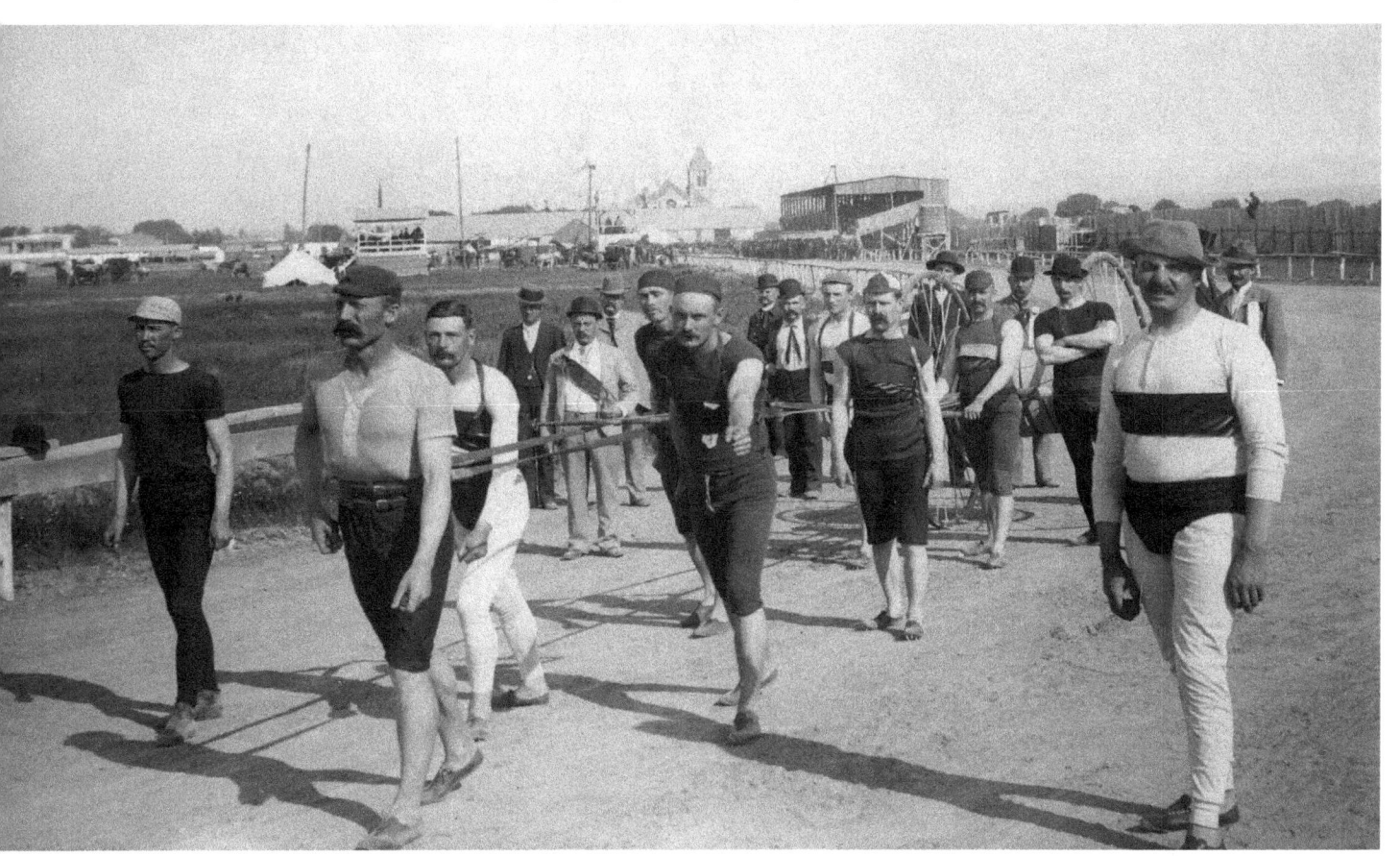

The starting lineup is ready for a footrace at the Territorial Fair. The men from the volunteer fire department are ready to run. The crowd watches as the racers wait for the official to fire the starting pistol. The fair was held every year, and there was betting on all the races.

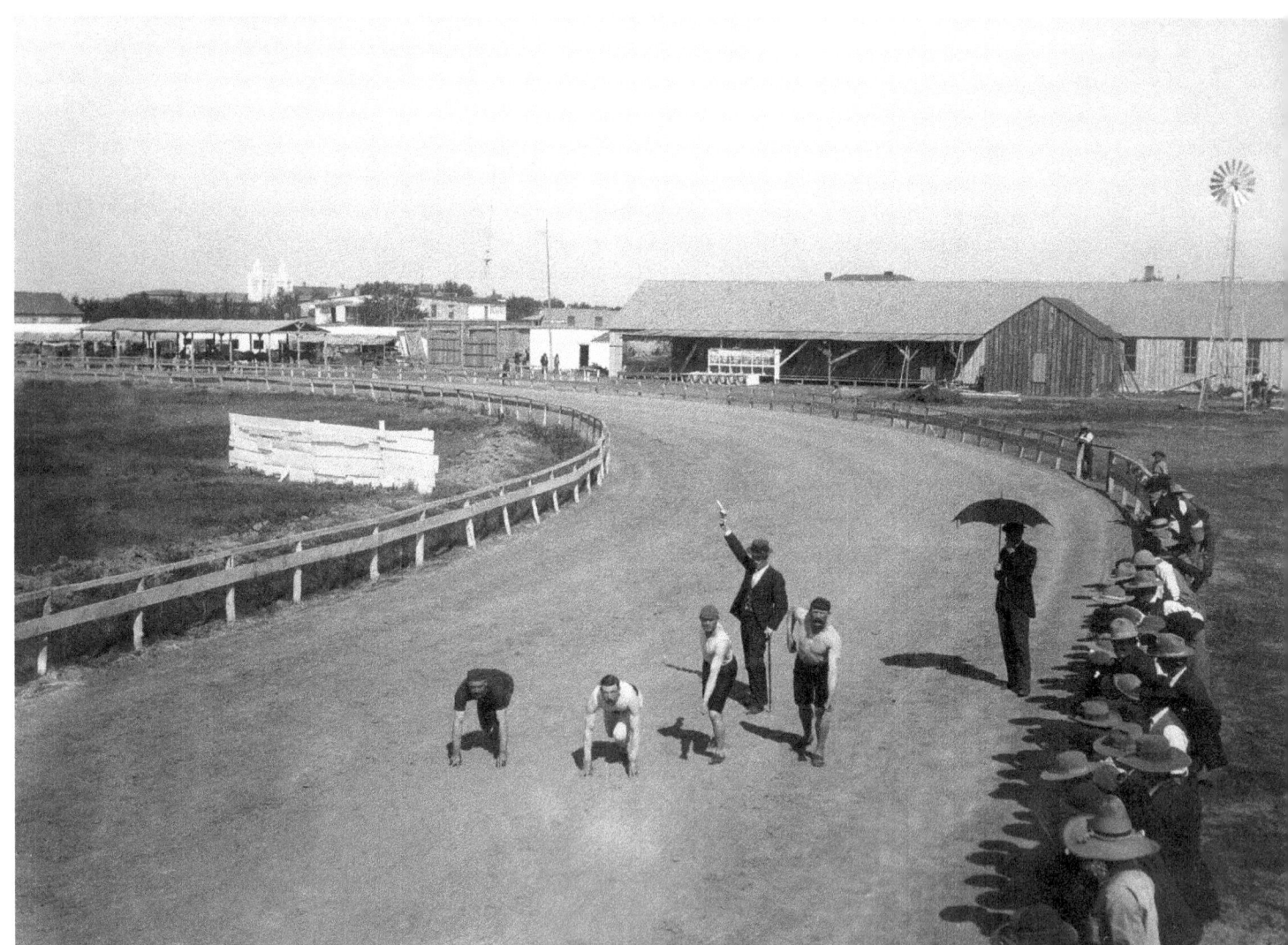

The Albuquerque Guards were the local militia unit, who wore showy blue uniforms. They did military drills, chased outlaws, and escorted the territorial governor in the parade that opened the fair. The writing on the item one of the militia men is holding says Dave Griego.

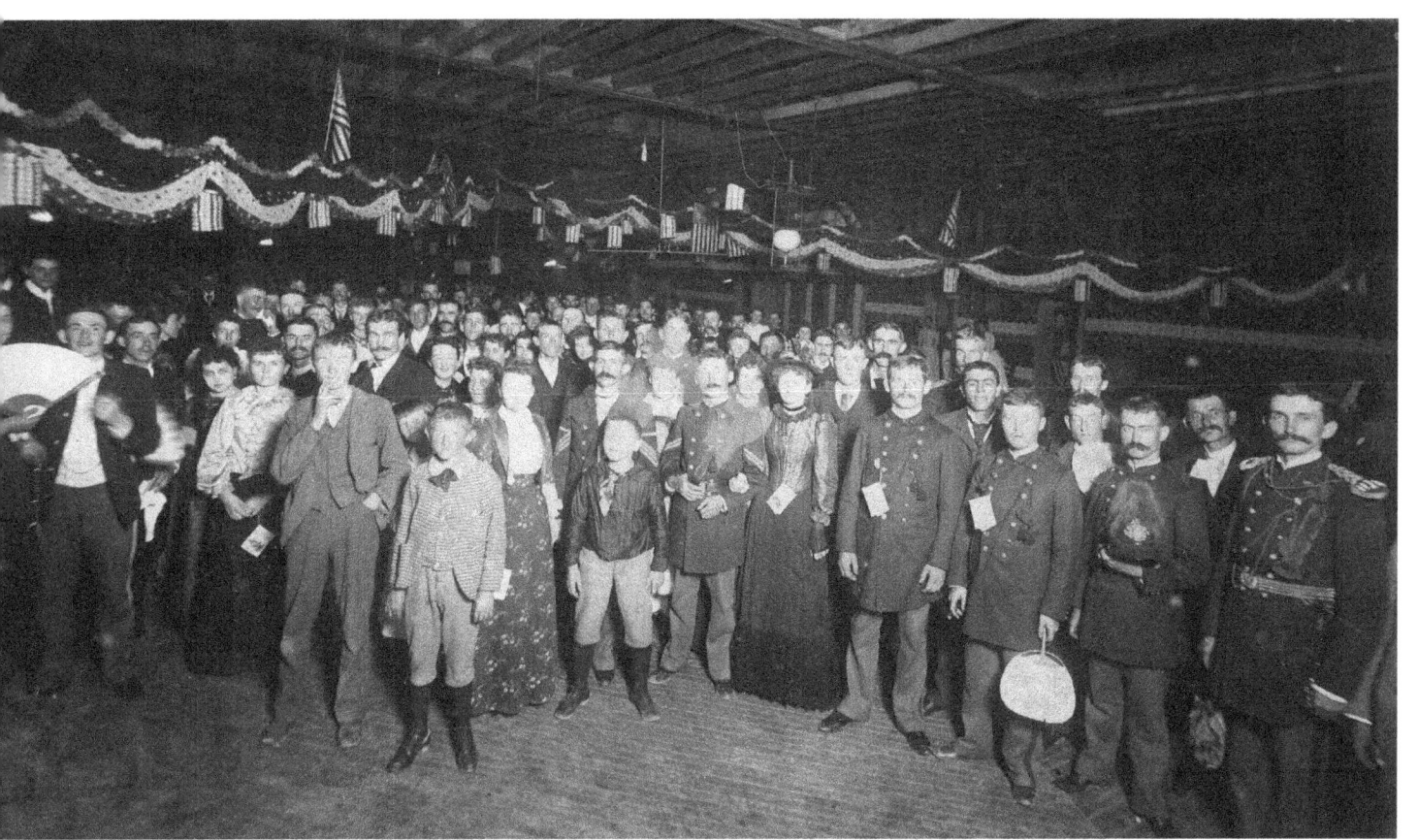

The San Felipe Hotel, at the corner of Gold Avenue and Fifth Street, took two years to build, at a cost of $103,000. It was owned by local businessmen, who organized as the Albuquerque Hotel Company in 1882. It had 80 rooms and was a luxury hotel, with a separate ladies entrance, a library, and bridal parlors. The hotel burned down in 1899.

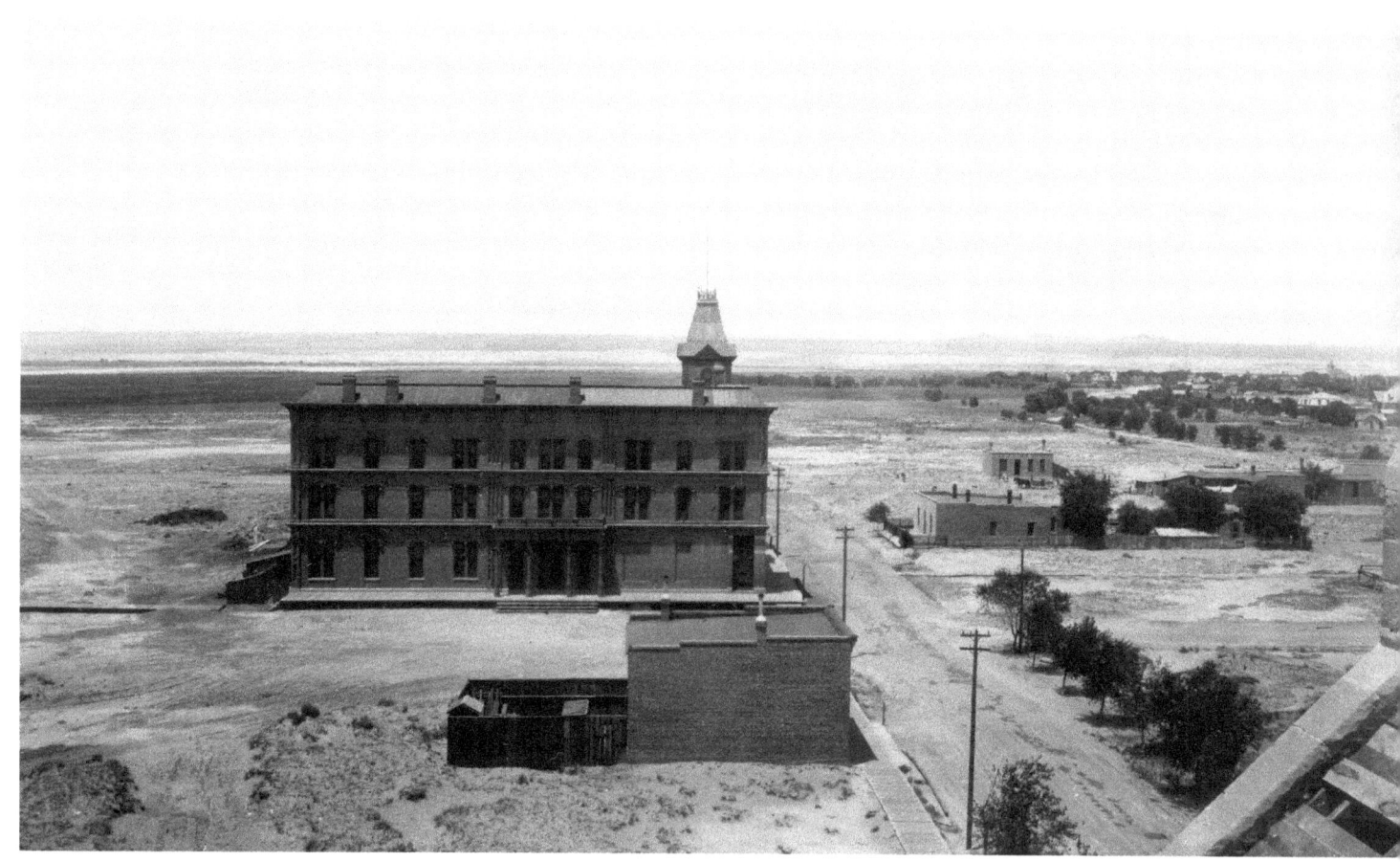

The Fergusson Hook and Ladder Company was named for Harvey Fergusson, who moved to Albuquerque in 1883 and set up a law practice. He became district attorney in 1885. In 1887, he married Franz Huning's daughter, Clara. Fergusson was a champion of lost causes. He defended the weak and believed in public service. The 1898 Fergusson Act in Congress set aside four million acres of public domain in New Mexico for schools.

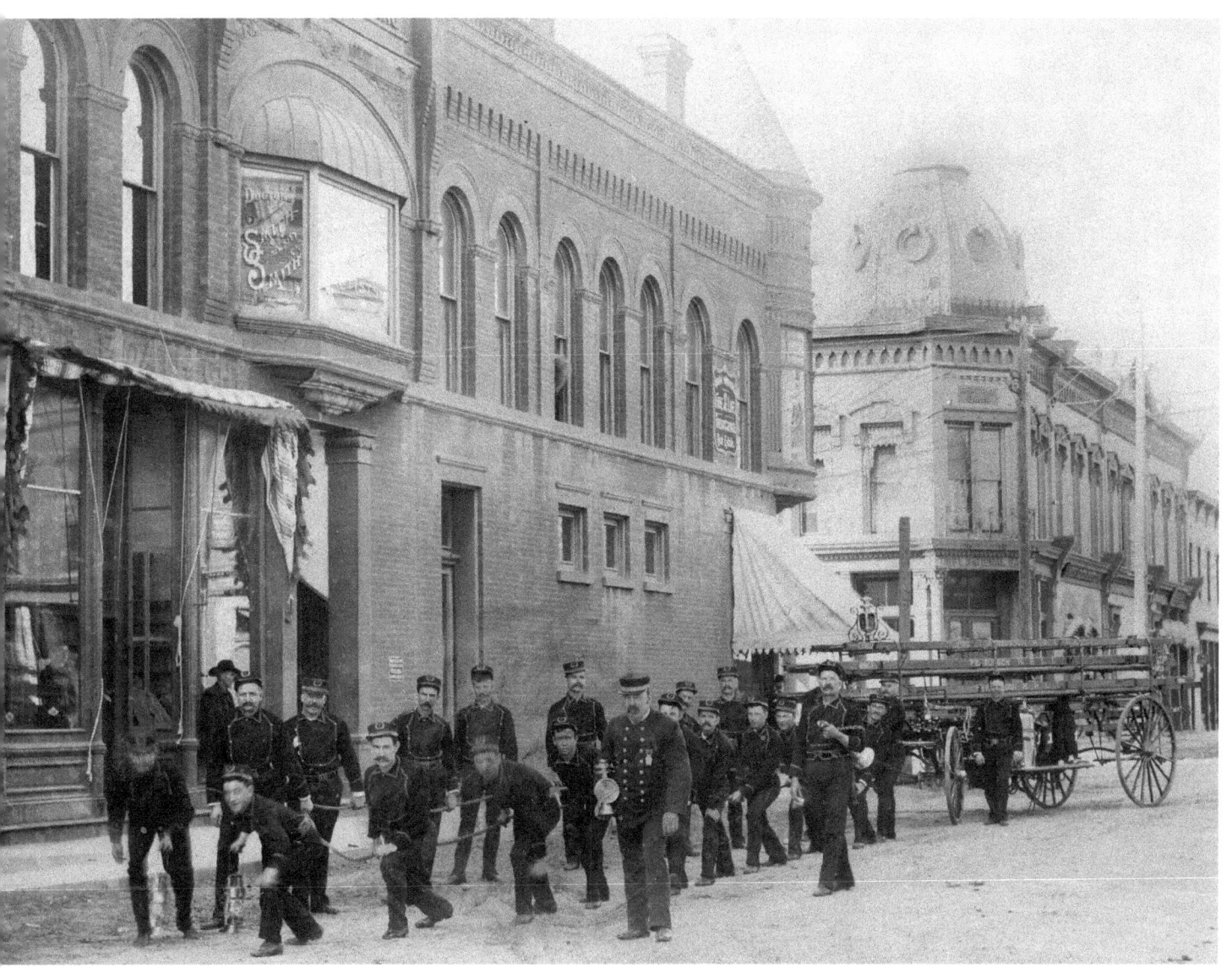

Baseball has always been big in Albuquerque, and many teams competed here. The first professional baseball team was started in 1890 by W. T. McCreight, a former major league player with the St. Louis Browns. This team photograph of the Albuquerque Maroons included Messrs. Timmons, Murry, Riecke, Shannon, Hagel, Lockhart, McCann, Knight, and their mascot.

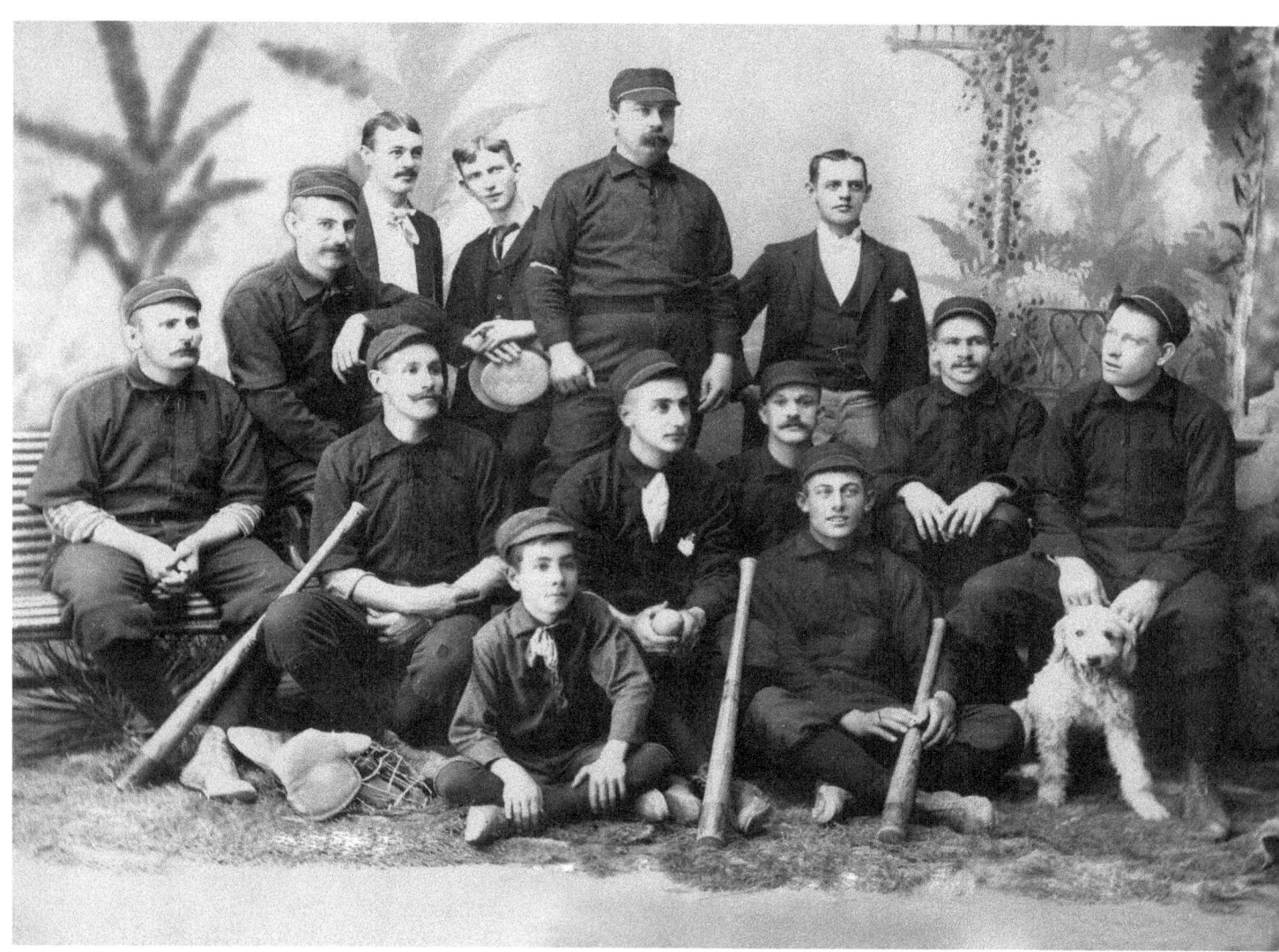

The 1892 Territorial Fair Parade went down Gold Avenue. There were horse-drawn floats and marching bands. Onlookers cheered from the boardwalk.

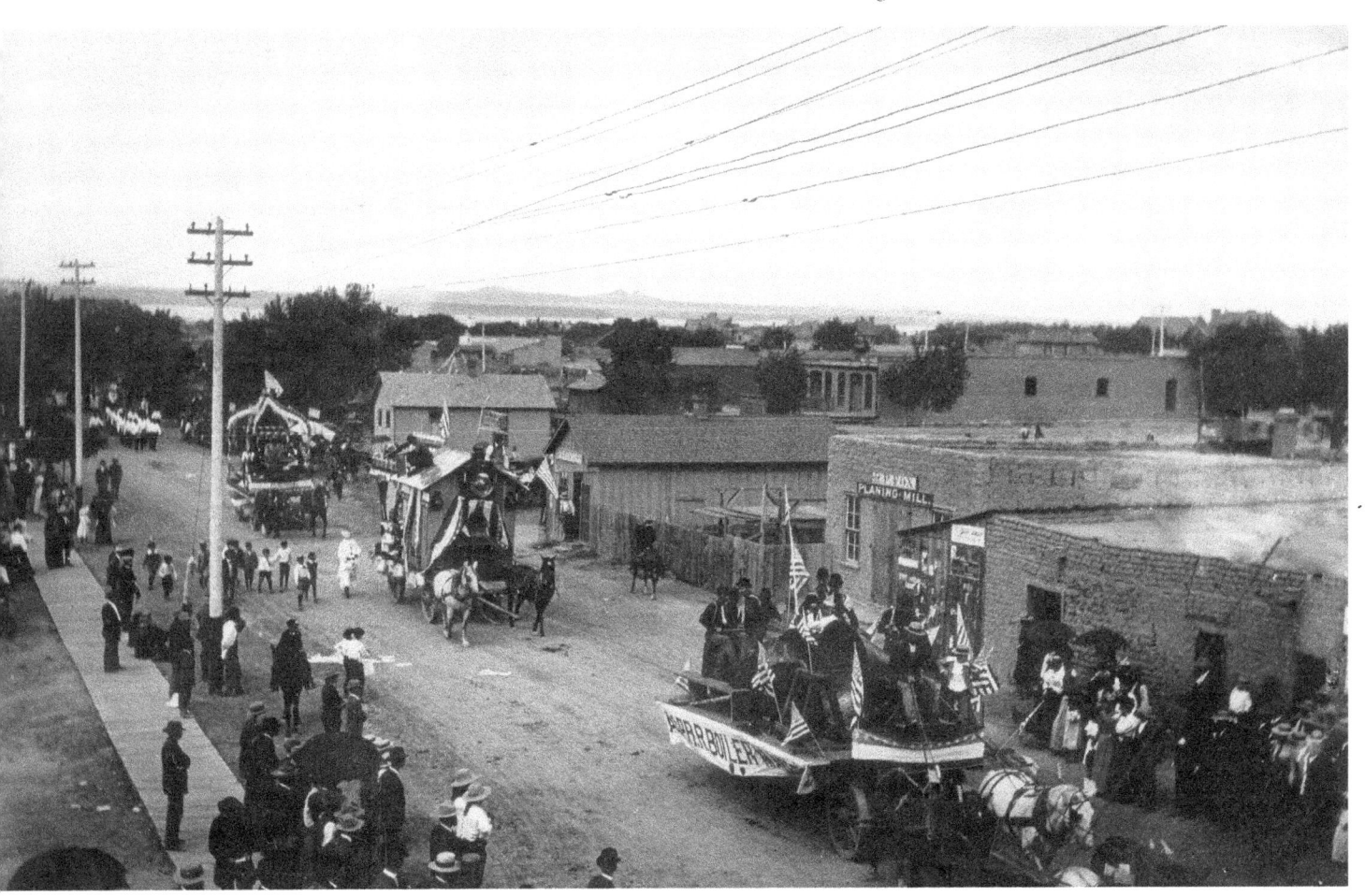

Here, the 1892 fair parade is near the office of the Albuquerque *Daily Citizen*, which was co-owned and edited by Tom Hughes. Hughes was one of the many men who helped start the Territorial Fair, seeing it as a chance to promote business.

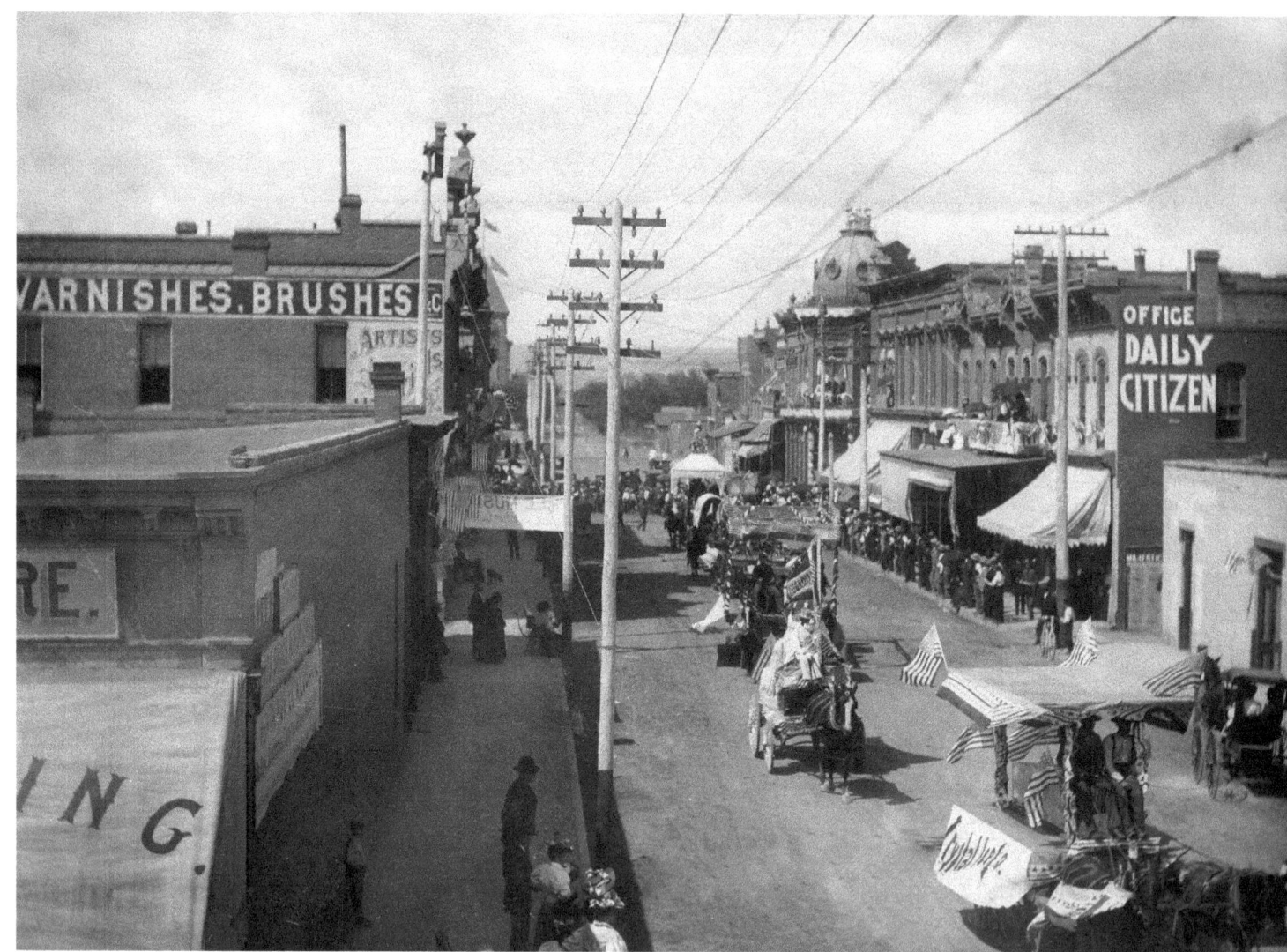

The parade is going past the Commercial Club, on the left. A cavalry troop is riding on Gold Avenue. The territorial fair was always the high point of the year in Albuquerque.

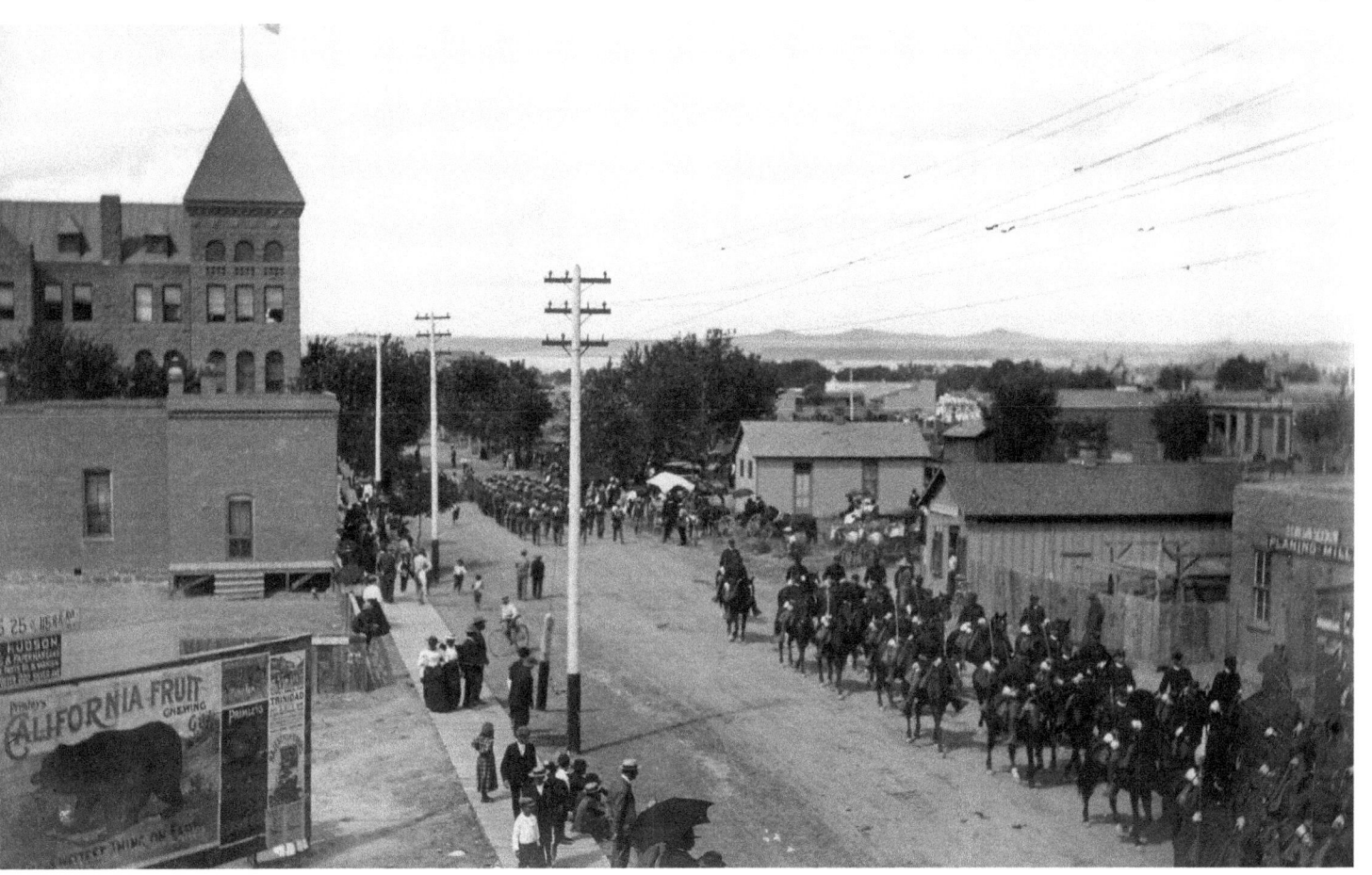

The Santa Fe Railway created the narrow Depot Park along the tracks. It had a stone fountain, two bronze statues, and gas lanterns. It was demolished when the Alvarado Hotel was built.

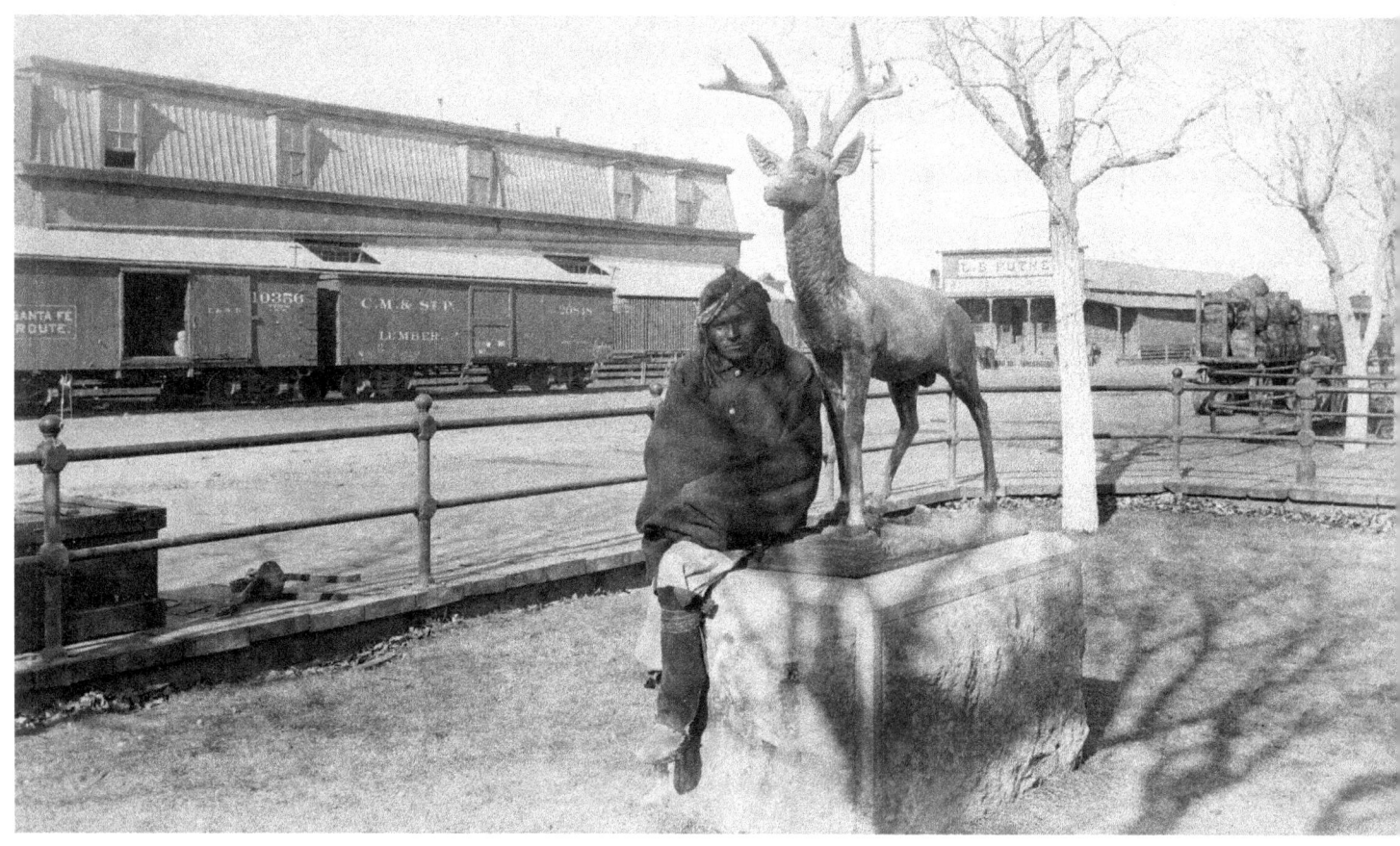

The Albuquerque Guard was a militia unit led by Captain J. E. Westlake. They were always popular at the Territorial Fair and took part in competitive drills. The man who took the photograph, W. Calvin Brown, was a lieutenant in the Territorial Militia in 1882. In the late 1880s, he became an Albuquerque town marshal.

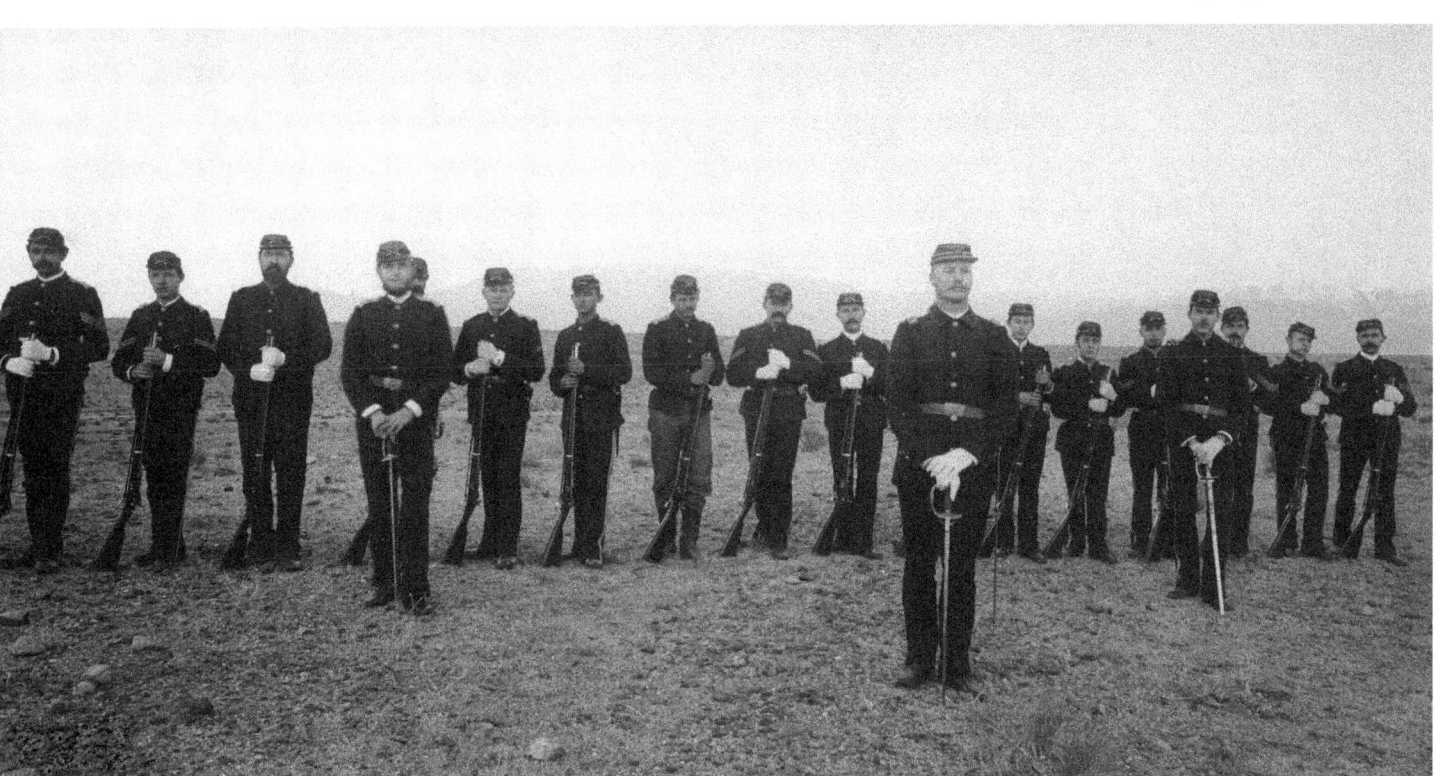

The Isleta Pueblo San Augustine Church is about thirteen miles south of Albuquerque. The Isleta Pueblo was established around 1300 AD. The church, established in 1612, still exists on its main plaza. *Isleta* is from the Spanish and means "little island."

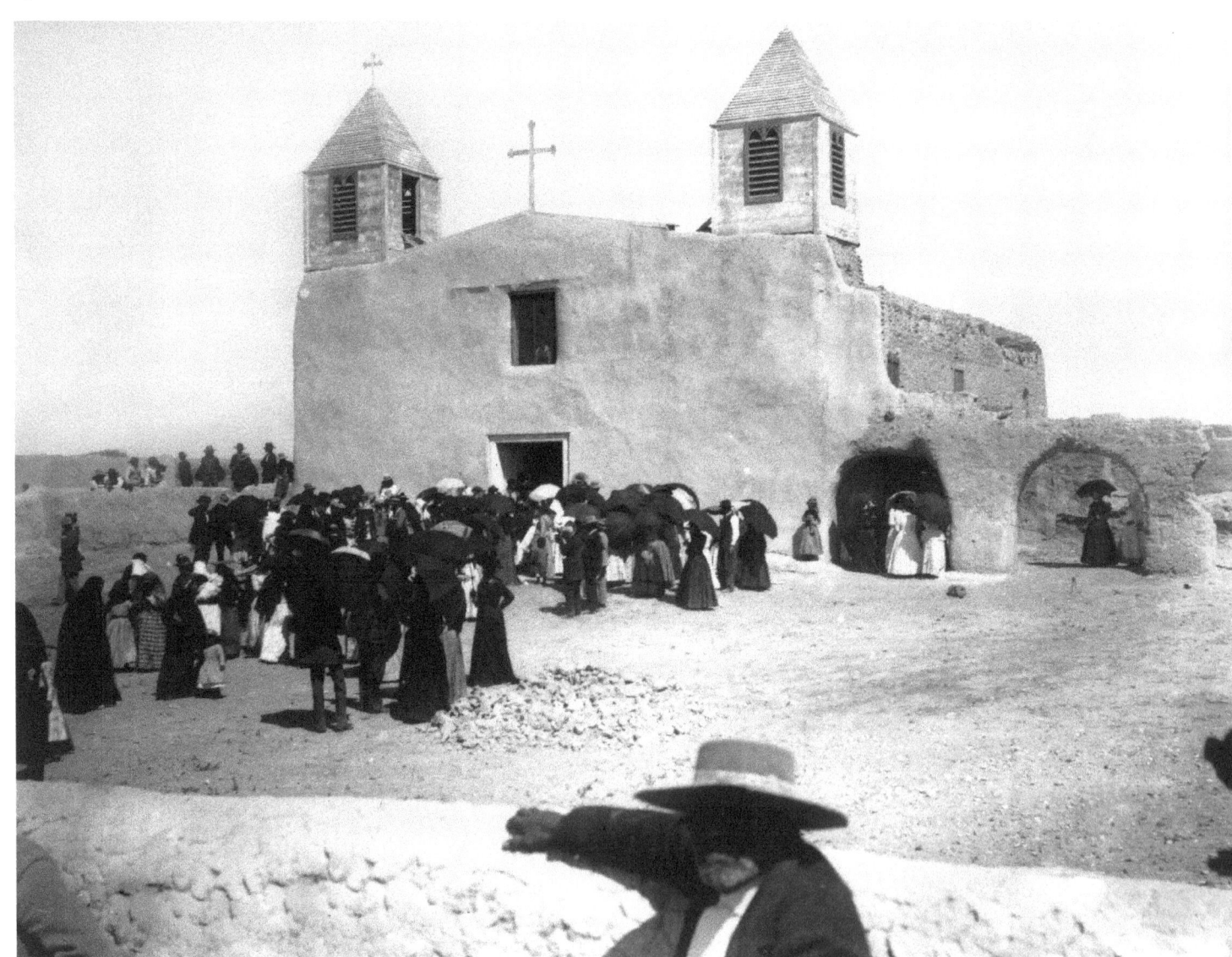

A man is standing on the top of the building being constructed at Second Street and Railroad Avenue in 1892. The N. T. Armijo Block was dedicated to the memory of Nicholas T. Armijo by his wife and was there until 1971. Albuquerque's first Walgreen's store was in this building.

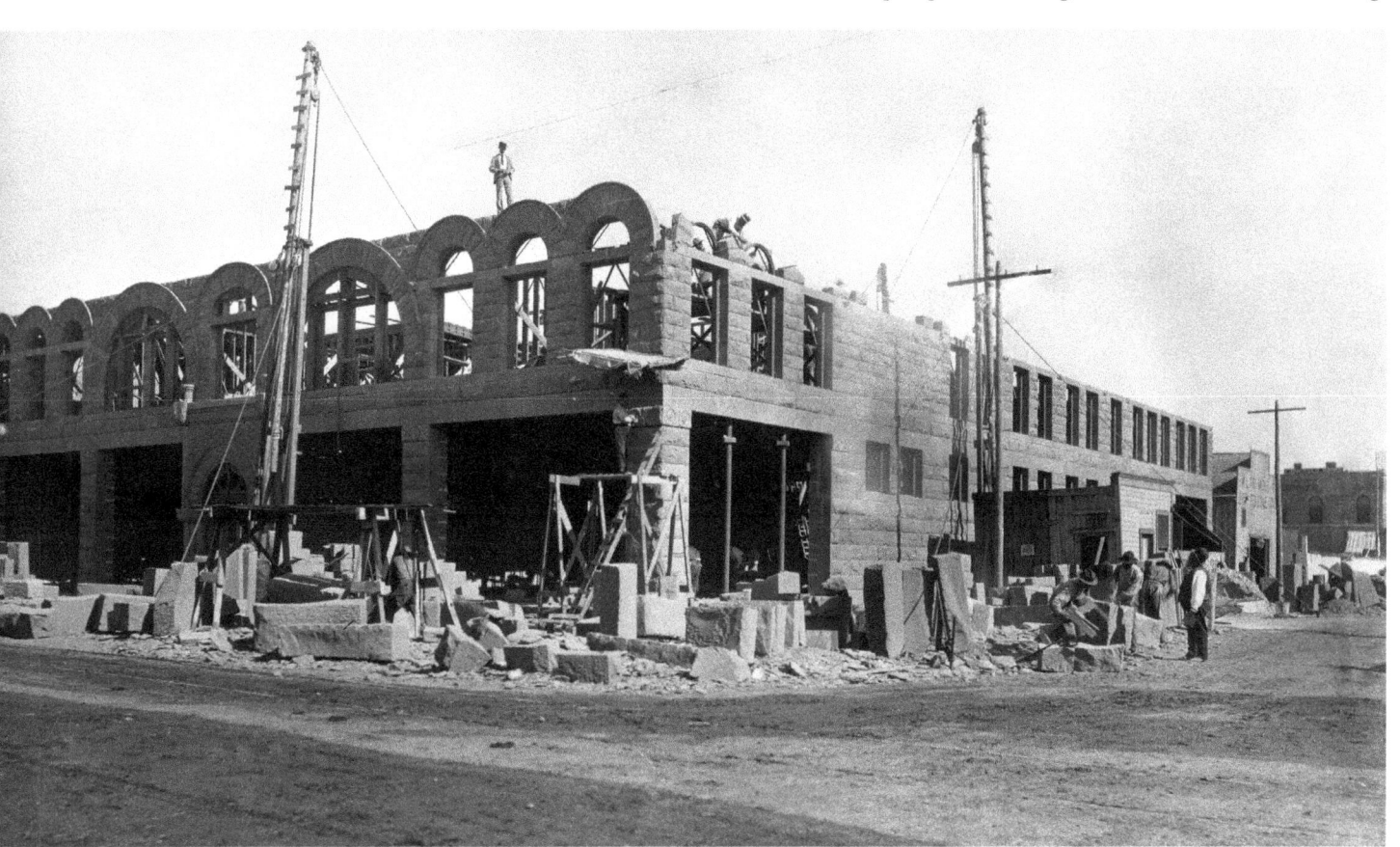

The photographer was looking east from Second Street, on Gold Avenue, in about 1892. This area was called Banker's Corner as the Central Bank, the Albuquerque National Bank, Montezuma Trust, and the Whiting Building were on the four corners. This was the heart of the business district. Most of the businesses were locally owned.

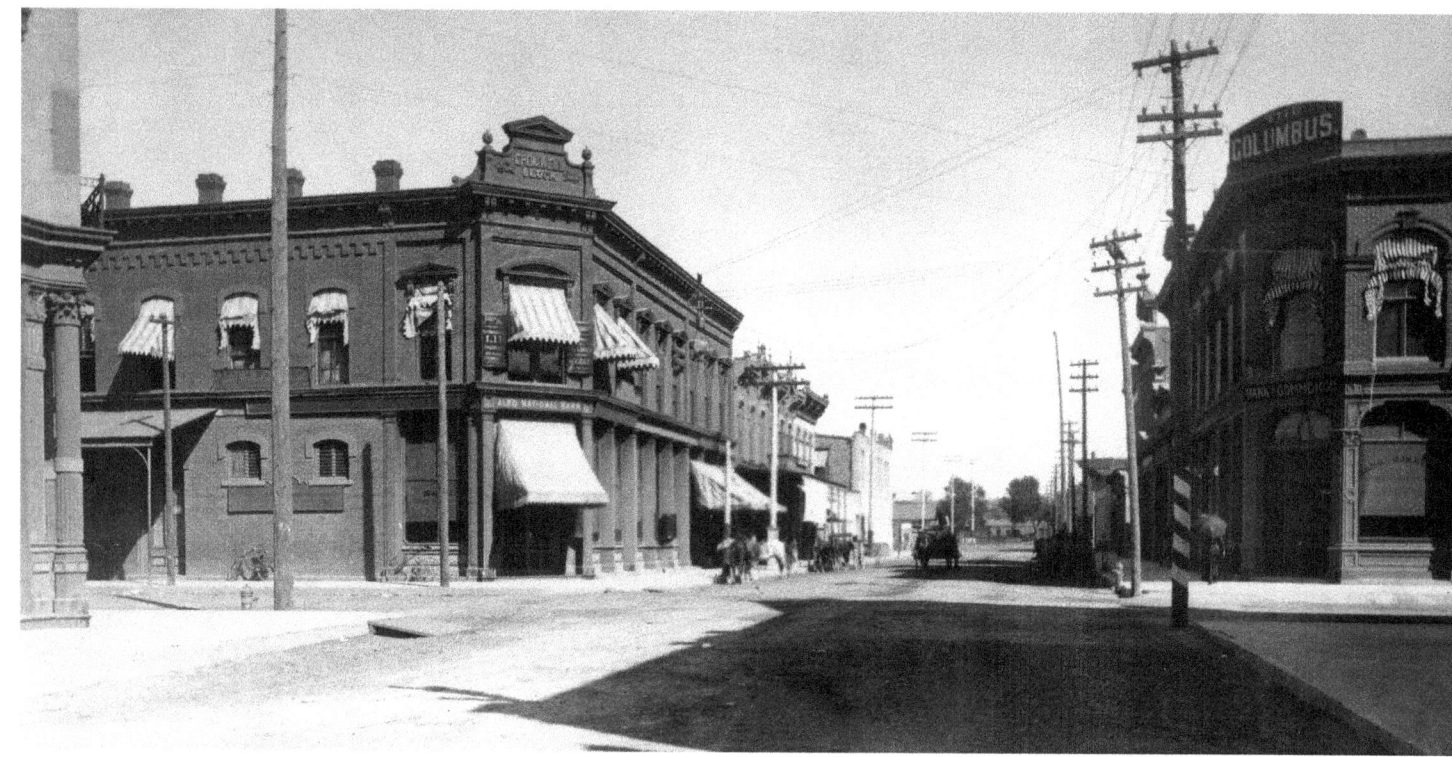

At the 1892 Territorial Fair, the trapeze artist was performing above the crowd and beside the grandstand. The New Mexico Territorial Fairgrounds was at what is now W. Central Avenue and Rio Grande Boulevard. The Territorial Fair became the New Mexico State Fair after New Mexico attained statehood on January 6, 1912.

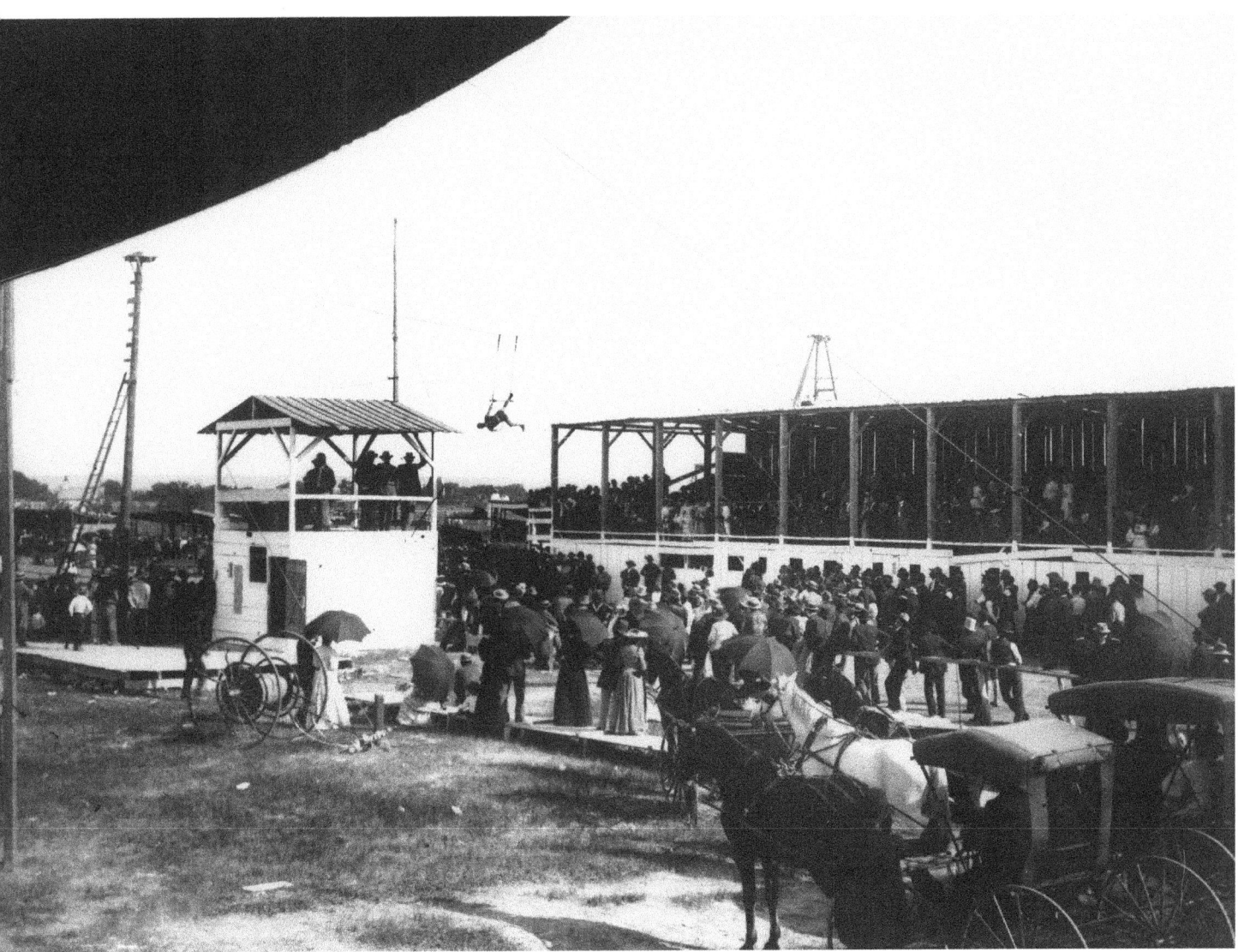

The Commercial Club, at the southwest corner of Gold Avenue and Fourth Street, was built at a cost of $70,000. The organization was established on May 21, 1890, to promote Albuquerque's business potential, climate, and cultural assets. The building had offices, a ballroom, clubrooms, and bachelor apartments. It boasted more than 200 members and published booster booklets.

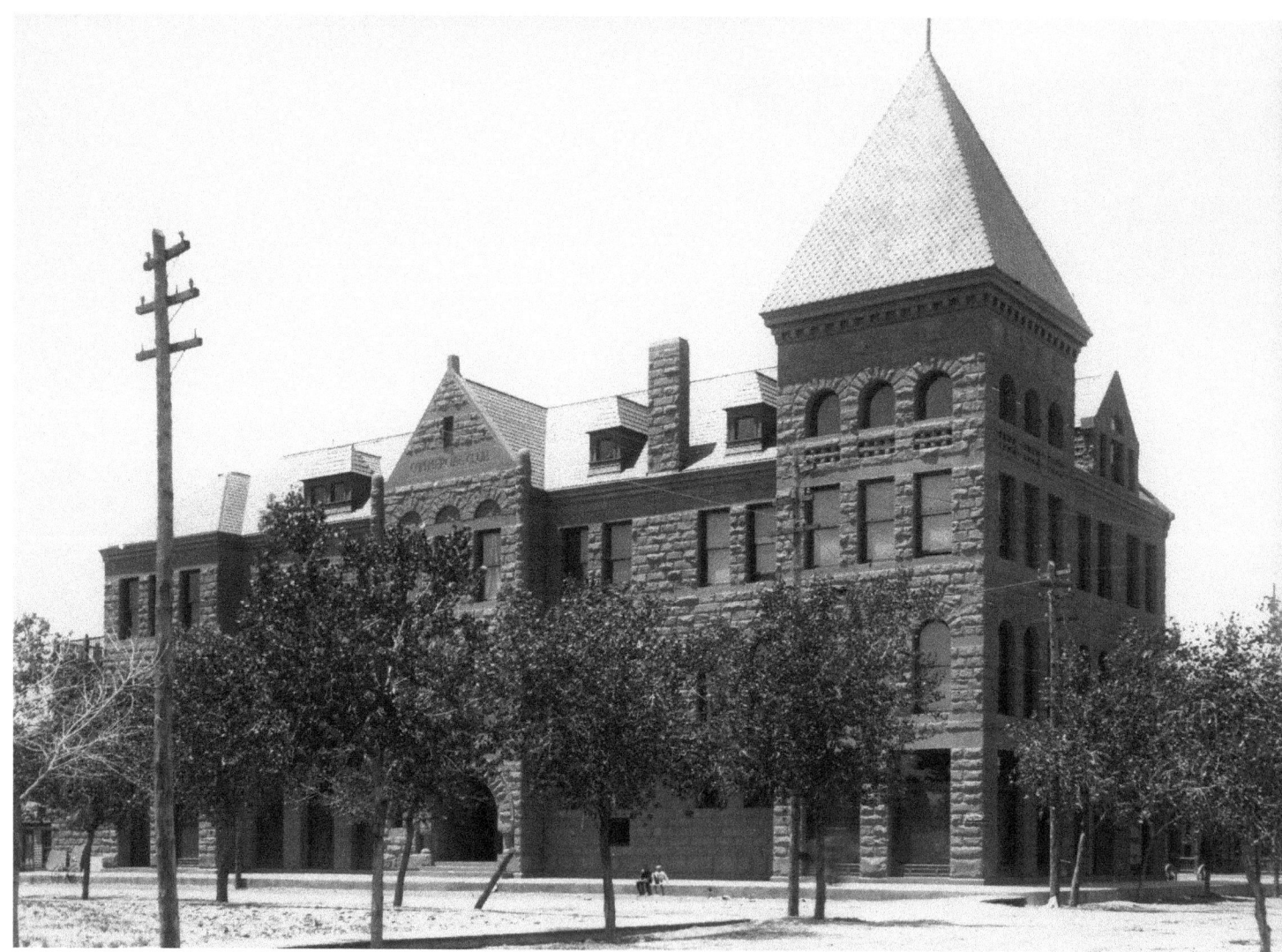

The Boss Saloon gambling and concert hall was at 115½ Railroad Avenue. The St. Louis Restaurant was to the left of it. The railroad workers and cowboys brought cash to Albuquerque. Gambling and saloons were open twenty-four hours a day.

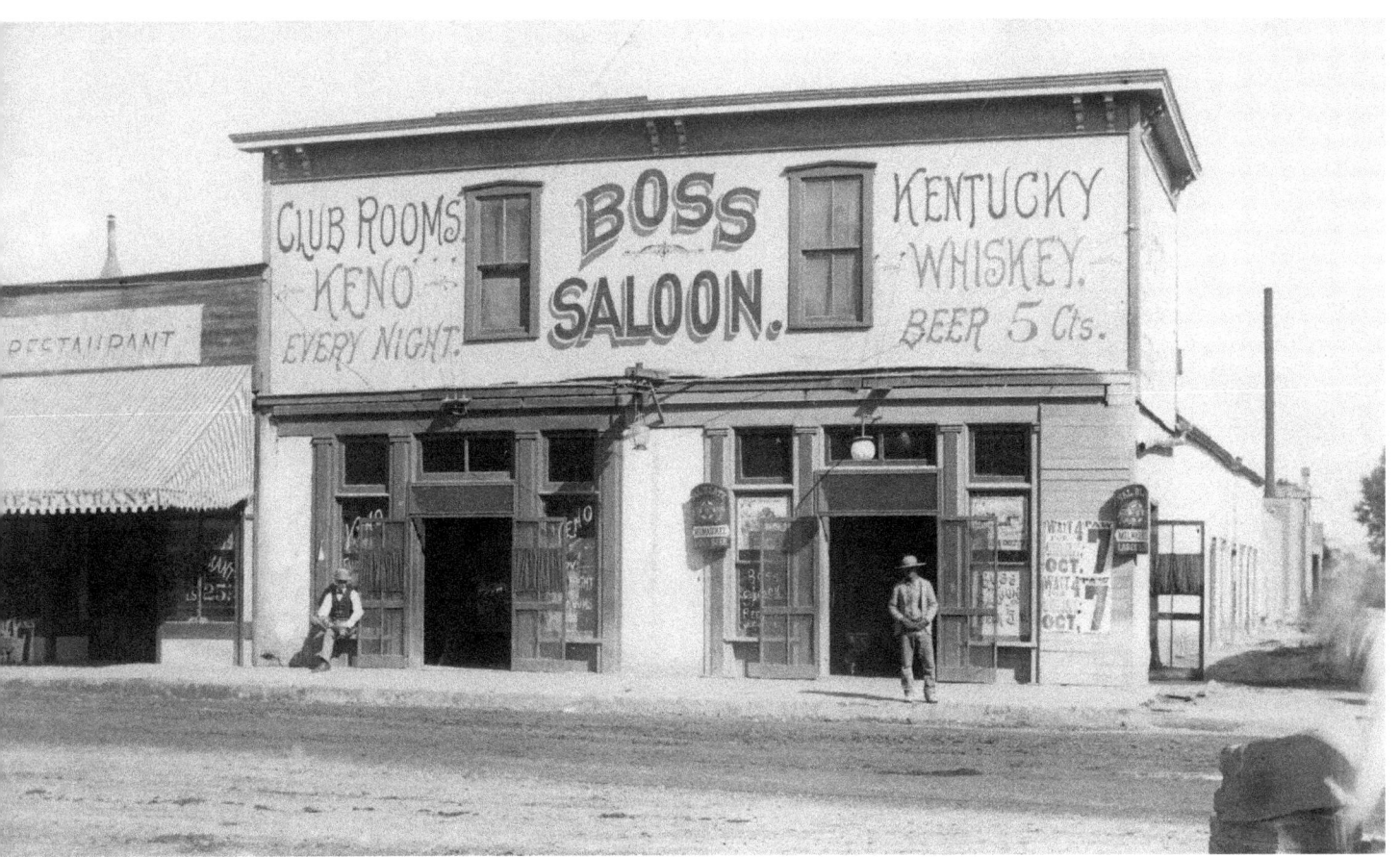

The Huning Highland Addition, east of the railroad, was Albuquerque's first subdivision, and its location made it a nice area. Franz Huning and Thomas F. Phelan were behind the development. The houses were Victorian style.

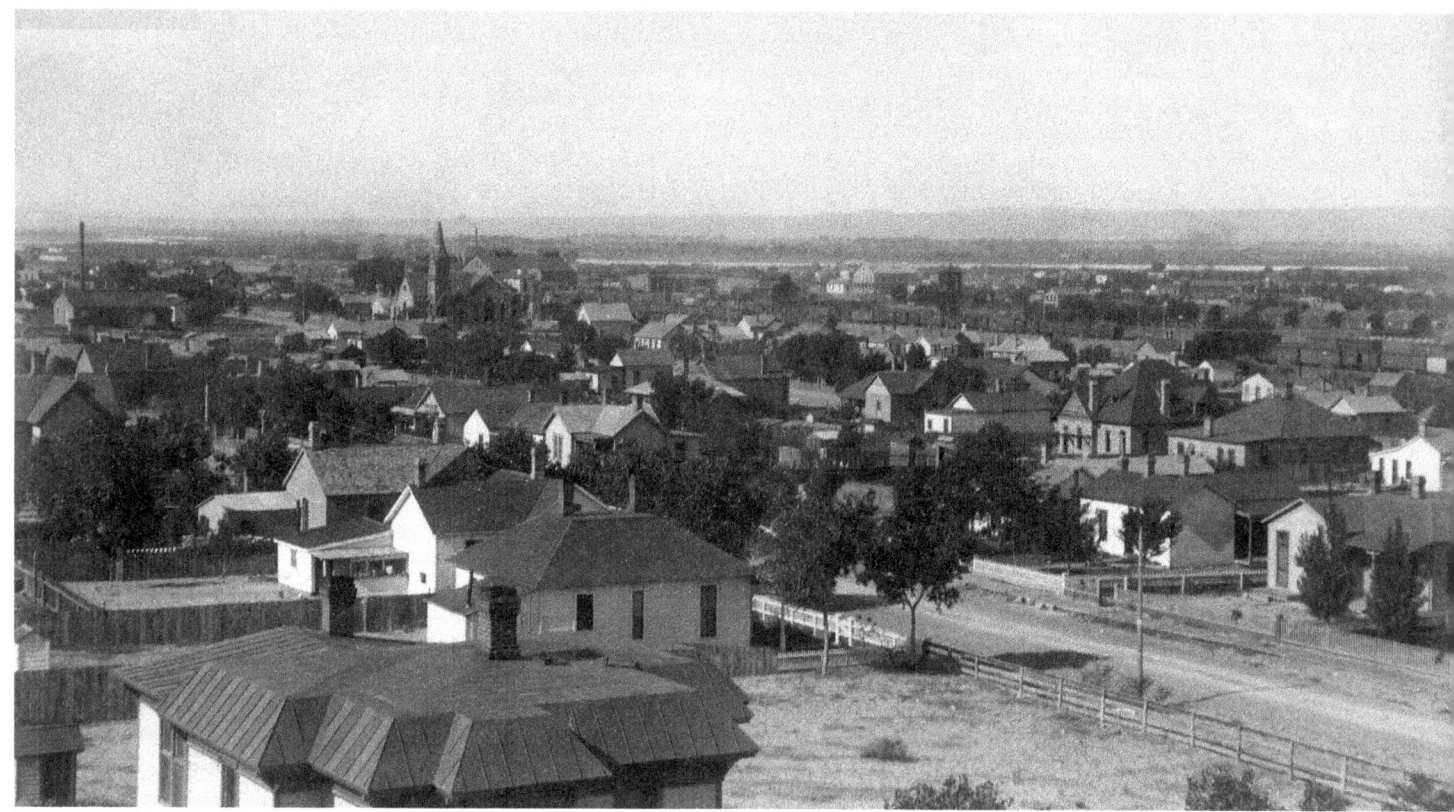

A horse-drawn carriage sits in front of Smith and Prieston New Mexico Novelty Works and the W. J. Tway Wallpaper, Paint, and Signs, at 216½ South Second Street. F. W. Smith was the manager of the Atlantic and Pacific Railroad, but t is not known if the store owner was the same Smith.

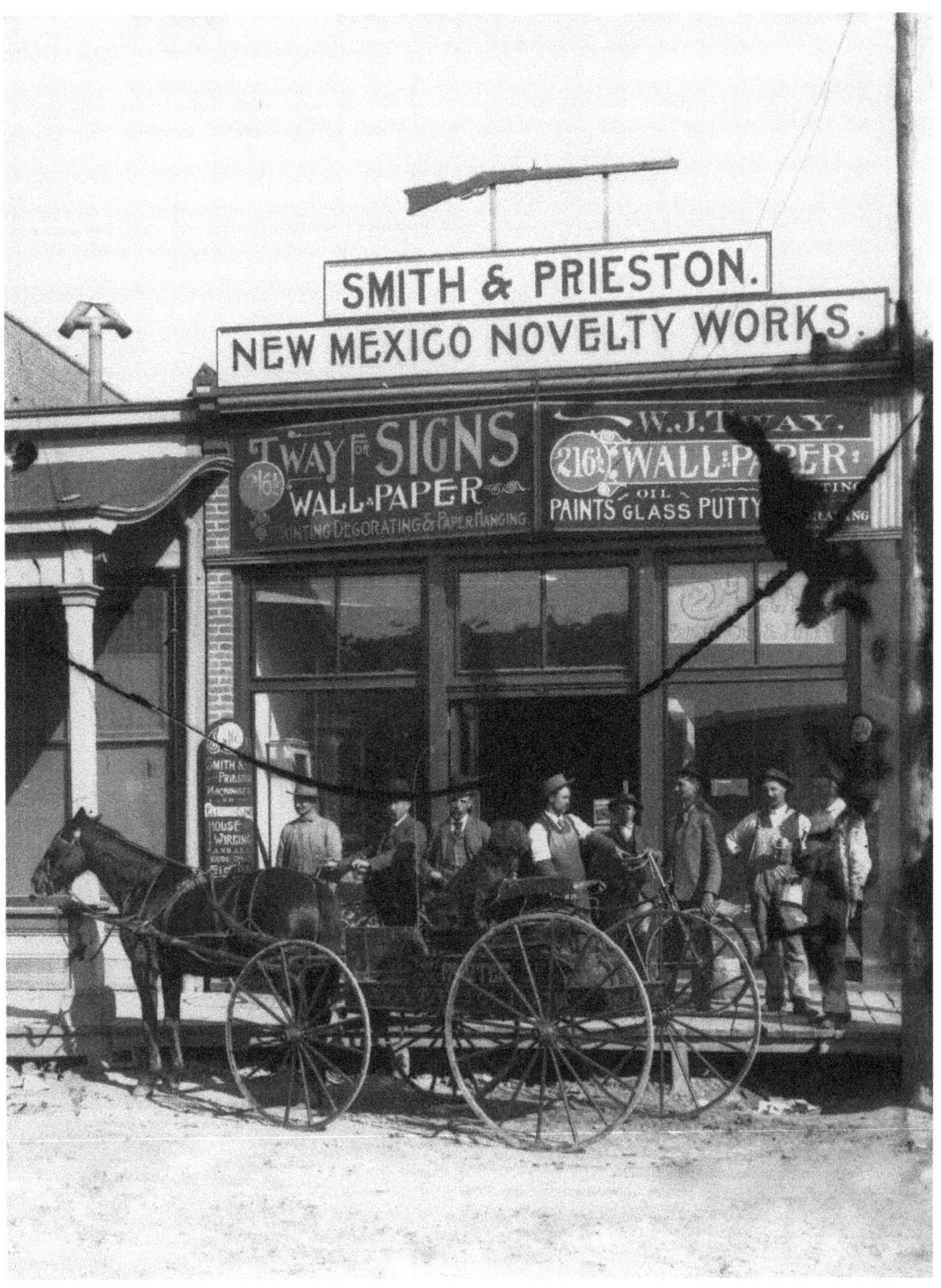

Standing in front of the Montezuma Saloon is the Albuquerque Fire Department crew, which was one of three volunteer fire departments in 1882. William Sanguinette was a saloon owner and the first elected fire chief. In 1900 the city government took over the fire department and had a station at 302 N. Second Street. Bernard Ruppe was the first professional fire chief.

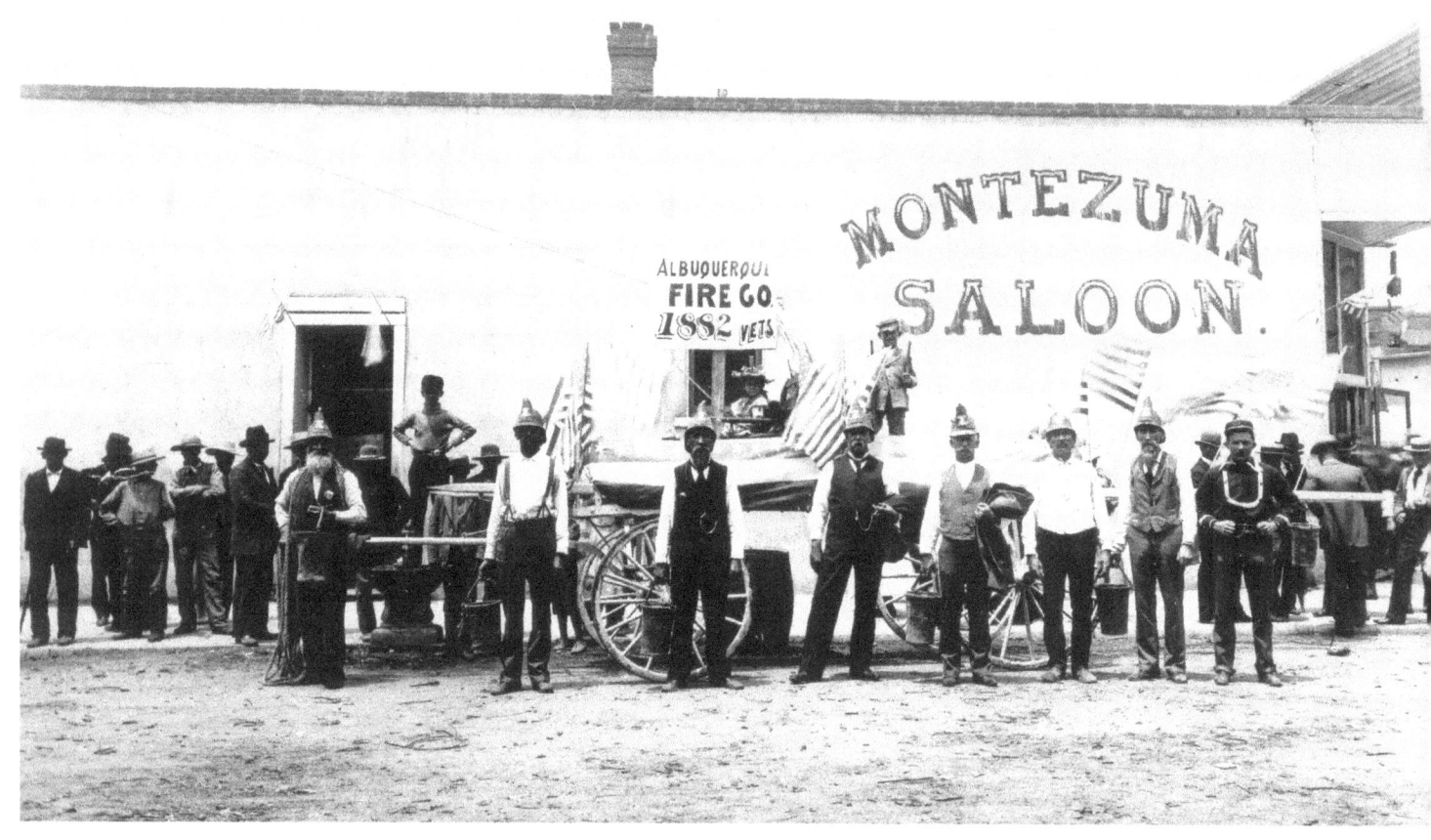

The men and their horses are on the 200 block of Gold Avenue. The Home Restaurant and the Star Furniture Company are behind the men. The Central Bank at the end of the block, on the corner of Gold and Second, was constructed in 1881. Harvey B. Fergusson had his law office above the restaurant. Harvey Fergusson was the father of the writers Erna and Harvey Fergusson Jr.

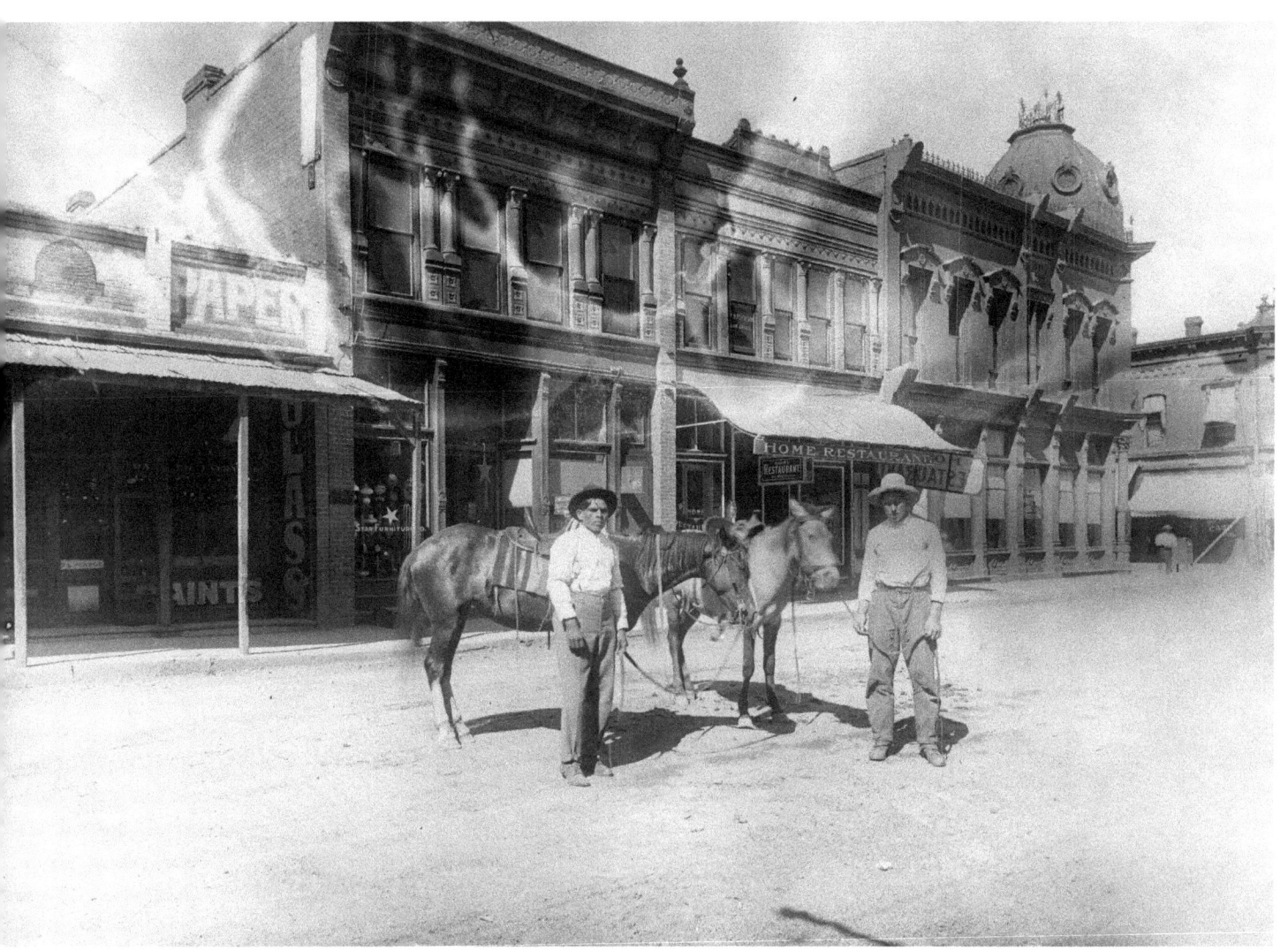

The Progress Dry Goods and Notions Store, a typical shop of the time,
was the low-cost store in Albuquerque.

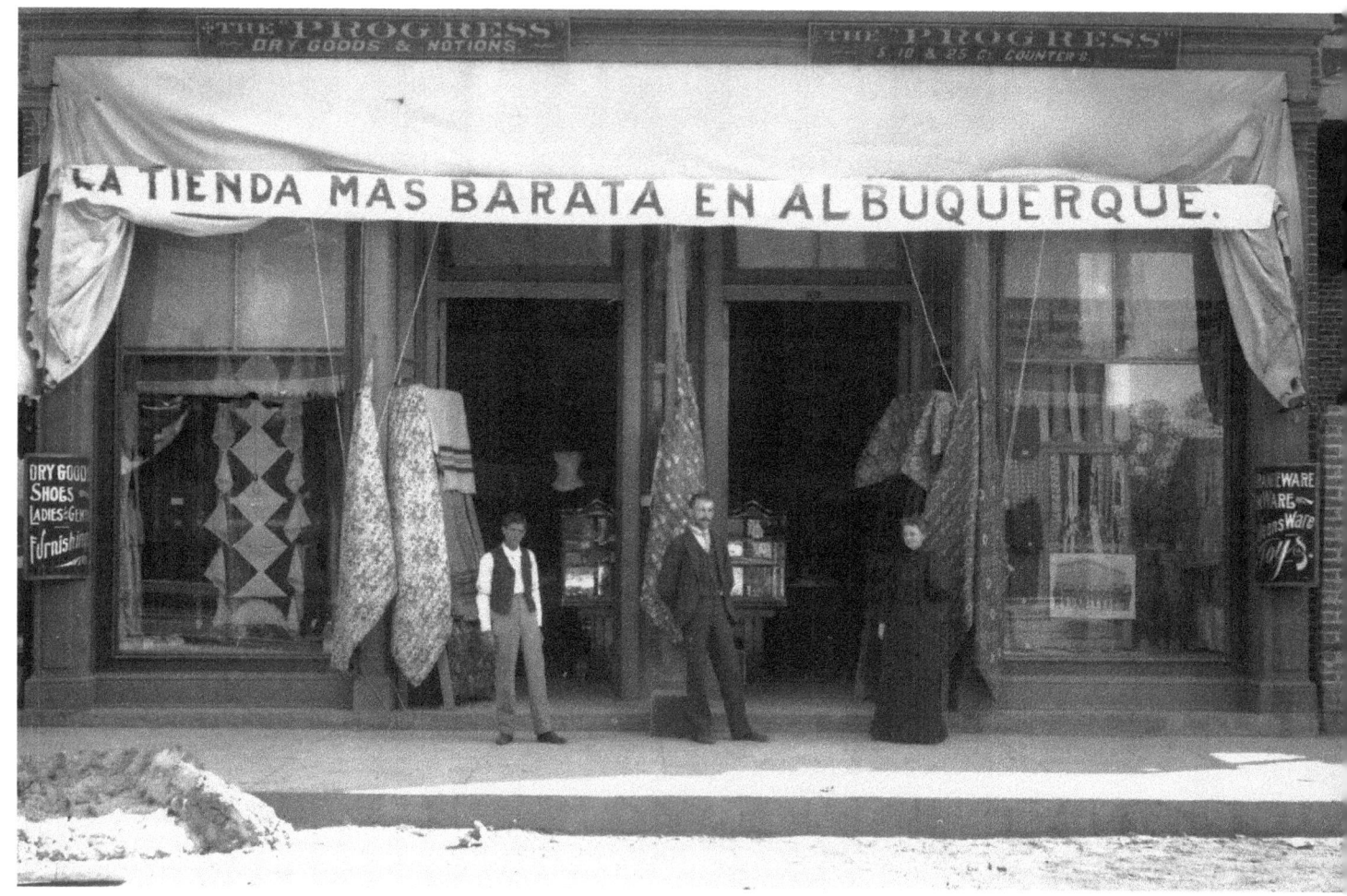

Frank and Eakin Wholesale Liquors and Cigars, at 111 South First Street, was across from the railroad tracks. Business was good, and the train brought new items daily to be sold throughout the area.

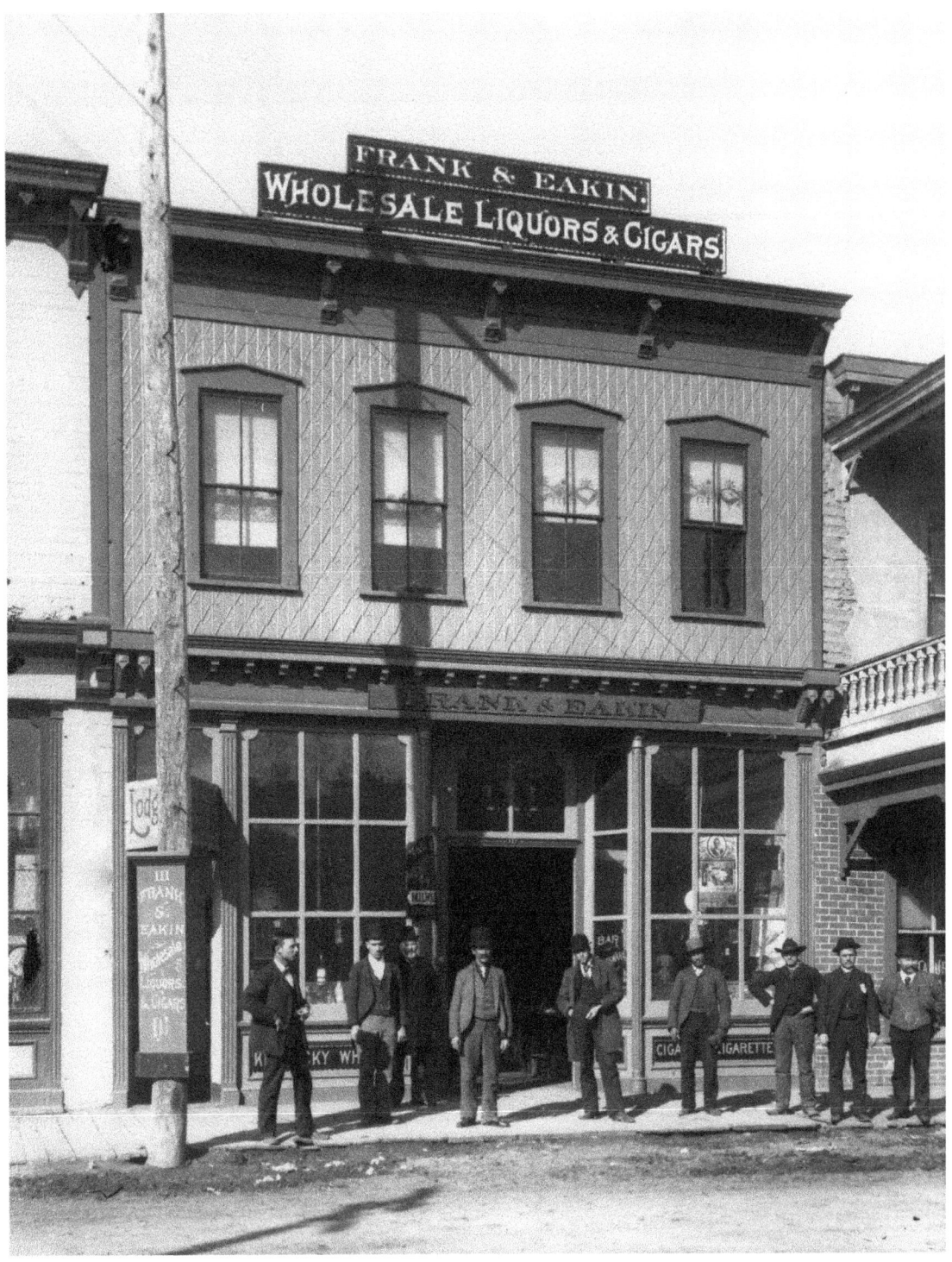

The Congregational Church started out with three members. This building was dedicated in April 1881. It was brick, with gothic elements and stained glass windows. William Henry Cobb took this photograph, at the corner of Broadway and Coal, in the Huning Highland Addition.

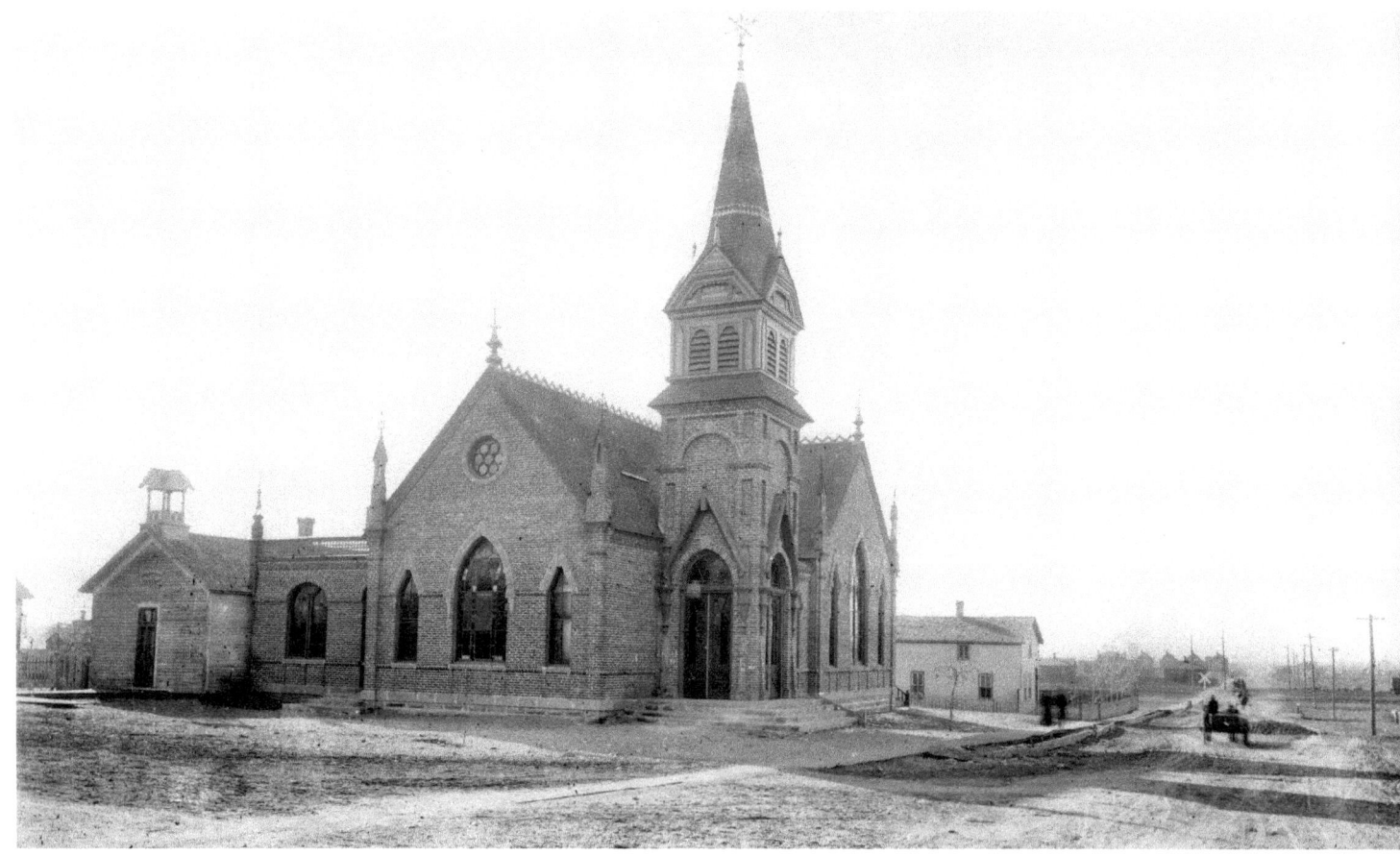

The Columbus Hotel, at Gold Avenue at Second Street, had George W. Hickox and Fox Jewelry Store downstairs, with Henry Lockhart Insurance and Real Estate upstairs in 1890. To the left are the Western Hardware Store and the Postal Telegraph Office.

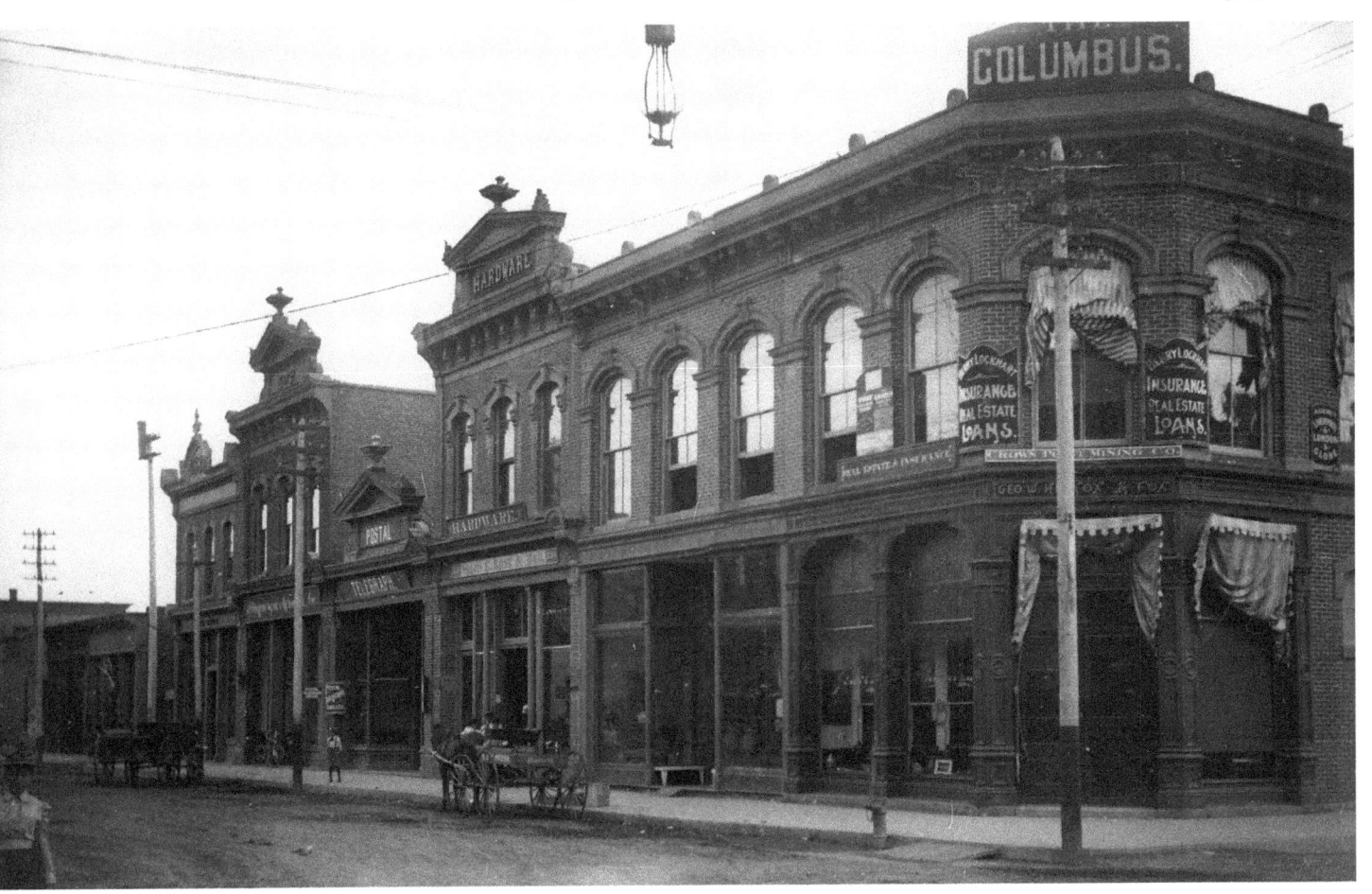

In 1881, W. L. Trimble and Company Livery, Feed, and Sale Stable became the first livery stable in Old Town. Trimble was from Kentucky, had fine horses, and liked to stand in front of the stable and greet people. He was very prosperous and opened a new stable at 113 N. Second Street. He rented ambulances, coaches, wagons, and tallyhos.

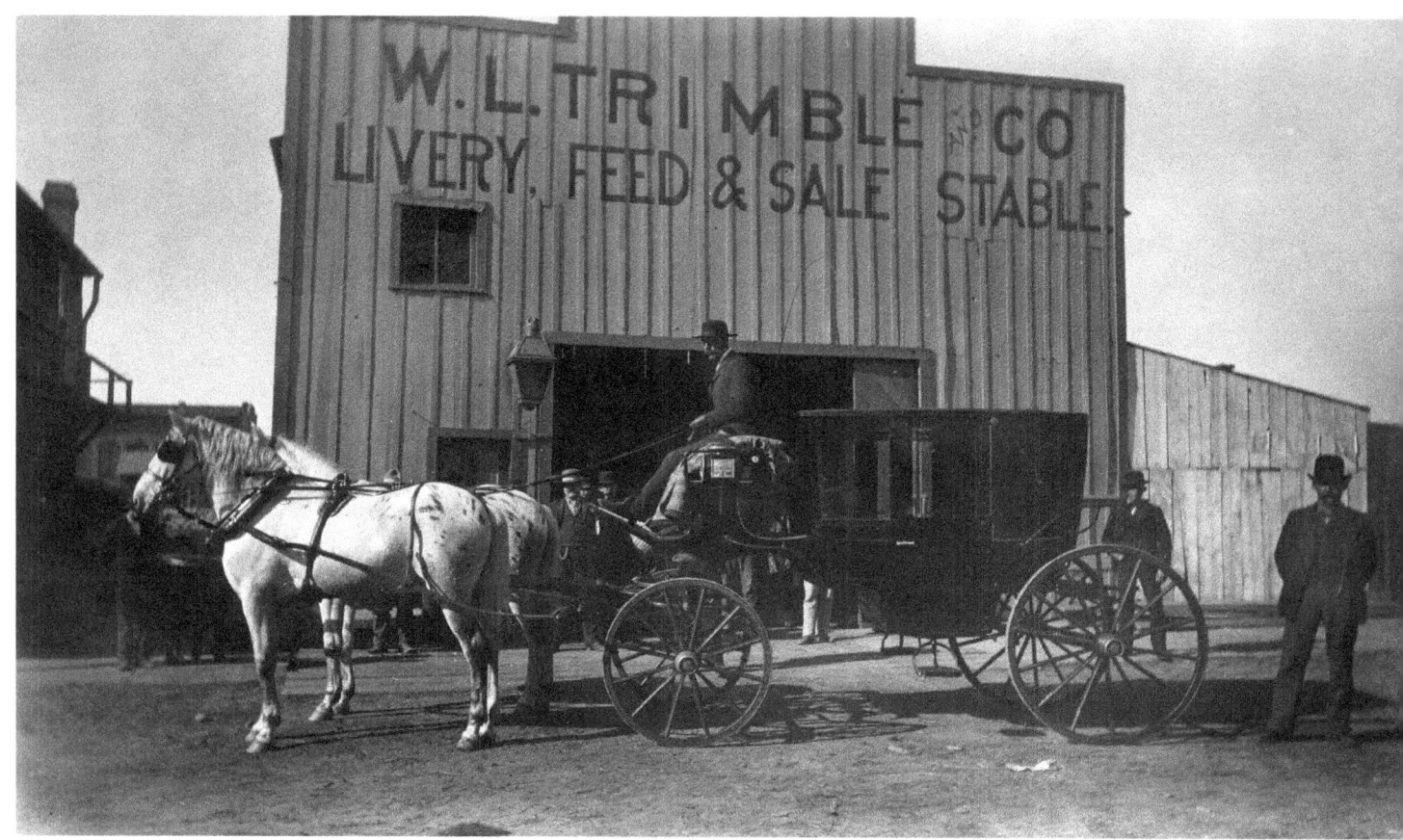

This was a typical adobe residence of the area. An adobe brick is made of sand, clay, and straw and dried in the sun. Such buildings are very durable and are well insulated.

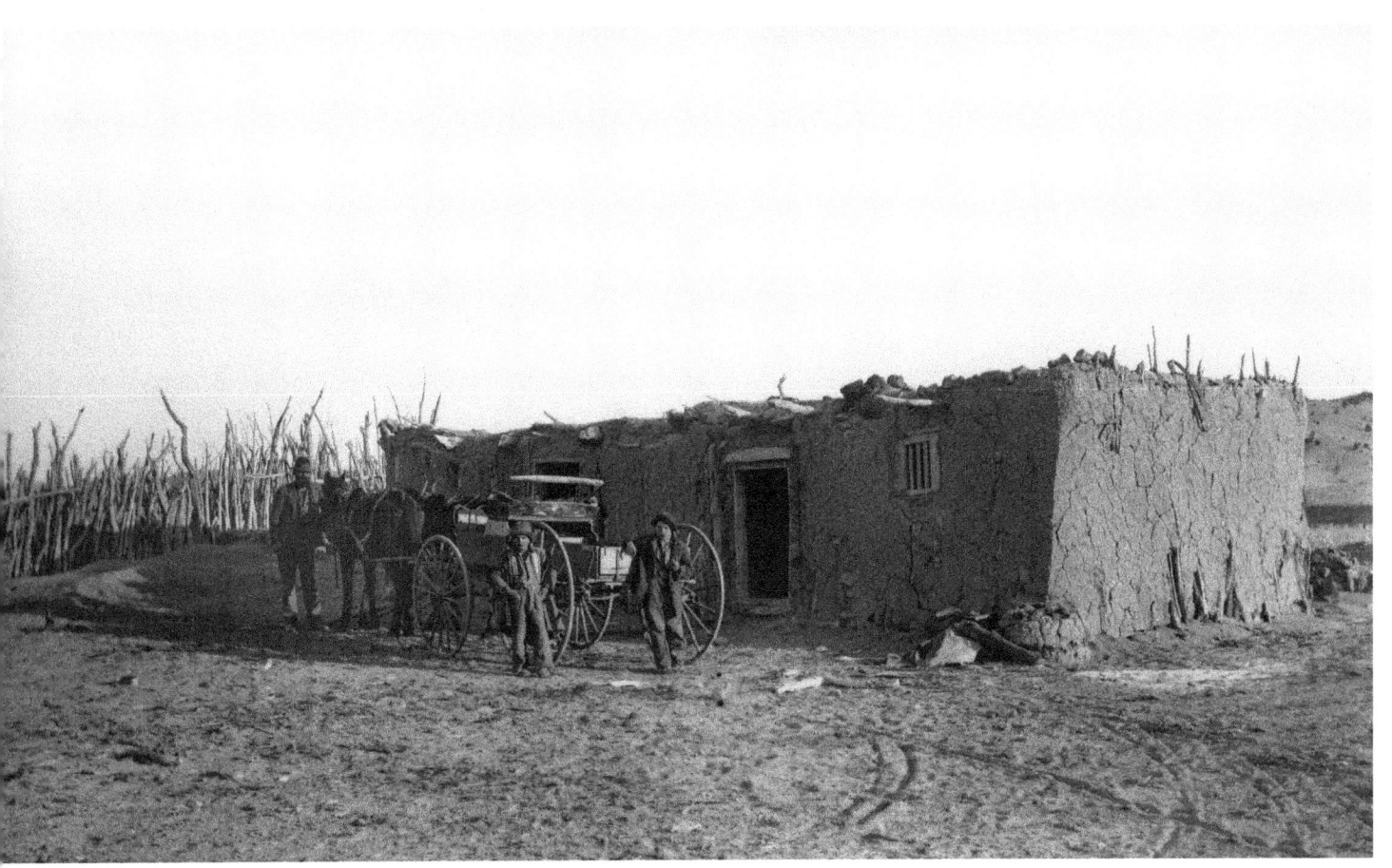

Albuquerque had a Presbyterian Church in 1883. The First Presbyterian Church pictured was on the corner of Silver Avenue and Fifth Street. The building was brick, with a crenellated bell tower and gothic windows.

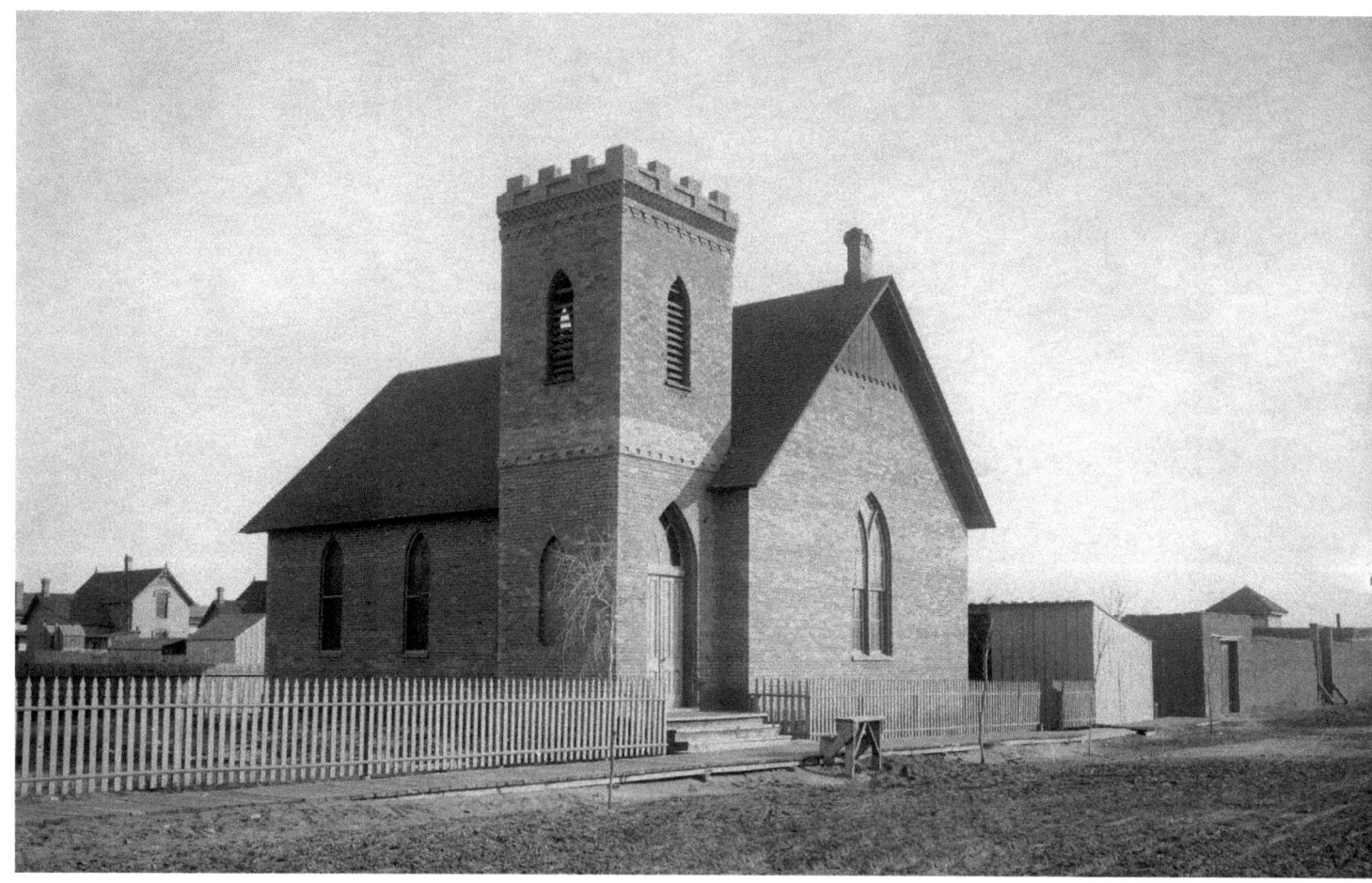

The William T. Keagy family in a horse-drawn buggy. William Keagy was a railroad brakeman and lived at 510 S. Edith Street. The railroad yard and a train can be seen in the background.

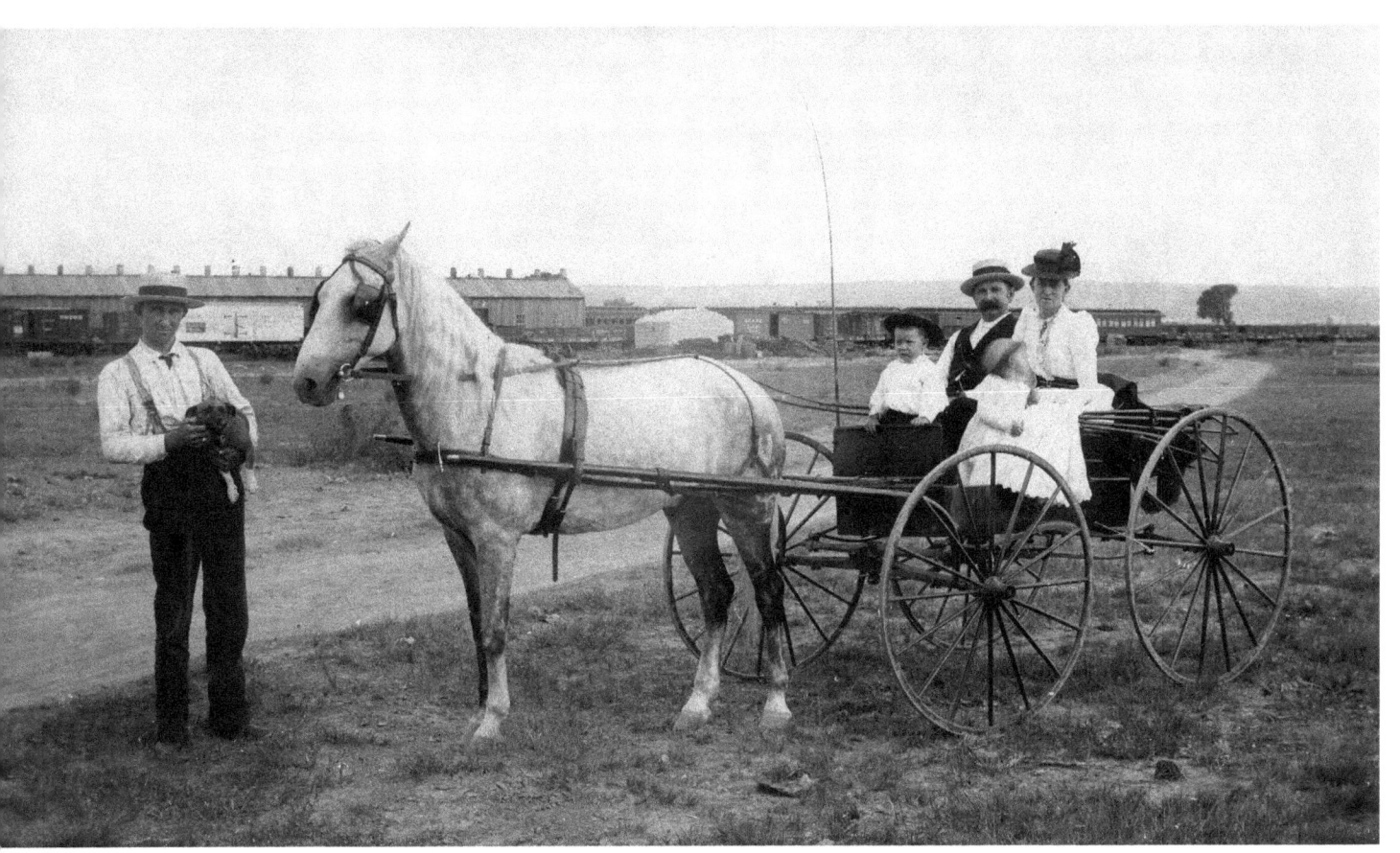

Passmore and Son Blacksmith and Horseshoing Shop, at 414 S. Second Street. The owners and employees shown are identified as Lu Kuhn, Peter Thomas, Thomas J. Passmore, Jr. and Thomas Passmore, Sr. The tracks in the front of the building are for the trolley. Gertrude Zachary Antiques is there now.

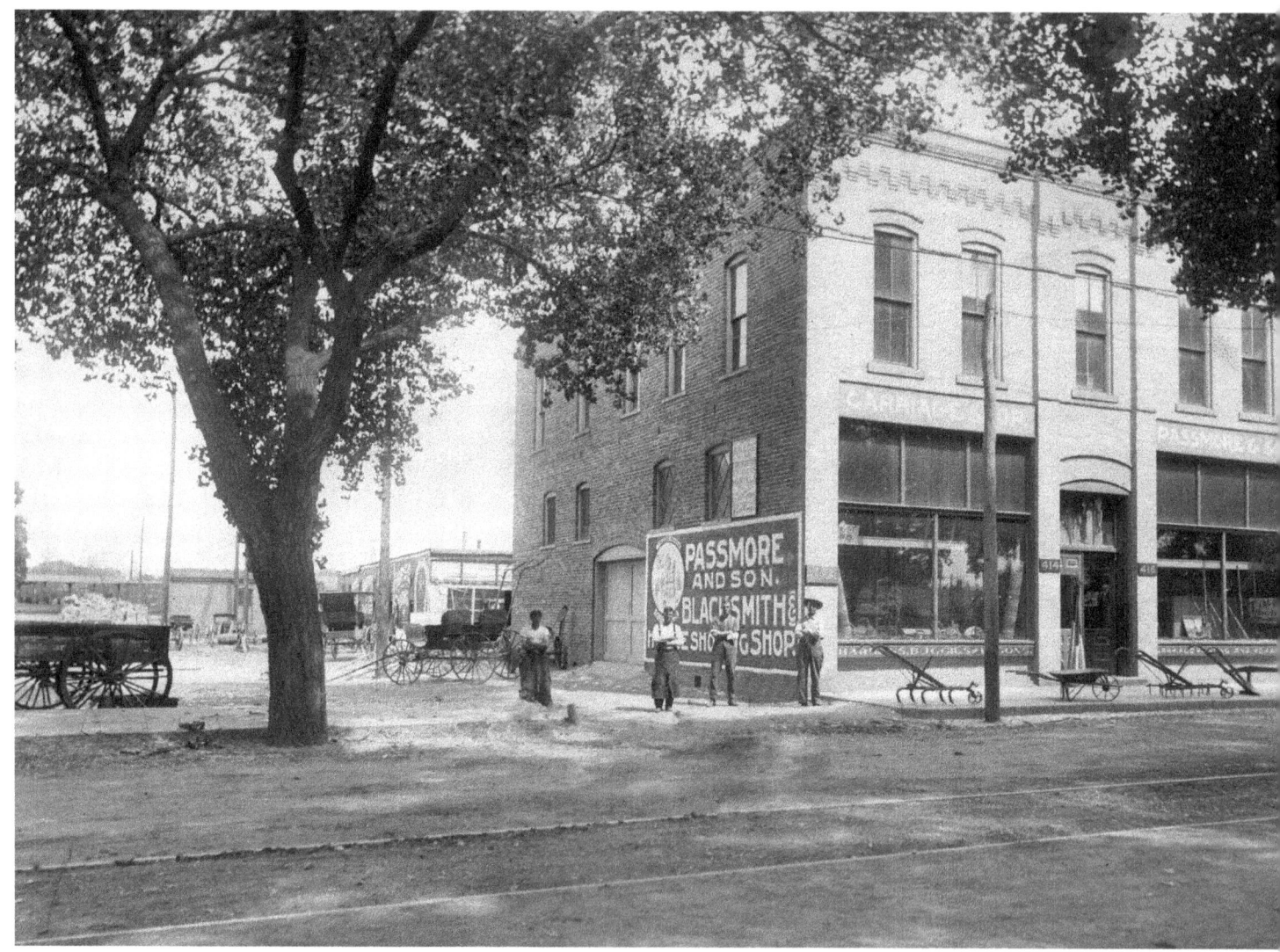

E. L. Washburn and Company Store, on S. Second Street, in the Cromwell Building. Writing on the photograph identifies the men, starting on the left, as Jake Gainsley, an unidentified Gainsley, Elmer Washburn, and Gus Gainsley.

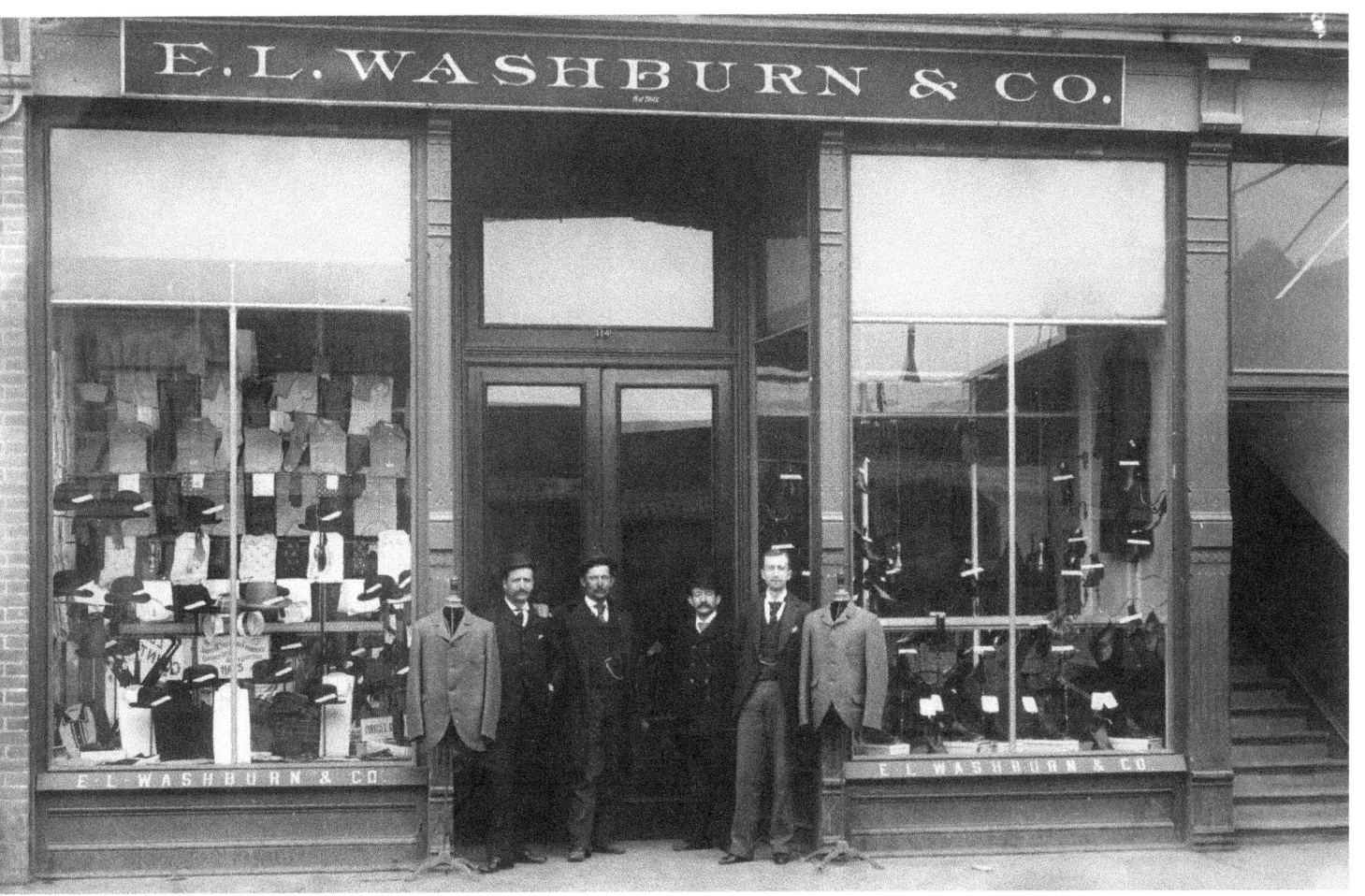

Immaculate Conception Church, built in 1882, with Saint
Mary's School next door, in the 200 block of S. Sixth Street.

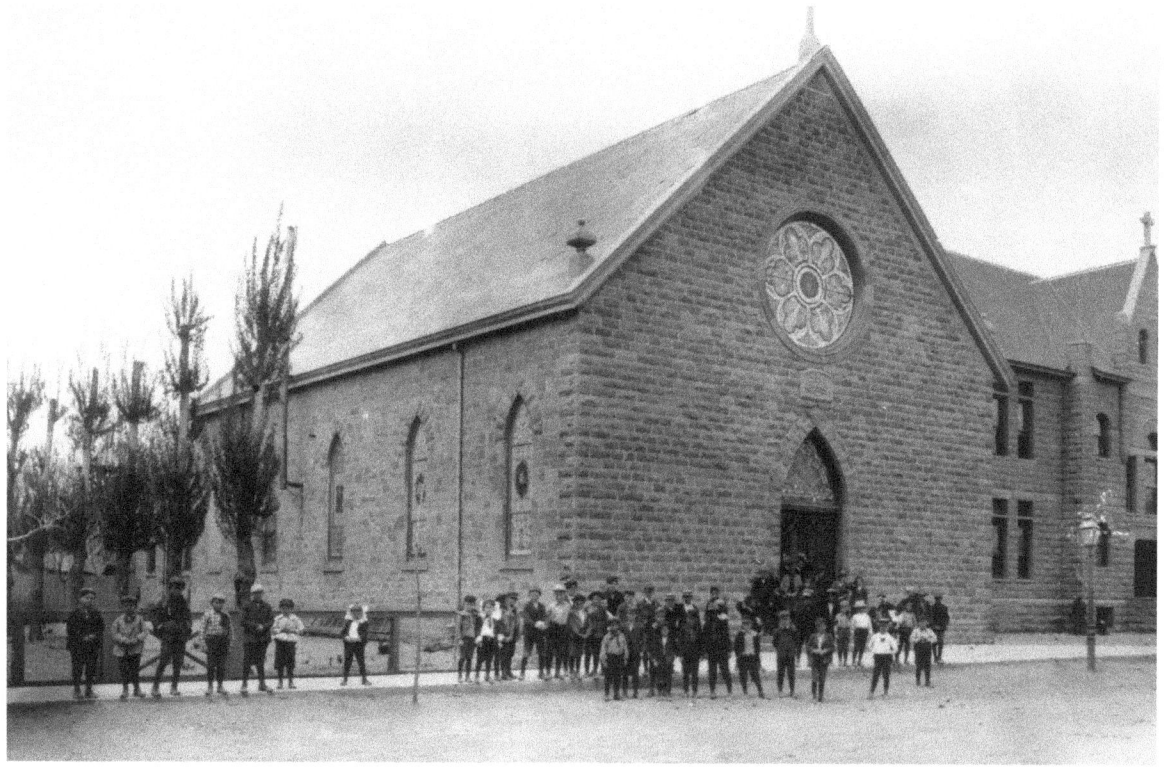

Albuquerque *Daily Citizen*, at 113 Gold Avenue, published the newspaper and did printing jobs from 1886 to 1909. To the left of the boys in the burro cart is the Cobb Studio, at 115 Gold Avenue. William Henry Cobb or his wife, Eddie Ross Cobb, took many of the photographs in this book.

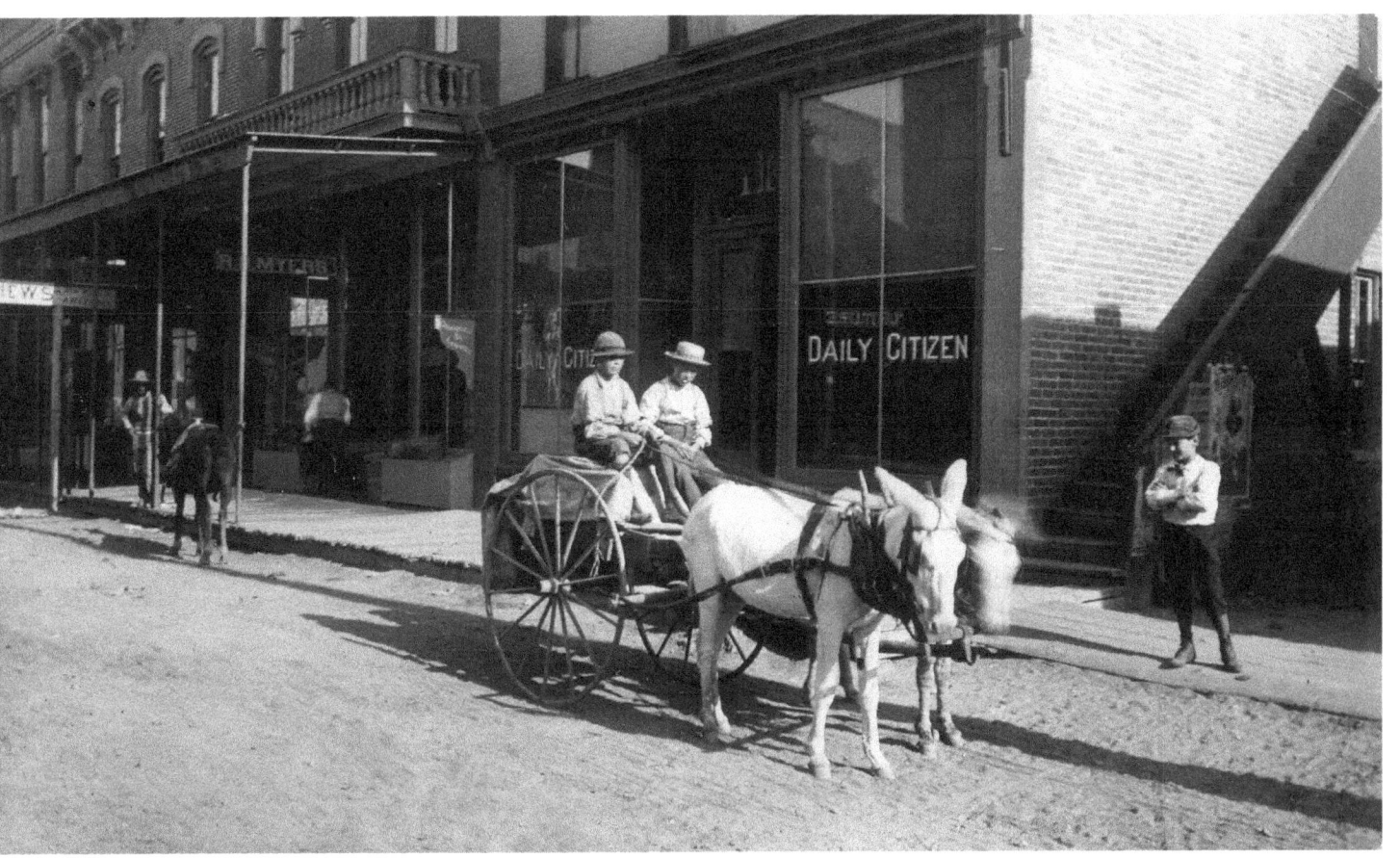

Train stopped at Albuquerque railroad station, with the European Hotel in the background. Gate towers were used to control the traffic and allow the train safe passage before the underpasses were built in the 1930s.

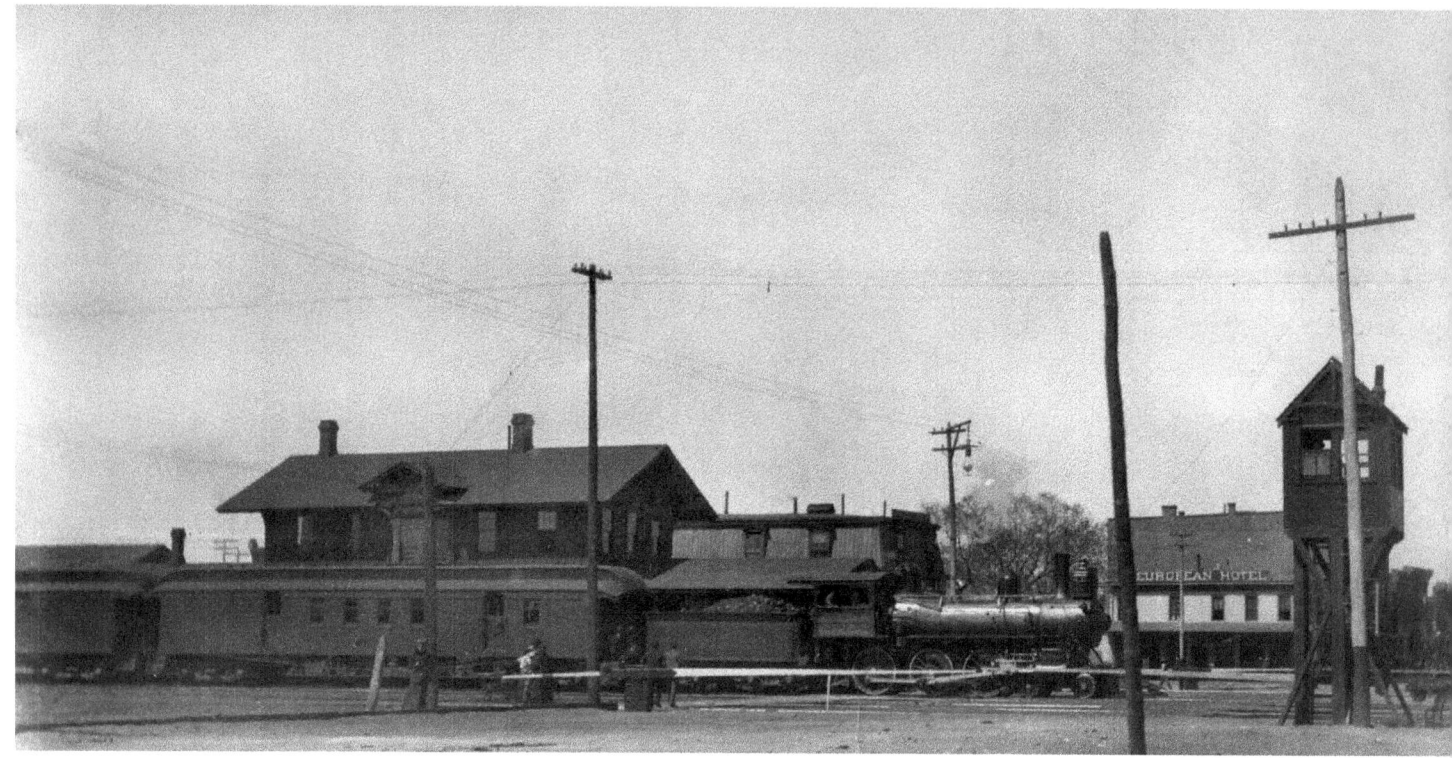

Looking north along Second Street, from Silver Avenue, is an interesting business area. The Post Office is on the left side, in the Barnett Building, and a sign on the corner says Imperial Laundry. A Sanborn Fire Insurance map shows there were four Chinese laundries in this block.

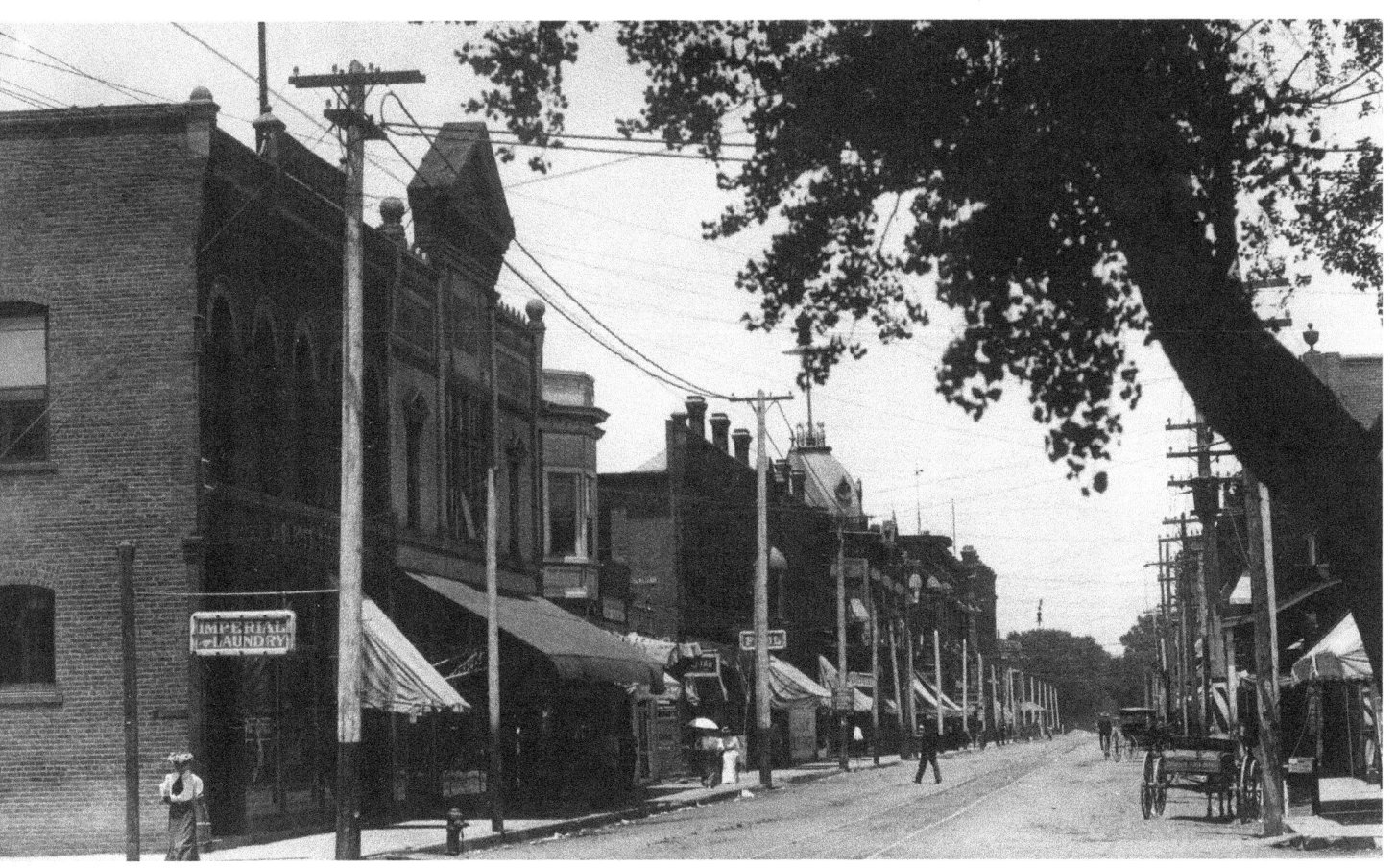

The M. B. Howard Studio took this picture of the women's football team
in front of Hodgin Hall, at the University of New Mexico.

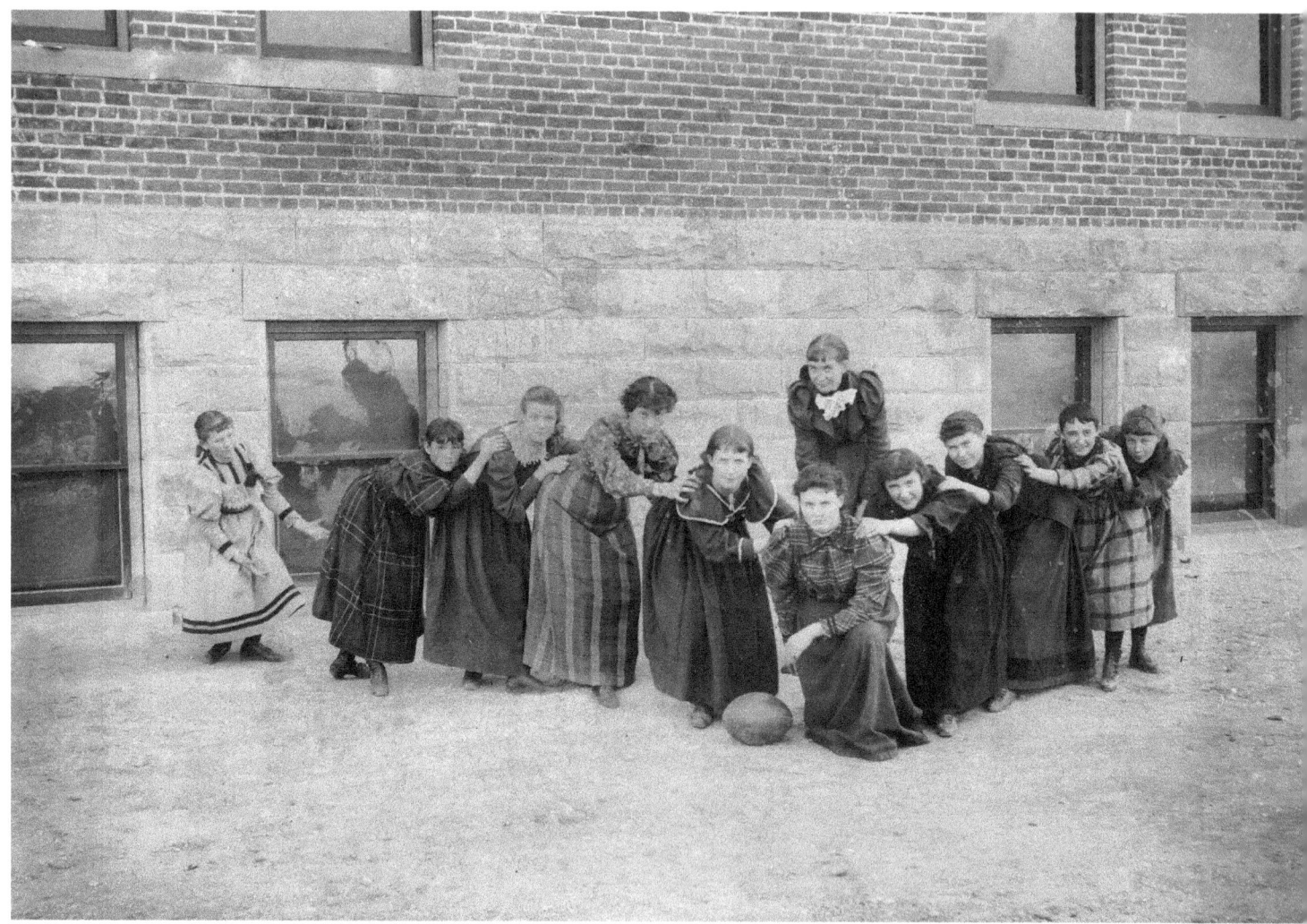

The Whiting Building, on the left, was at the corner of Gold Avenue and Second Street. The San Felipe Hotel is in the background, at the corner of Gold and Fifth. The three-story hotel burned down, even though twelve-year-old Will Keleher pulled the alarm at the red fire-alarm box and the volunteer fire fighters got there quickly.

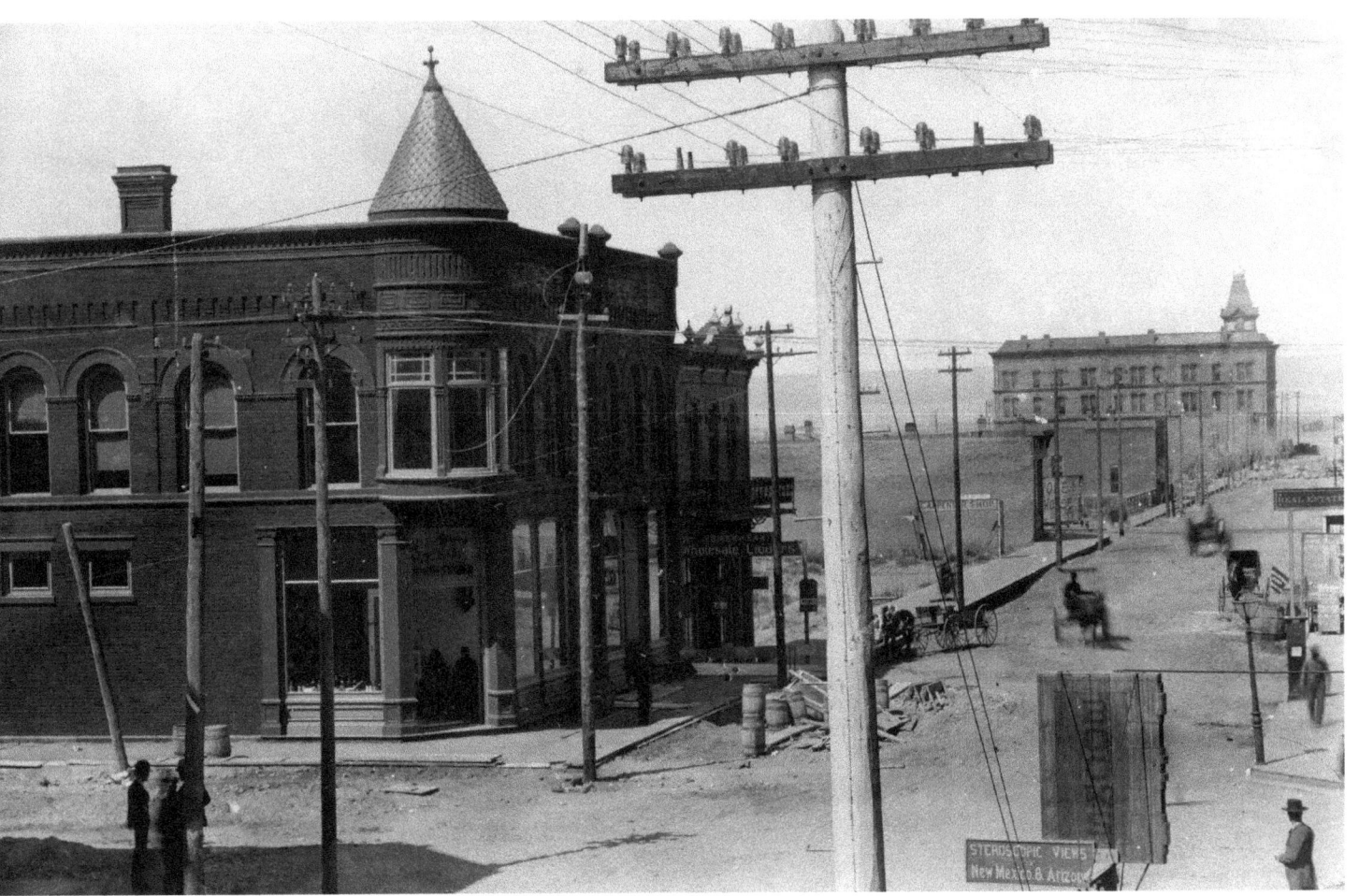

Looking west on Gold Avenue, the Commercial Club is on the left side of the street at the far end and the Whiting Building is also shown. On the right side of the street are the Grunsfeld Building, the *Daily Citizen*, and the Cobb Studio. William Henry Cobb and his wife, Eddie Ross Cobb, lived above the studio at 115 W. Gold Avenue.

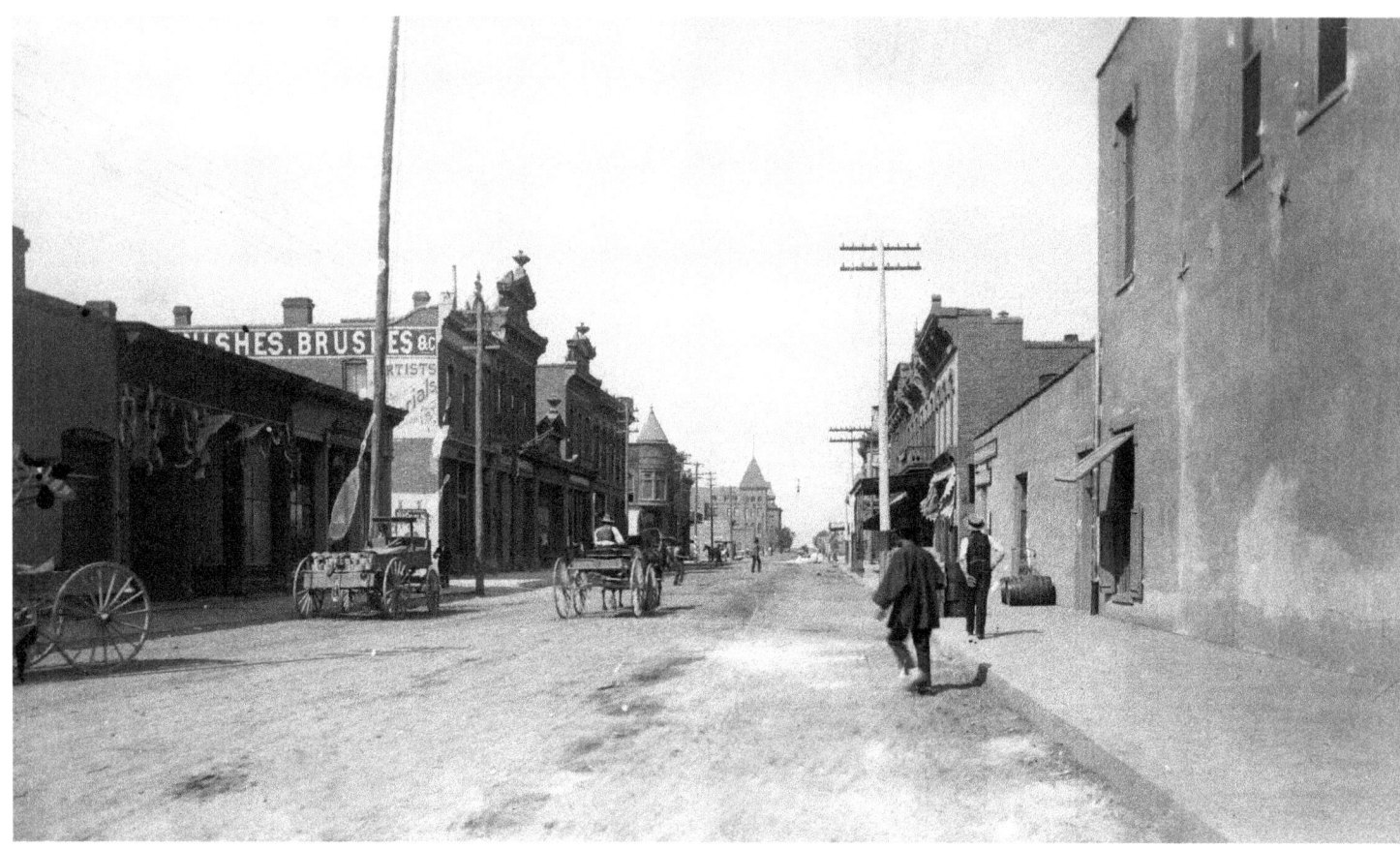

Eight men and a dog in front of the infamous White Elephant Saloon. The saloon had a huge solid mahogany bar that could accommodate fifty men. One of the men is Col. J. G. Albright, so Emma L. Albright was probably the photographer. Joe Barnett tore the saloon down after Prohibition and erected the Sunshine Theater building.

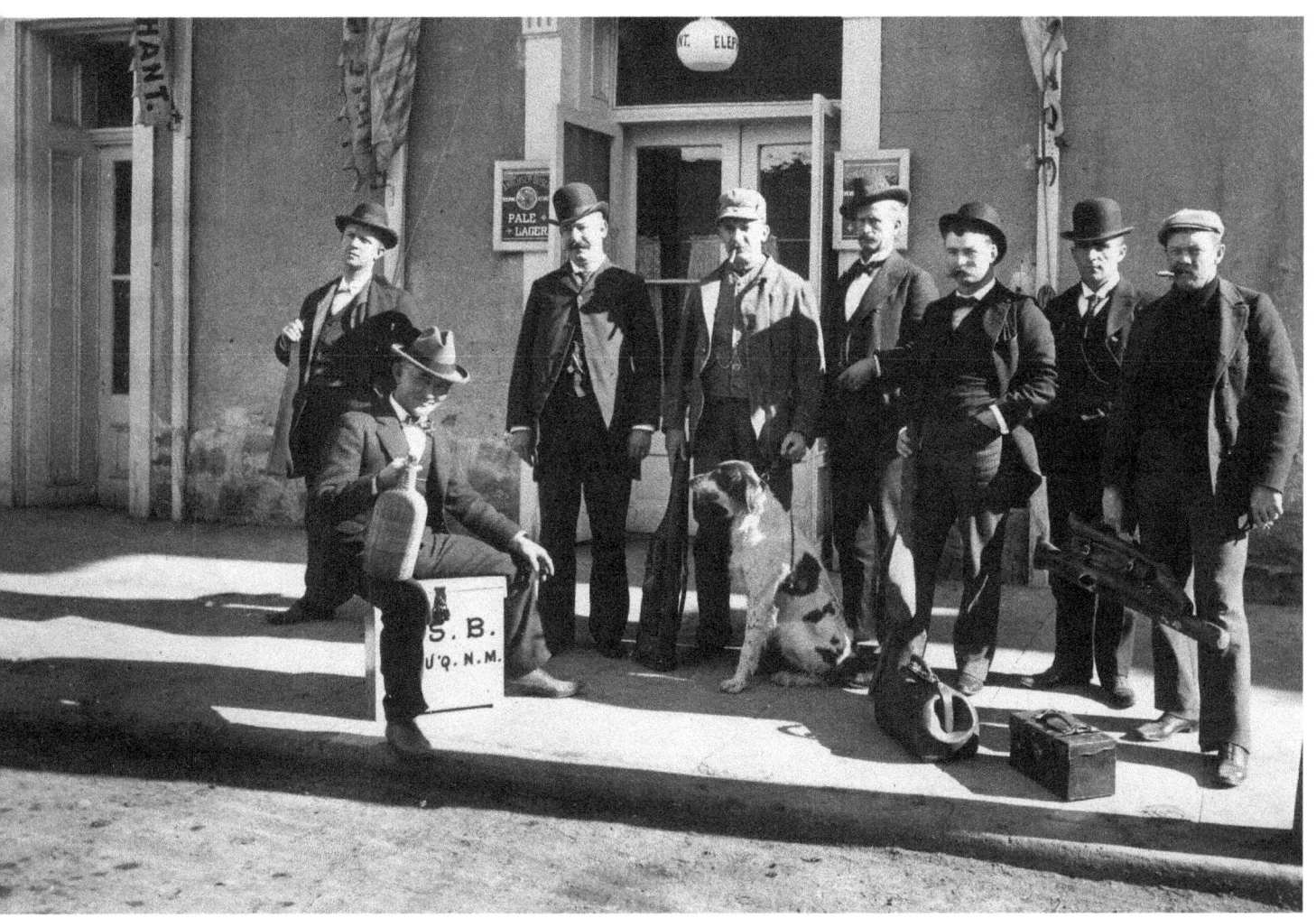

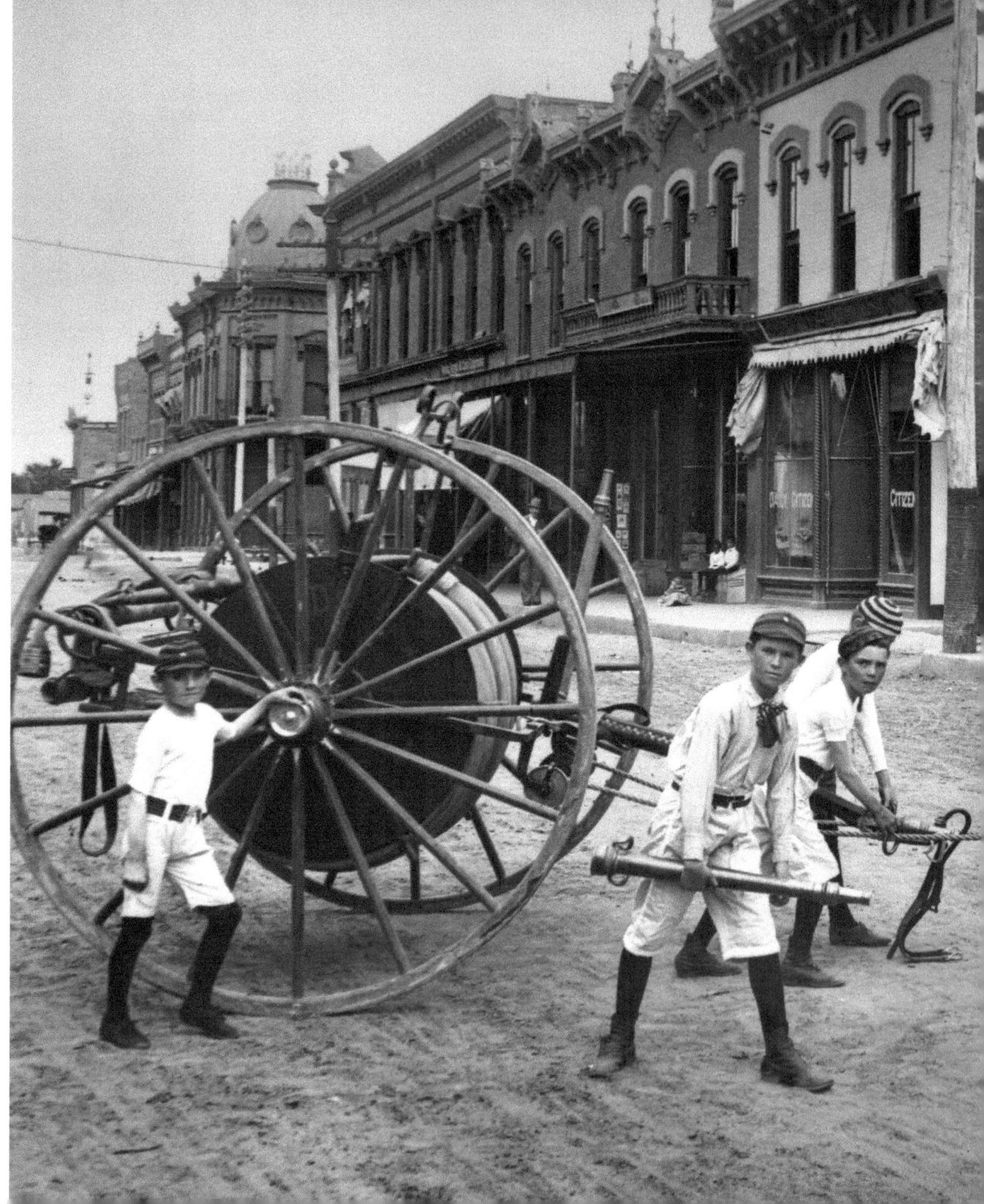

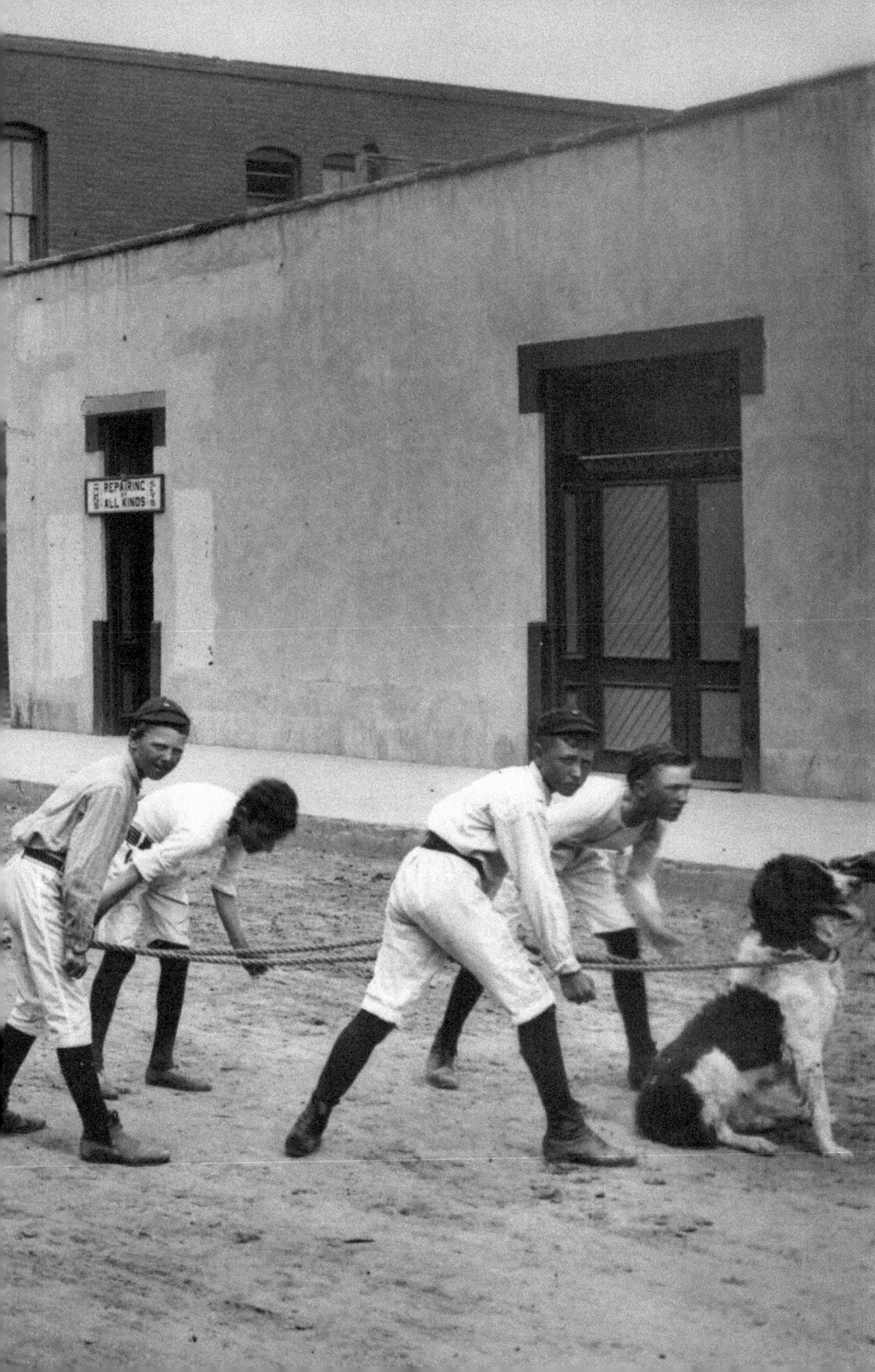

Volunteer Fire Department Youth Hose Cart Team, near the 100 block of W. Gold Avenue. From the left are Jack Harnett, Lawrence Walsh, Bob Archer, Bob Hart, Joe Helwig, Billy Wilson, Morris Hartnett, and Fidel Romero.

Fergusson Volunteer Hook and Ladder crew at the corner of Gold Avenue and Second Street, near the Whiting Building. Calvin Whiting, a lawyer, had this building built by 1887, and it was there until 1962. When the city took over fire fighting on June 6, 1900, they replaced the hand-drawn hose carts with a horse-drawn vehicle. The horses were named Slim and Frisky.

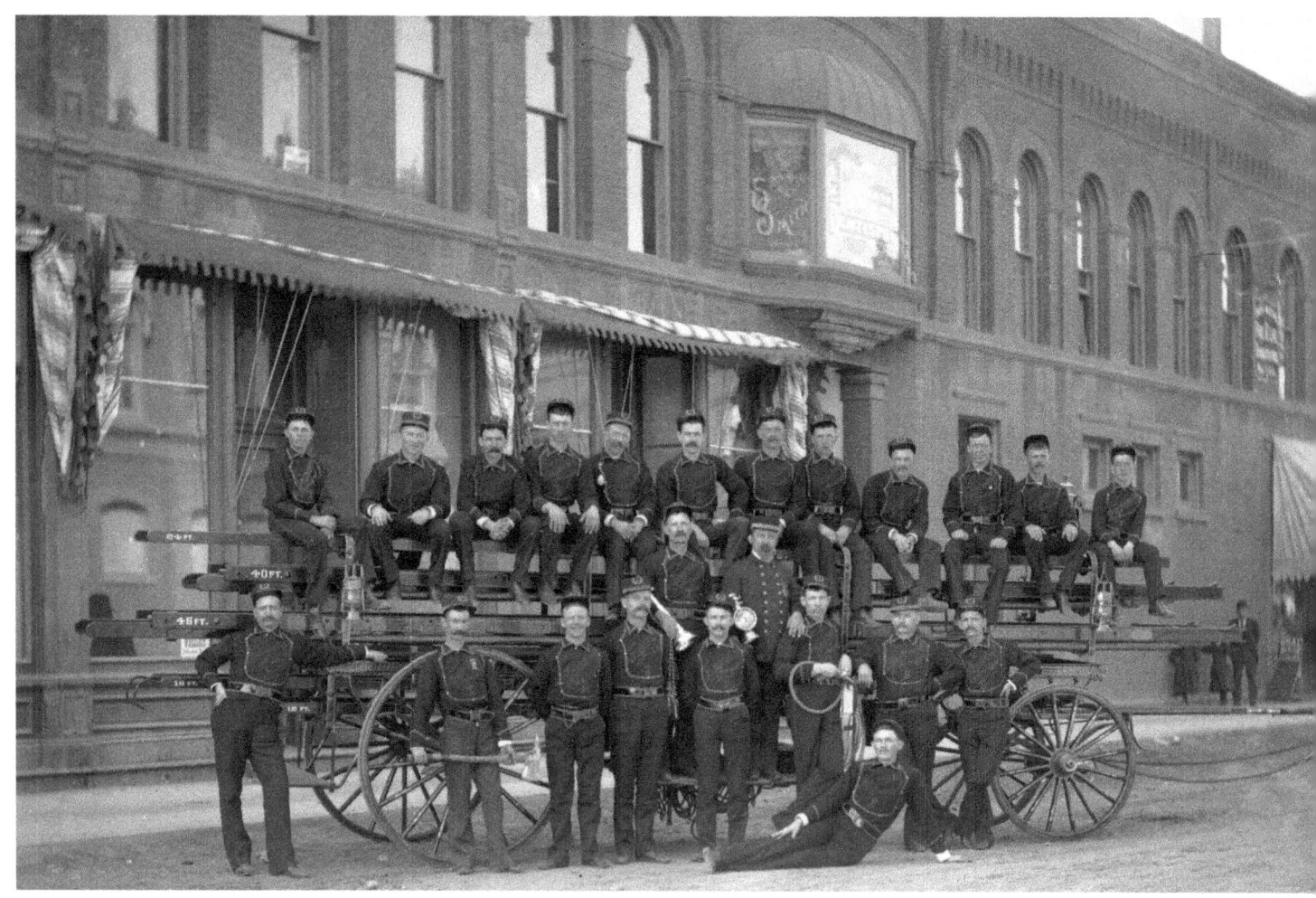

Badaracco's Summer Garden, a beer garden, was on Mountain Road and Fifteenth Street. The Badaraccos were an Italian family. People used to go up Mountain Road for picnics in the country.

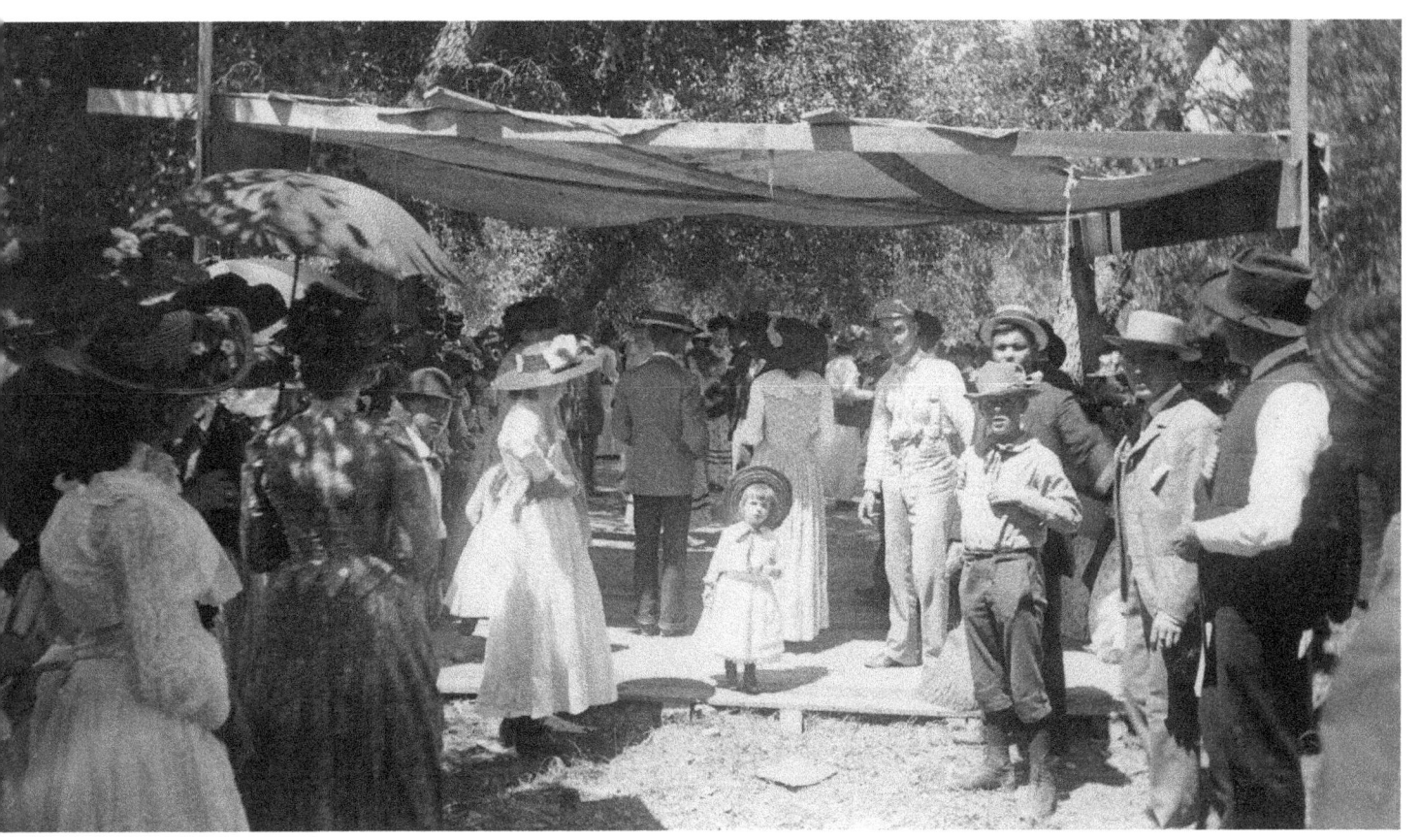

The Cactus Roadhouse with a large group of men, a horse-drawn wagon, and a dog in front.

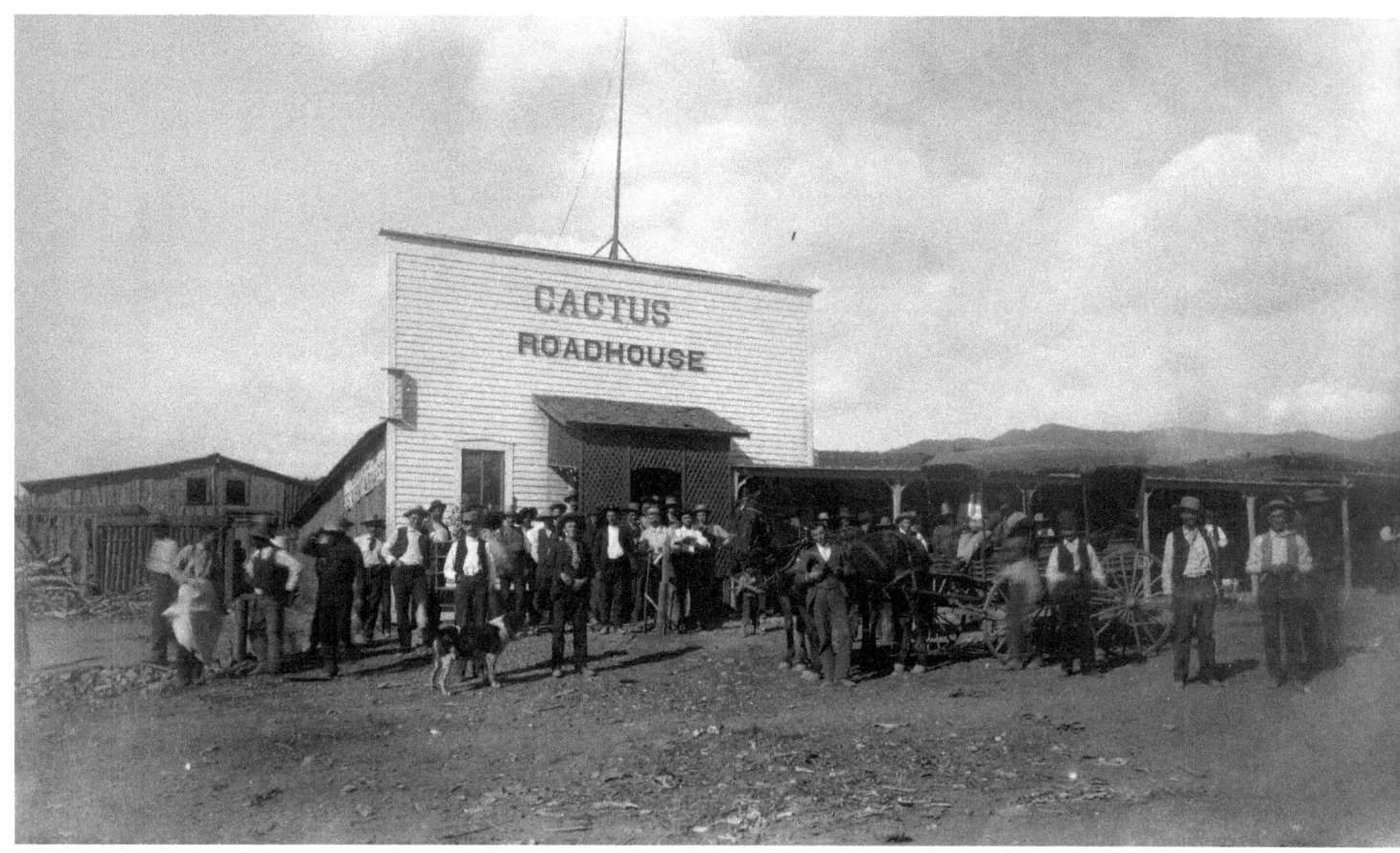

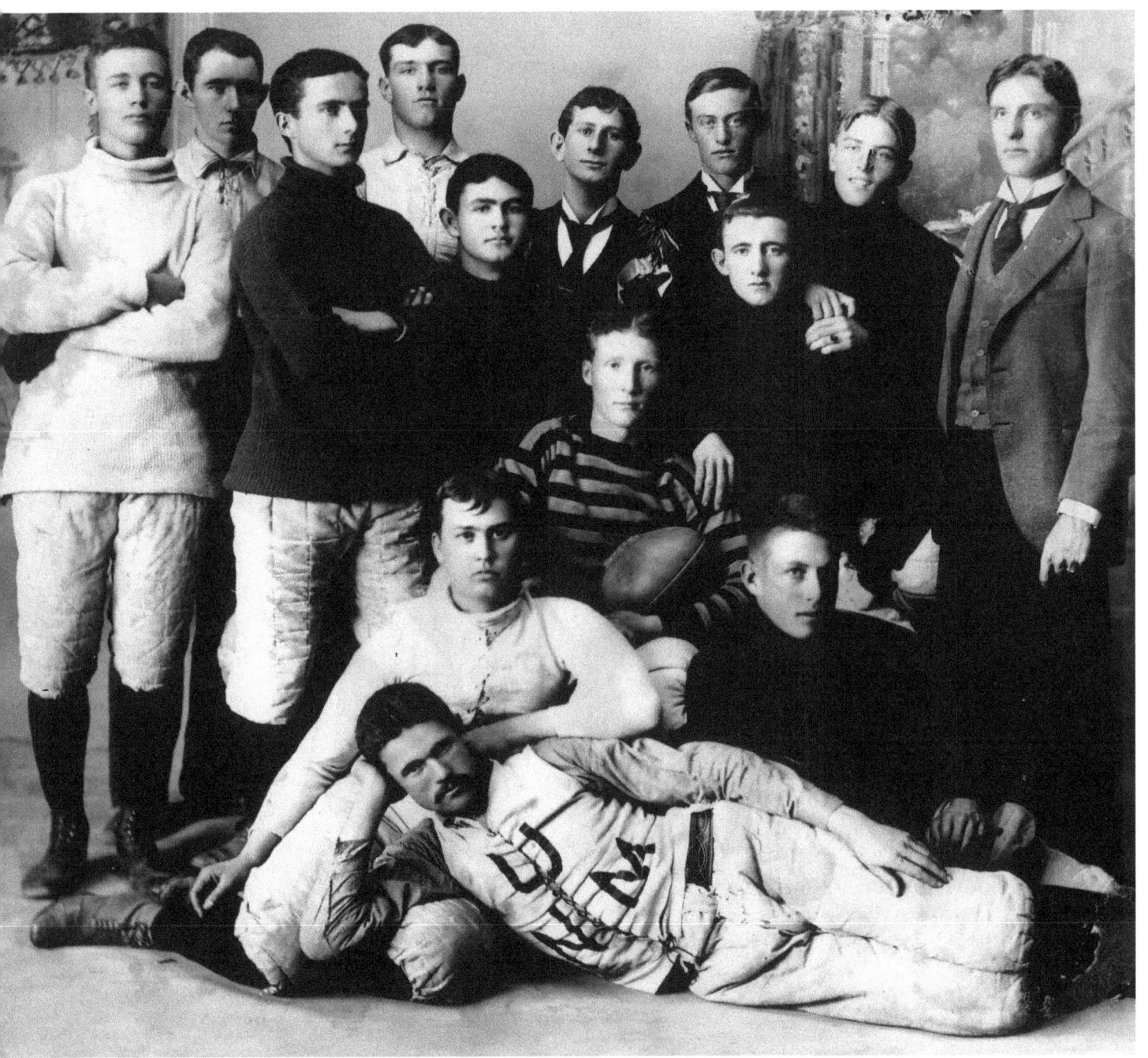

The 1894 University of New Mexico football team.

The first automobile in Albuquerque was a Locomobile Steamer, owned by Mr. Dobson, a bicycle shop proprietor. He drove it from Denver to Albuquerque in November 1897. It was the first car to cross over the Raton Pass. Dobson became the first car dealer in town.

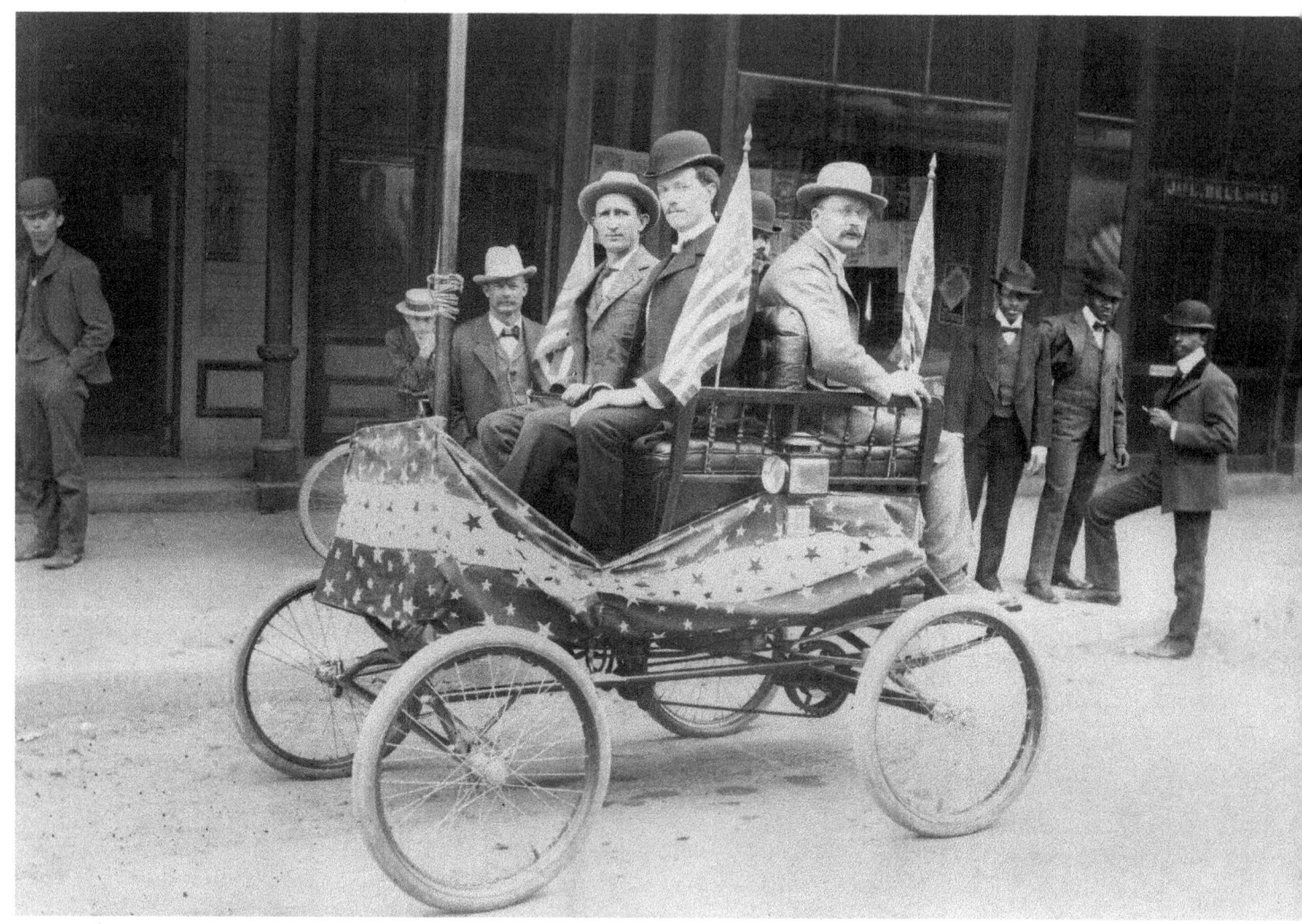

CHIEF CITY OF A NEW EMPIRE

(1900–1919)

"Chief City of a New Empire in the Great Southwest" is the subtitle of a 1908 booster booklet published by the city and the Commercial Club. They had high expectations for Albuquerque. Panoramic photographs in the booster booklet prove the city was experiencing amazing growth. The American Lumber Company was the second-largest employer and the railroad was the first. Albuquerque had the second-largest repair shops on the Santa Fe Railway, and in 1914 the railroad built more shops south of New Town Albuquerque. A thirty-two-stall roundhouse was built in 1914–1915. There was even talk of building a seventy-five-stall roundhouse.

The population had doubled in five years, and the Sixteenth National Irrigation Congress was deemed a success. Albuquerque had four banks, modern utilities, Western Union, and the Federal Building, and 232 building permits were issued in fiscal year 1907. Professional police and fire departments, a library system, and public education system were in place.

There were clubs, including the Commercial Club, Woman's Club, an Elks Theater, and Columbo Hall. The fine year-round climate was promoted, with sanitaria, health cottages, health resorts, and hospitals. A French magazine even mentioned New Mexico as the area with the least tuberculosis (then known as consumption). The photographer William Henry Cobb settled in Albuquerque due to a near fatal bout of tuberculosis in 1889 and lived for more than twenty years. Many patients who were cured, or had the disease in check, added a sophisticated element to the city, such as the leading architect of Spanish Pueblo-style buildings, John Gaw Meem. Future governor of New Mexico Clyde Tingley came to Albuquerque from Ohio because Carrie Wooster, the woman he was courting, was chasing the tuberculosis cure. When her mother became sick en route to Phoenix, they stopped in Albuquerque for medical care, and all three stayed after discovering the outstanding health facilities. Clyde Tingley and Carrie Wooster were married by Dr. Hugh Cooper, founder of the Presbyterian Sanatorium, and lived in a small health-seekers cottage on Iron Avenue.

Bicycles were very big in Albuquerque. Men rode them to work, women rode them shopping, and children rode them to school. The sandwich board in front of Muggley's Confectionery, beside The Model Baking Co., says "Ice Cream today."

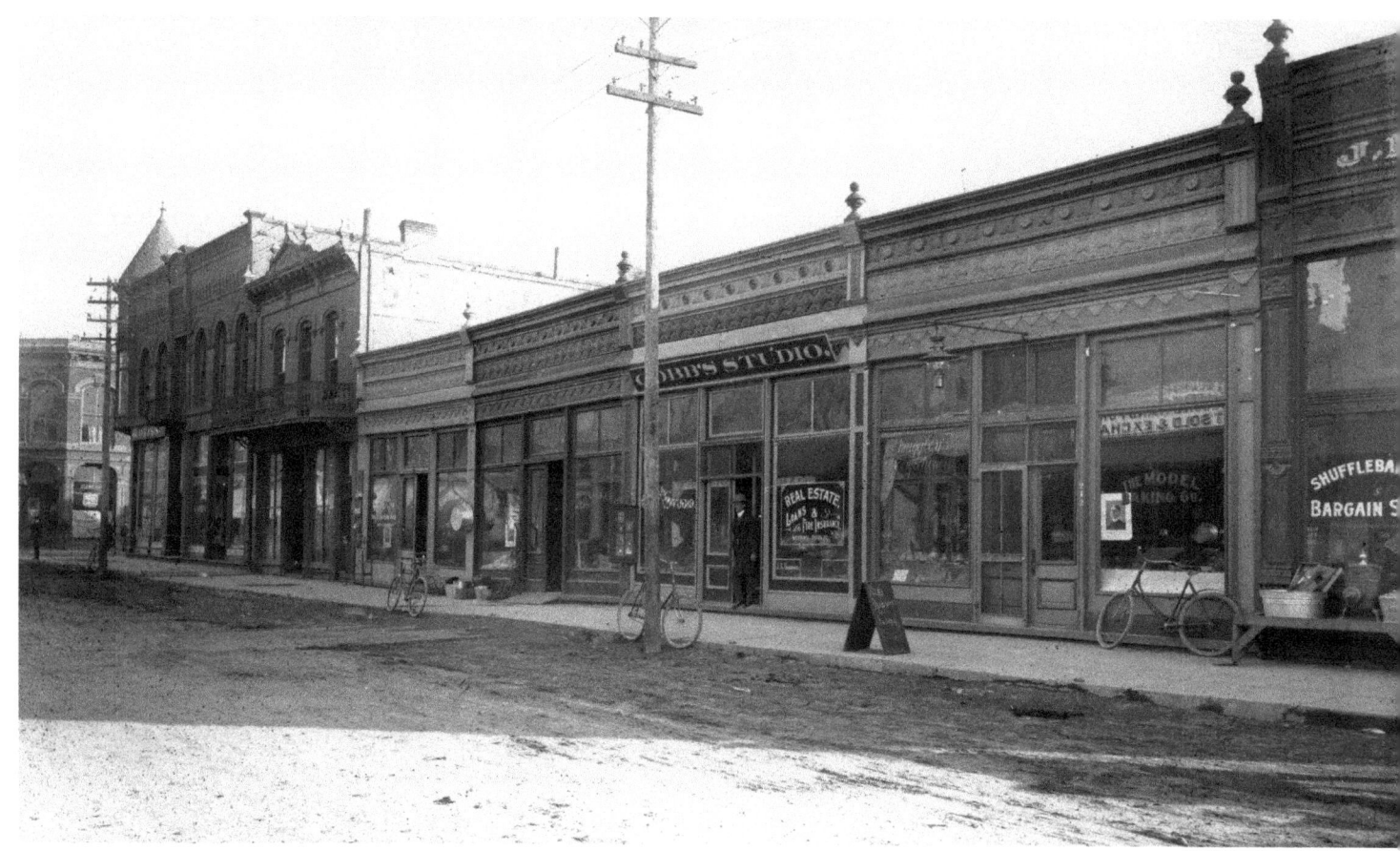

At Third Street and Railroad Avenue, this parade went past the Rosenwald Brothers Hardware Store, the N. T. Armijo building, and the Zeiger building. Captain John Borradaile, of the Albuquerque Guard, led the horsemen.

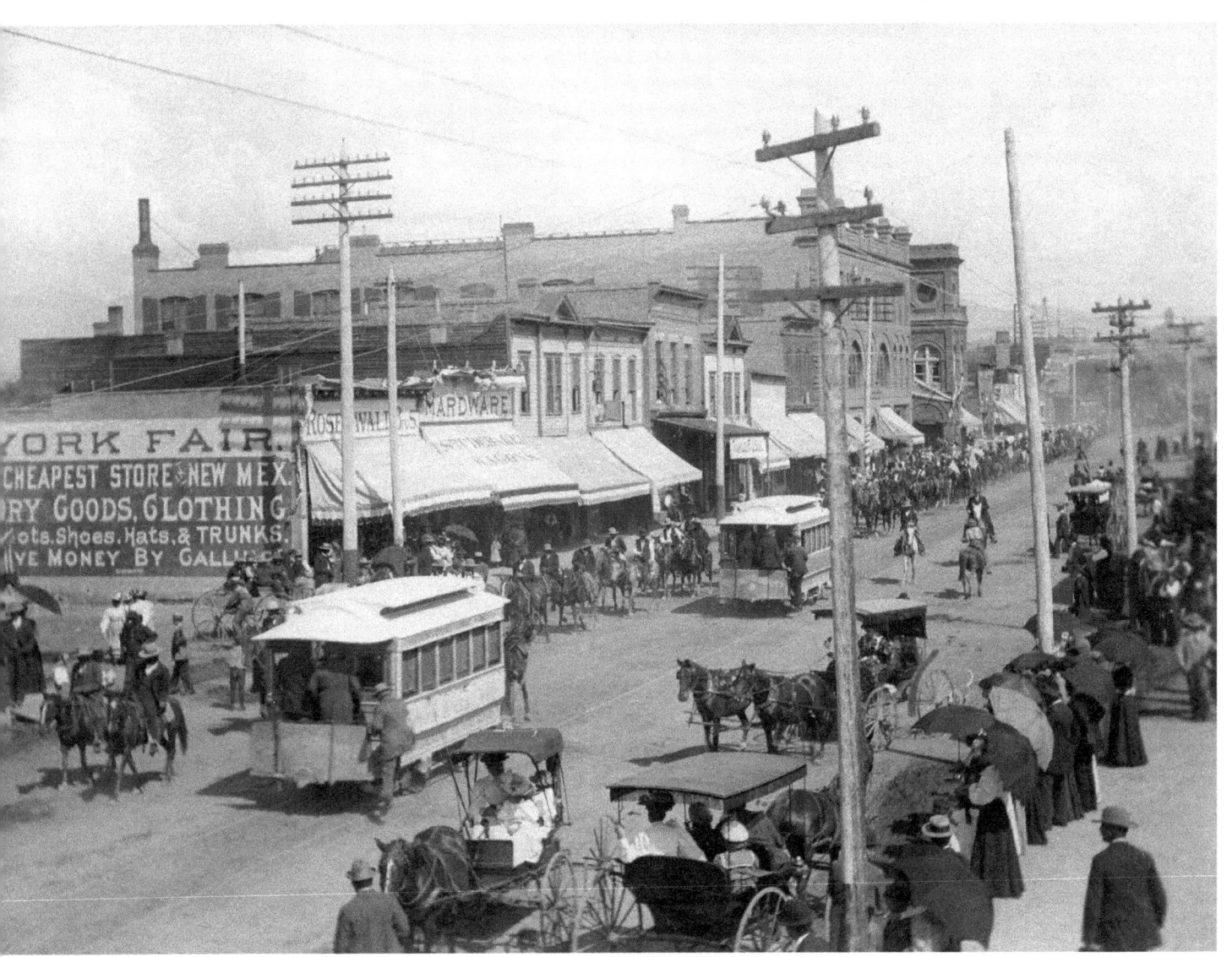

Ed Pickard, an Elks Burlesque Circus parade clown, was photographed in a horse cart on November 9, 1900.

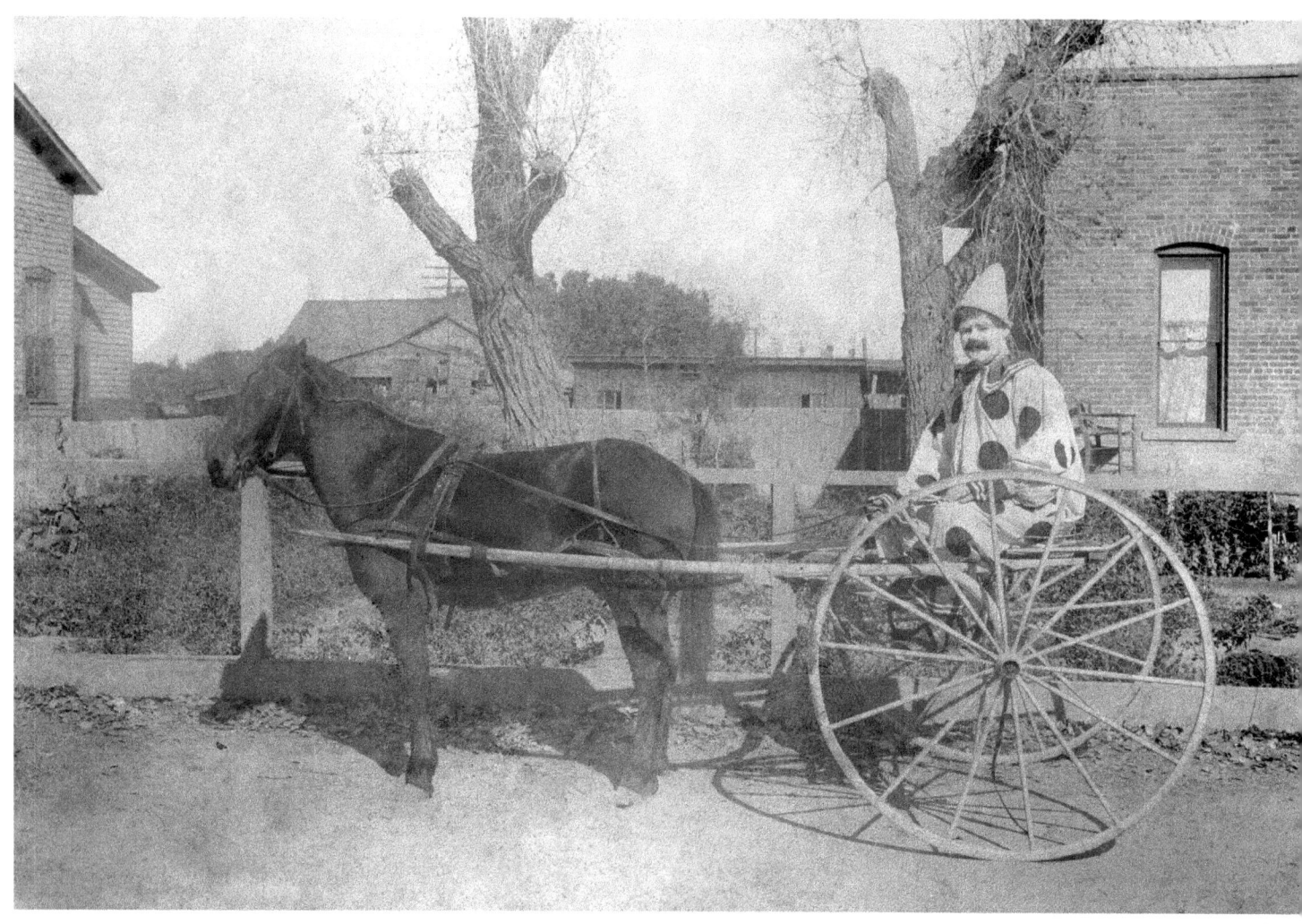

The Elks Burlesque Circus parade on November 9, 1900, included two people in a giraffe costume, a clown on a burro, and a man in a Turkish costume. The Gloria Saloon behind them was at 217 N. Third Street. Pasquale Cutinoli was its proprietor.

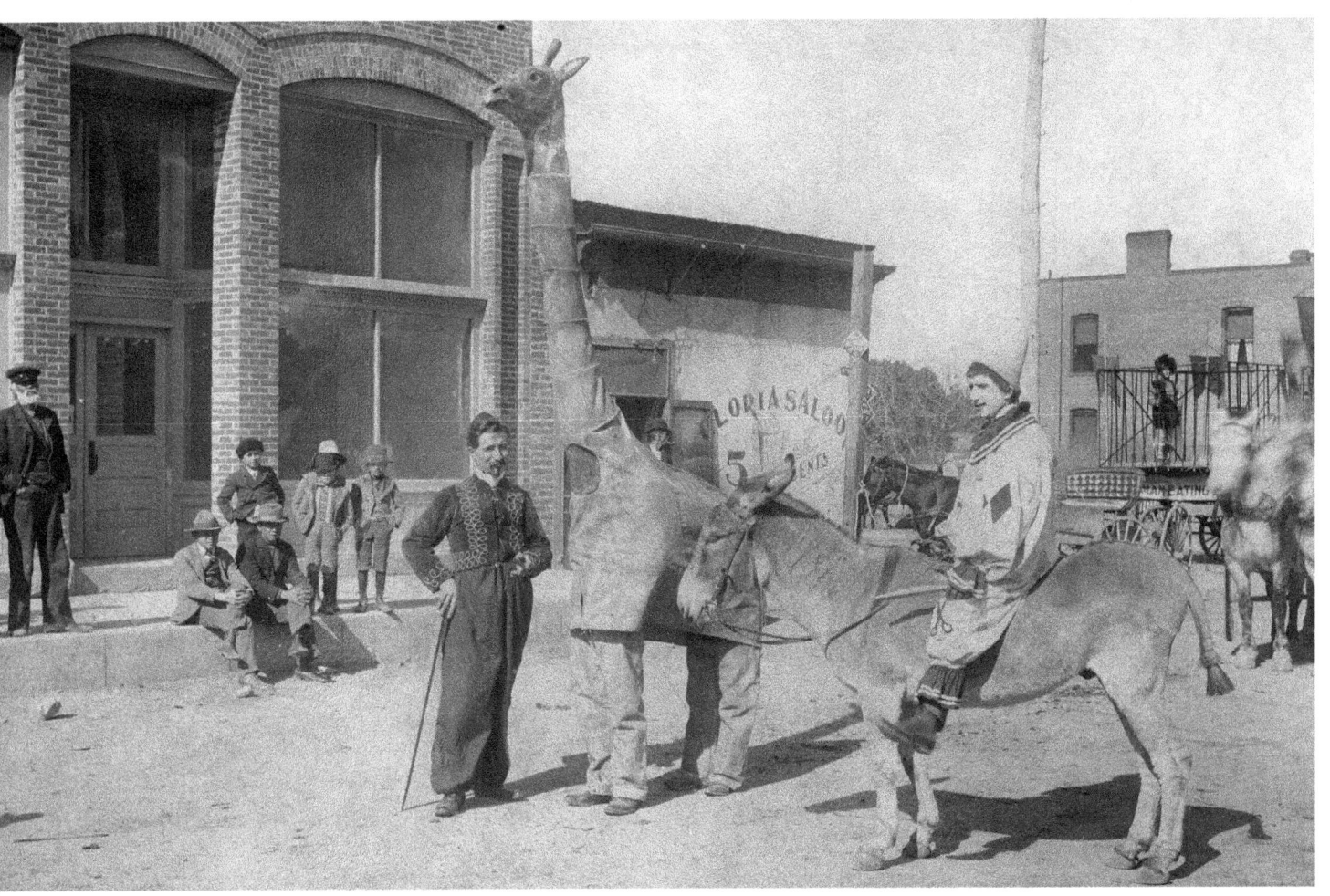

"Miss Annie Oakley" banner on a horse-drawn wagon in the Elks
Burlesque Circus parade.

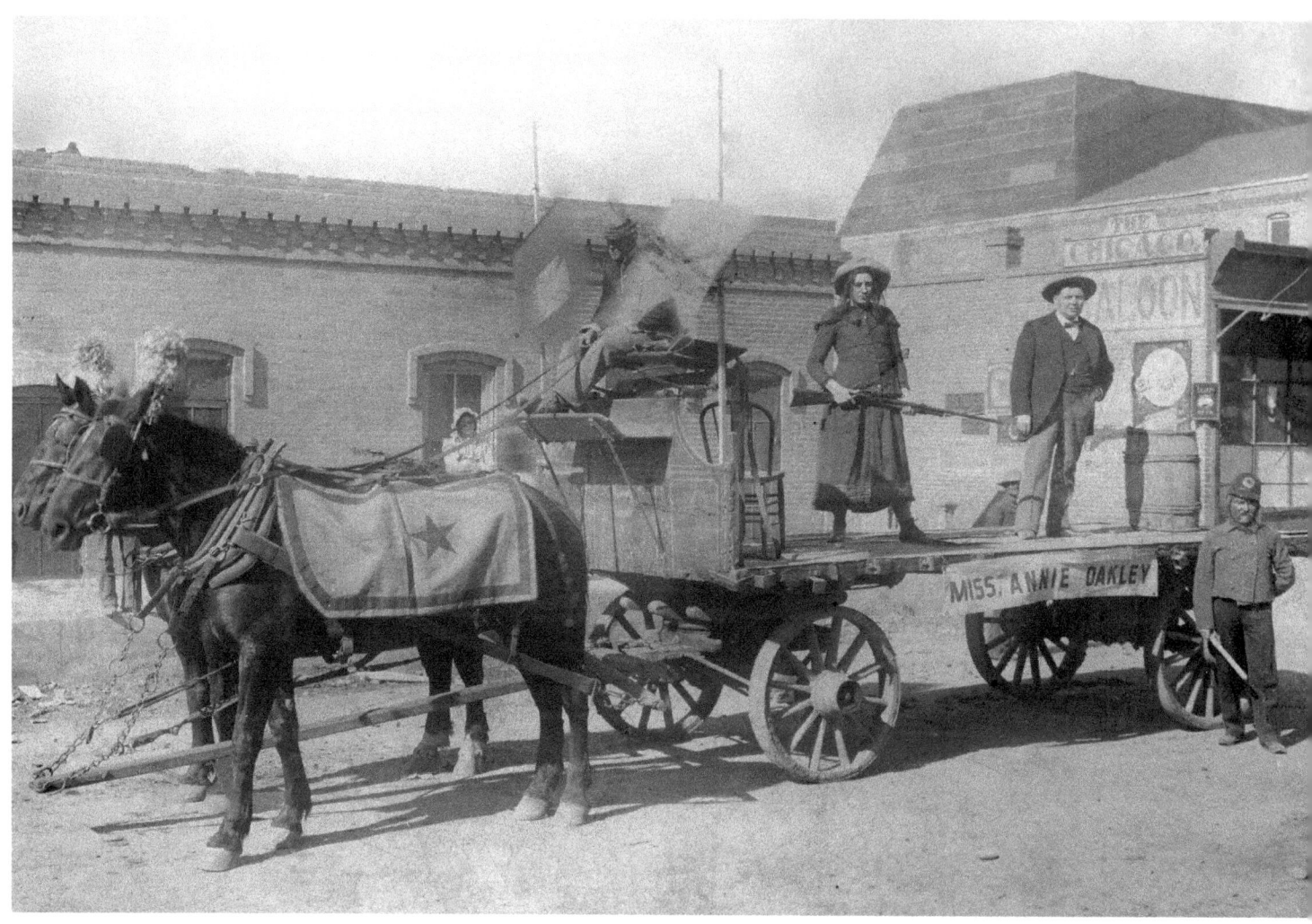

Hodgin Hall, University of New Mexico, in June 1902. Hodgin Hall sits on the mesa, with the Sandia Mountains in the background.

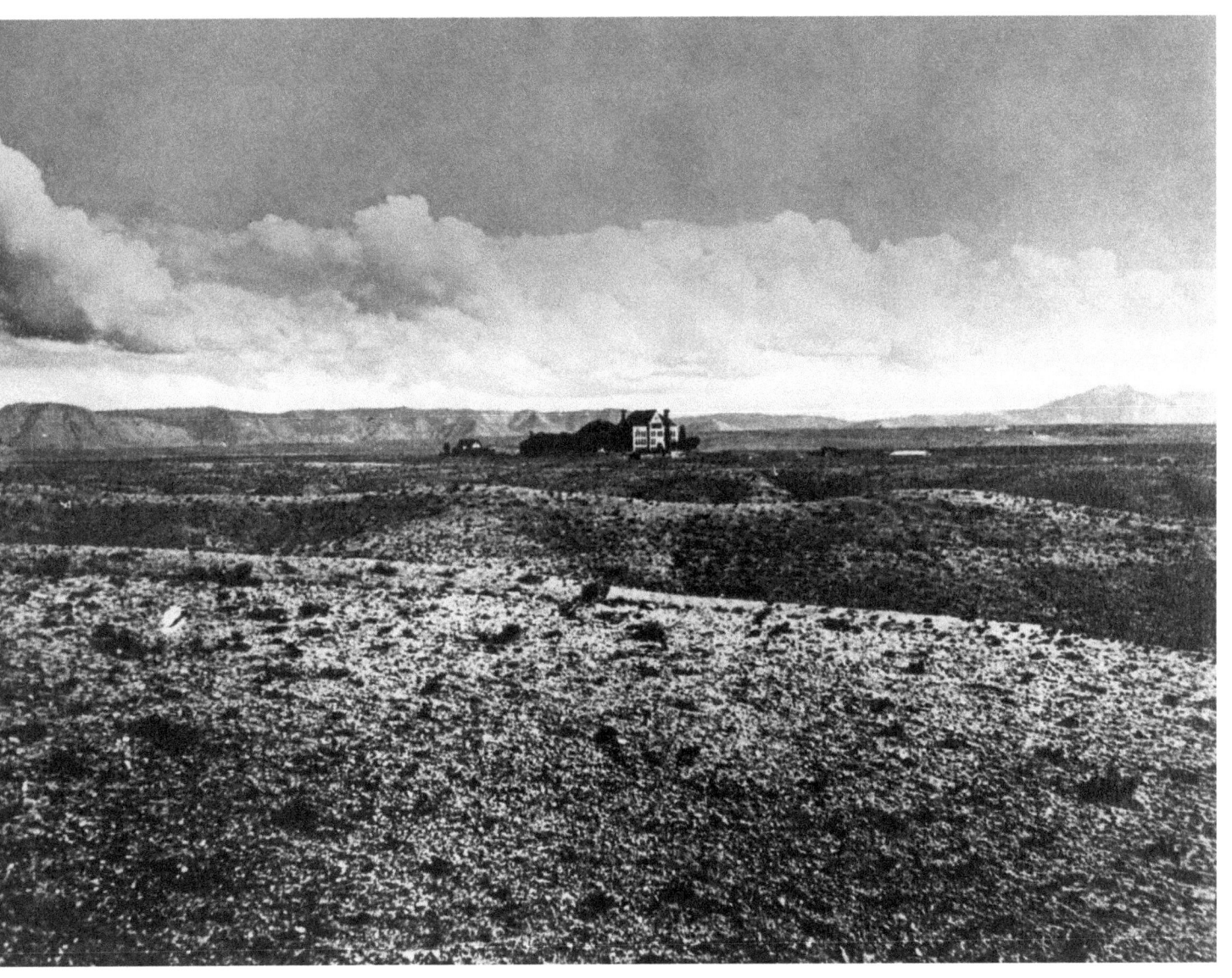

The Santa Fe Railway Station was built in 1902 as a passenger complex that included a baggage handling facility, restaurants, newsstand, Fred Harvey Indian Building, and the Alvarado Hotel. Architect Charles Whittlesey designed the complex for the railroad, which used the California Mission Revival Style architecture in many of its new buildings.

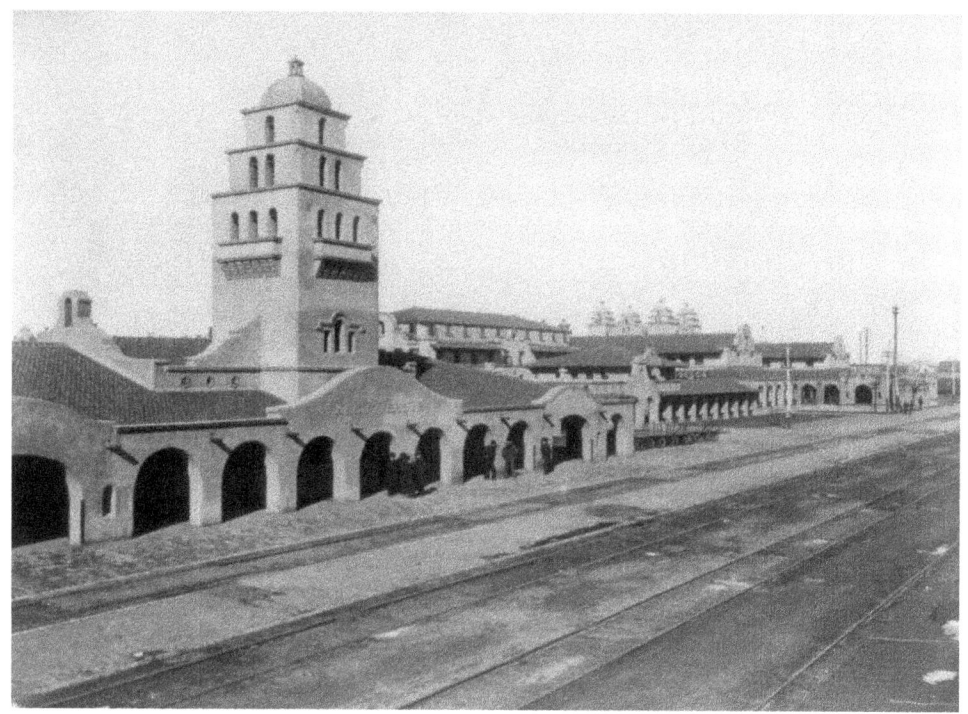

The Barelas Bridge was destroyed by the floodwaters of the Rio Grande. Before the bridge, there was a ferryboat that was government-owned, but operated by local residents for more than twenty years. The ferry was built by a former ship carpenter named Private Church, under the command of Major James Carleton. The ferry carried passengers, stagecoaches, livestock, and freight.

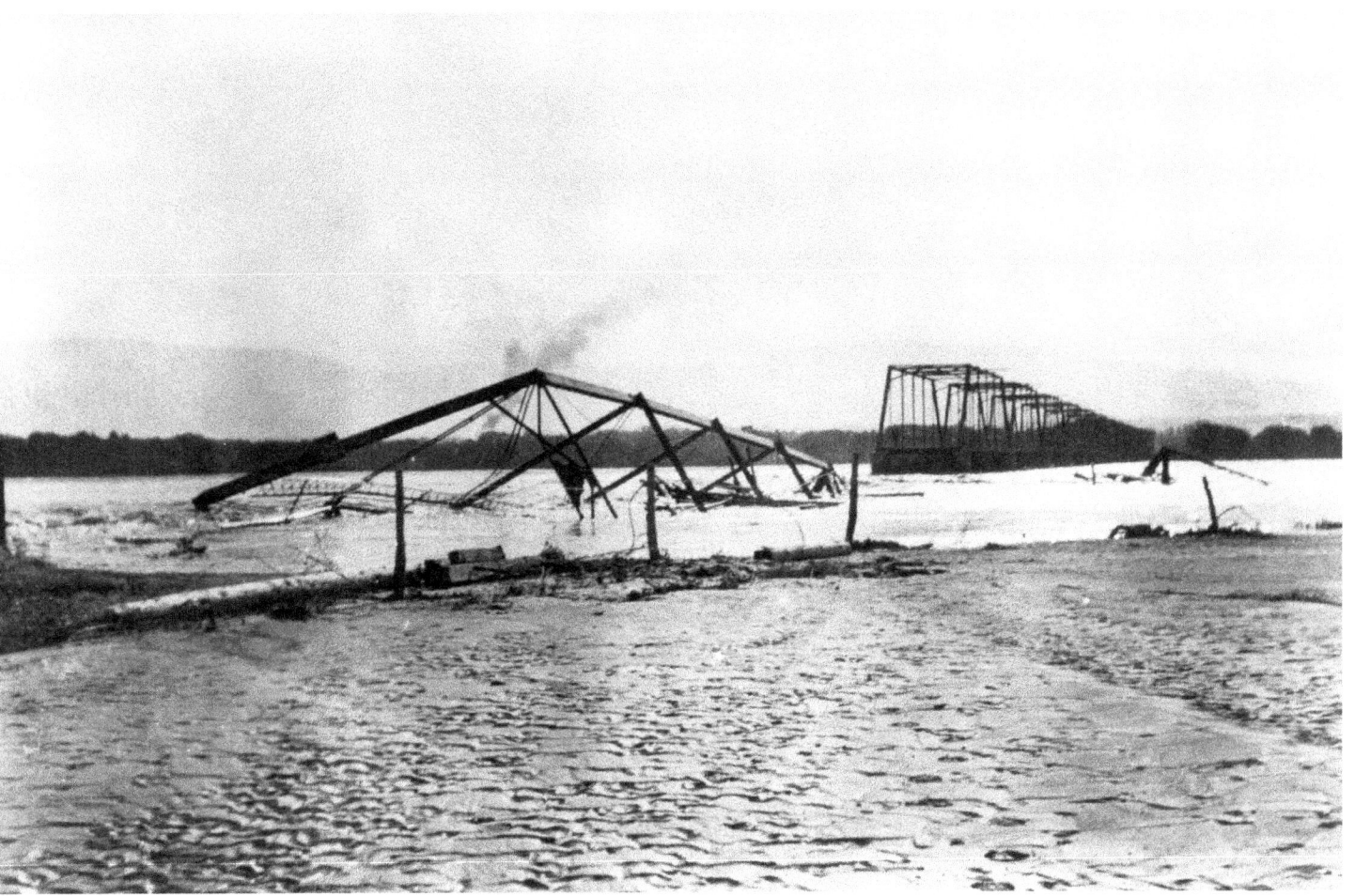

Seventh-grade class at St. Vincent's Academy, at the corner of Sixth and New York Avenue (Lomas), in 1906. The 1901 Albuquerque City Directory listed Sister Dolasco as the supervisor.

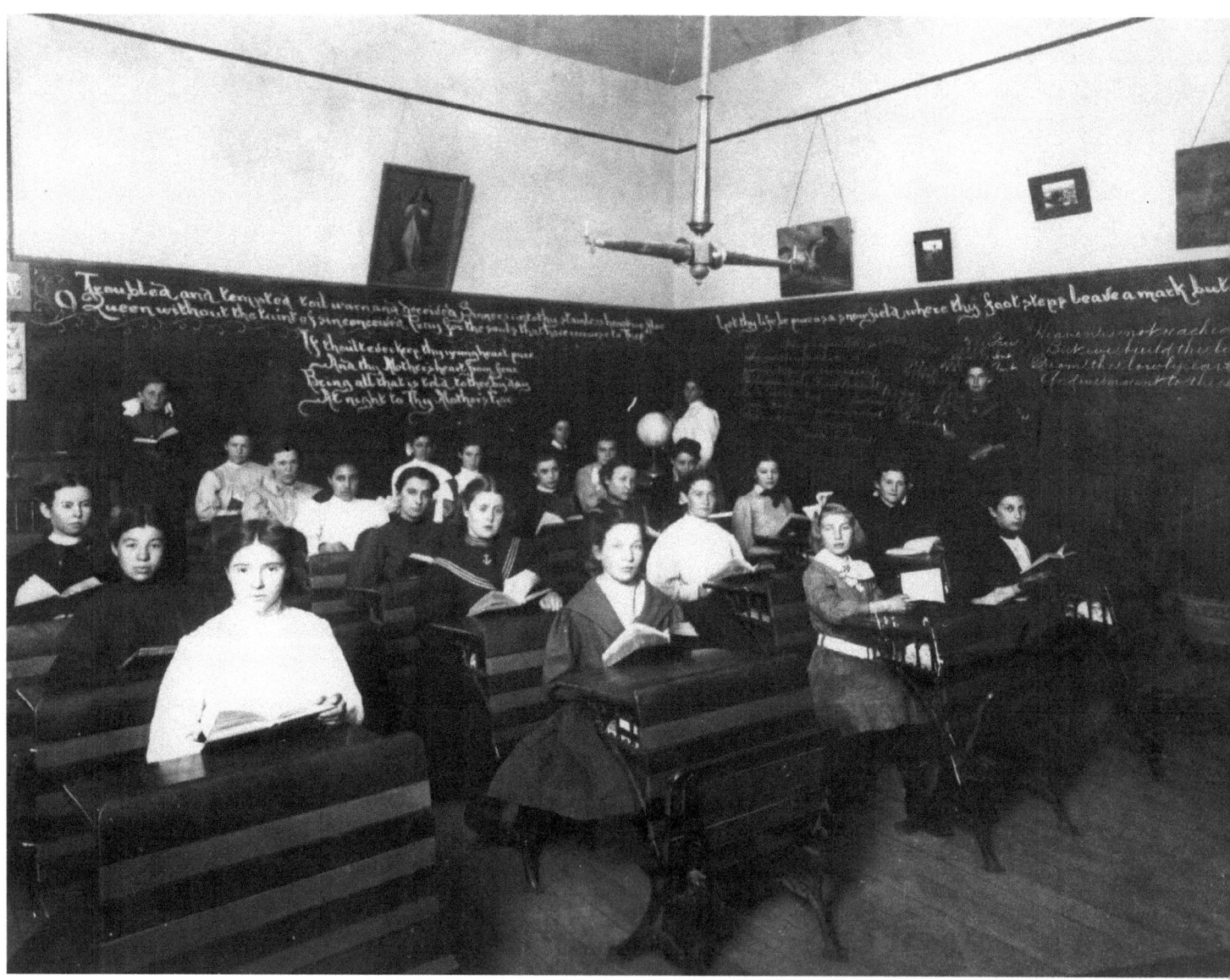

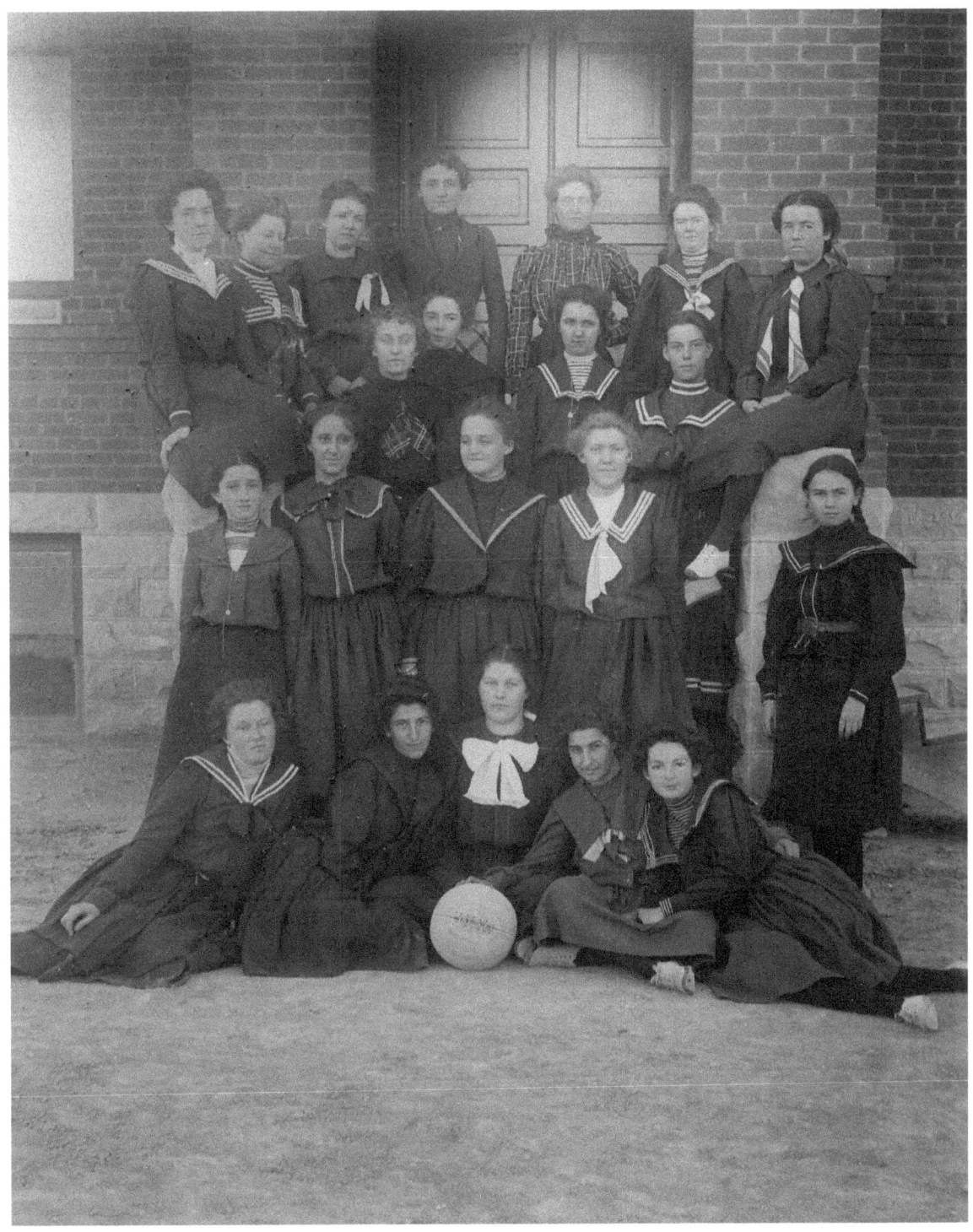

The University of New Mexico women's basketball team in 1902.

An Arbor Day celebration, in front of the University of New Mexico's
Hodgin Hall, on April 3, 1903.

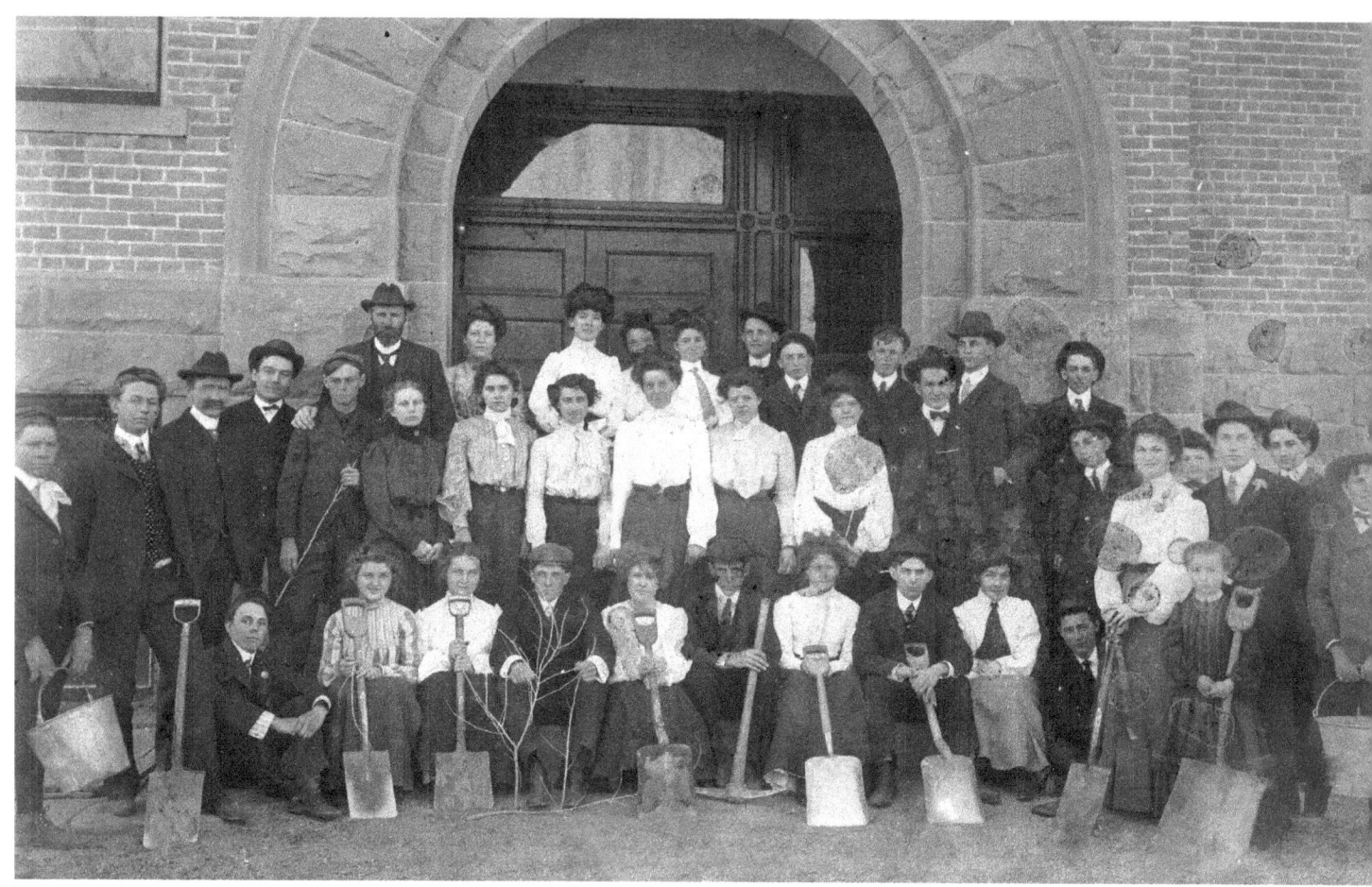

President Theodore Roosevelt came to Albuquerque on May 5, 1903. Welcomed at the Santa Fe depot by dignitaries and brass bands, he spoke from a platform set up near the Alvarado Hotel, while the Rough Riders stood guard. He toured city, led by the bands and Troop F of the Fourteenth Cavalry from Fort Wingate.

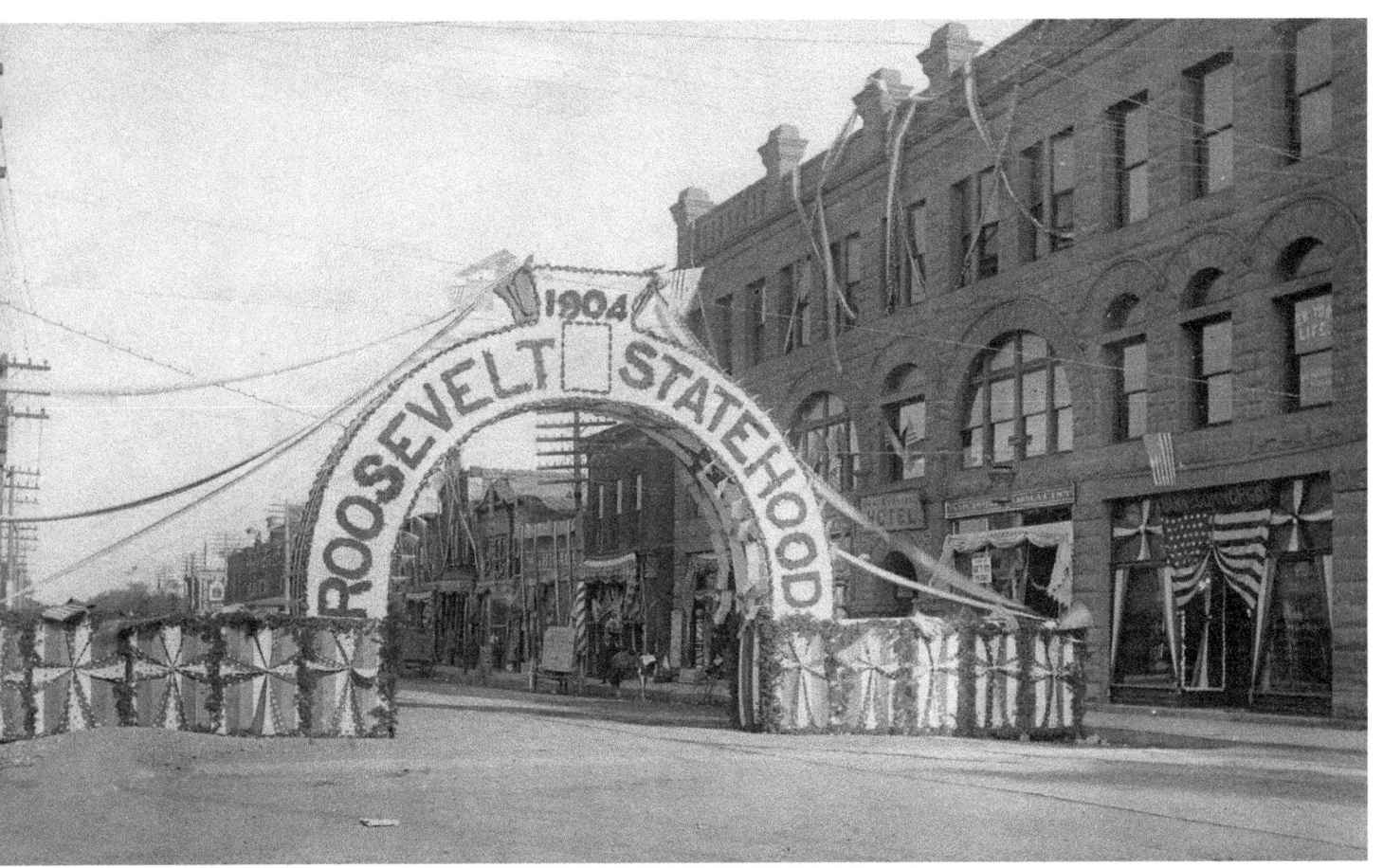

Looking east on Railroad Avenue. A well-dressed crowd at Fourth and Central waits for the parade. On the left are the Selvia Hotel, Giomi Building, N.T. Armijo Building, and the Zeiger Building.

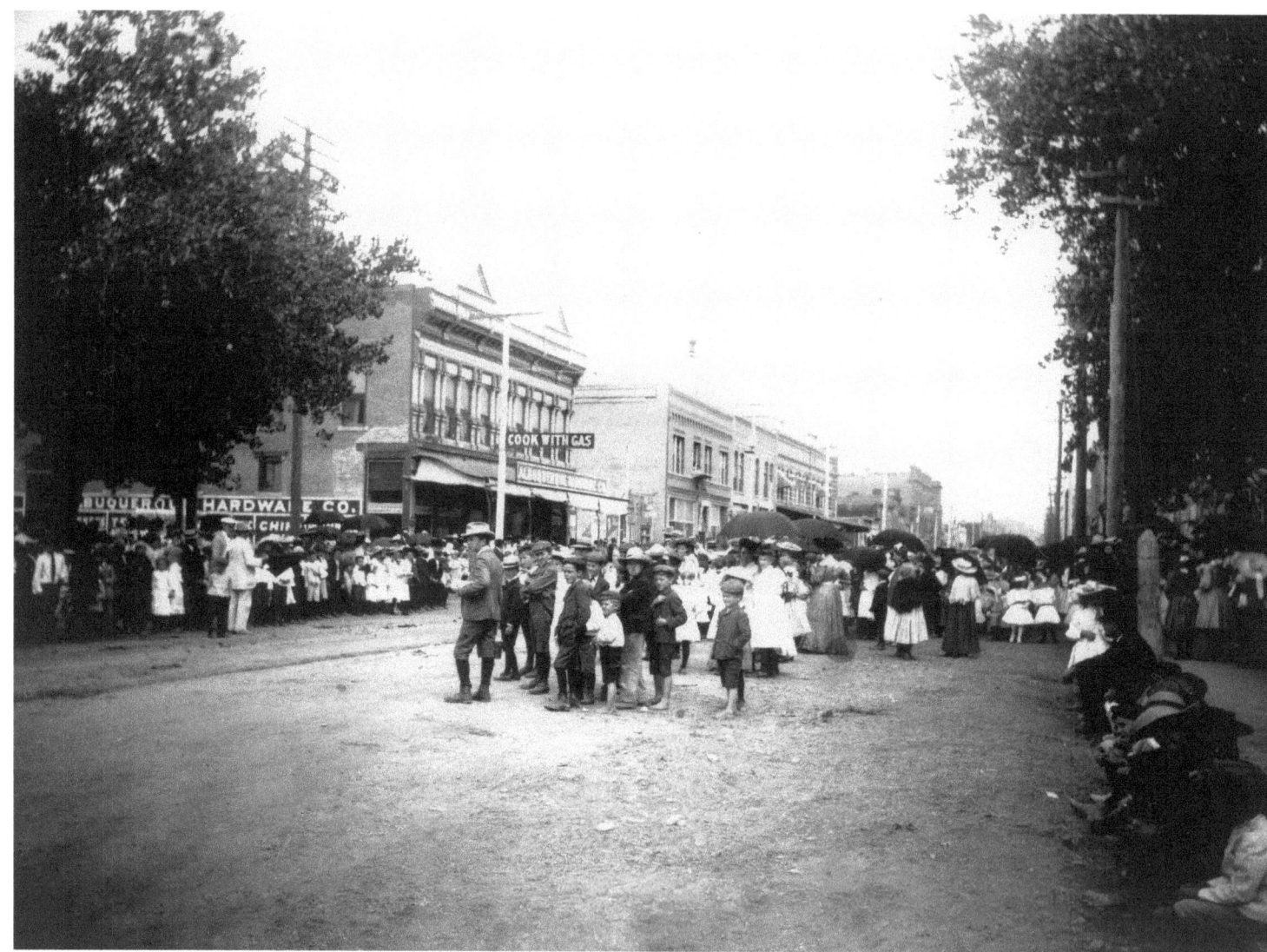

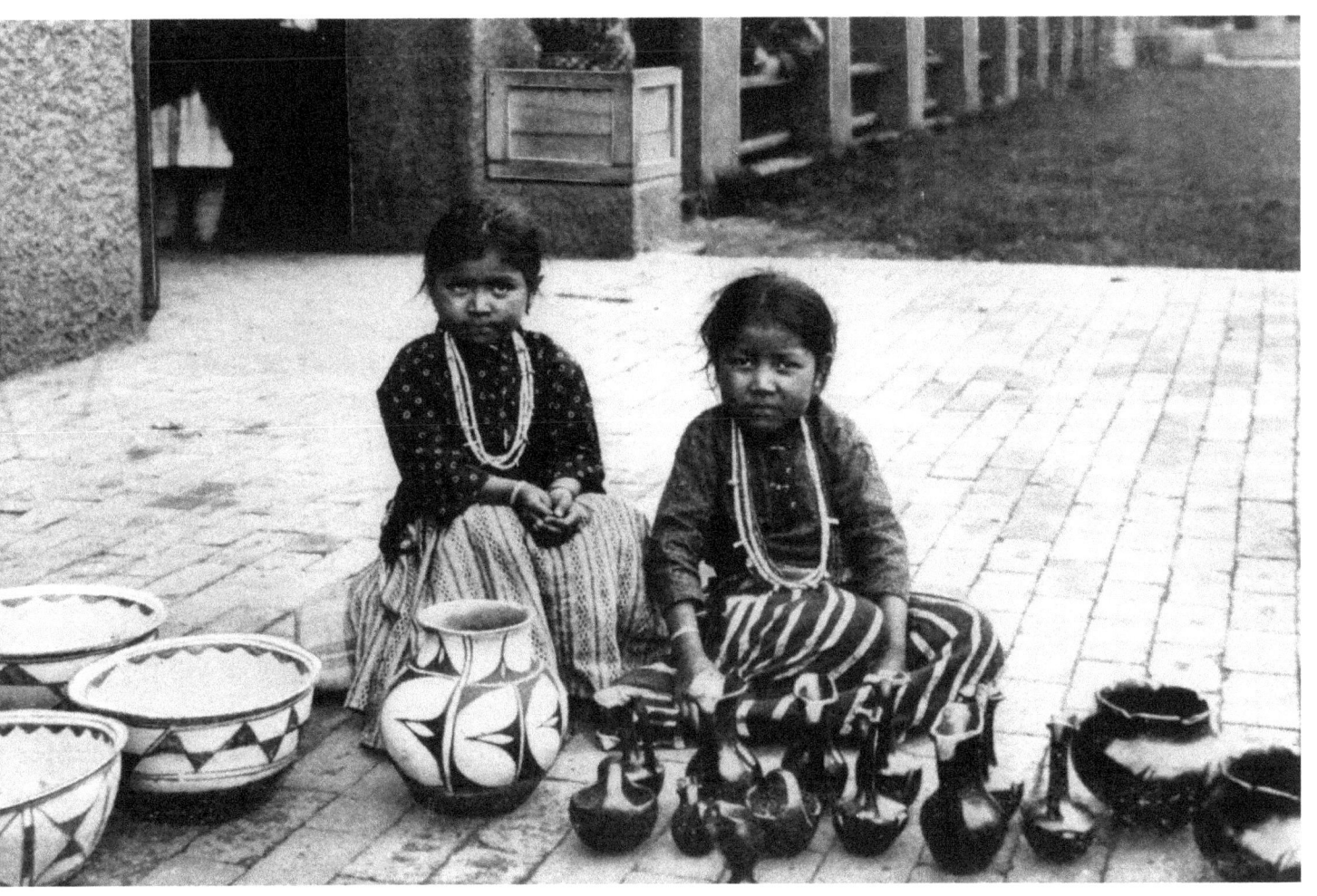

Two girls selling pottery at the railroad station (ca. 1905).

This 1905 horse-drawn streetcar is decorated for a parade, possibly a Fourth of July event or a carnival. The tallyho is packed with people.

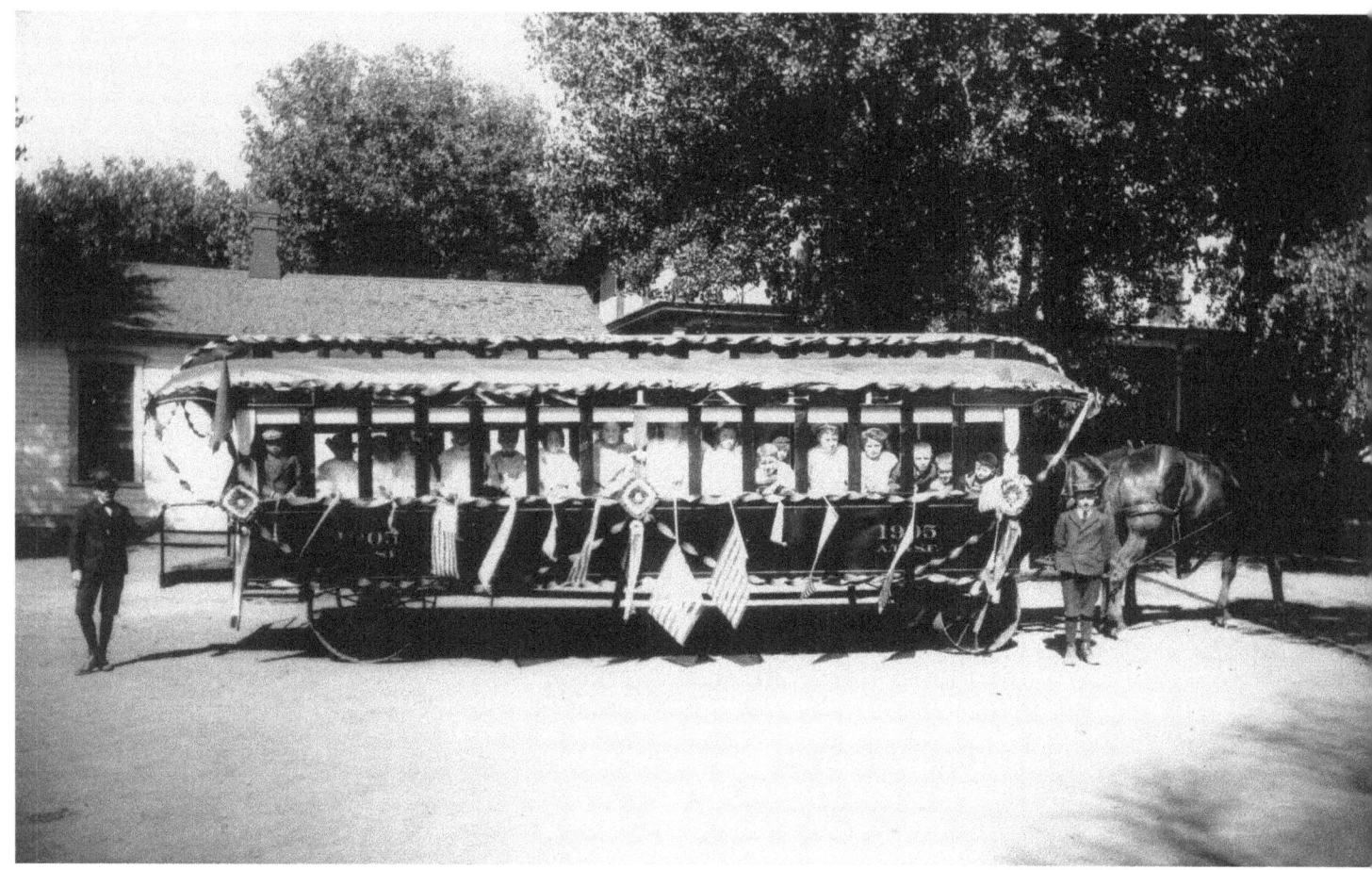

Hodgin Hall, on the left, was the University of New Mexico's first building and was remodeled in a Pueblo Revival Style. Hadley Hall, on the right, the science building, was built in 1900. It was destroyed by fire in 1910. The Sandia Mountains can be seen in the background.

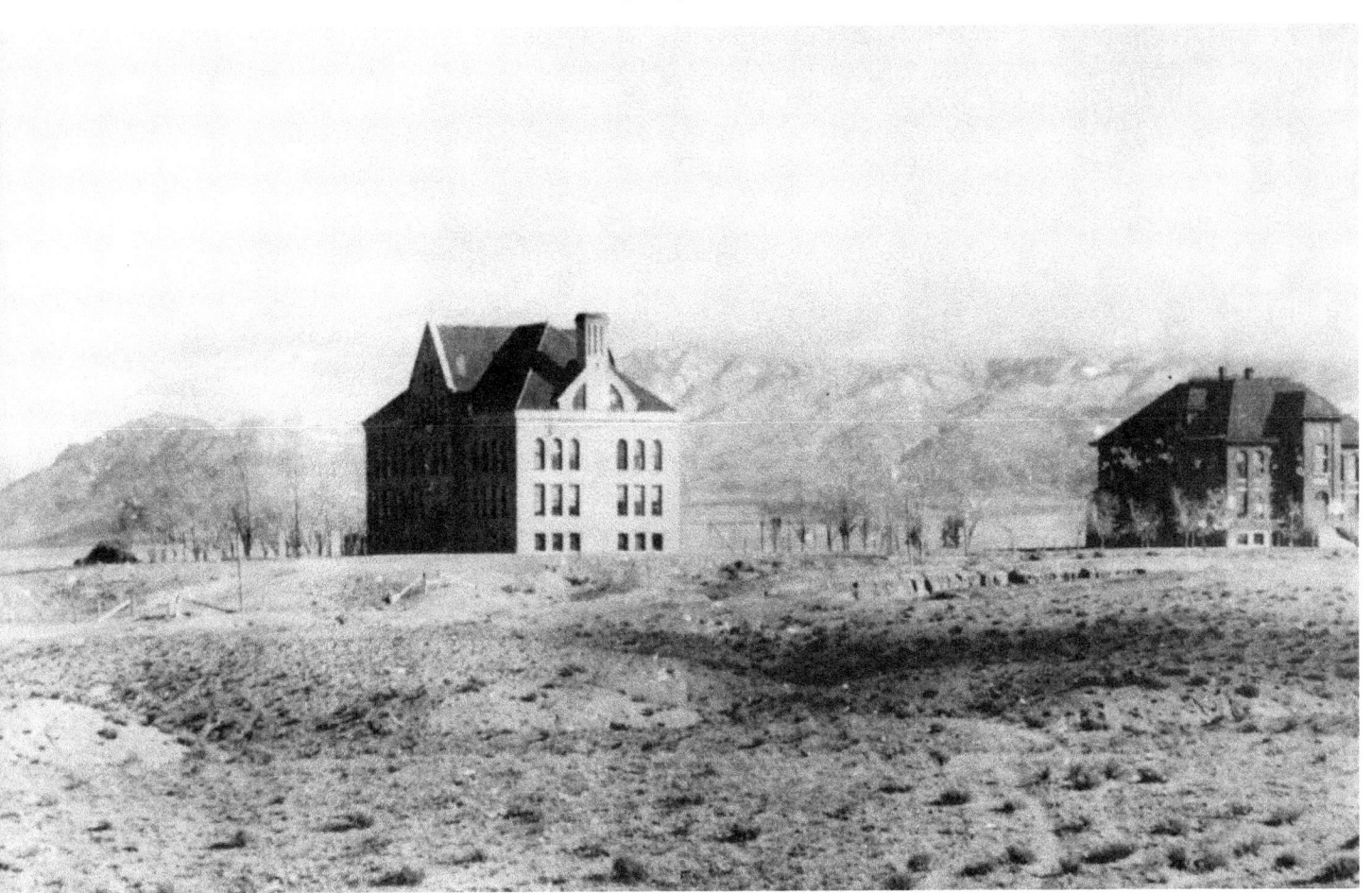

Hodgin Hall, with horse-drawn hacks in the front of it. Most students and faculty lived in downtown Albuquerque and paid five cents to ride the hack two miles to the university. When this Victorian-style building was remodeled with vigas, balconies, and stucco, people were outraged. In 1927, the Board of Regents decided the campus would be Pueblo Style.

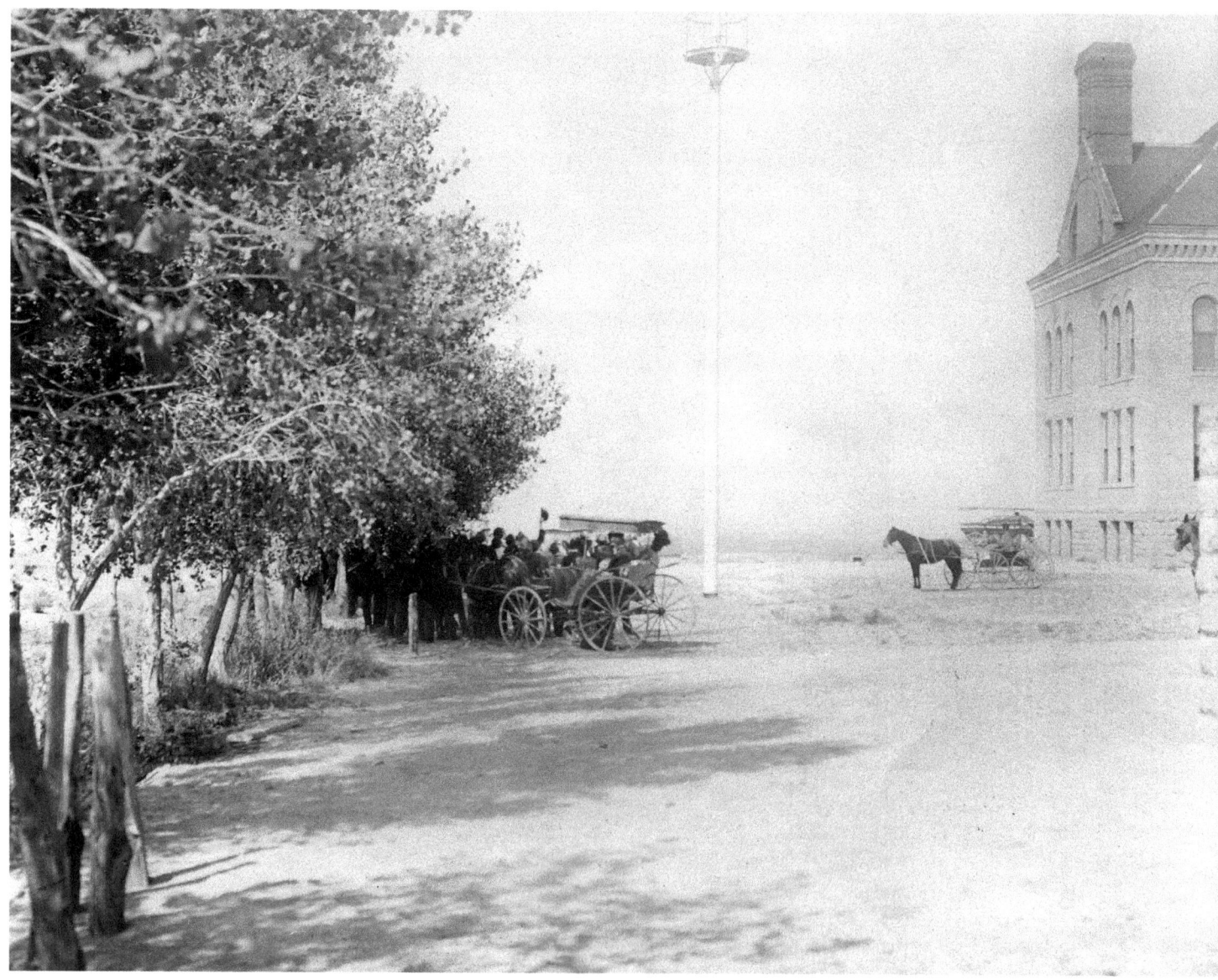

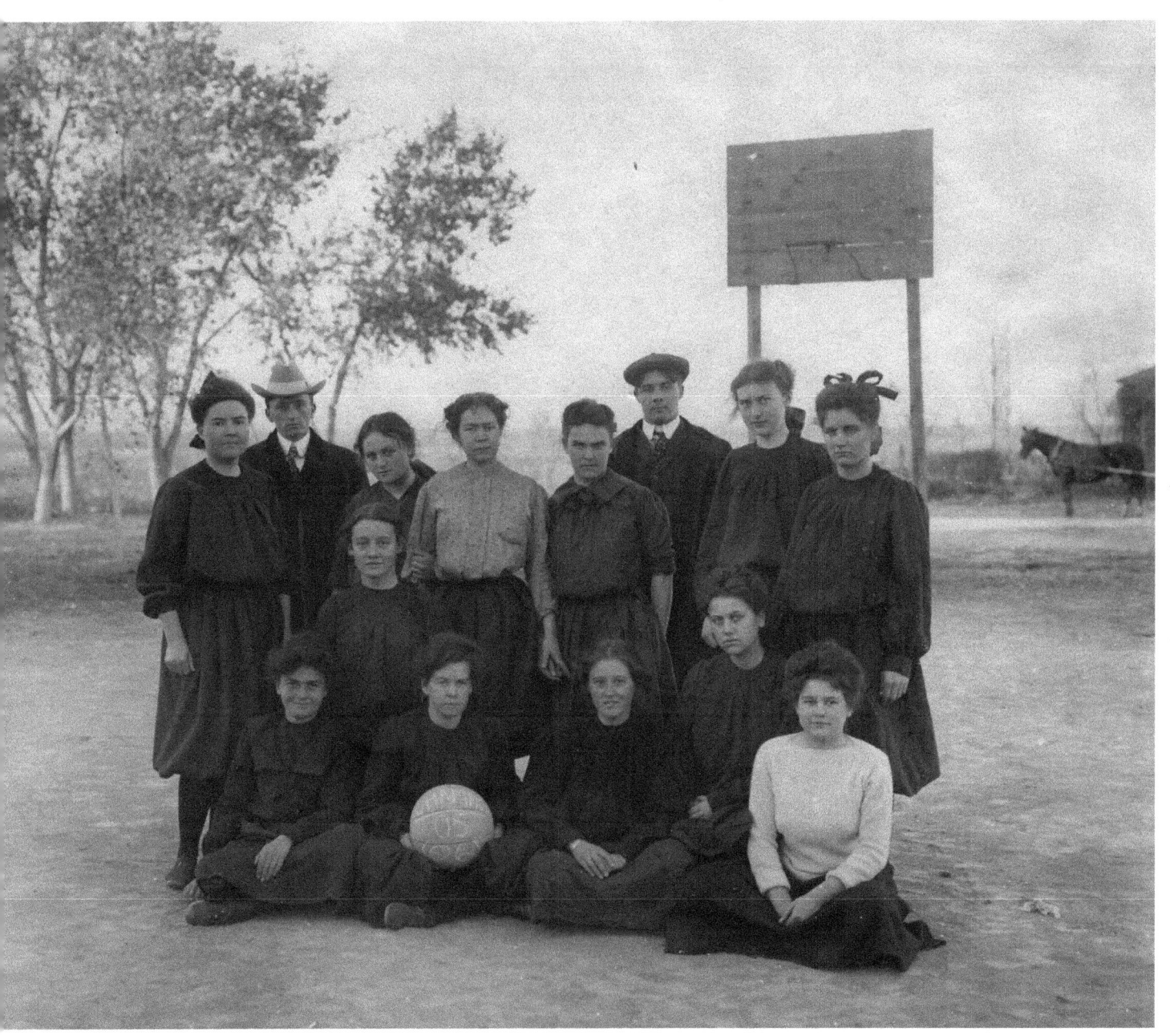

University of New Mexico's women's basketball team in 1906.

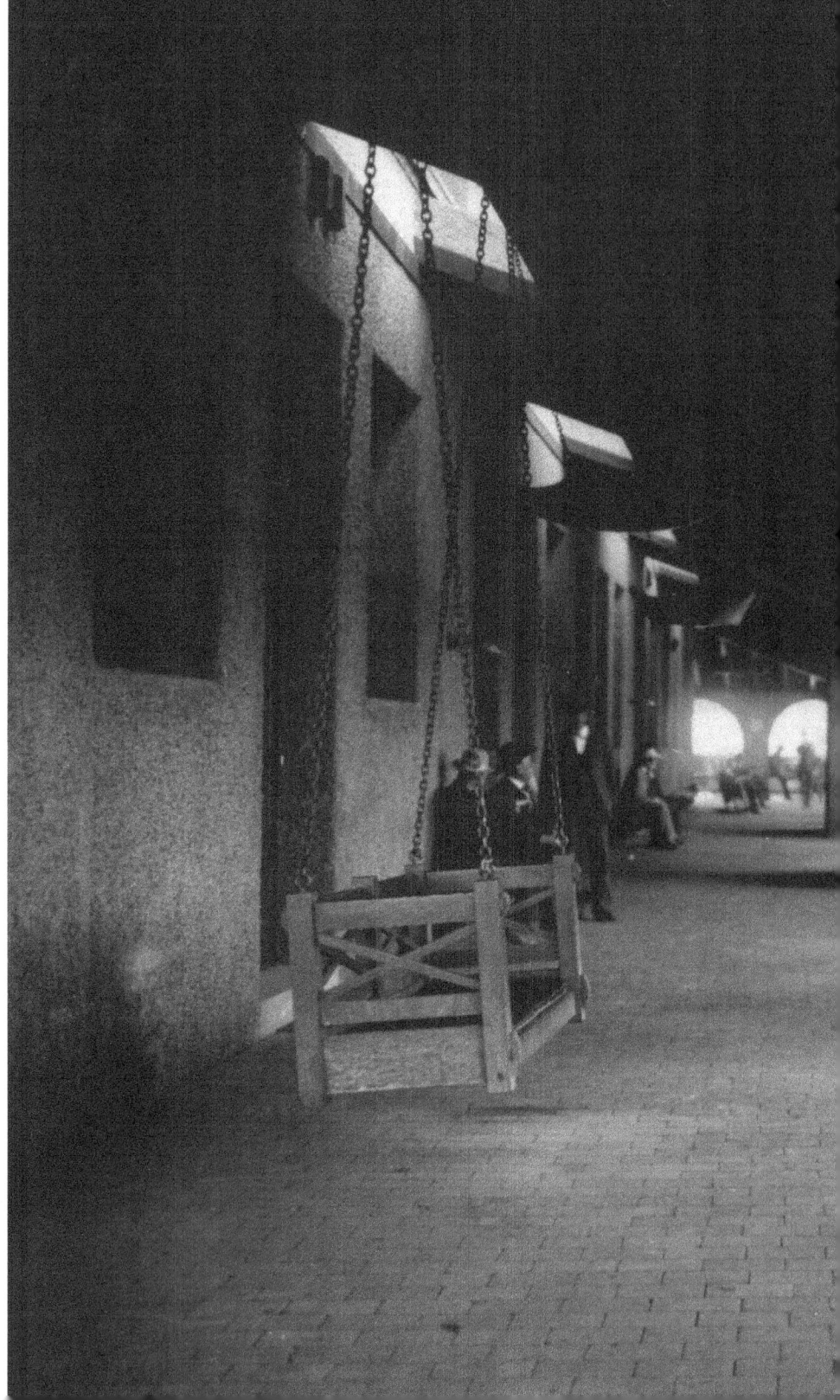

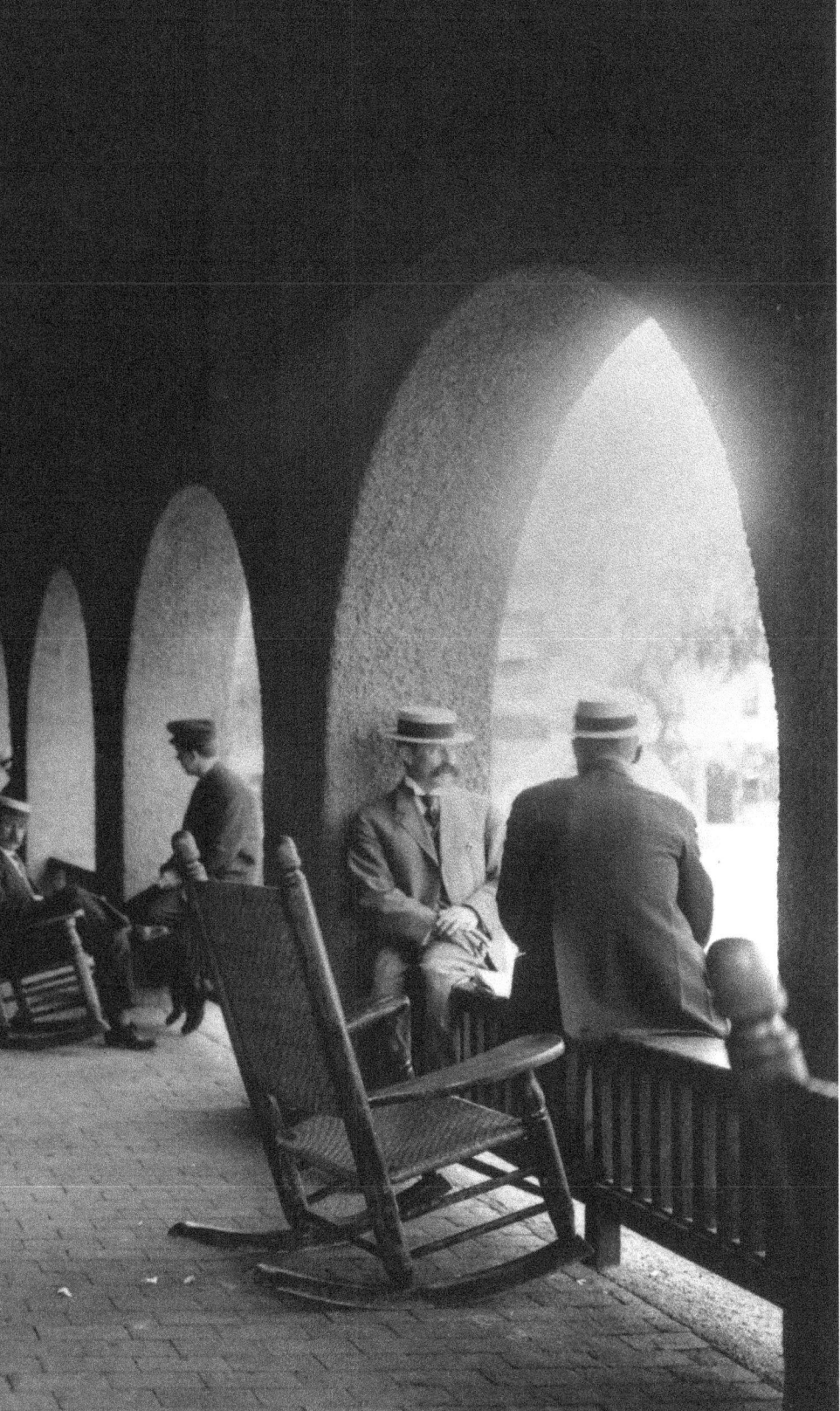

This classic William Henry Jackson photograph of the Alvarado Hotel verandah was taken in 1908. The Alvarado was the social hub of Albuquerque. Residents strolled along its walks hoping to see movie stars and celebrities getting off the train. The verandah was a comfortable place to sit and watch people walk by.

This was one of the first horseless carriages in town. In 1910, the entire
New Mexico Territory had only 470 automobiles.

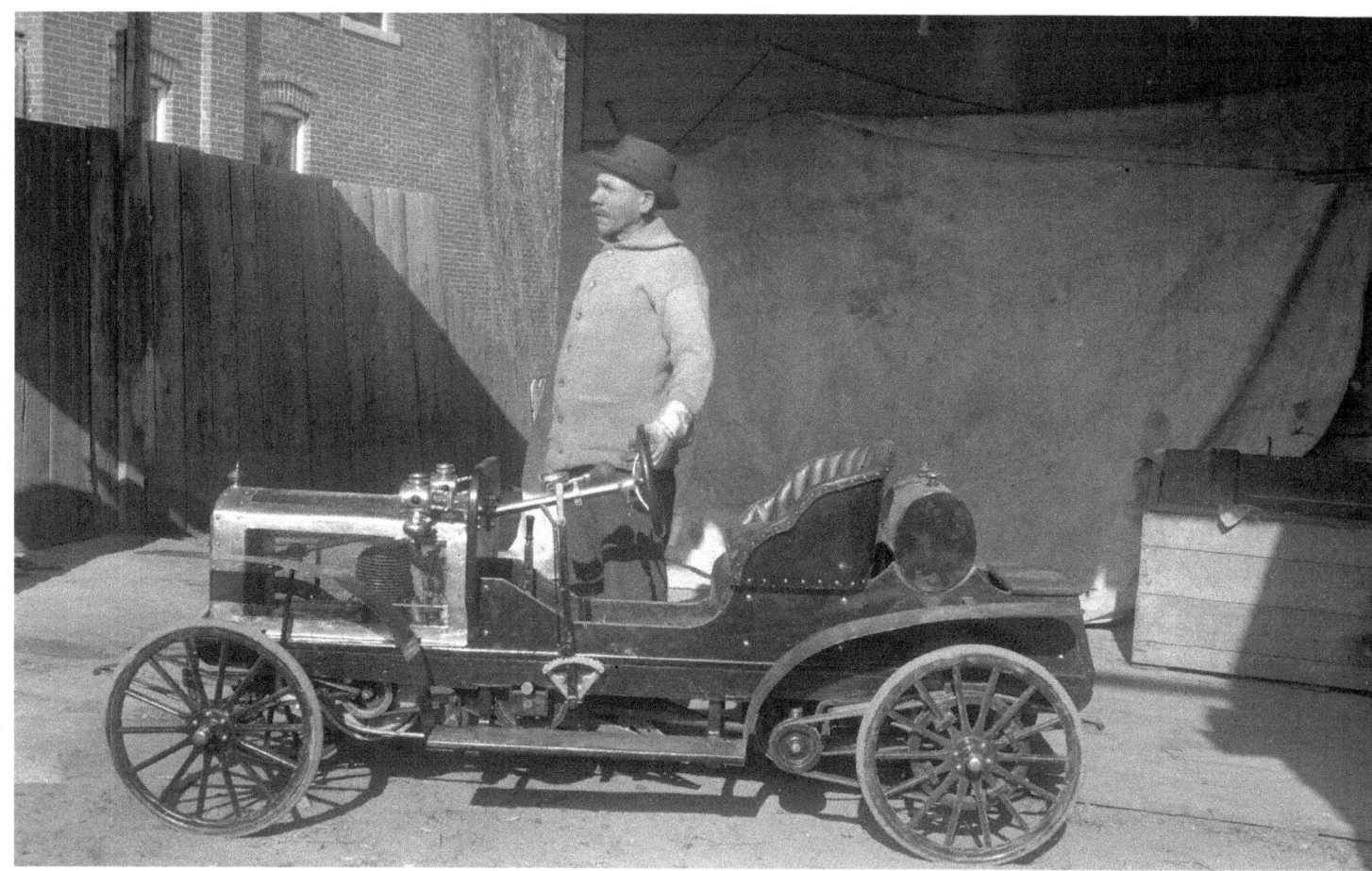

The Sixteenth National Irrigation Congress and Interstate Industrial Exposition, held in 1908, was a proud time for Albuquerque to share the wonders of the area and to showcase local products with people from other states and countries.

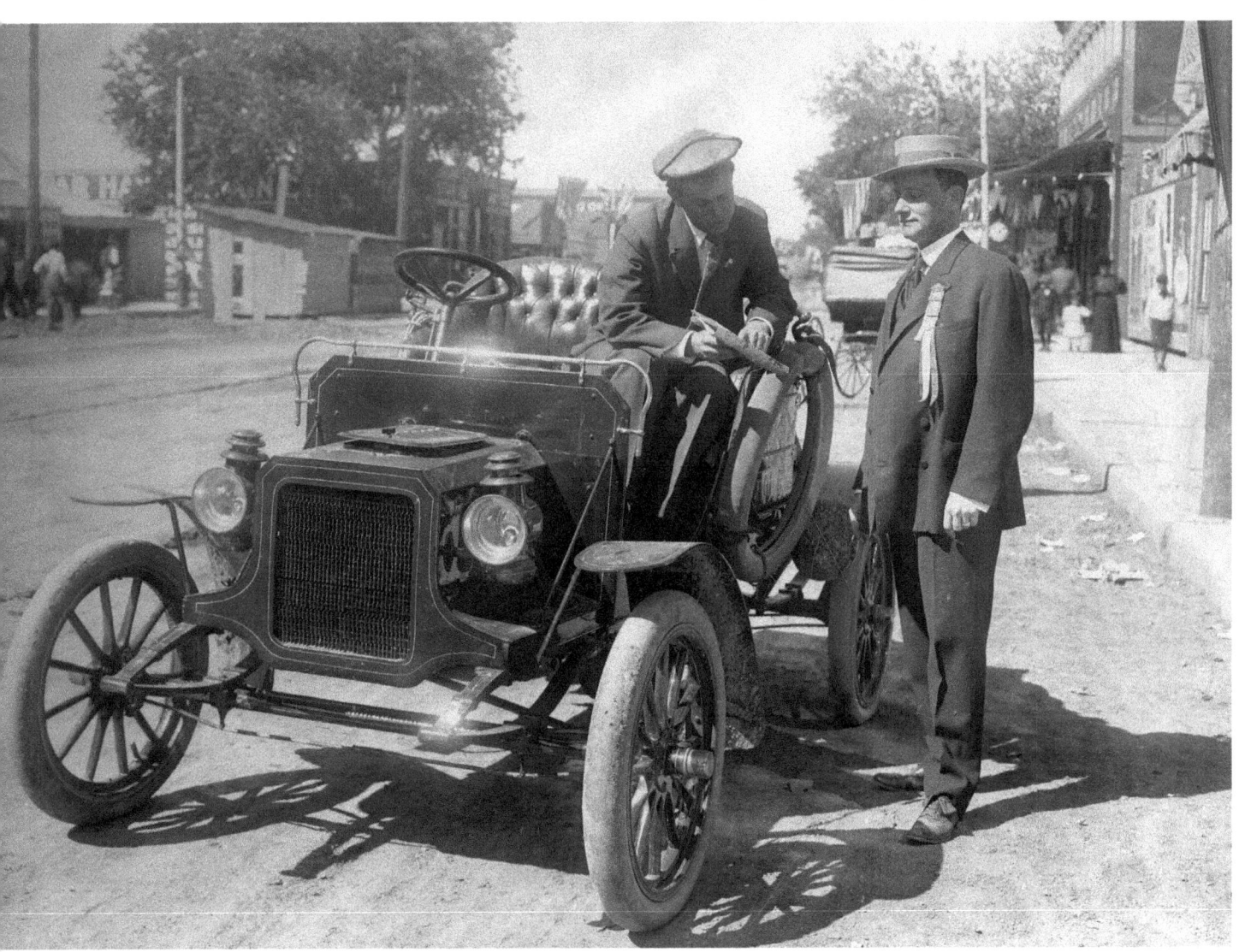

The photographer took this picture of a group of International Industrial
Exposition of 1908 parade participants and another photographer.

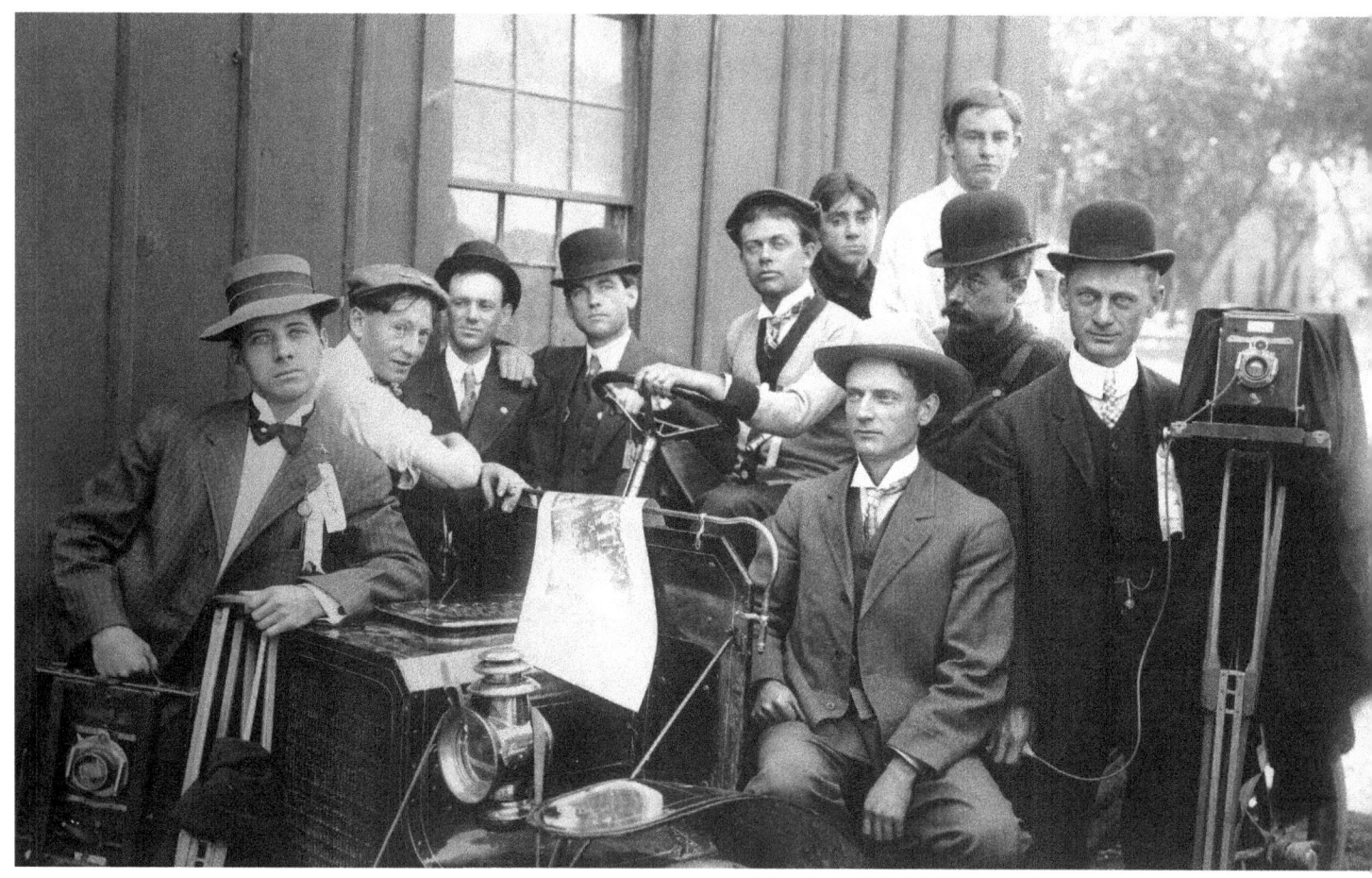

The "All the Way" float in the 1908 International Industrial Exposition parade.
This may have been a float to celebrate the early settlers who came west.

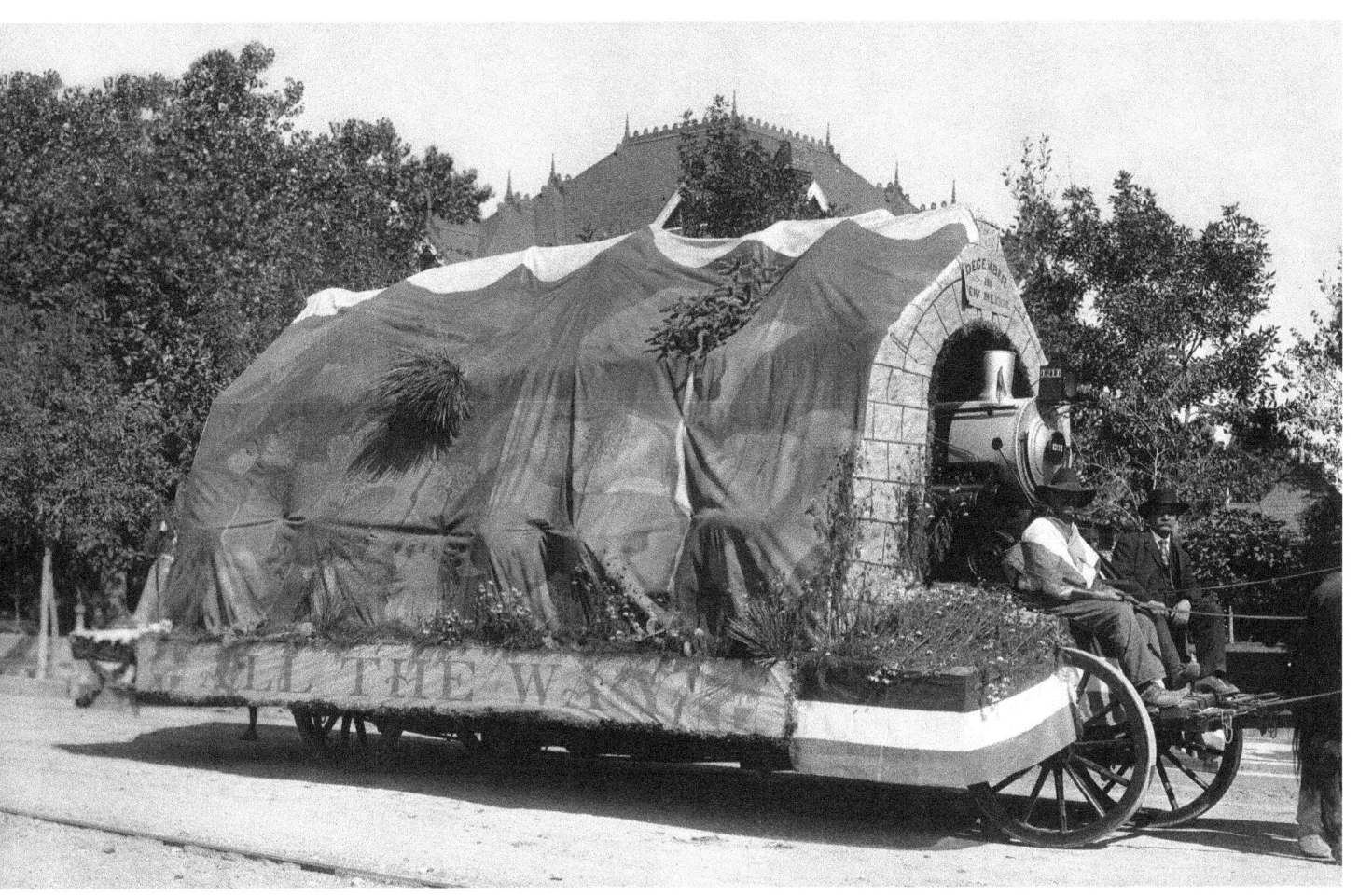

The 1908 International Industrial Exposition was underwritten by the United States government, and $30,000 was appropriated for it. AT&SF had special trains for the expo, and 4,000 people attended. There were booths for arts and crafts, electric motors, agricultural products, and lumber products.

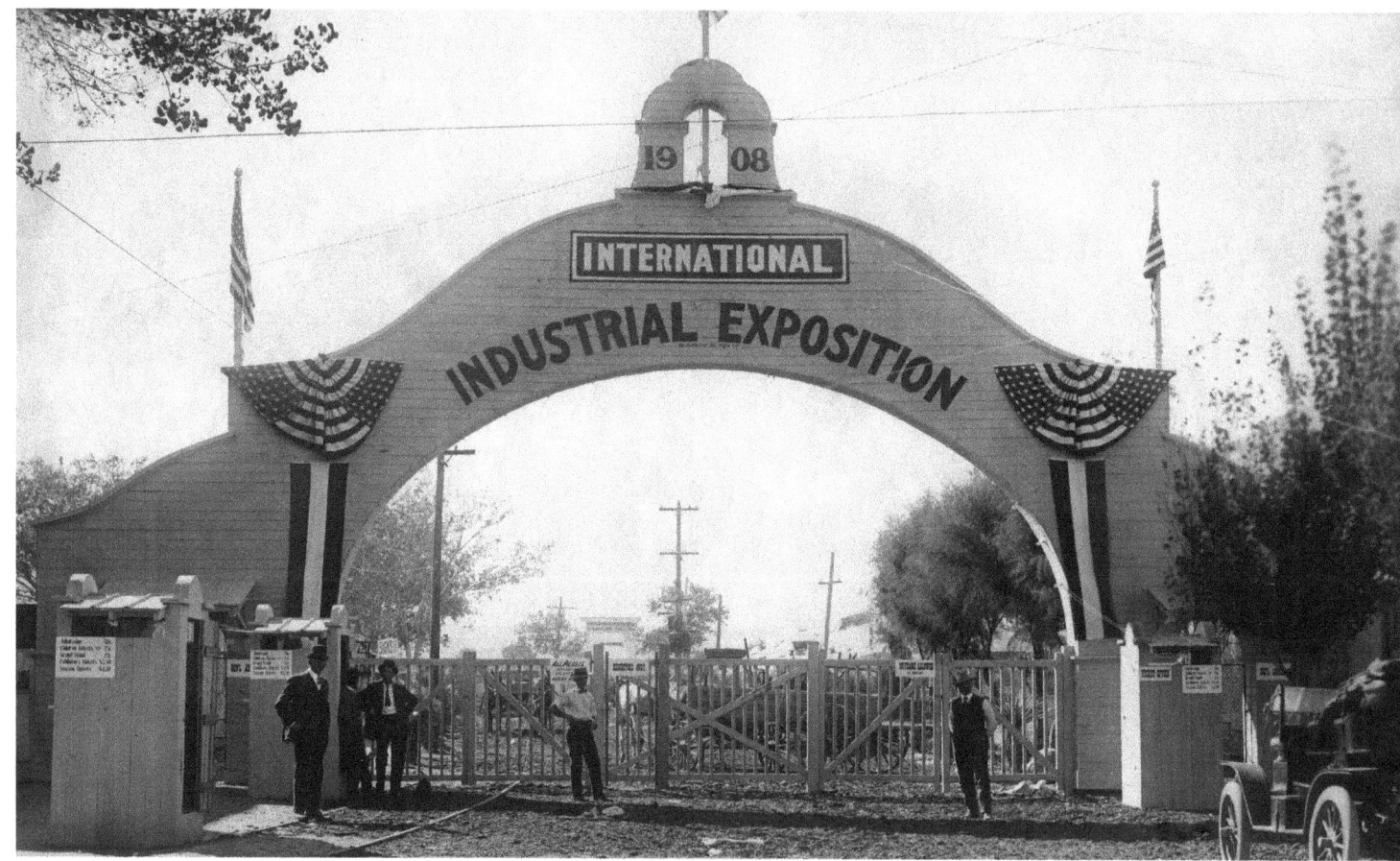

This group is inside the Armory, which was built at Fifth and Silver for the 1908 International Industrial Exposition. It served as a concert venue and wrestling arena until the Civic Auditorium opened in the mid-1950s.

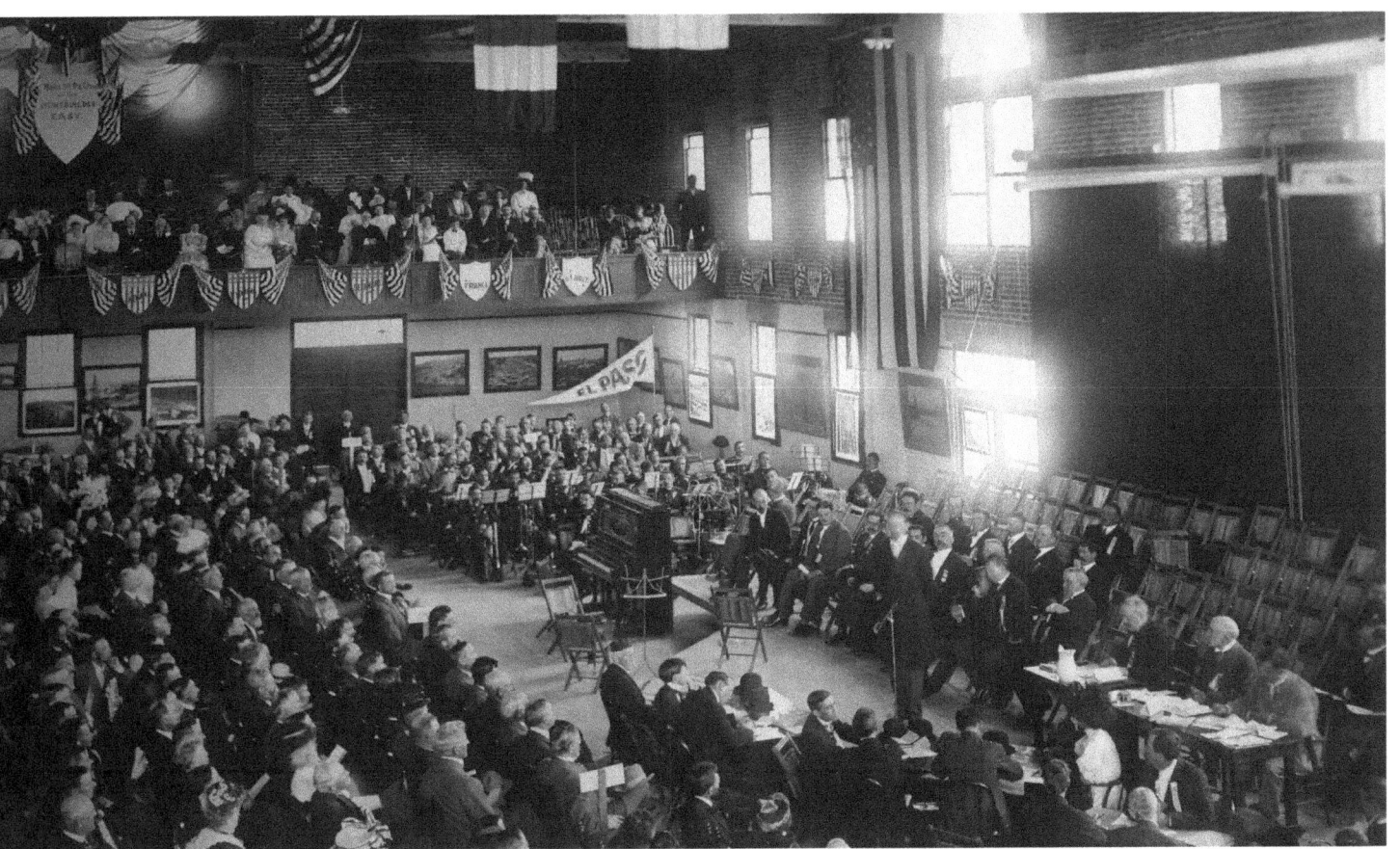

An interesting slice of history is preserved in this photograph of one of the agriculture booths at the International Industrial Exposition. The Sisters of Loretto Academy, Mesilla Park Agricultural College, and Herman Blueher's Old Town Market Garden also had agricultural booth displays.

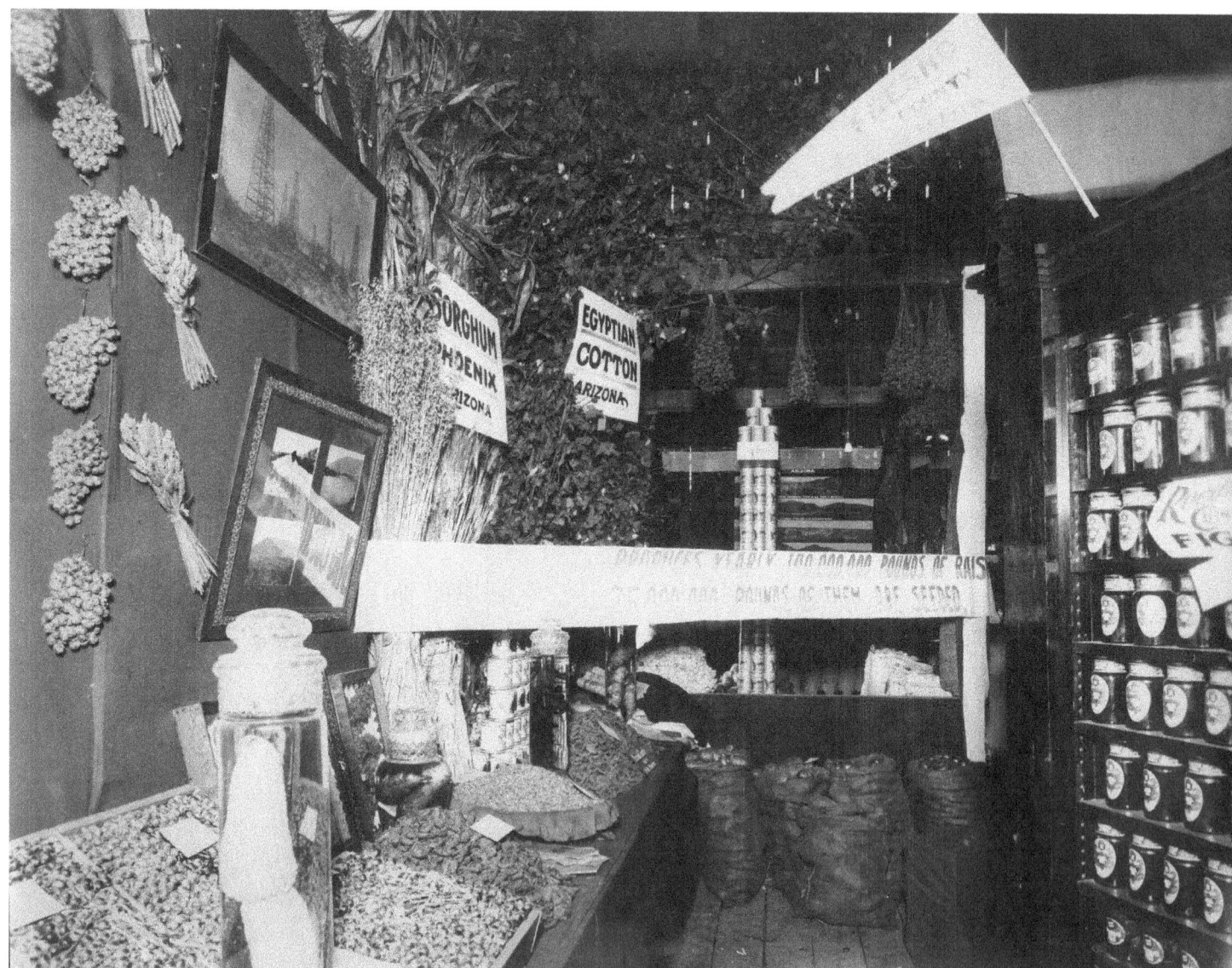

Tree-lined Copper Street, a residential neighborhood, was shot from Eighth Street by William Henry Jackson in 1908. Many people who moved to Albuquerque planted trees to enhance the area. John Collins, a Buffalo Soldier, arrived in the late 1860s and was known for planting trees along Railroad Avenue in the 1870s.

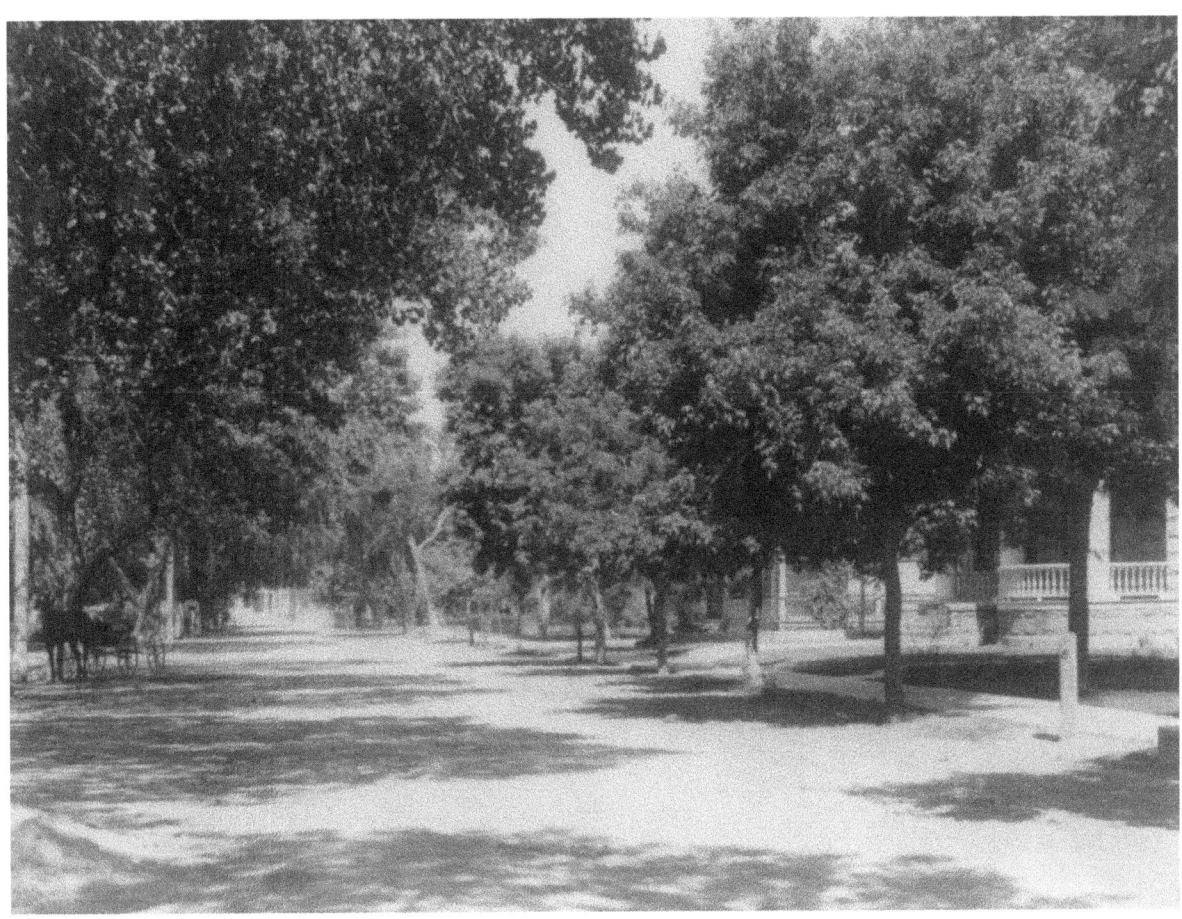

Old Town Plaza in 1908, with the distinctive San Felipe de Neri showing behind the trees. On the left is El Parrillan, 201 Romero Street, which was built in the 1890s and housed a saloon and barber shop. The Territorial Style building is still standing and now has a second story. The photographer was William Henry Jackson.

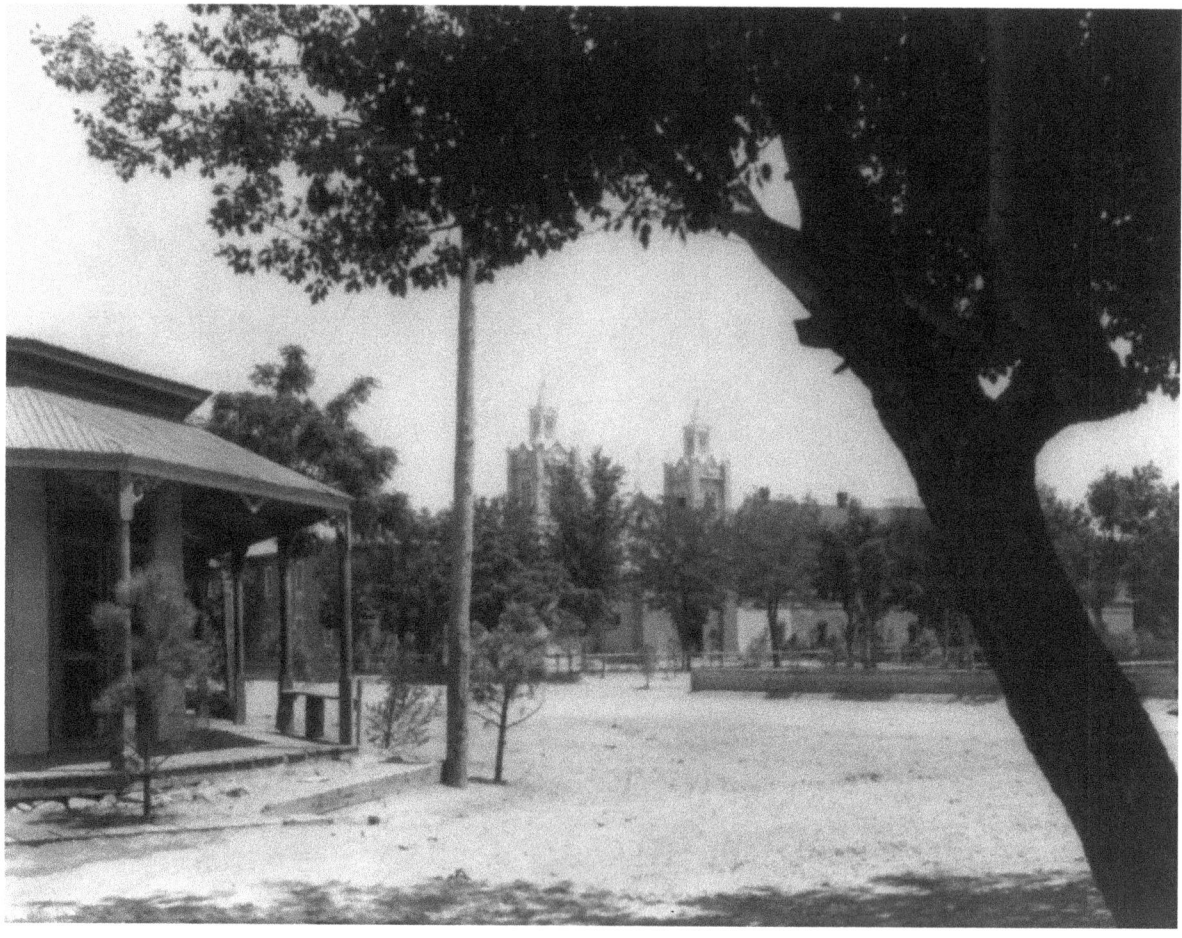

First Street, 1908, with the Alvarado Hotel on the right. Just to the right of the utility pole is the Metropolitan Hotel. This tranquil setting is what people saw when they stayed at the hotel and strolled along the streets. This is one of just a few photographs of the First Street side of the Alvarado and was taken by William Henry Jackson.

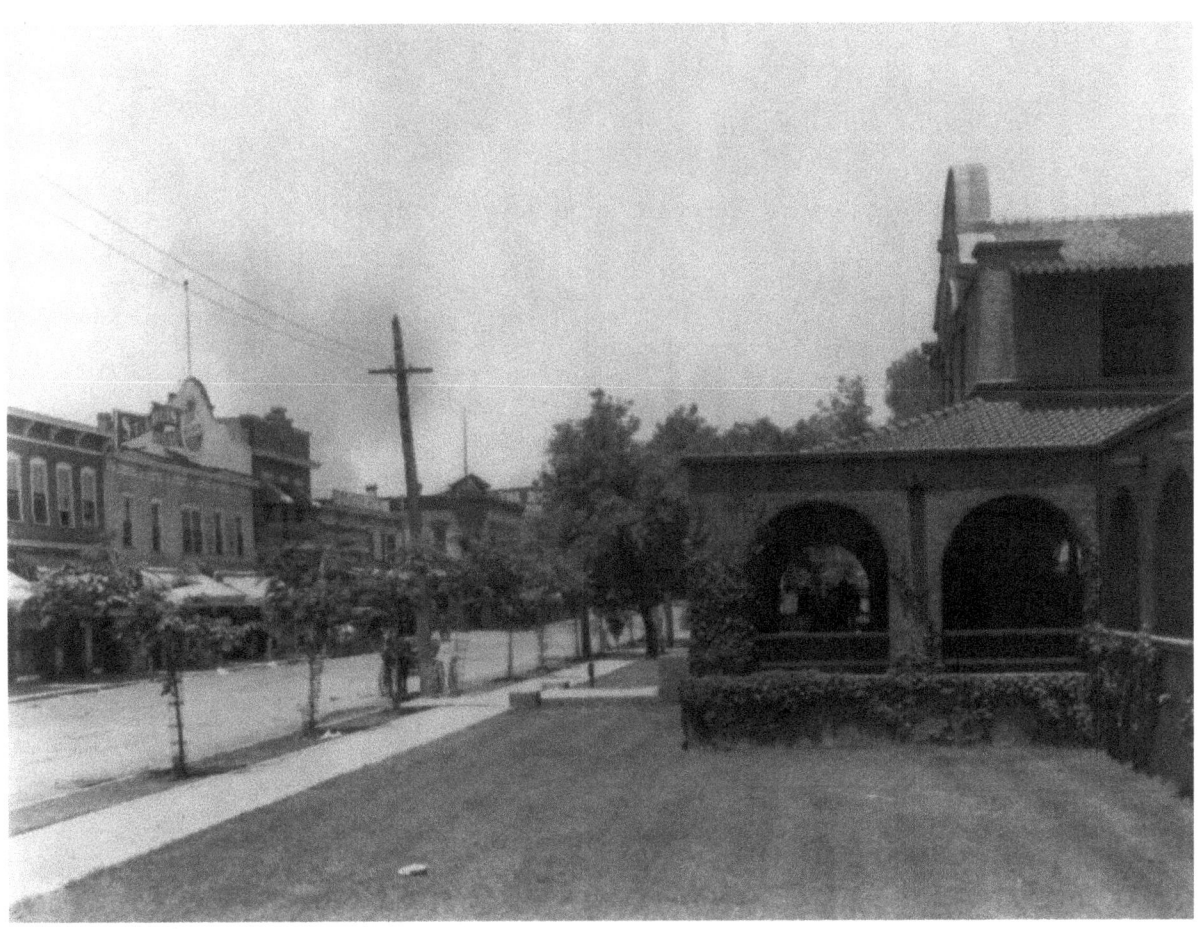

The Bernalillo County Courthouse, built in 1886, was southeast of the plaza in Old Town. The cast stone building was demolished in 1959.

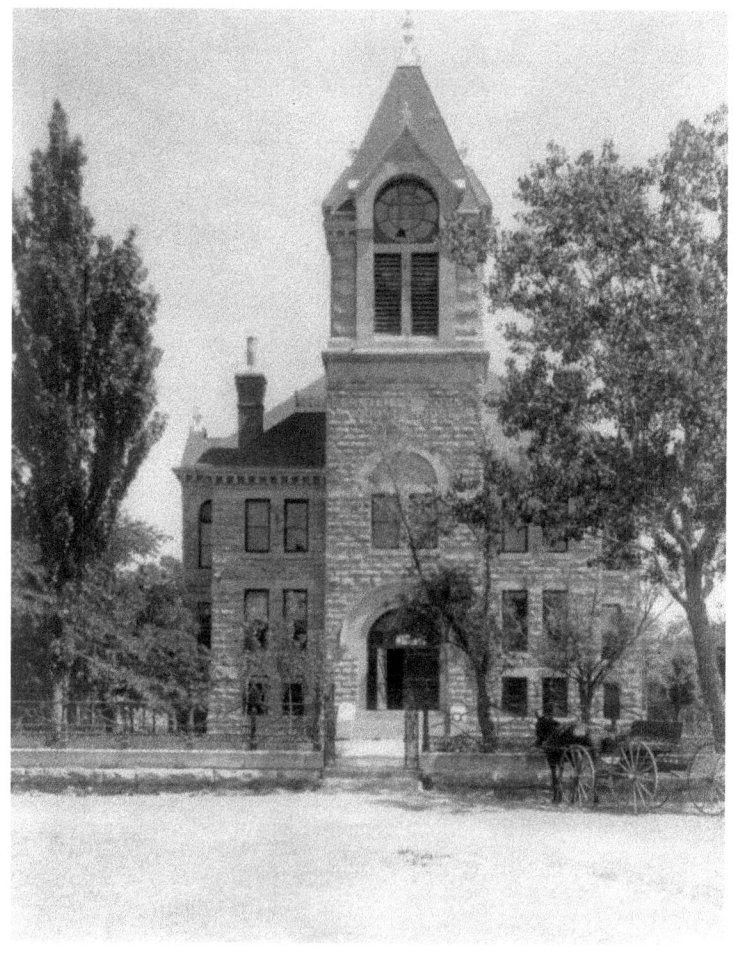

The Benevolent & Protective Order of Elks No. 90 Pueblo Band and committee members pose in front of the Alvarado Hotel Lunch Room. The woman on the left is a vendor. There were always vendors at the Alvarado Complex to greet tourists and sell handcrafted items.

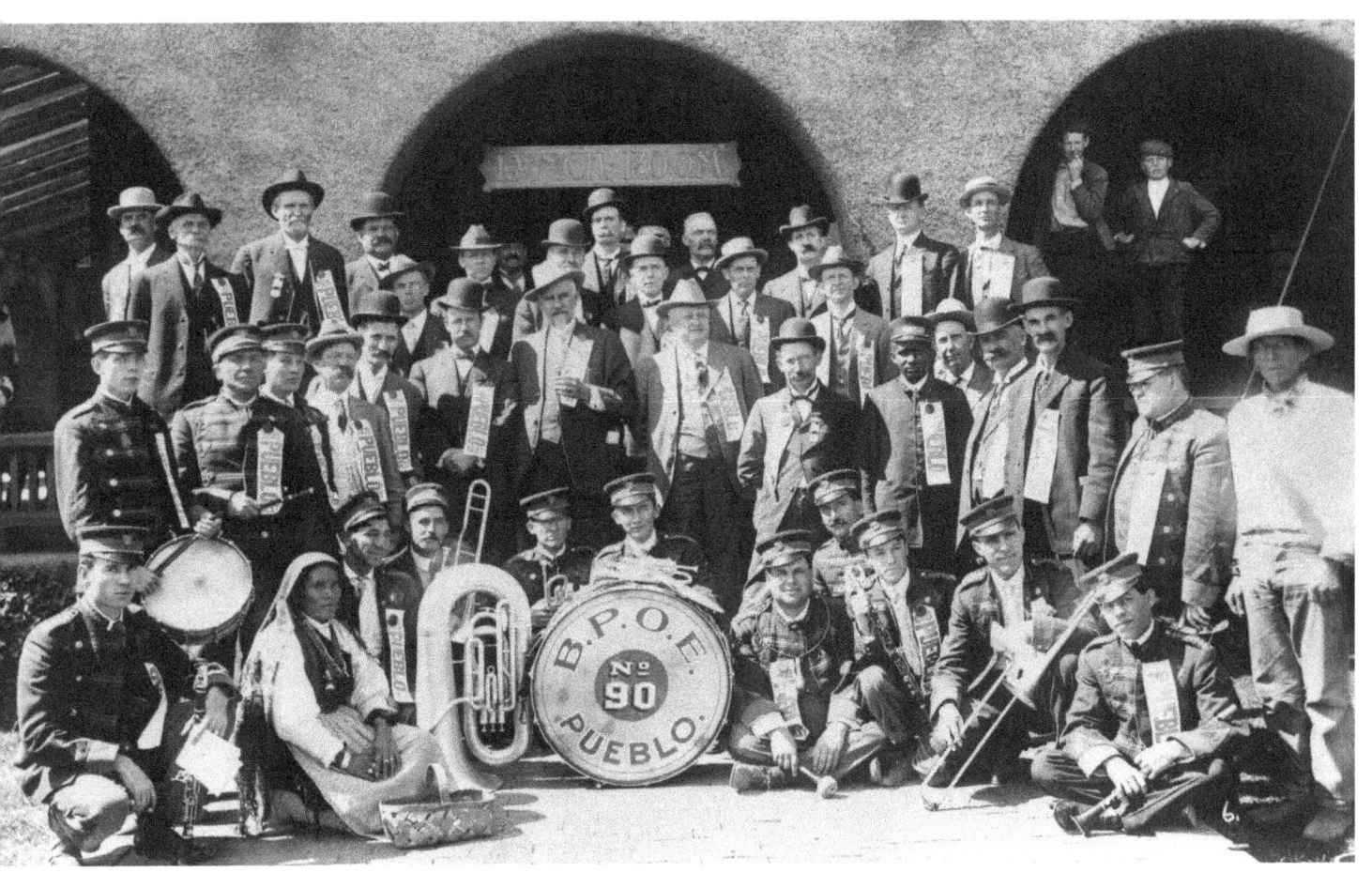

Tom Insley, the driver of this rental car, owned Tom Insley's Bicycle Shop on W. Gold Avenue. He always kept busy with local competitions, and children loved to hang around his shop. He ended up in the penitentiary in Santa Fe for shooting his brother-in-law with a double-barreled shotgun.

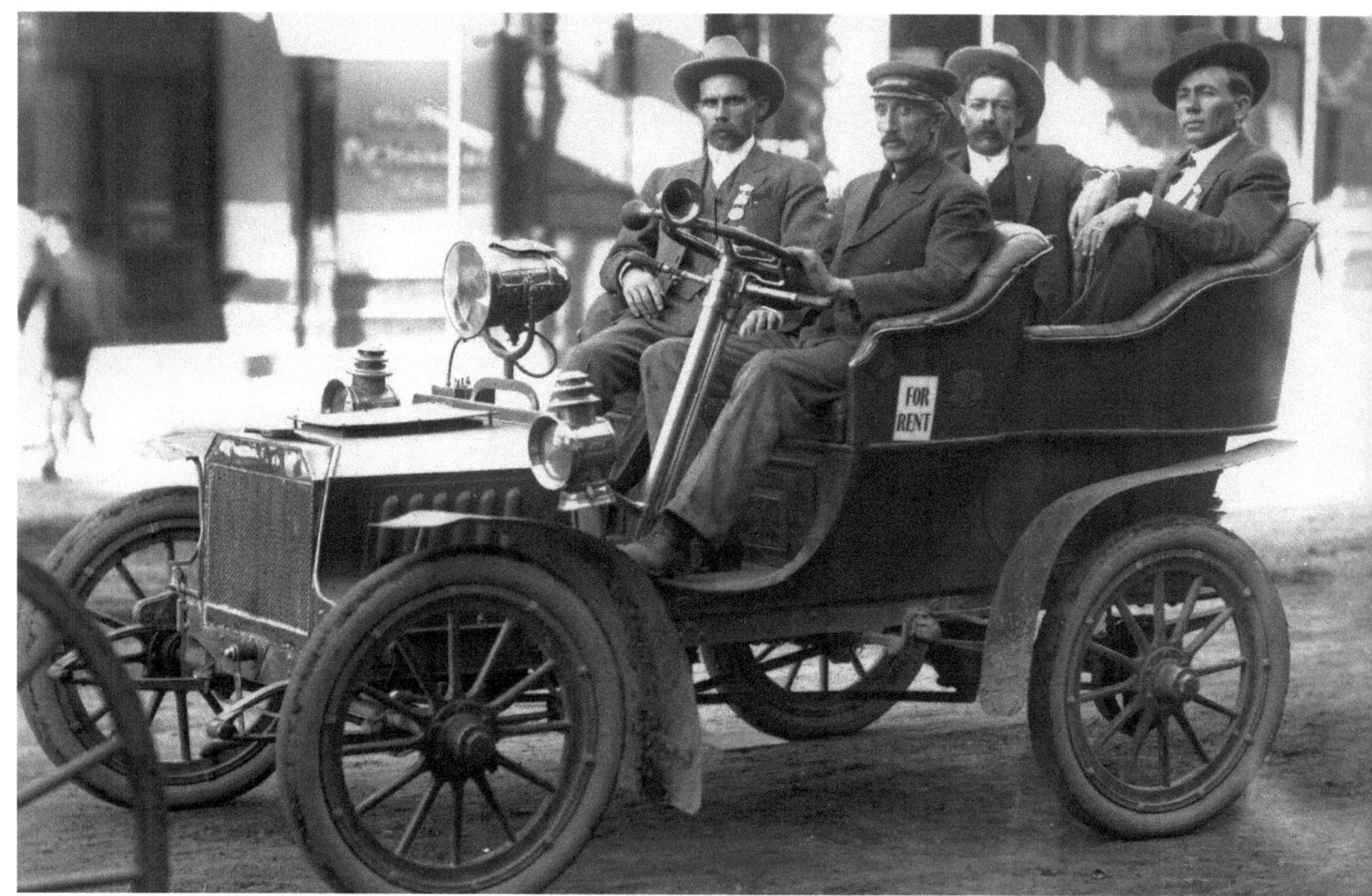

Castle Huning, at S. Fourteenth Street and W. Central Avenue, was the dream house of Franz Huning. It was made of terrones or sod blocks, dug up from a meadow. It took three years to build and was finished in December 1883. The castle sat on 400 acres.

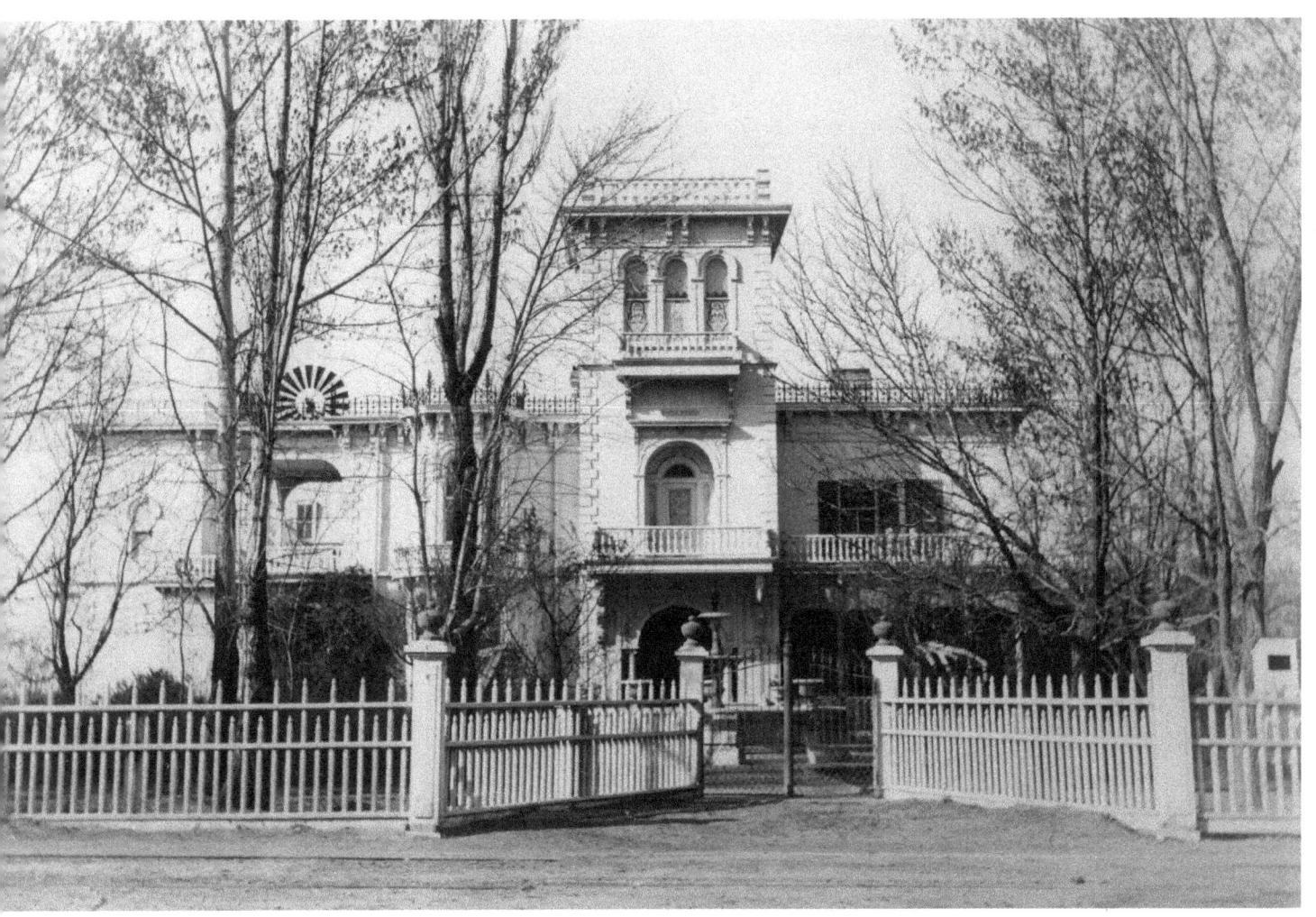

Lincoln Beachy, one of the best-known exhibition flyers, flew this Curtiss pusher biplane in 1912, taking off from the New Mexico State Fair. He made two flights on opening day and buzzed the crowd as he flew over the baseball games. On the next day, he got caught in a downdraft and crashed into a fence. It is not known where this picture was taken.

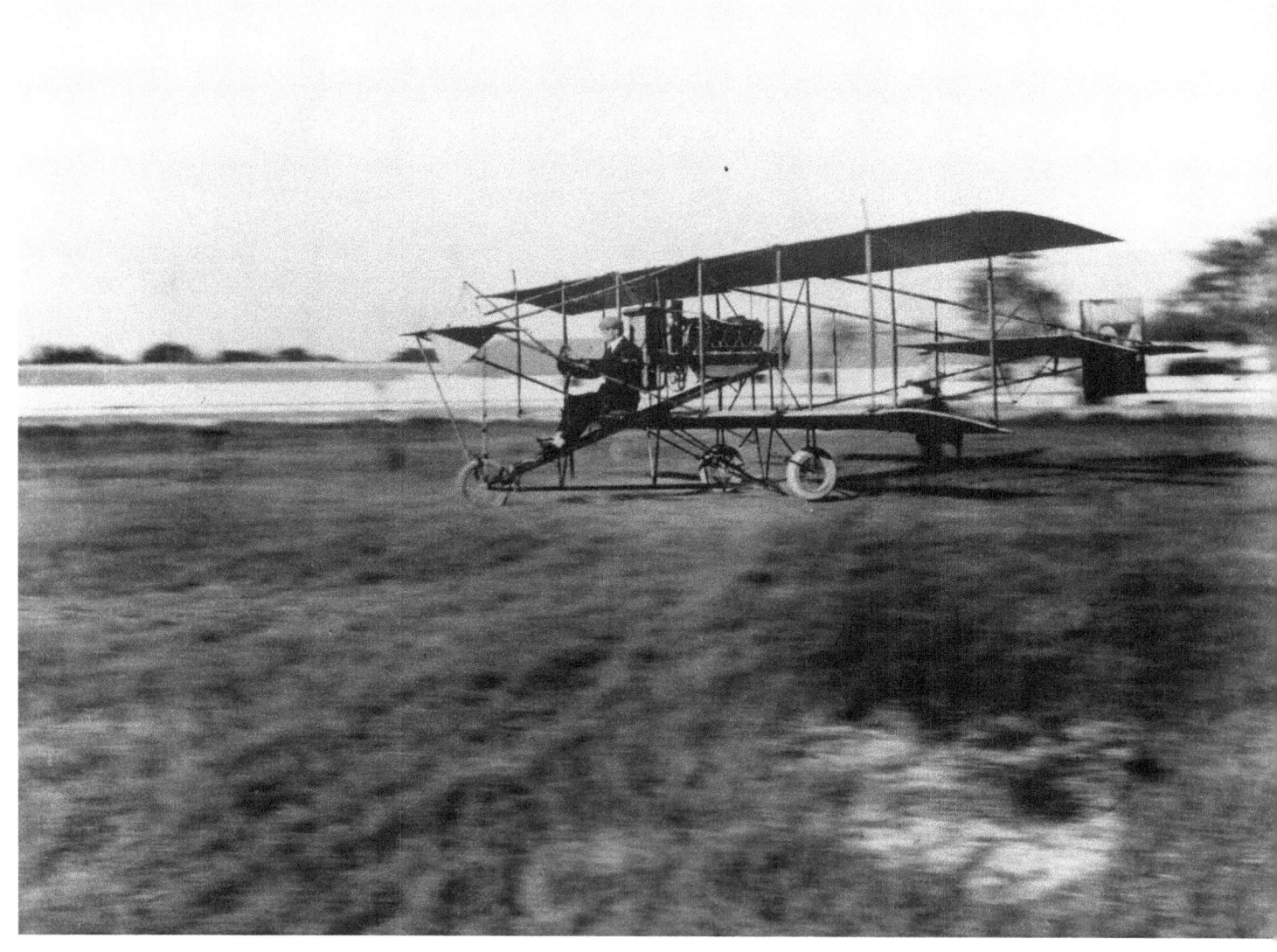

Charles F. Walsh, from San Diego, flew for the Curtiss Exhibition Company. On October 12, 1911, in a Curtiss Model D pusher, he flew about 1,000 feet above the crowd at the New Mexico Territorial Fair. He went over the Rio Grande and came back to land on the baseball diamond. While he was in town, Ray Stamm, Roy Stamm, and Joe McCanna went on flights with him.

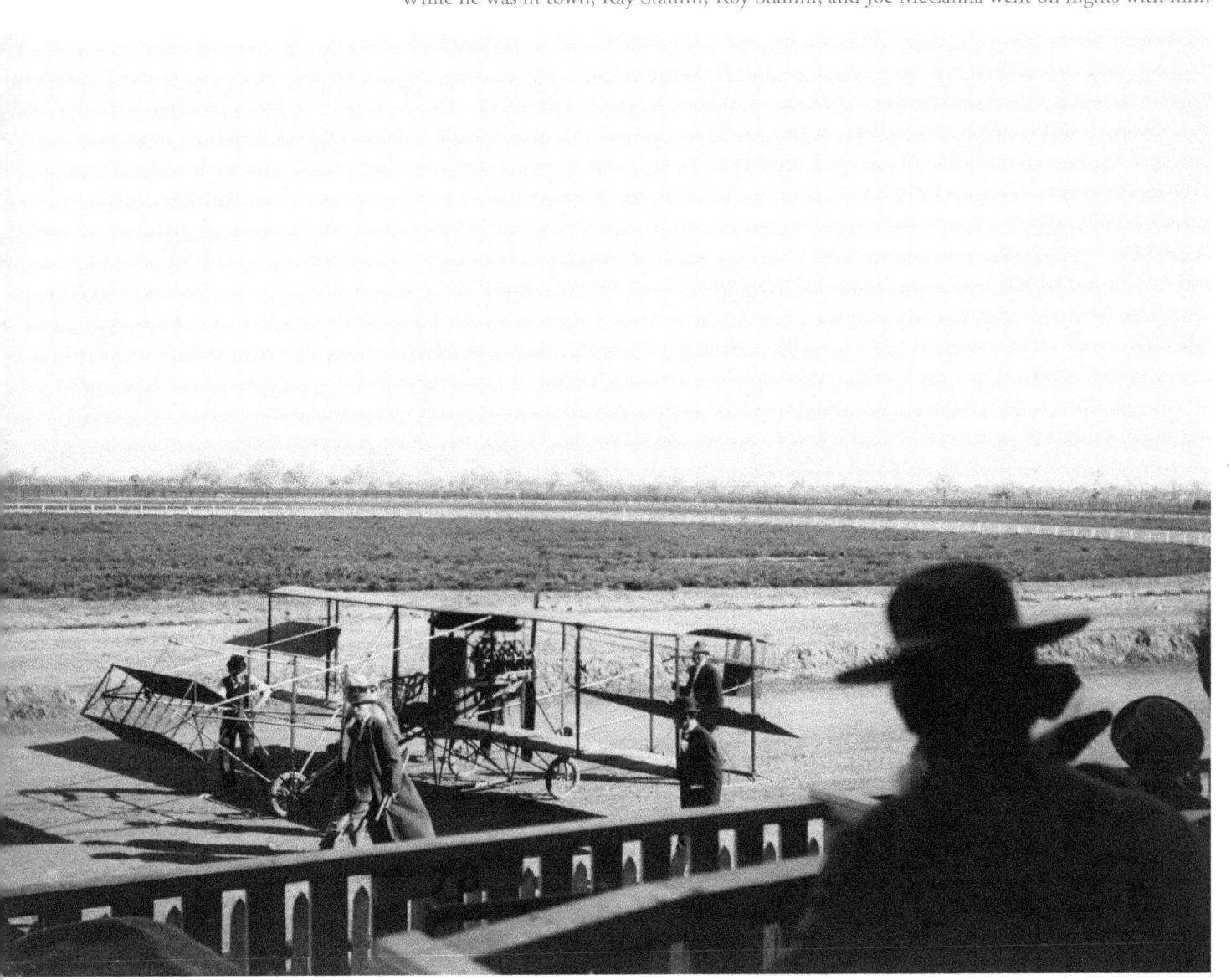

Children's Day at the Orpheum Theatre, 502 S. Second Street. The building started out as the William V. Futrelle Furniture Store. In 1911, after a fire, he rebuilt it as the Orpheum Theatre, offering silent films and vaudeville. The building is still standing.

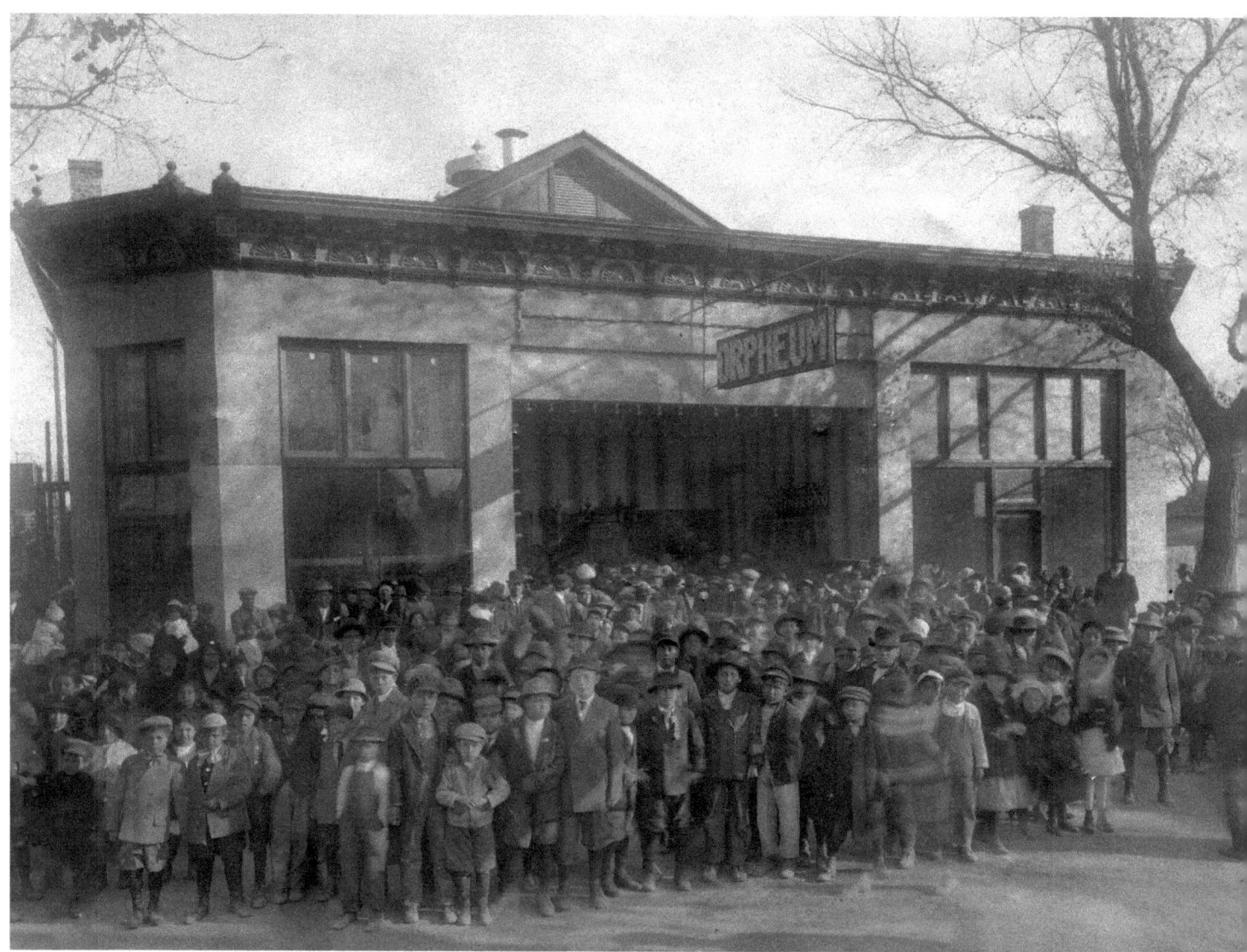

The Barelas Bridge crossed the Rio Grande between Barelas and the South Valley. Barelas was a farming community, with adobe and stone homes. From 1880 to 1948, it was a railroad neighborhood, and many of the workers built homes and lived there.

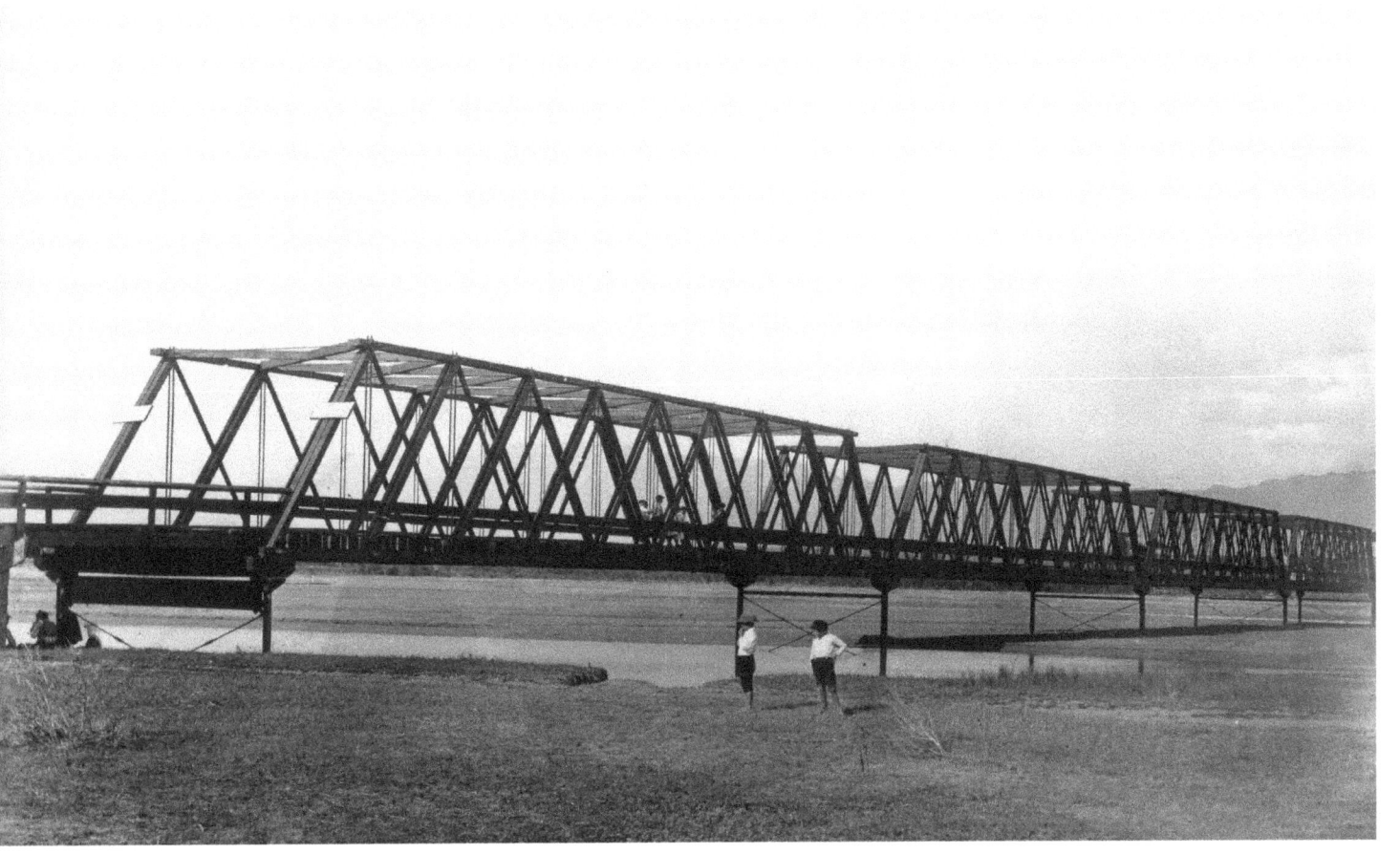

Bryant Company Delivery Service, at 222 W. Gold Avenue, was owned by General N. Bryant. The buildings on the left are still there, and the Gold Street Caffe is in the two-story building on the far left.

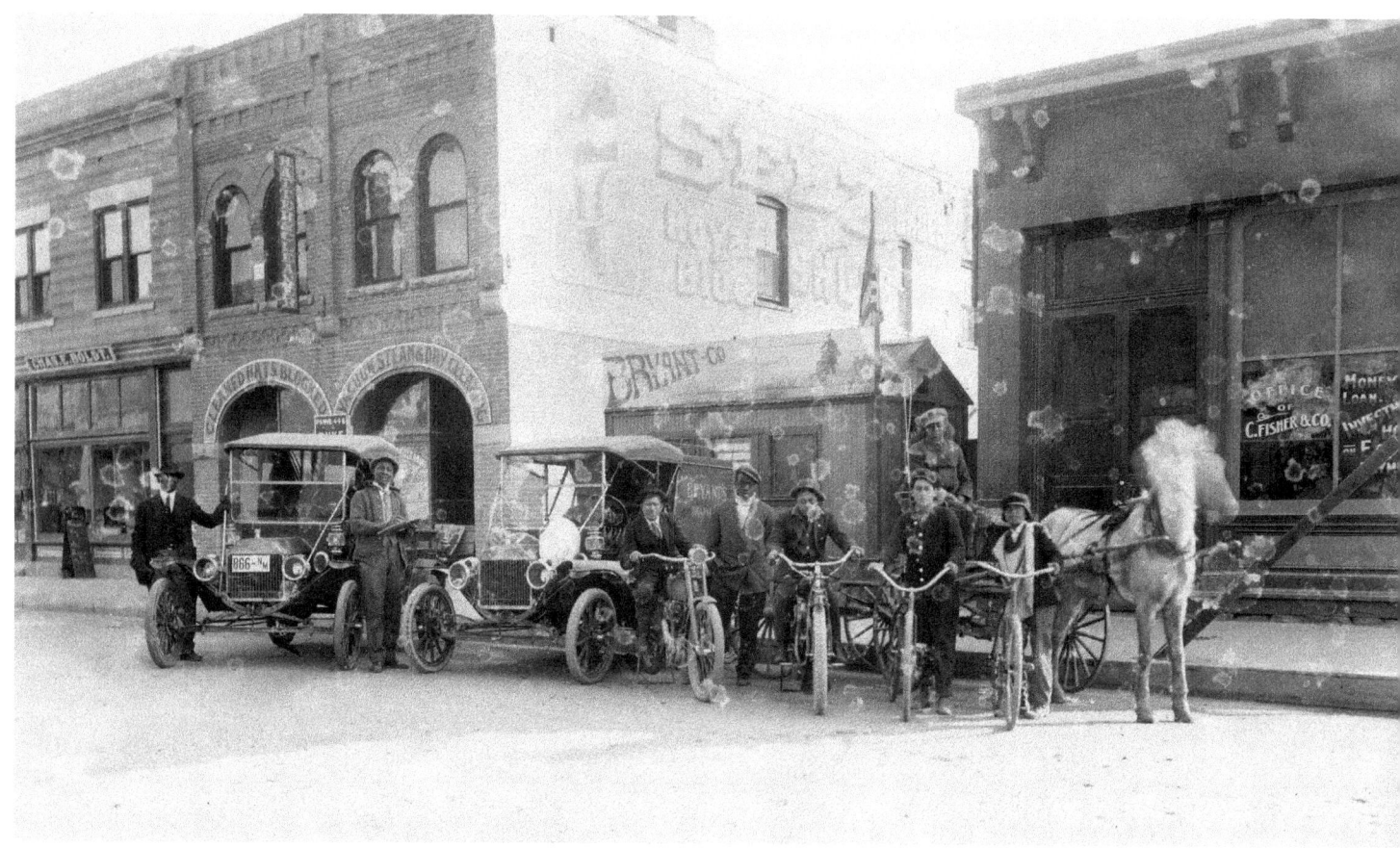

The University of New Mexico library was housed in Hodgin Hall and shared the room with the post office. The university opened its first real library in 1926, east of Hodgin Hall. In 1938, Zimmerman Library, designed by architect John Gaw Meem, opened with a parade and a marching band led by UNM President James Zimmerman.

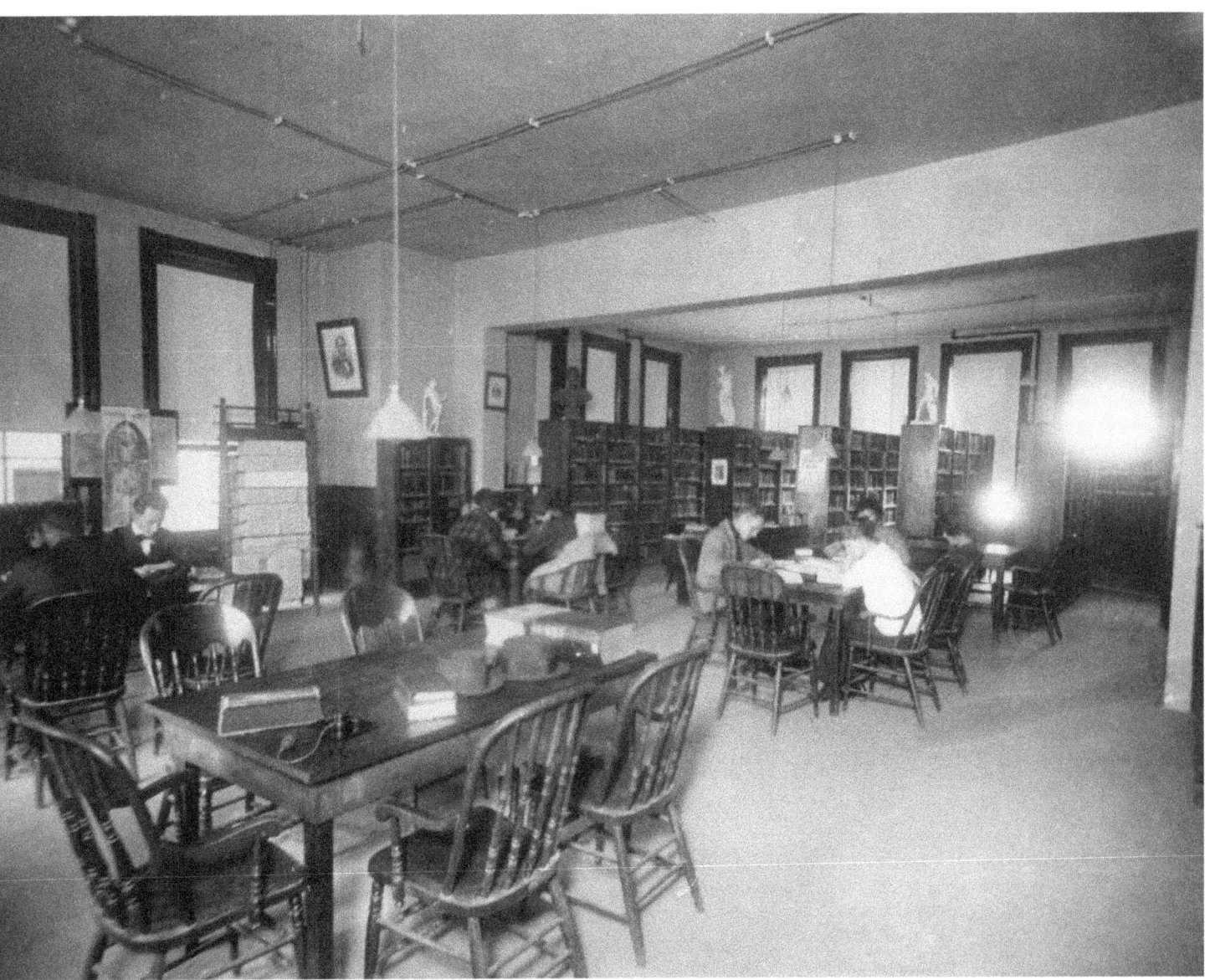

A crowd is gathered for the groundbreaking ceremony of the YMCA in June 1915. The vacant lot was used for carnivals and the circus before the YMCA was built. The Ilfeld Building can be seen in the background.

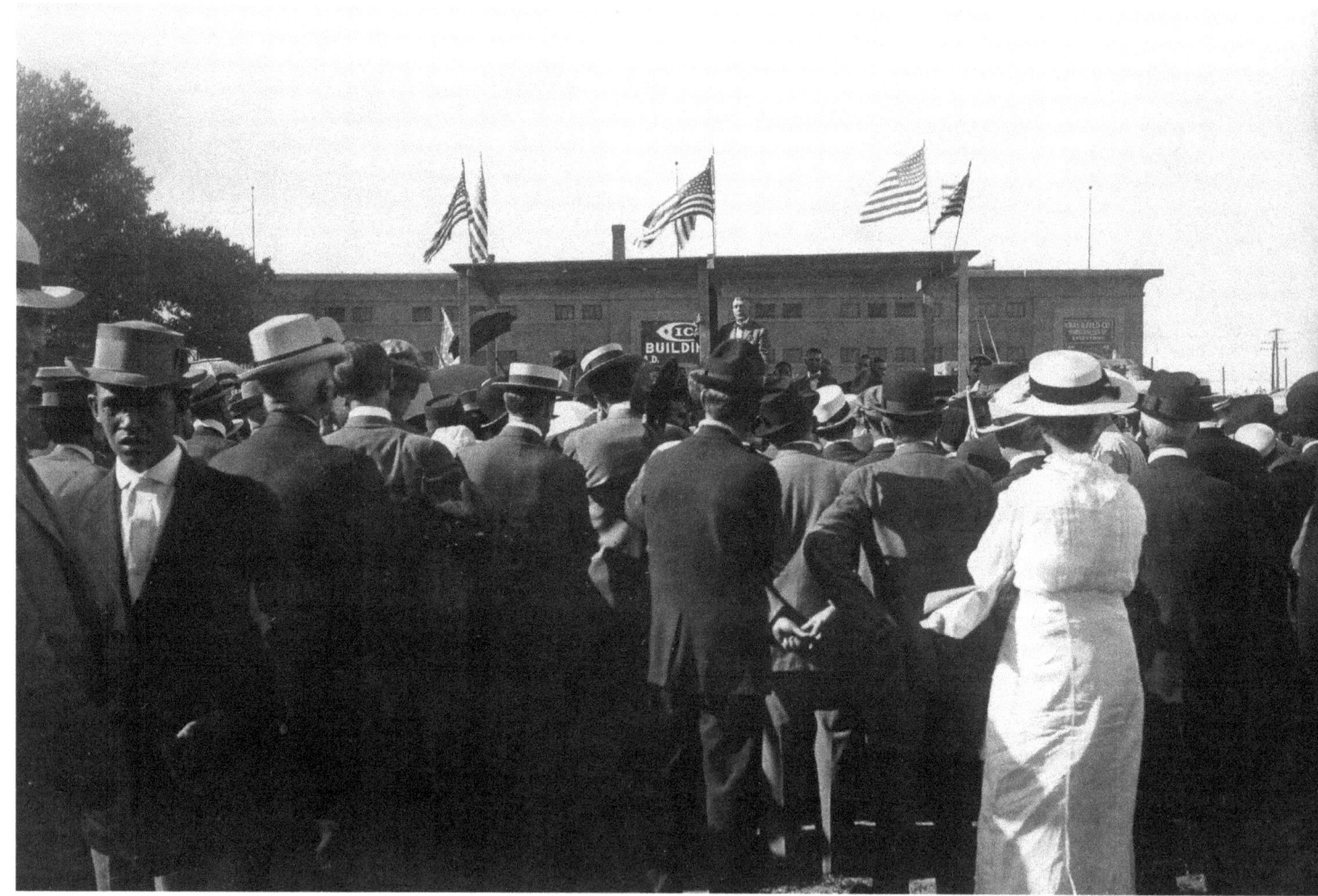

The Alvarado Hotel was always the center of activity. It is seen here with a group of
Native Americans on horseback, onlookers and tourists in the background.

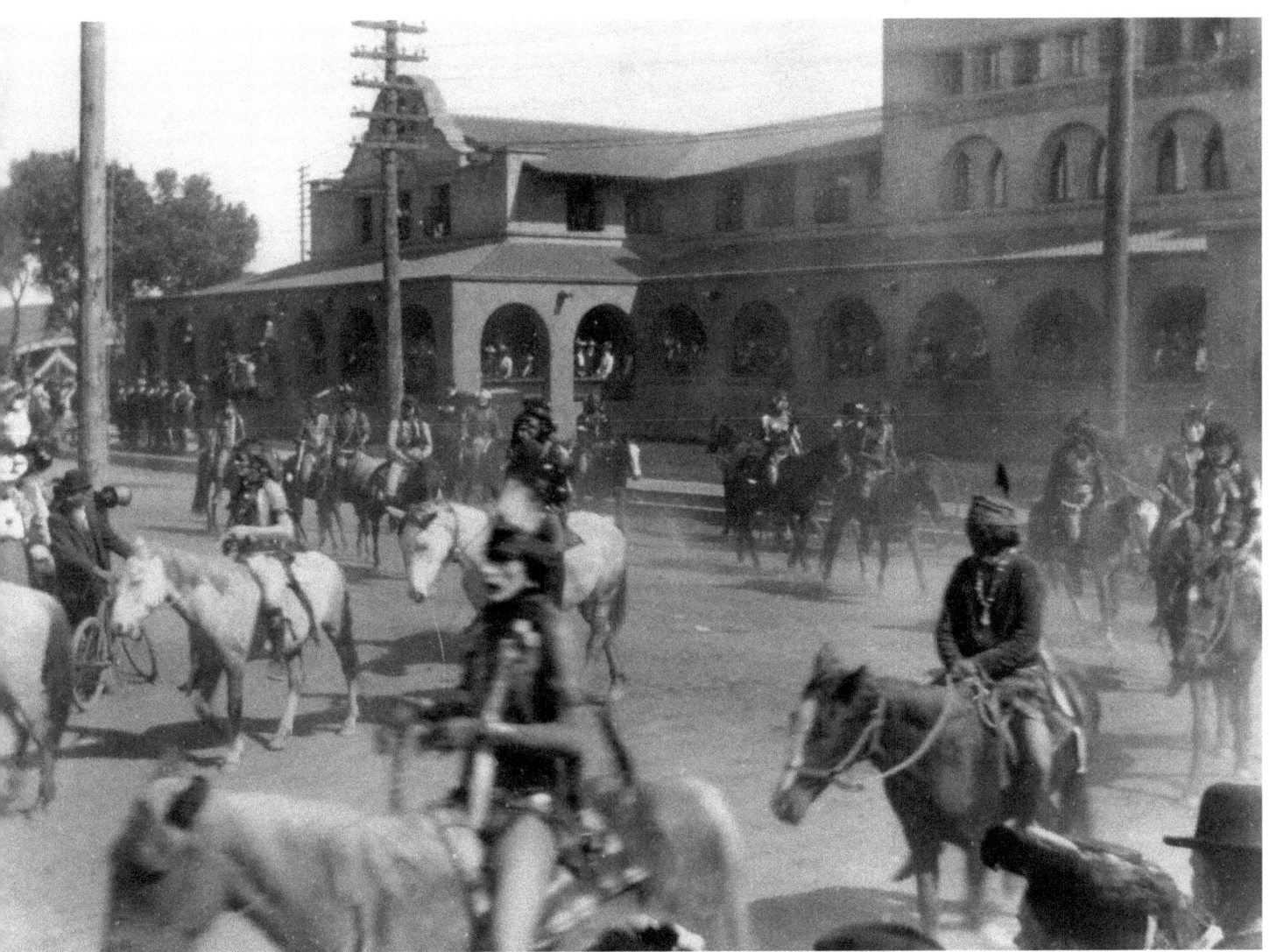

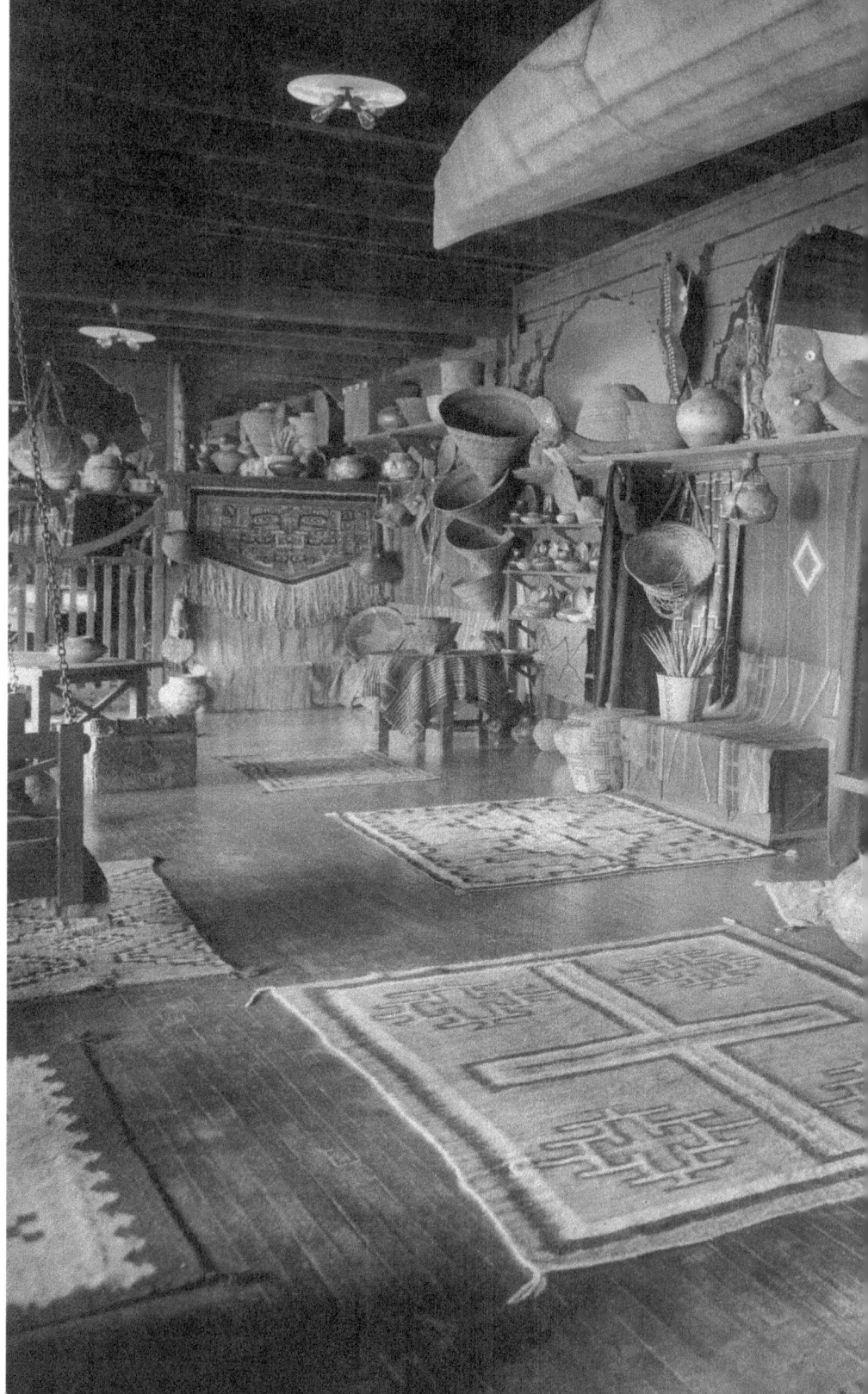

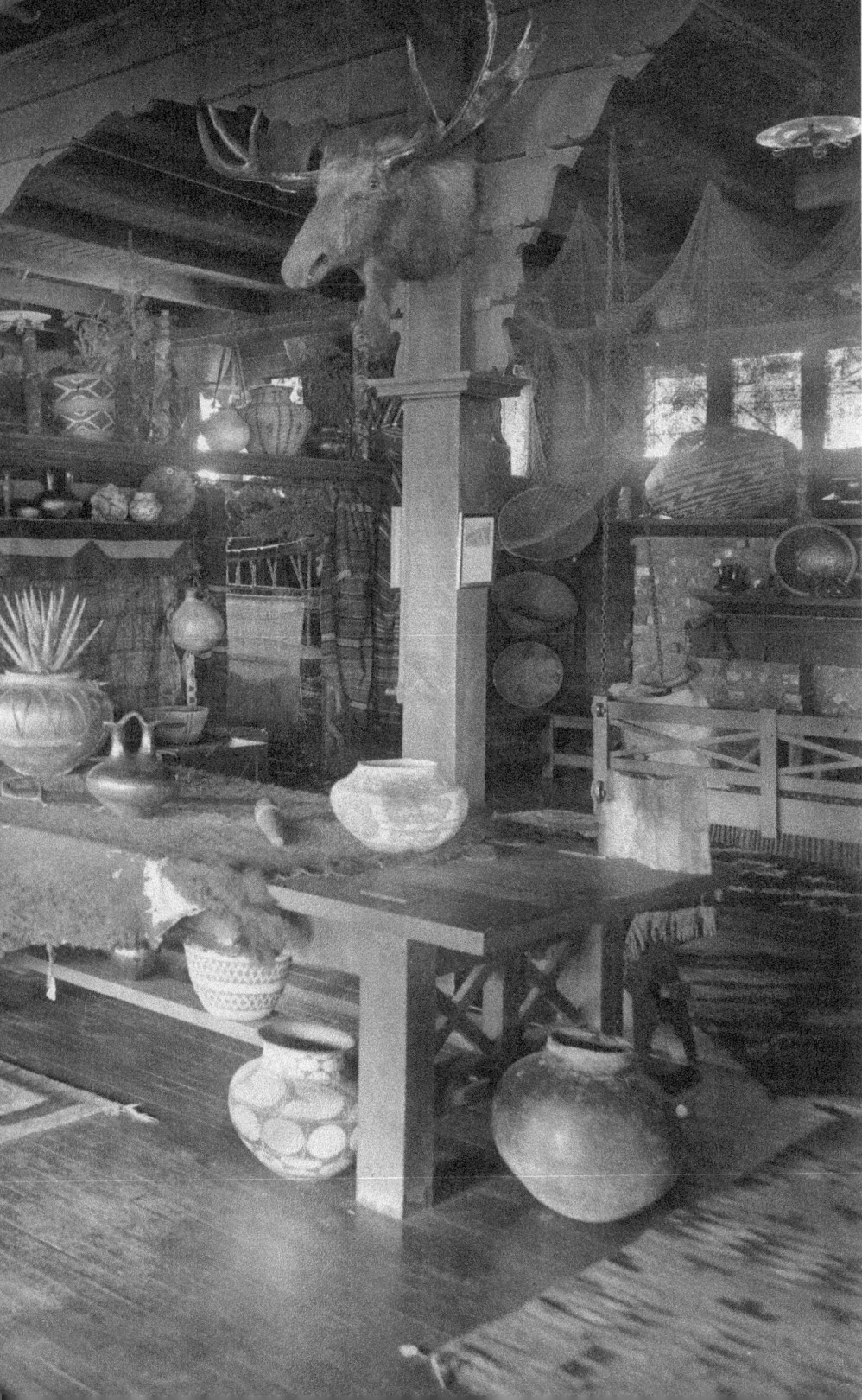

Many of these items went home on the train with the visitors to Albuquerque. The Fred Harvey Indian Room at the Alvarado Hotel was designed by architect Mary Jane Colter. She is credited with putting the Fred Harvey Hotels and the Santa Fe Railway tours of the southwest on the "must-do" vacation lists of the time.

The Korber Building at 214 N. Second Street, with the Korber Garage on the ground floor and the Albuquerque Business College on the upper floors. Jacob Korber came to Albuquerque in the 1880s and opened a blacksmith shop in Old Town. He later bought an entire block downtown, where he sold hardware, furniture, and cars.

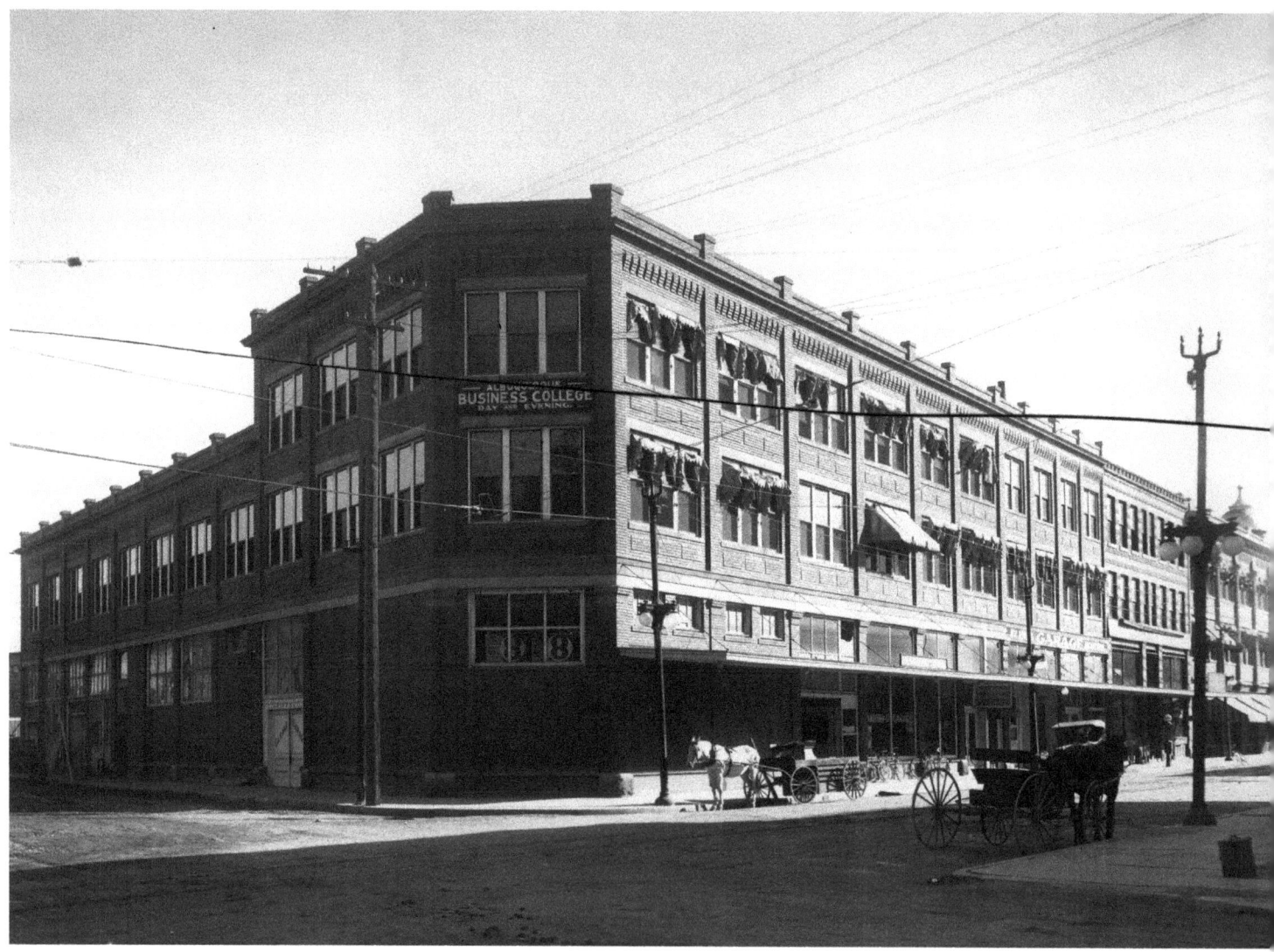

Korber Block tenants, 200-206 N. Second Street, were the Occidental Life Insurance Company and the Angelus Hotel. Many people lived downtown in second- and third-floor walk-ups and some of the rooms had kitchens. The building was there from about 1905 to 1975. The Charles Ilfeld Building is on the right side, in the background.

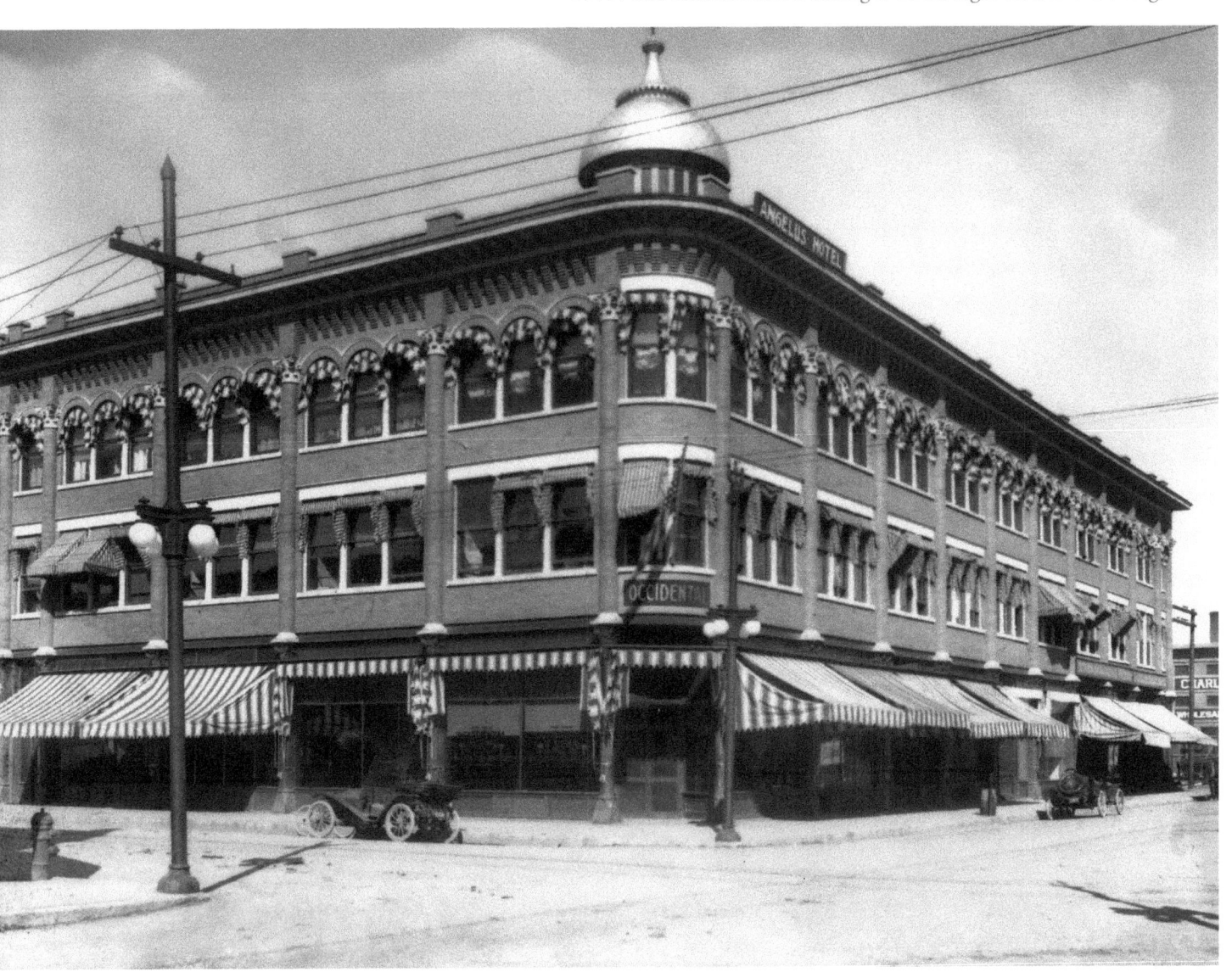

Jail, Old Town, 1916, Sheriff Deputy Elfego Garcia. The Bernalillo County
Jail, at Central Avenue and Rio Grande, was built in 1885, of brown
sandstone, in the same style as the Bernalillo County Courthouse.

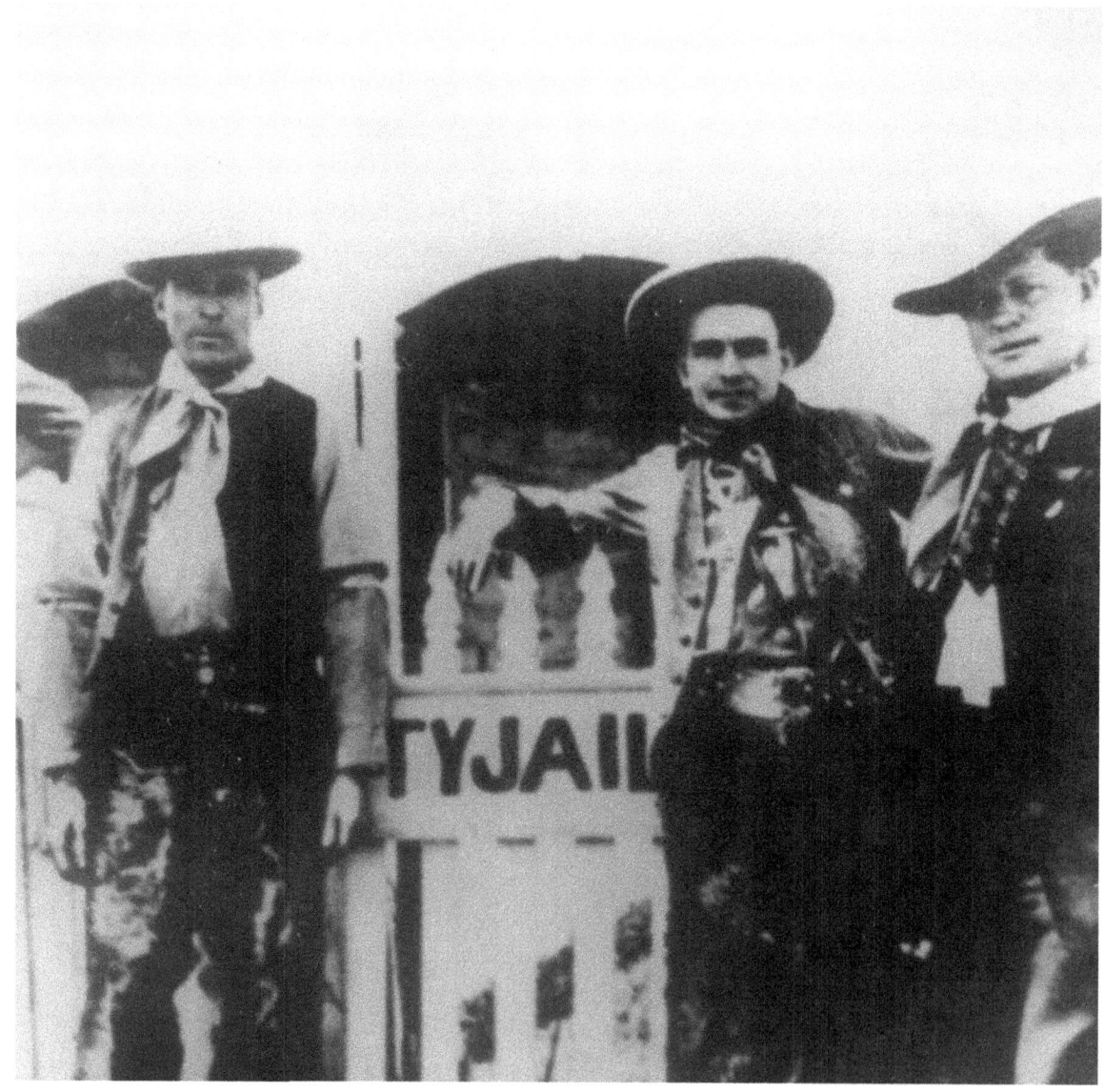

On March 9, 1916, Pancho Villa led Mexican rebels in an attack on the U.S. Army garrison at Columbus, New Mexico. In response, New Mexico, Arizona, and Texas Guardsmen were called into federal service on May 9. The entire National Guard, except coastal units, was called to duty on June 18, 1916.

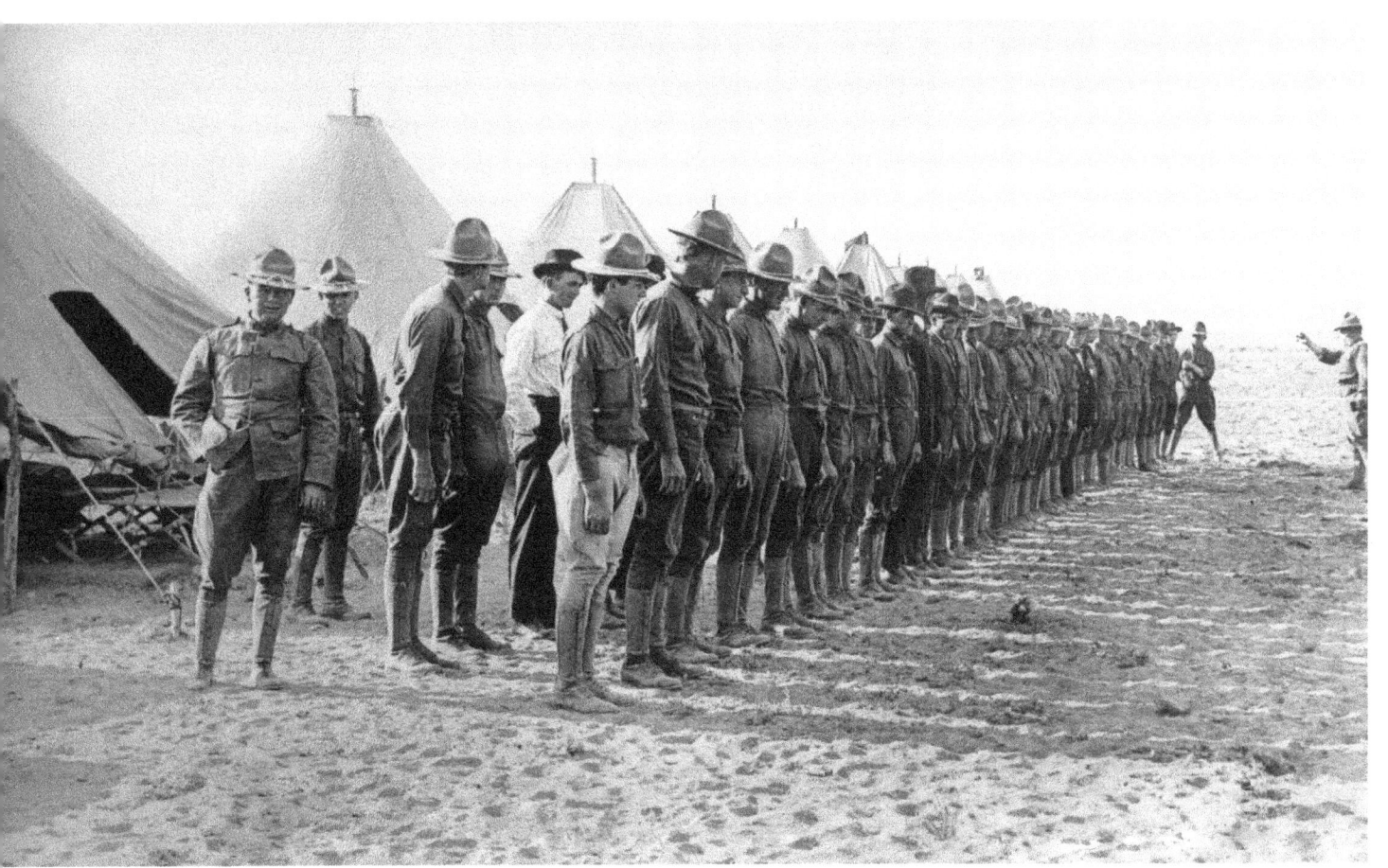

In 1918, local military men training for World War I march west on Central Avenue, crossing First Street. On the right is the Sturges Hotel, first known as the European Hotel, one of the "perhaps houses."

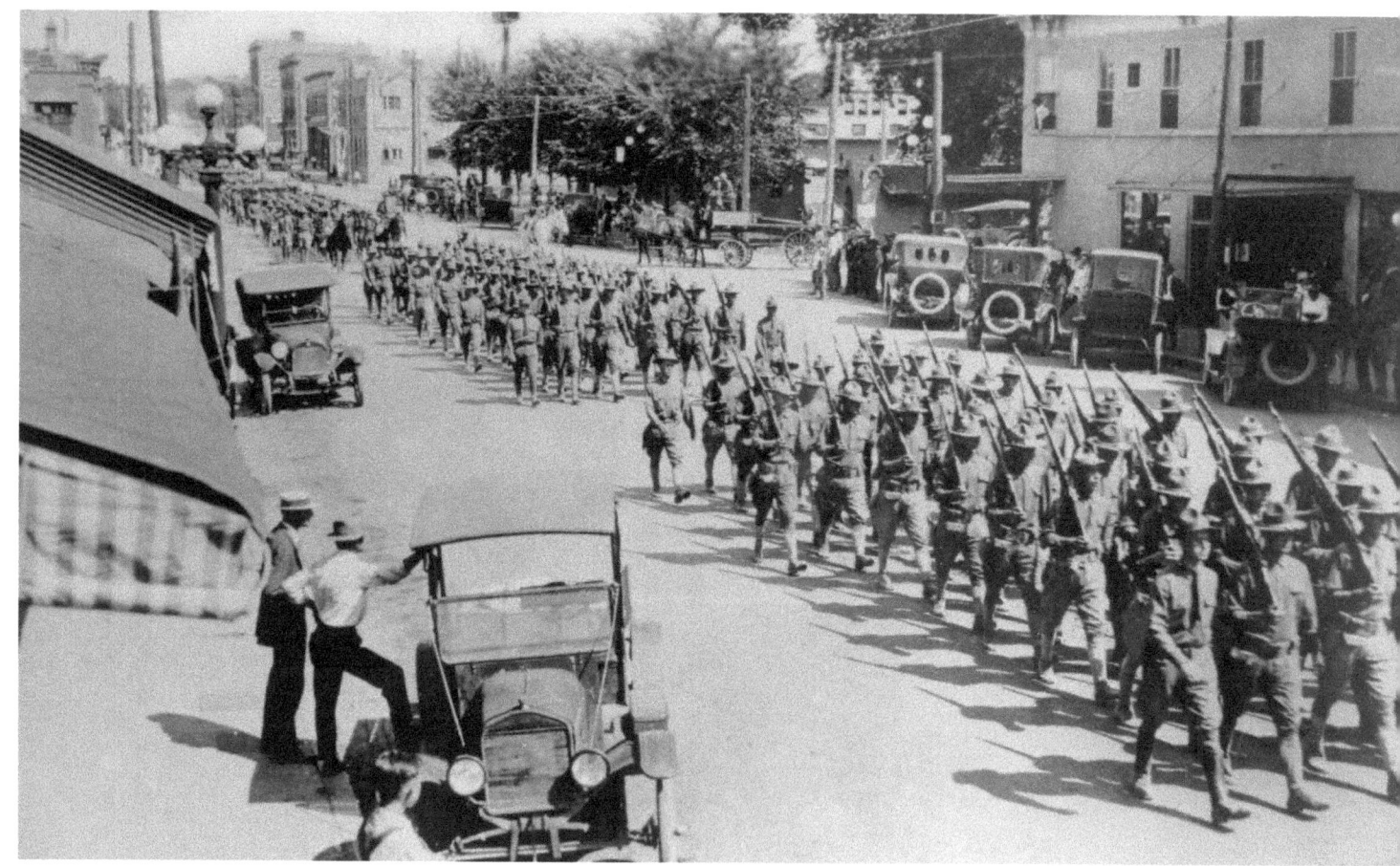

An Albuquerque Streetcar motorette is standing on W. Central Avenue, near First Street. Women drove the streetcars, because the men were off to World War I. The Metropolitan Building can be seen behind the streetcar, with the Metropolitan Cafe. A Henry Mathews Transit Truck and a bicycle share the road.

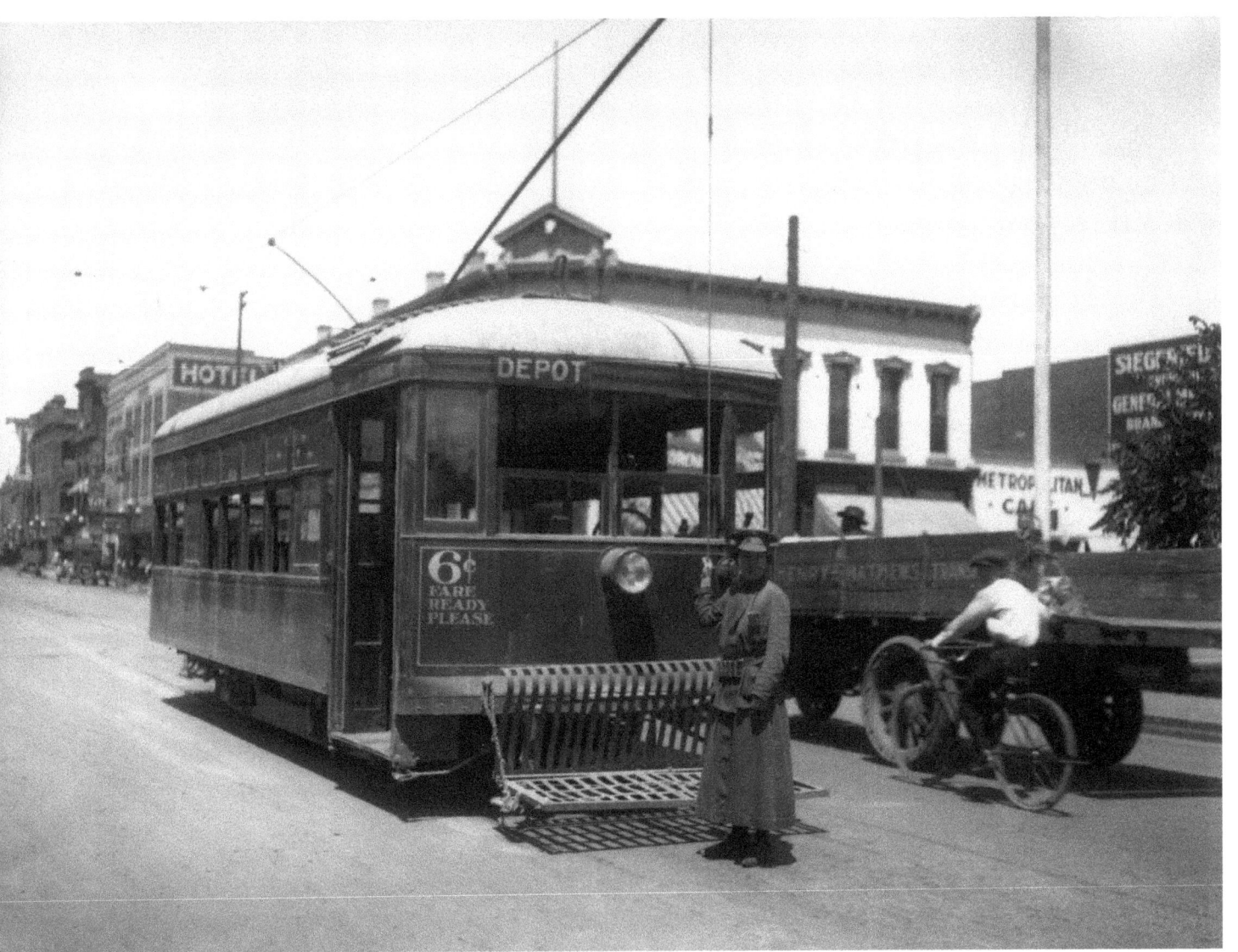

University Of New Mexico Student Army Training Corps, assembled in front of Hodgin Hall during World War I. A military encampment known as Camp Funston operated from the University of New Mexico campus during the war.

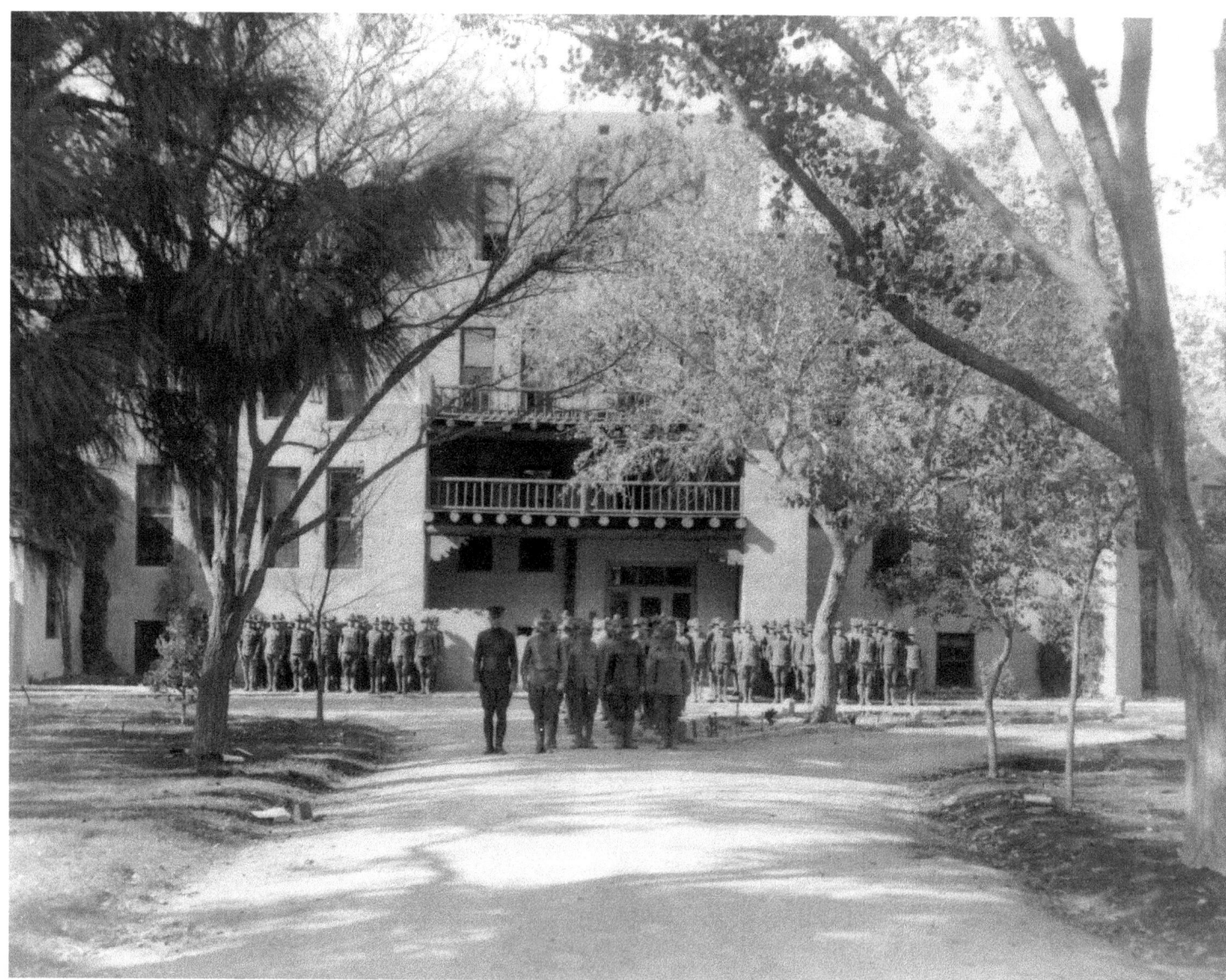

TOURISM BRINGS CHANGES AND CELEBRITIES

(1920–1939)

The Territorial Fairs always promoted aviation, and the State Fairs continued that tradition until World War I, when the fairs were discontinued. After William Franklin and Frank Speakman leased 140 acres and graded runways on East Mesa, interstate flights began. Western Air Express and Transcontinental Air Transport began regular flights to Albuquerque in 1928.

Bond issues from 1912 and 1919 were used to expand the schools. In 1923, the Hotel Franciscan opened, capitalizing on the Pueblo revival style. As the economy recovered from the post–World War I recession, more people bought automobiles and started moving away from downtown. Two skyscrapers were built, the Sunshine building and the First National Bank. A new Bernalillo County Courthouse was constructed in 1926. The KiMo Theatre opened in 1927 using local motifs, and became a city landmark.

The Chamber of Commerce organized the First American Pageant, to compete with the Gallup Inter-Tribal Indian Ceremonials. The first one was in 1928. Its opening day was a business and school holiday, a street dance took place downtown, and the Hotel Franciscan hosted the Montezuma Ball. The pageant proved very popular and was repeated until the Great Depression ended it.

By 1933, the Depression started to affect Albuquerque, when the AT&SF railway laid off 40 percent of its work force. Transients started to arrive, and a shantytown arose south of town. President Franklin Roosevelt's New Deal programs were a great benefit to Albuquerque, so the slowdown wasn't as bad here as in other communities. The Civilian Conservation Corps, Public Works Administration, Civil Works Administration, and Federal Emergency Relief Administration brought big changes to the area.

Hospitals were built or expanded, including an Indian Public Health Hospital and Veterans Administration Hospital. WPA and PWA funds built more public buildings, including the Chamber of Commerce, Albuquerque Little Theater, and community centers. PWA funds also built a new fairground at San Pedro and Central. The University of New Mexico saw a building boom. Streets and utility projects expanded, including the construction of a viaduct over Coal Avenue, and the Central Avenue and Tijeras underpasses. Suburbs developed with the Federal Housing Authority offering low-cost loans.

The steel Barelas Bridge across the Rio Grande, with a newer concrete bridge beside it. Before it was rerouted down Central Avenue in 1937, Route 66 went down Fourth Street and crossed this bridge. So many cars crossed the bridge daily that the older one couldn't handle the traffic.

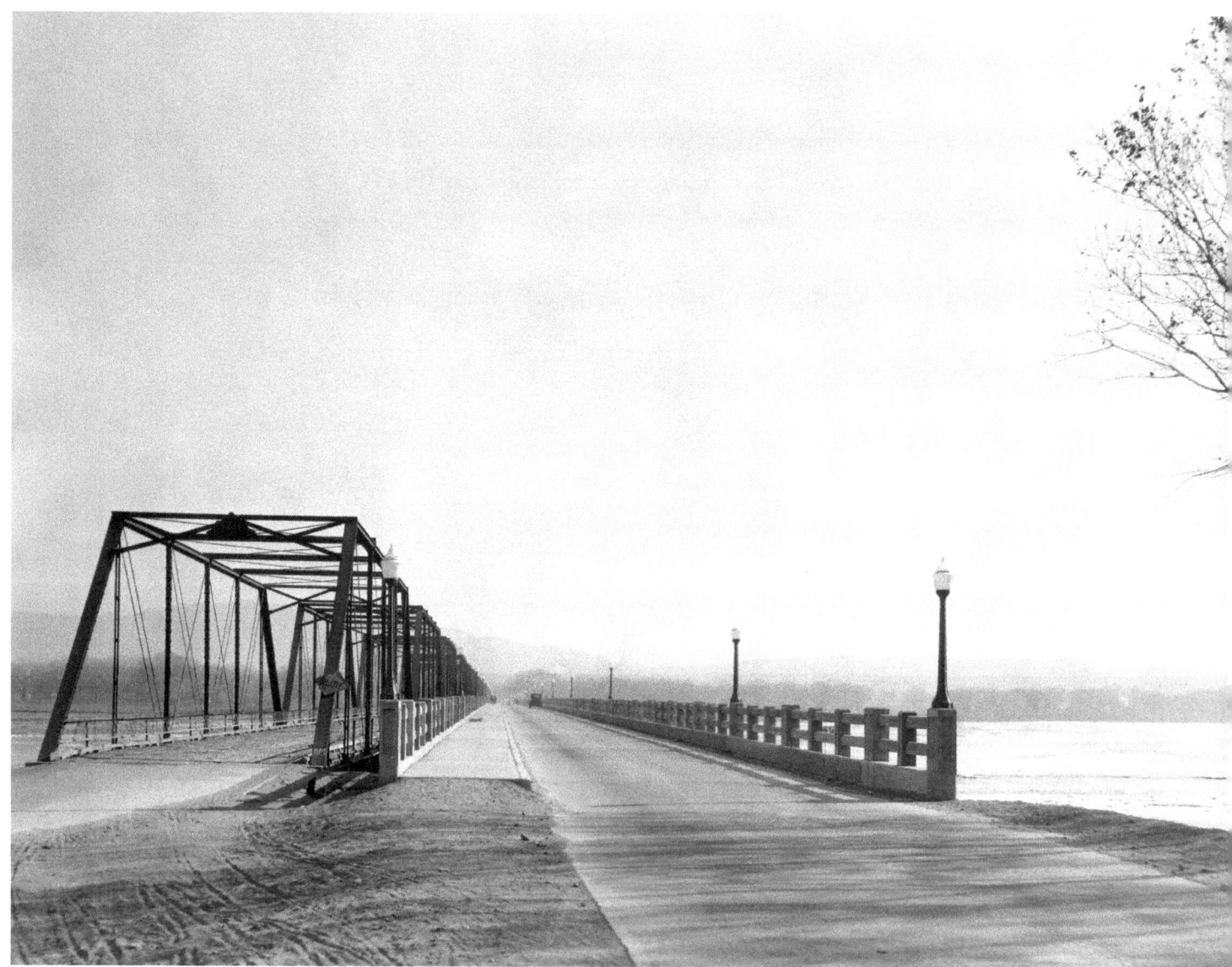

Hodgin Hall, at the University of New Mexico, is shown on a winter day. Charles E. Hodgin was the first superintendent of the Albuquerque Public Schools, from 1891 to 1897. Even though money was tight, he included instruction in music and manual arts in the curriculum. In 1897, he became head of the University of New Mexico Teachers Training Division.

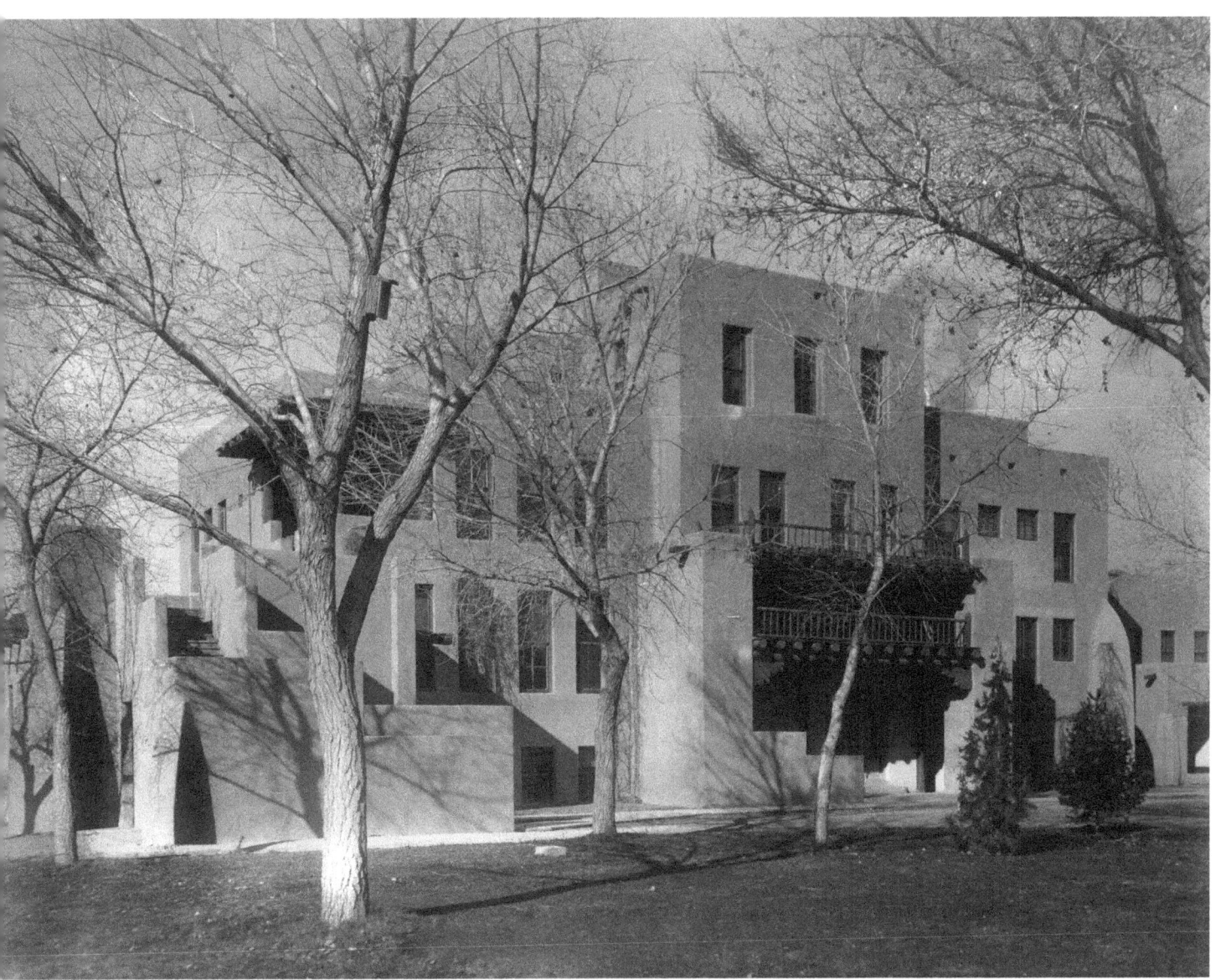

The San Ignacio Catholic Church, in Martineztown, at 1300 Arno Street, was built in 1916. It is still there and serves the Martineztown and Santa Barbara neighborhoods.

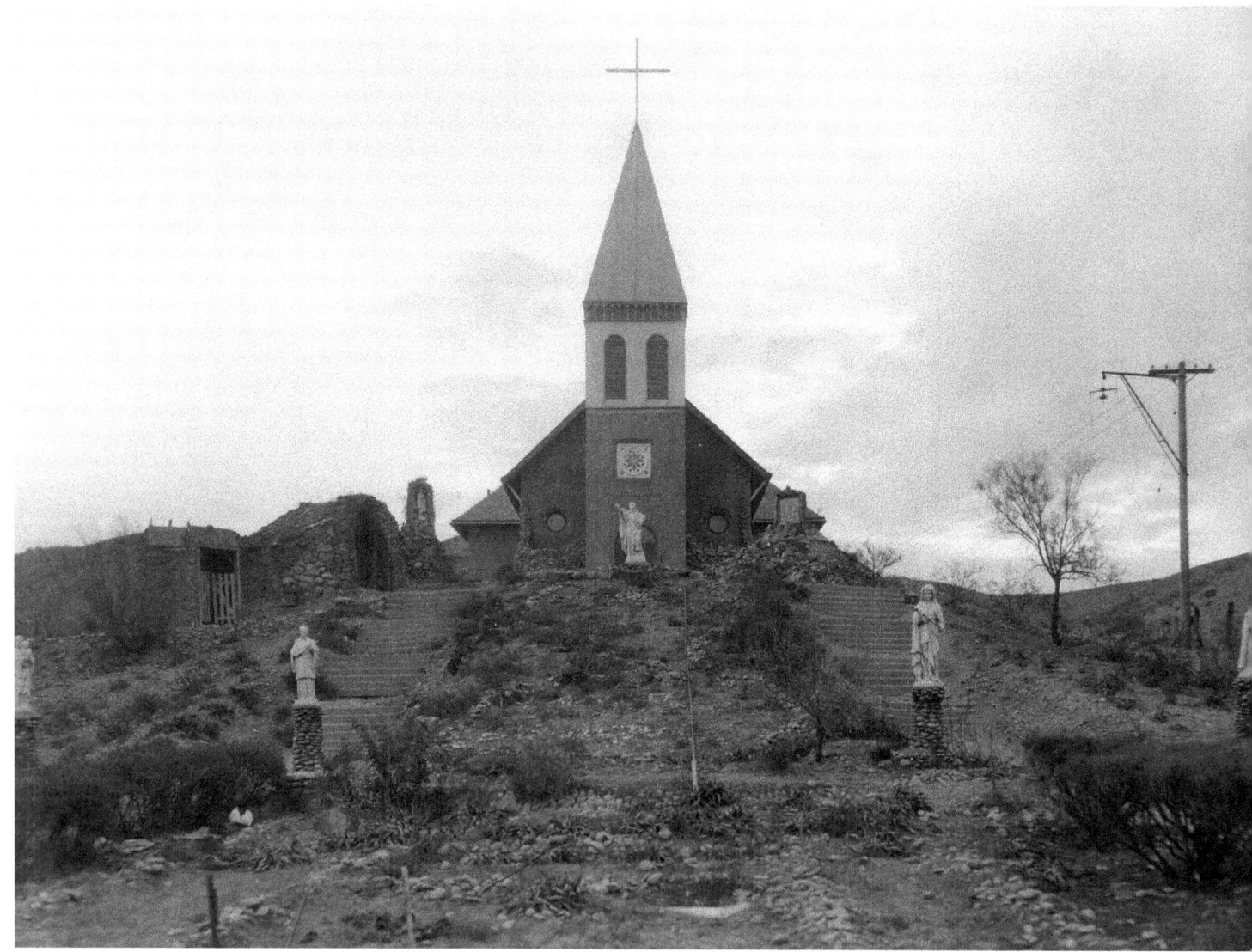

An electric streetcar and automobile share the road at First and Central, looking west. The city is presently trying to recreate this system of streetcars, complete with cowcatchers. The Metropolitan Hotel, behind the streetcar, no longer has the original 1880s decorative cupola.

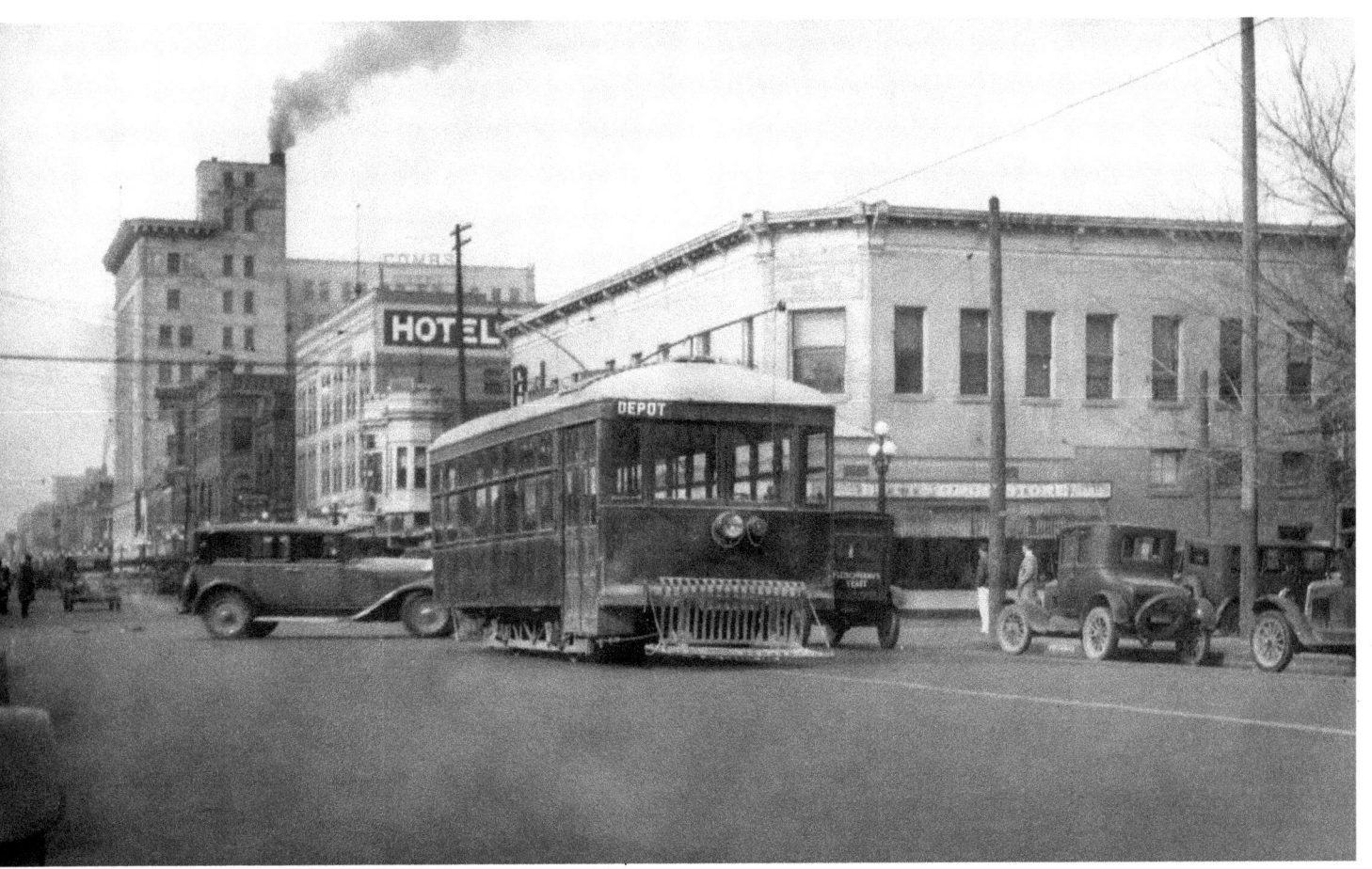

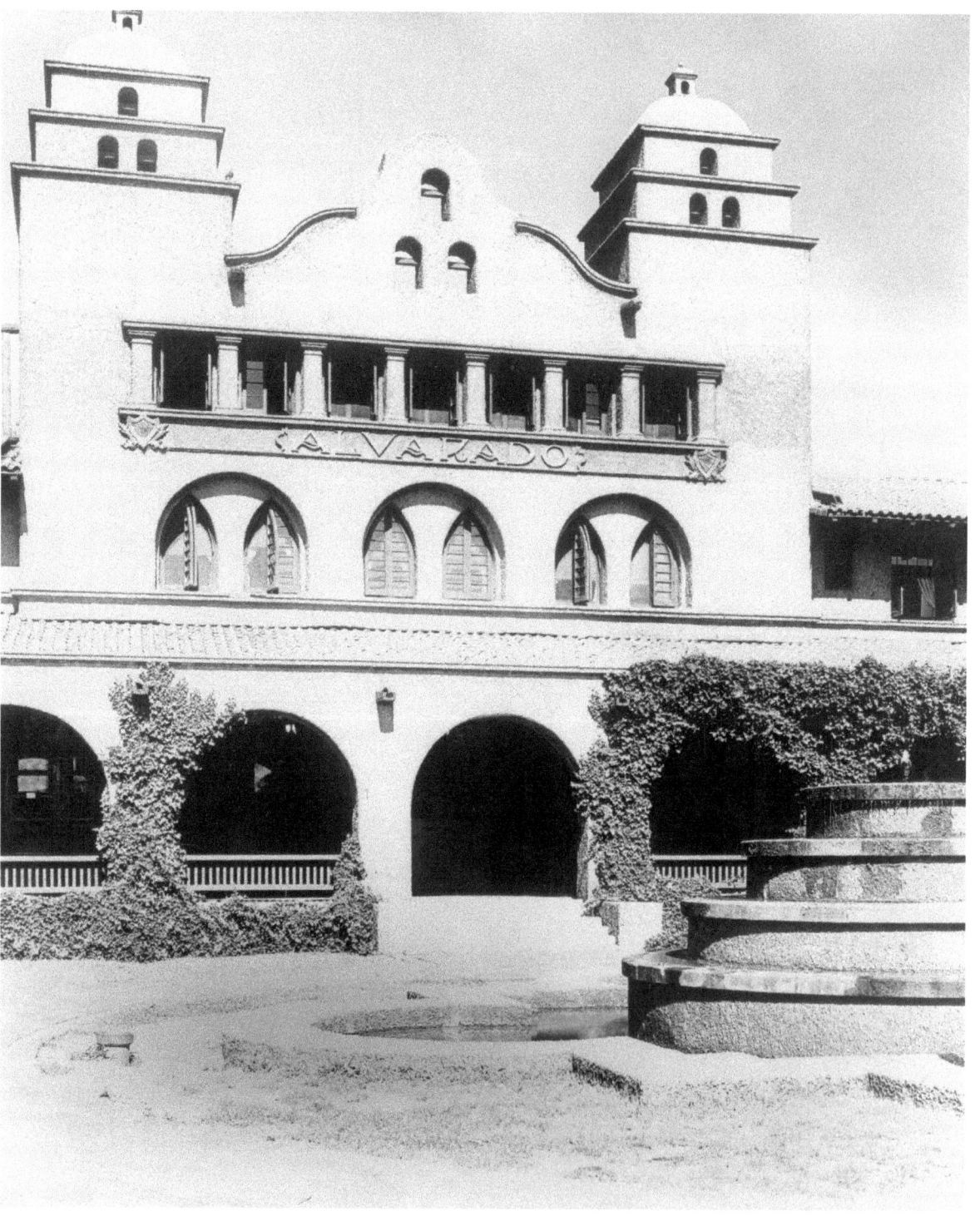

Many happy memories are relived when people talk about the Alvarado Hotel. The Courtyard fountain was a place where many men proposed to their sweethearts. Visitors always wanted a picture of themselves in front of the fountain.

The California Limited made a scheduled stop at Albuquerque. Passengers were given a thirty-minute break. At the Alvarado they could purchase arts and crafts from the Indian vendors outside, browse the shops inside, or have a quick meal served by a Harvey Girl. The train would receive any needed service, before it continued on its eastern run to Chicago.

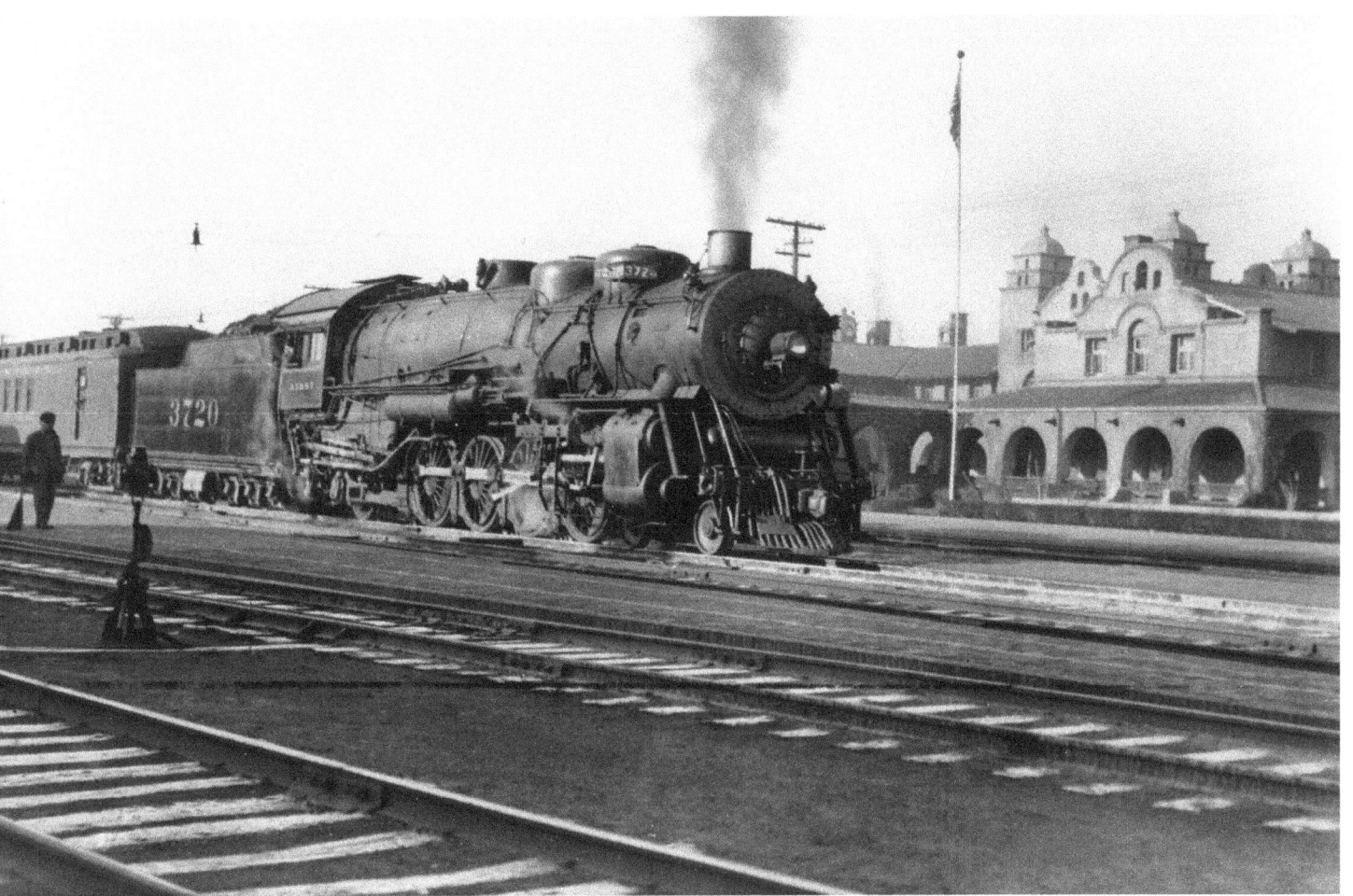

The Hotel Franciscan, at Central Avenue and Sixth Street, was very popular and a rival to the Alvarado Hotel. It was built by public subscription, because business people thought Albuquerque needed more rooms to attract more tourists and conventions. It was demolished in the early 1970s and became a parking lot.

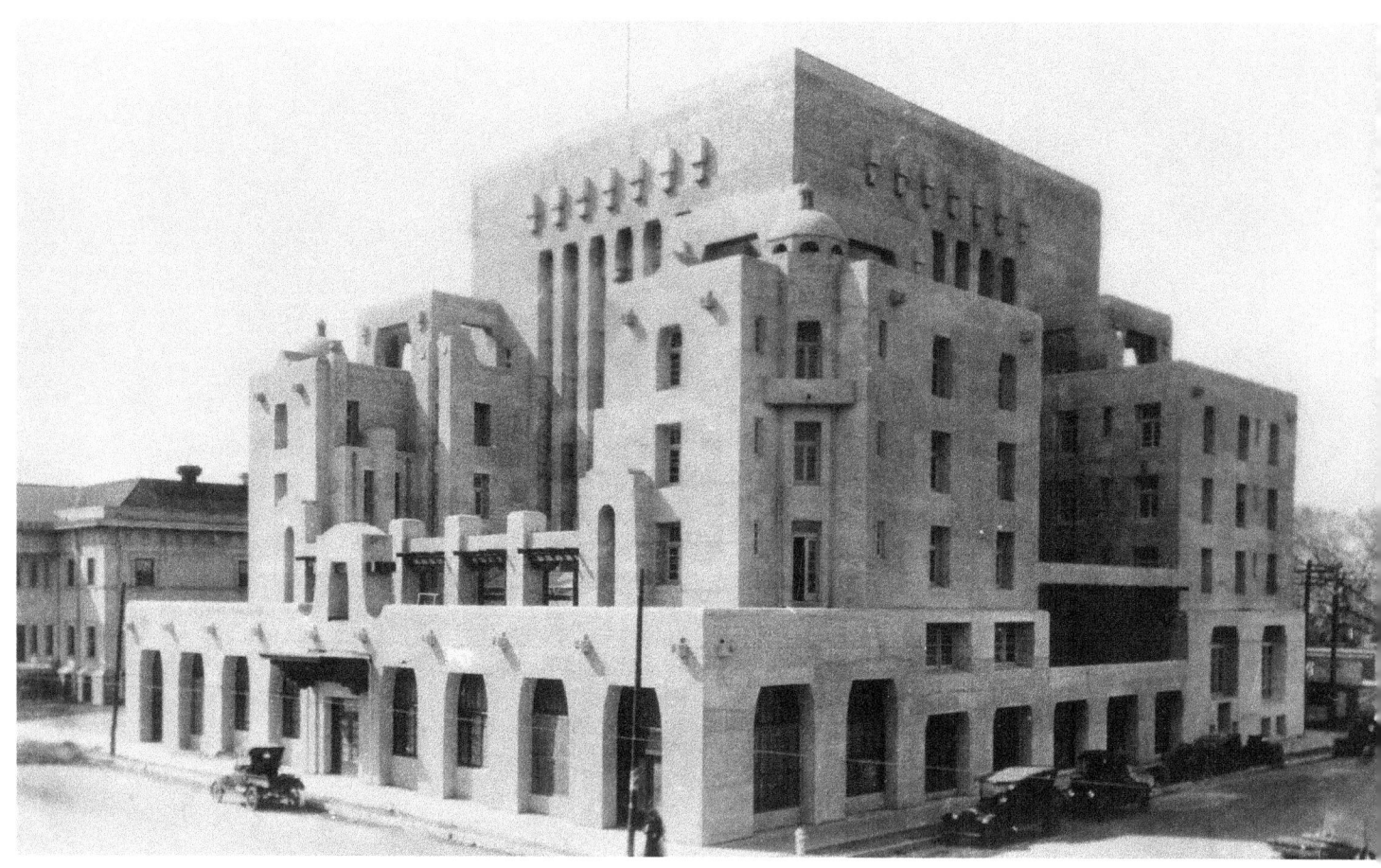

Rin Tin Tin, with owner Lee Duncan directly below him, at the depot. A five-day old puppy when Corporal Lee Duncan found him in a bombed war dog kennel in France, on September 5, 1918. Rin Tin Tin went on to make 26 movies for Warner Brothers and was considered one of Hollywood's top stars. The conductor next to "Rinty" is Hamilton J. Tompkins, who lived on W. Central Avenue.

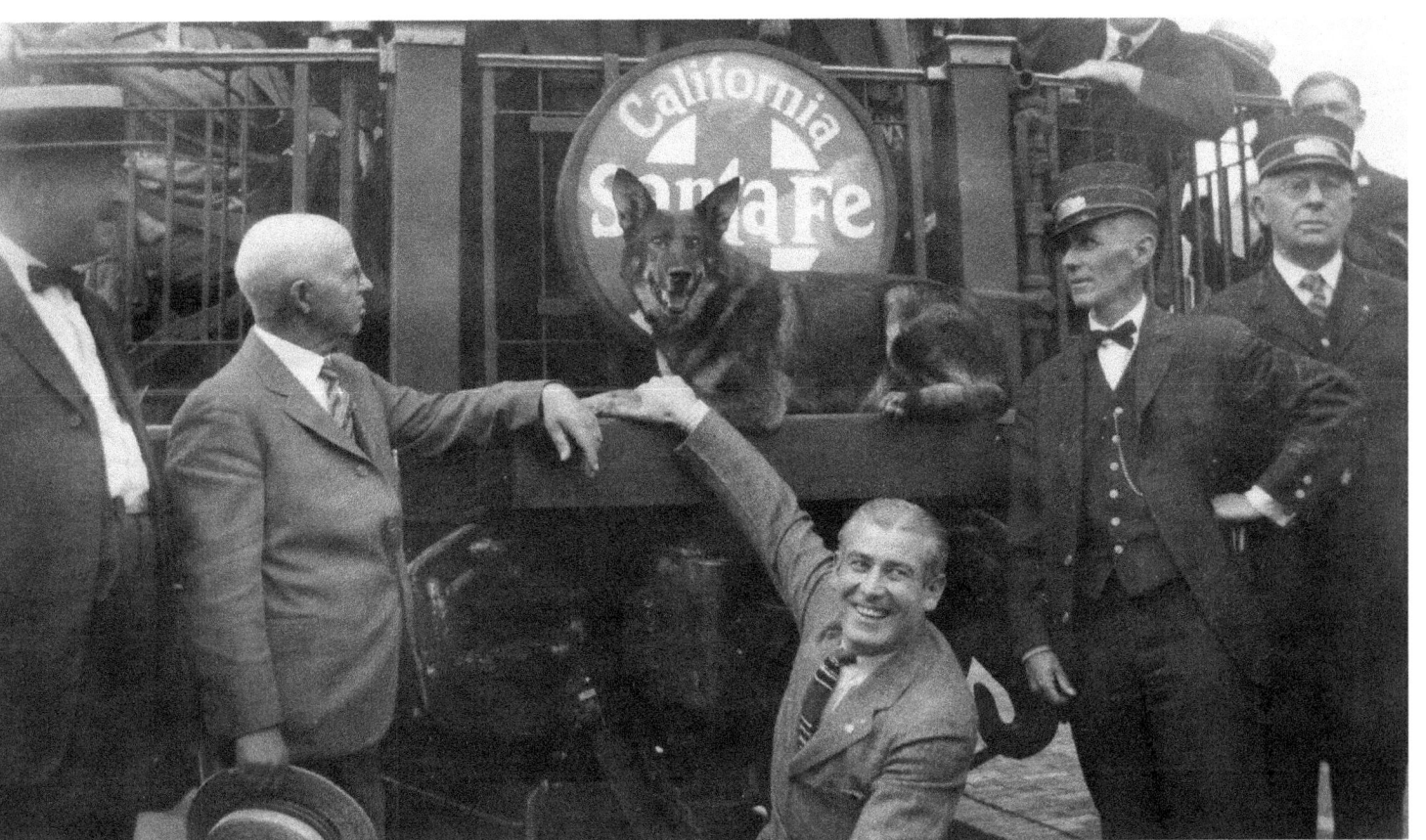

Movie stars and celebrities, like these young stars from Hal Roach's Our Gang Comedies, often stood on the observation car platform of the California Limited to greet their fans when the trains stopped in Albuquerque. Local resident William Steele Dean was frequently at the train station to take pictures.

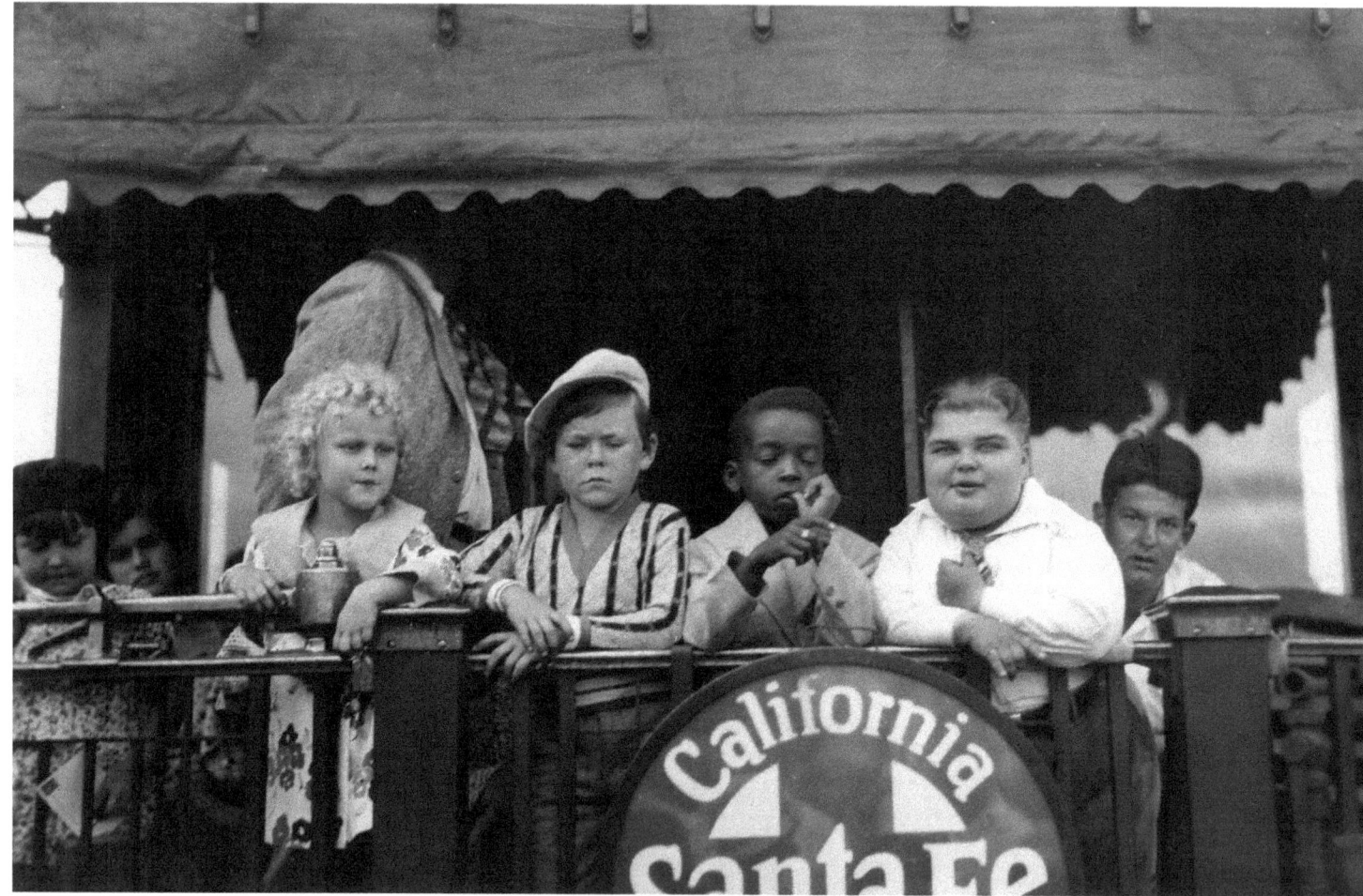

"Meet the Human Fly" during a promotion at the Chandler Salesroom, 218 N. Fourth Street. Chandler Motor Cars were sold and serviced at Malette Motor Company, 215 N. Fourth Street. In 1922, the Chandler Metropolitan Sedan retailed for $2,295.

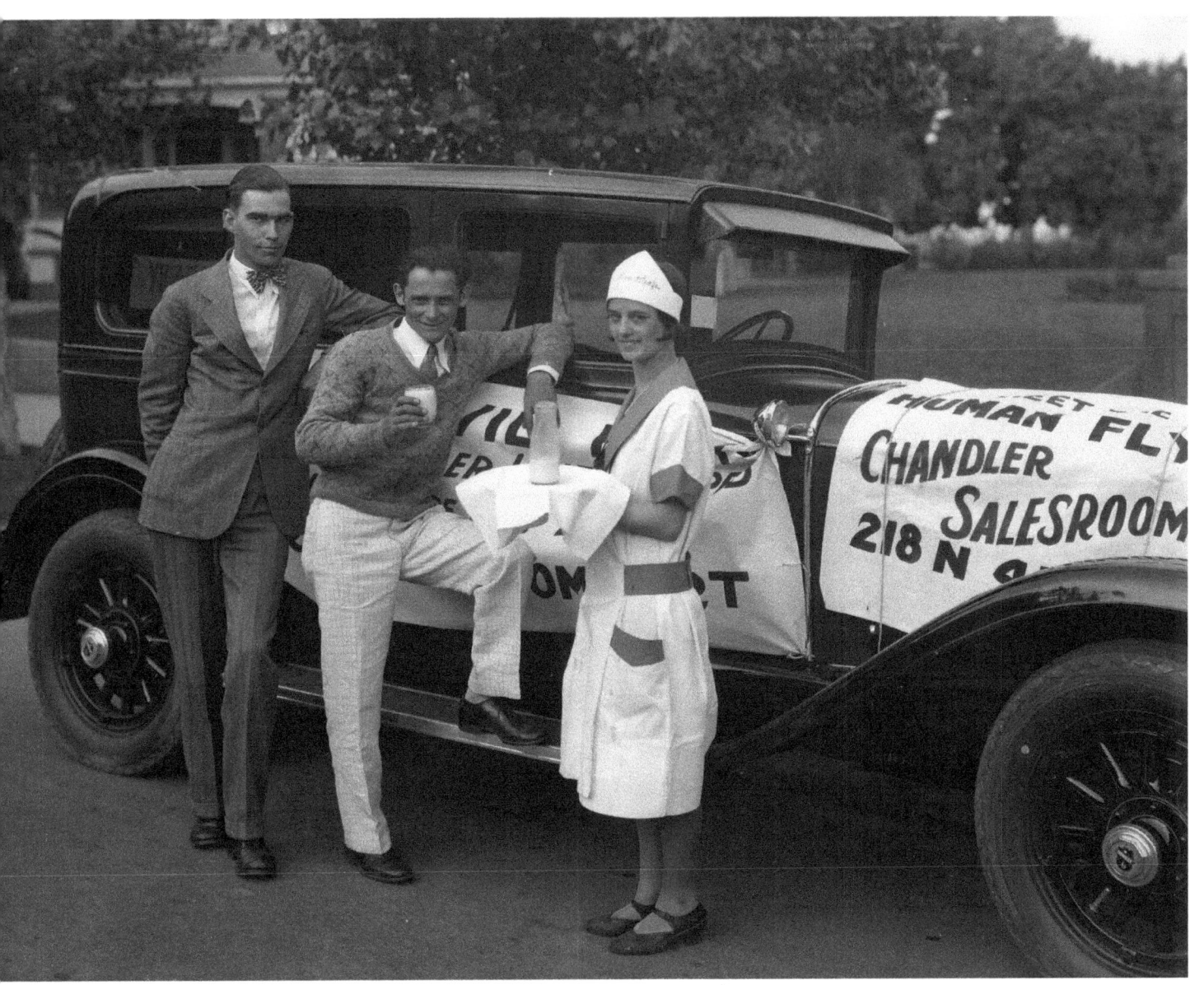

Two Hicks delivery trucks in front of the Albuquerque Public Library on Edith and E. Central. This was one of many North and South Valley dairies. Albuquerque High is just to the left of the library. The new Albuquerque Public Library opened in 1925, on the site of Perkins Hall.

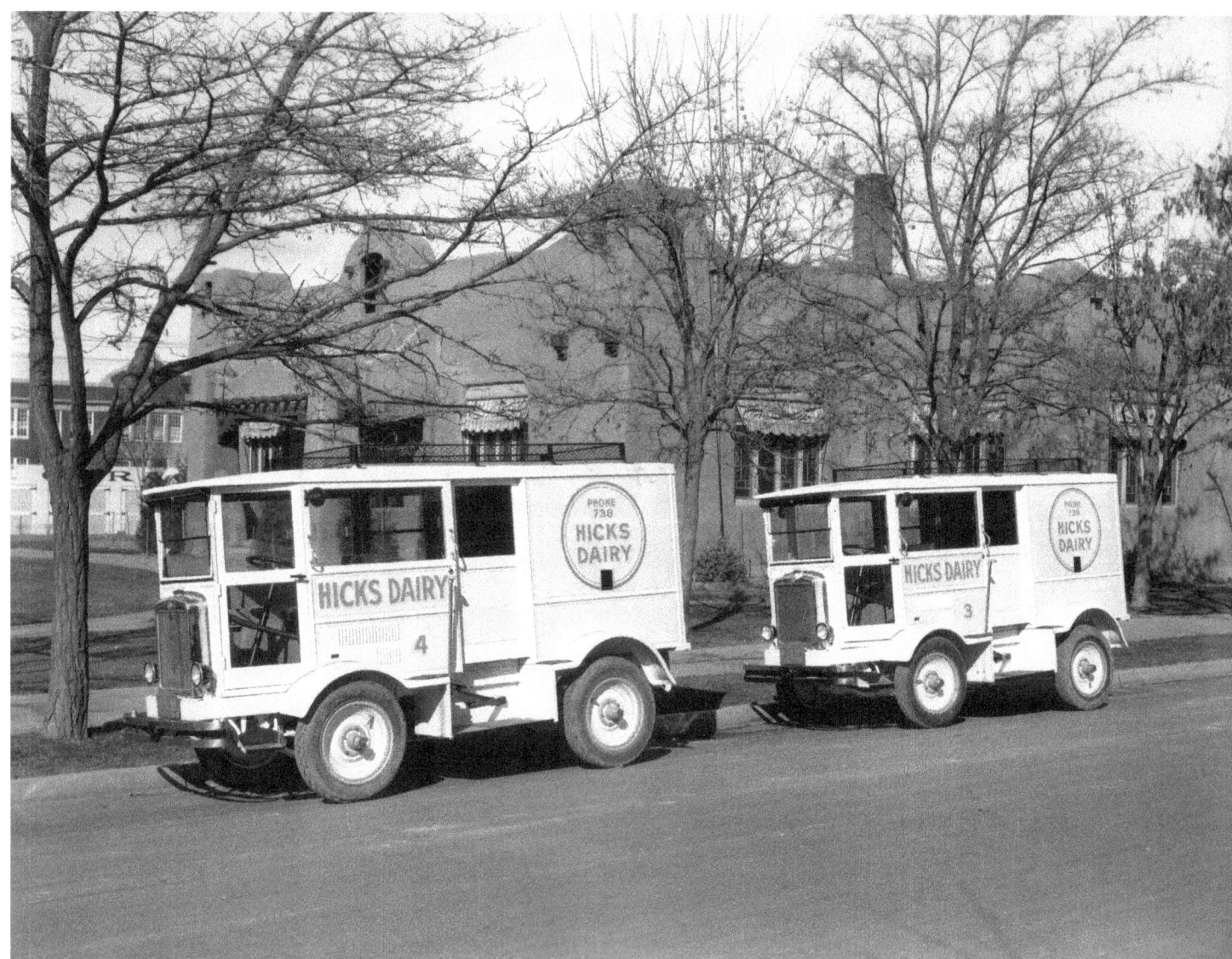

The signal pistol was still smoking as the runners left the starting position for this track event, held at the University of New Mexico.

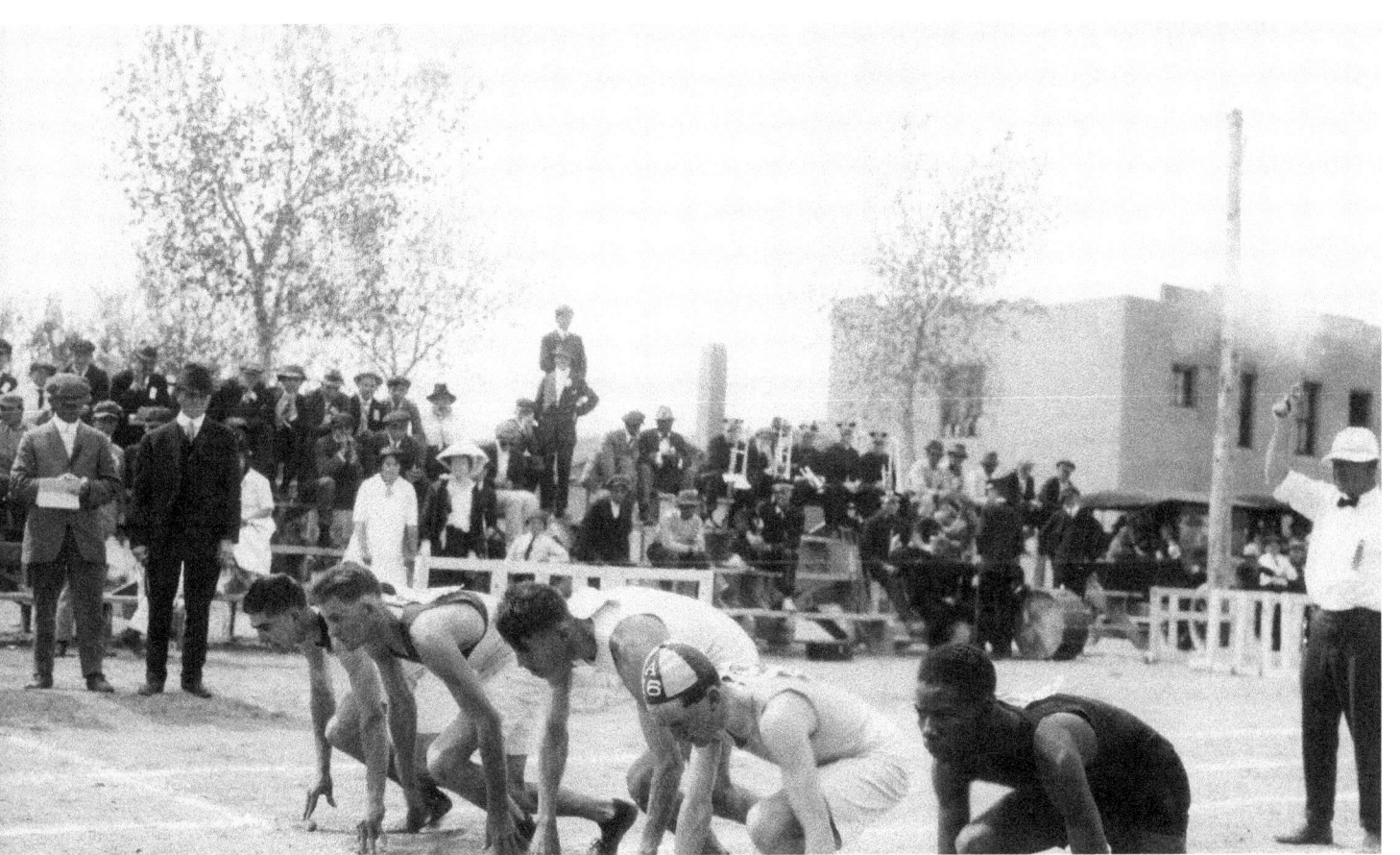

The largest soda fountain in New Mexico was the Albuquerque Pharmacy, at 324 W. Central Avenue. It had beautiful tile and woodwork. Soda fountains started in the 1800s, when pharmacies started to offer flavored carbonated soda waters as a healthful alternative to the hard liquors sold in saloons. In 1930, Albuquerque had five different soda fountains.

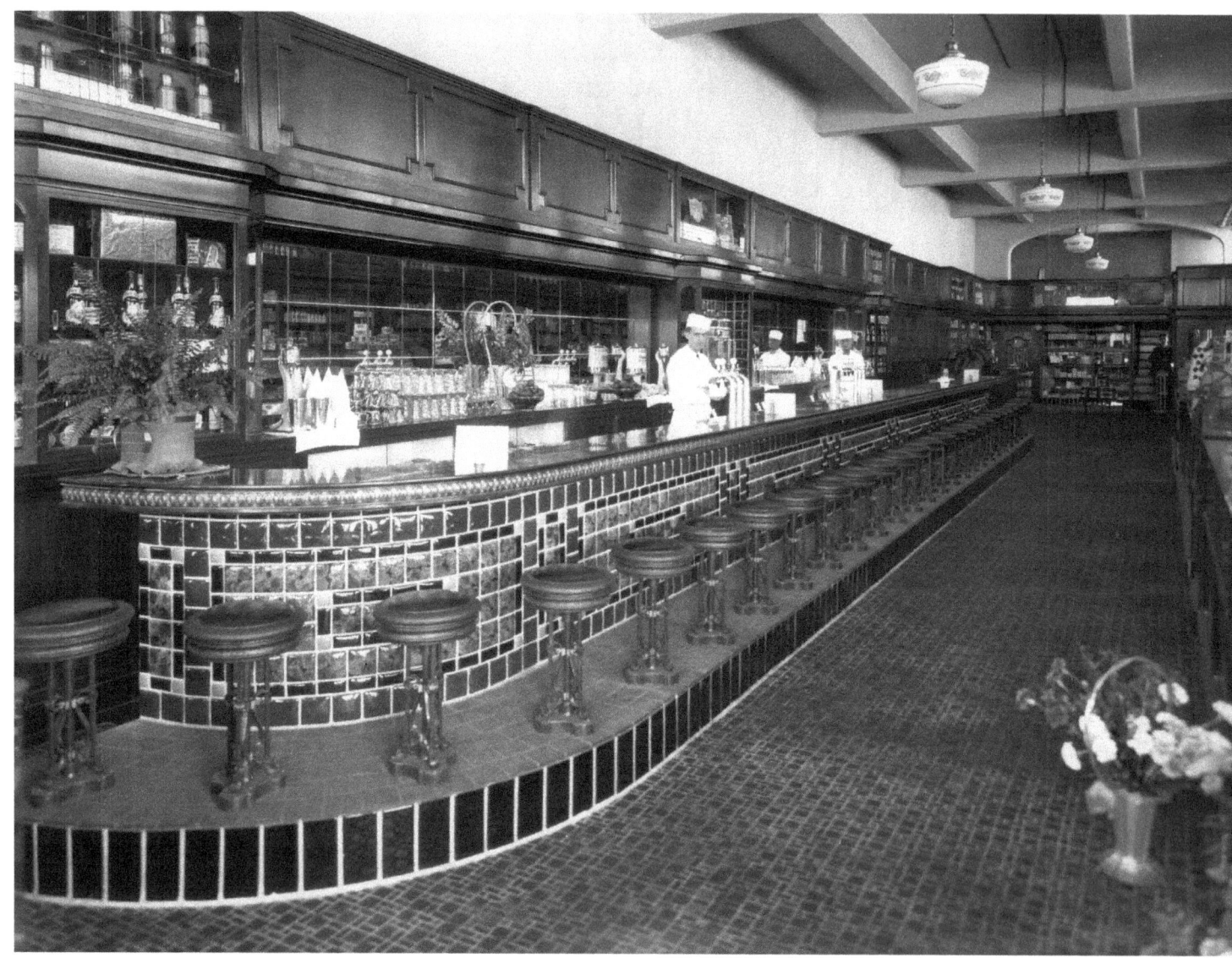

The Tom Thumb Golf Course, located at 501 W. Gold Avenue, in about 1929. Miniature golf was very popular during the Great Depression, and Albuquerque had several courses.

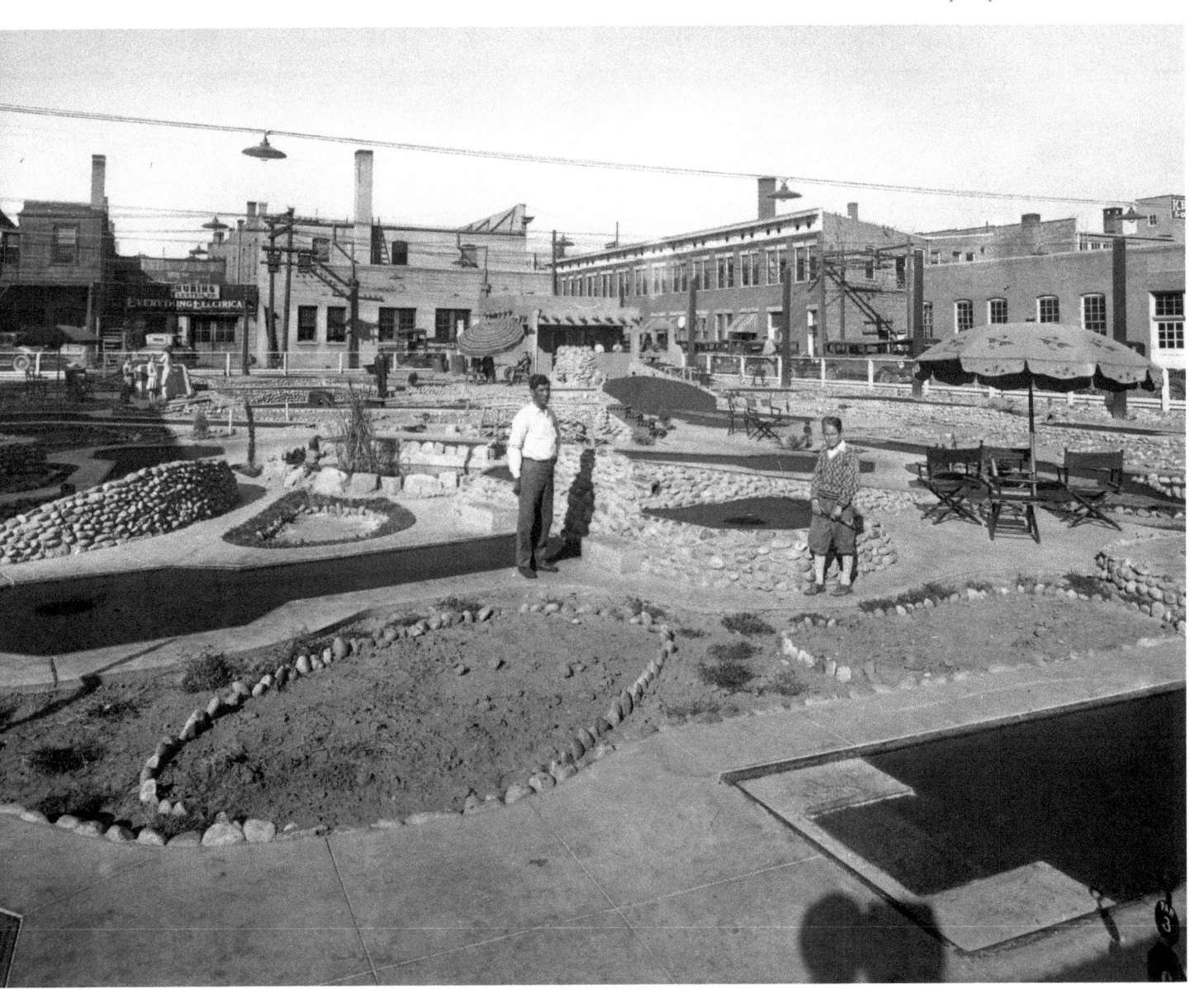

The Occidental Life Insurance Building, at Third Street and Gold Avenue, was completed in 1917. The architect, Henry C. Trost of El Paso, used the Doge's Palace in Venice as his model. The building was gutted by fire in 1933 and Occidental rebuilt it, with modifications. In 1981, a two-story office building was built inside the original walls and it still stands.

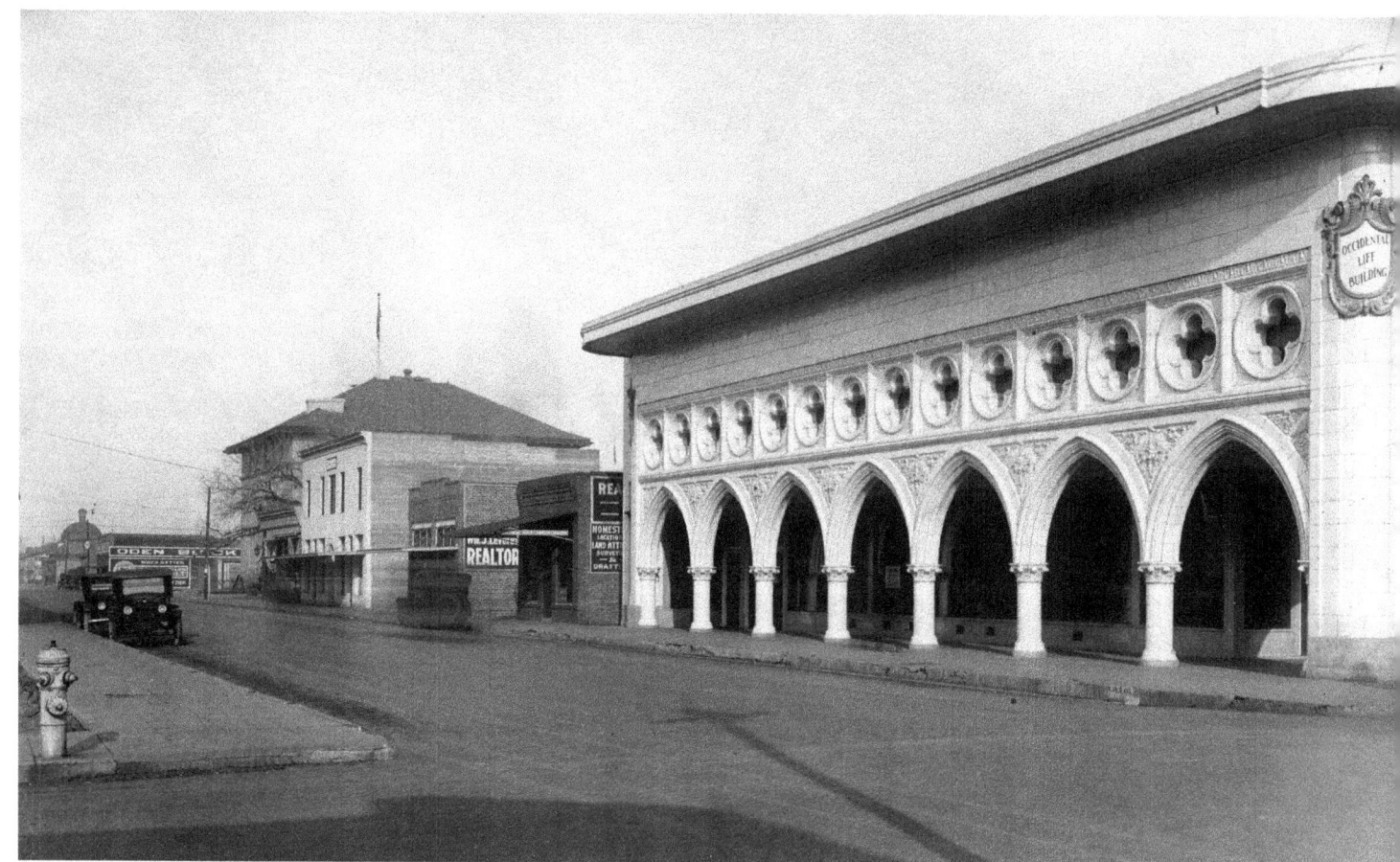

Hokona Hall Dormitory, the woman's dorm at the University of New Mexico, is behind the pole vault. *Hokona* means "butterfly" and the building now has two wings, Zuni and Zia. The old part of Hokona Hall, the Zuni wing, has been converted to an office building. The men's dorm was named Kwataka Hall.

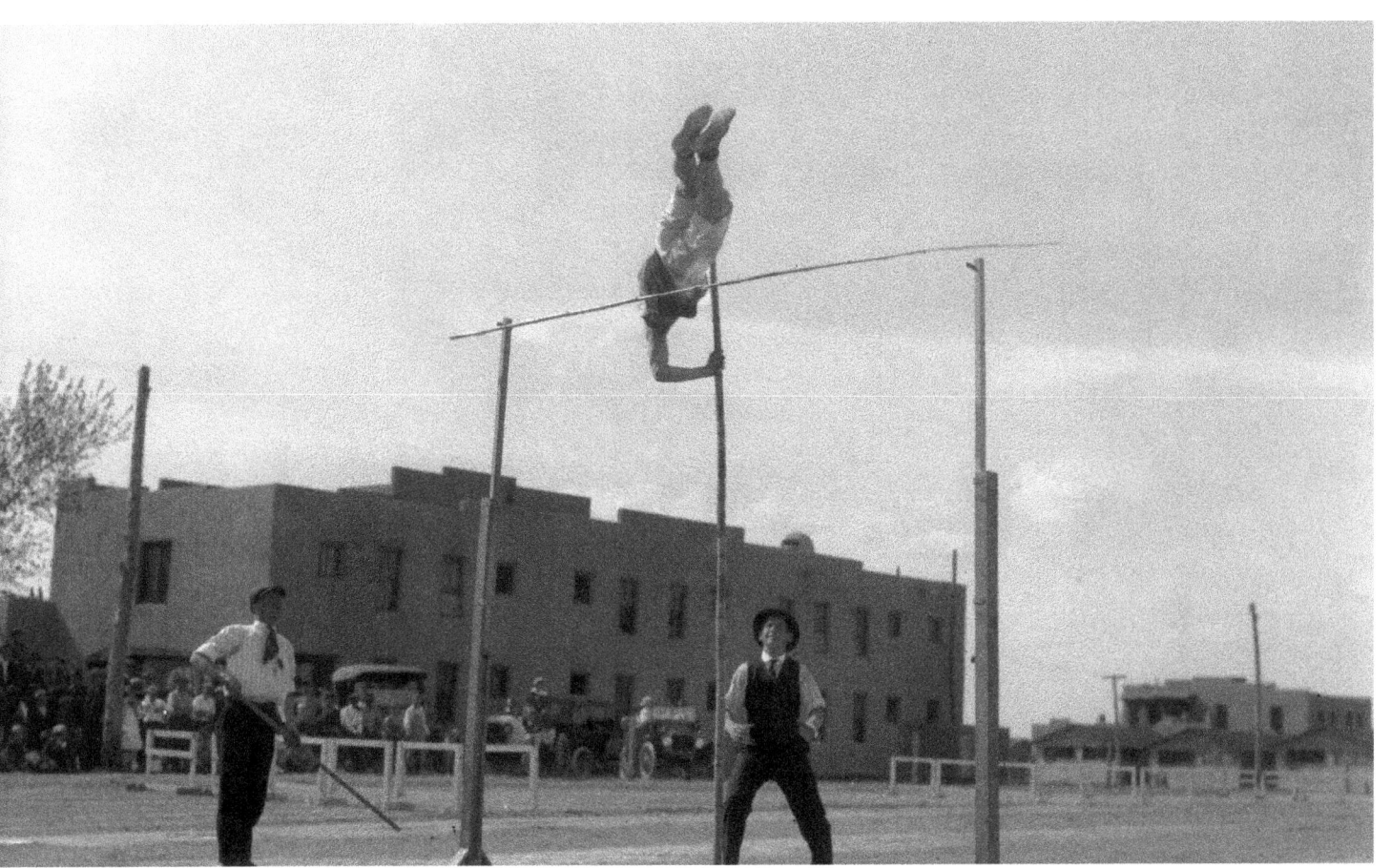

Boy Scouts of America, Troop 6, marching south on Seventh Street, past Central Avenue. The Masonic Temple is on the right.

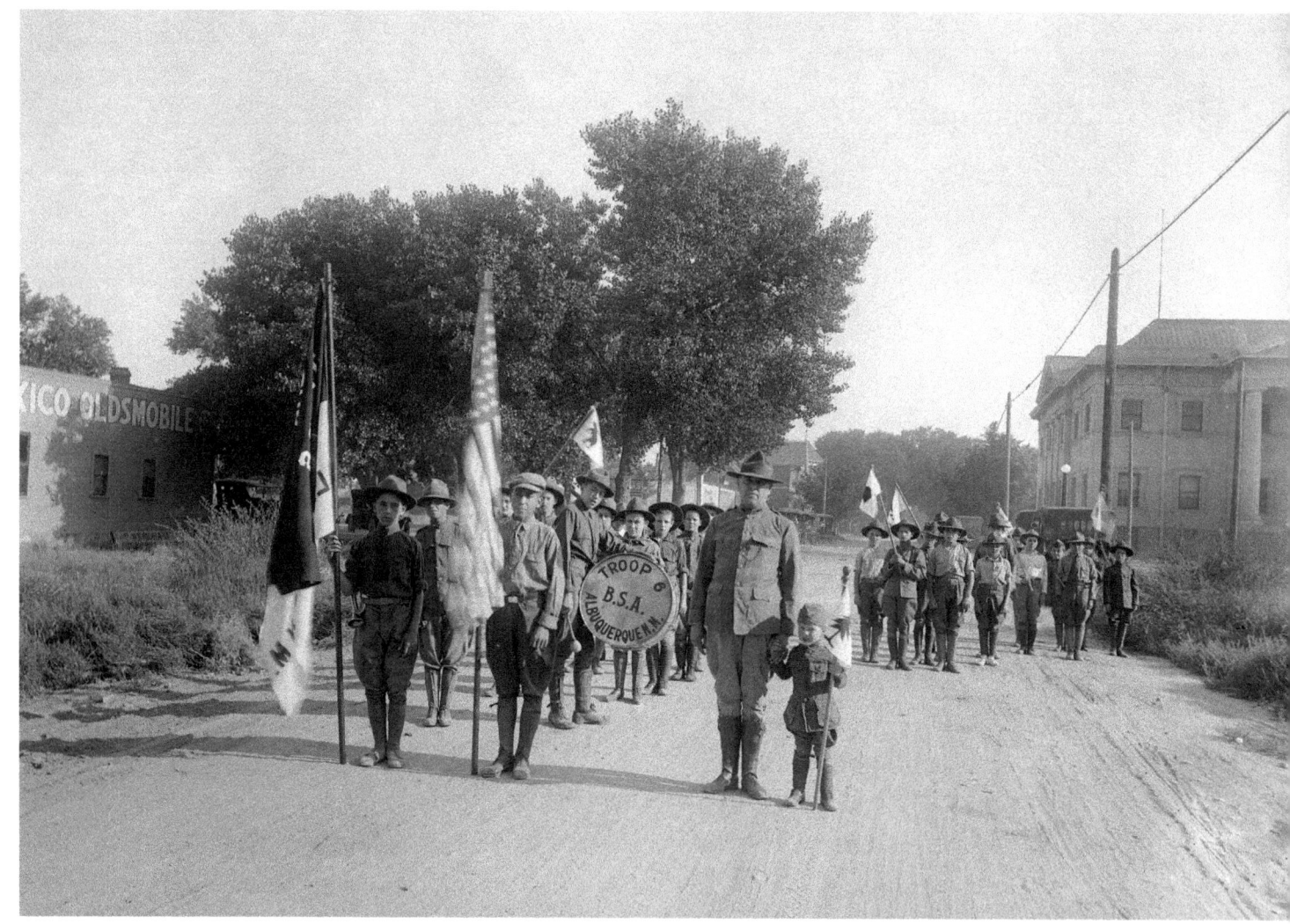

Central Avenue and Wyoming Boulevard was the location of the First American Pageant, a celebration of Native Americans and a tourist attraction. It featured a rodeo, Spanish fiesta, ceremonial dances, and a false front replica of an Indian Pueblo. It was an event for three years but stopped due to the Great Depression.

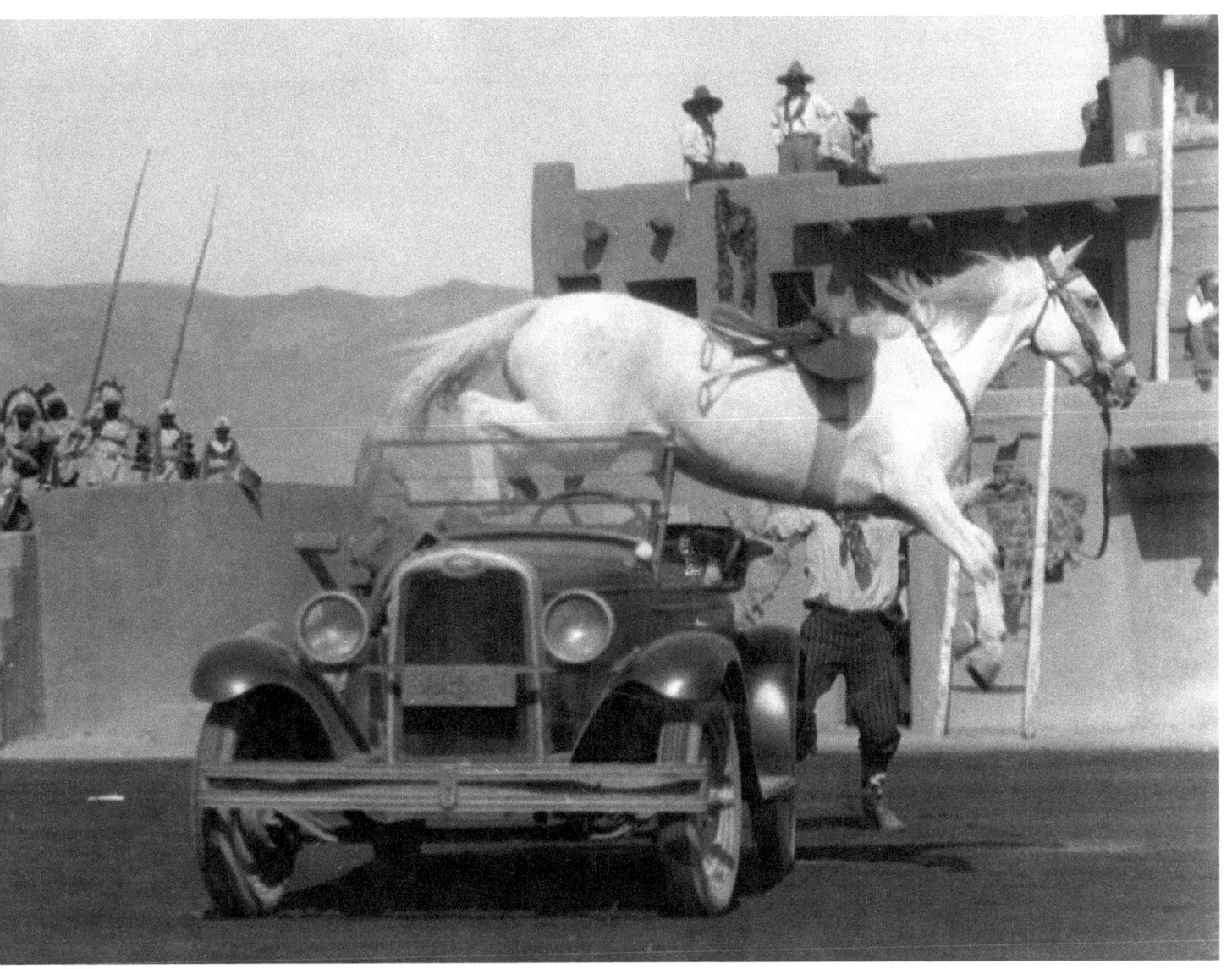

Amelia Earhart, the third woman on the left, and future governor Clyde Tingley, the second man standing on the right, in front of a T.A.T. Tri-motor airplane. Earhart was the best known of the aviatrixes who came to Albuquerque. This picture, taken on July 14, 1929, was a year after she became the first woman to make an Atlantic Ocean air crossing, as a passenger.

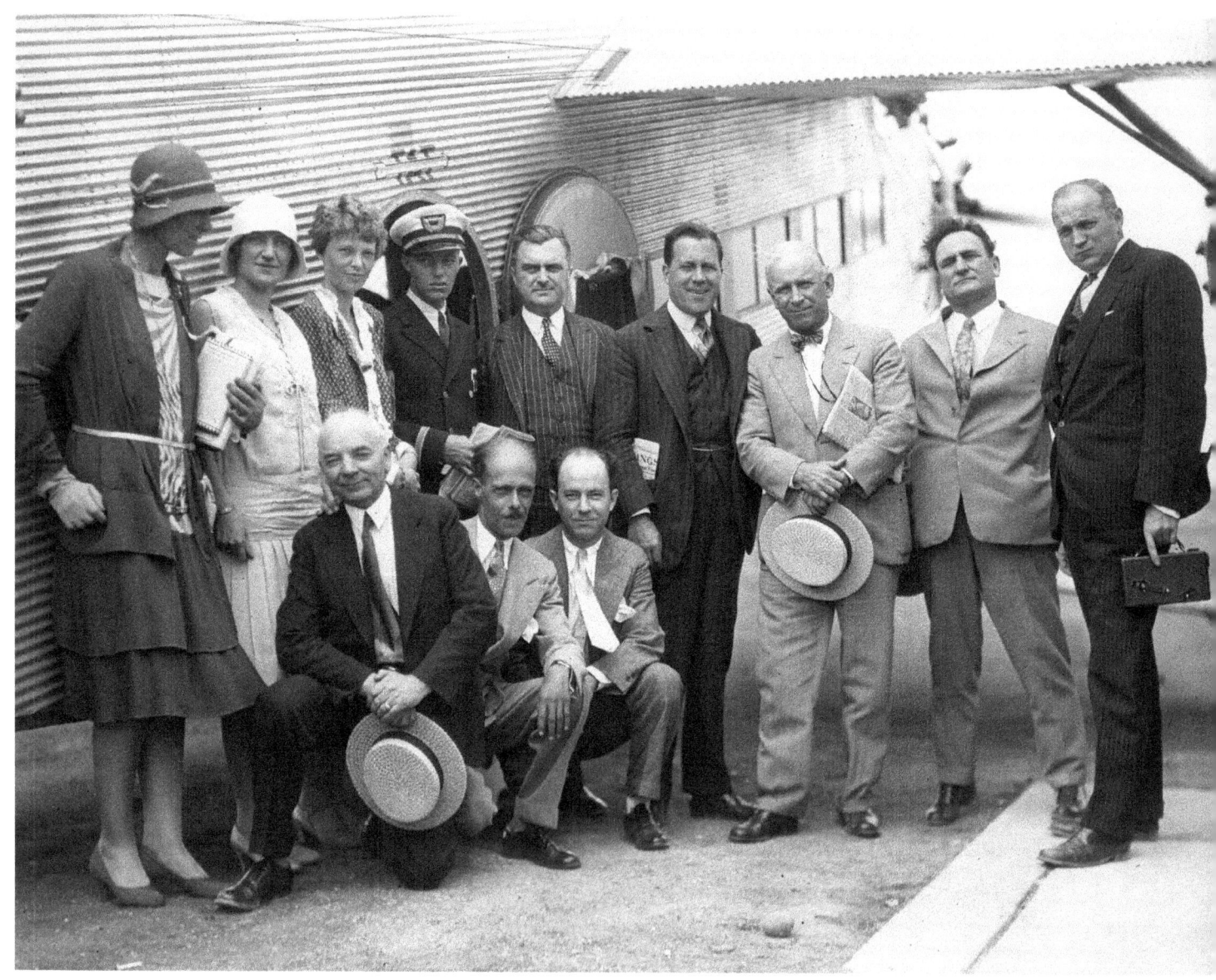

The University of New Mexico Lobo Football team took on their first flight to a game on October 10, 1929. Clyde Tingley and over 2,000 Albuquerque residents and students were at the airport to cheer them onto the Ford Tri-Motor airplane. They lost the game to Occidental College, at the Rose Bowl in Pasadena, 26-0.

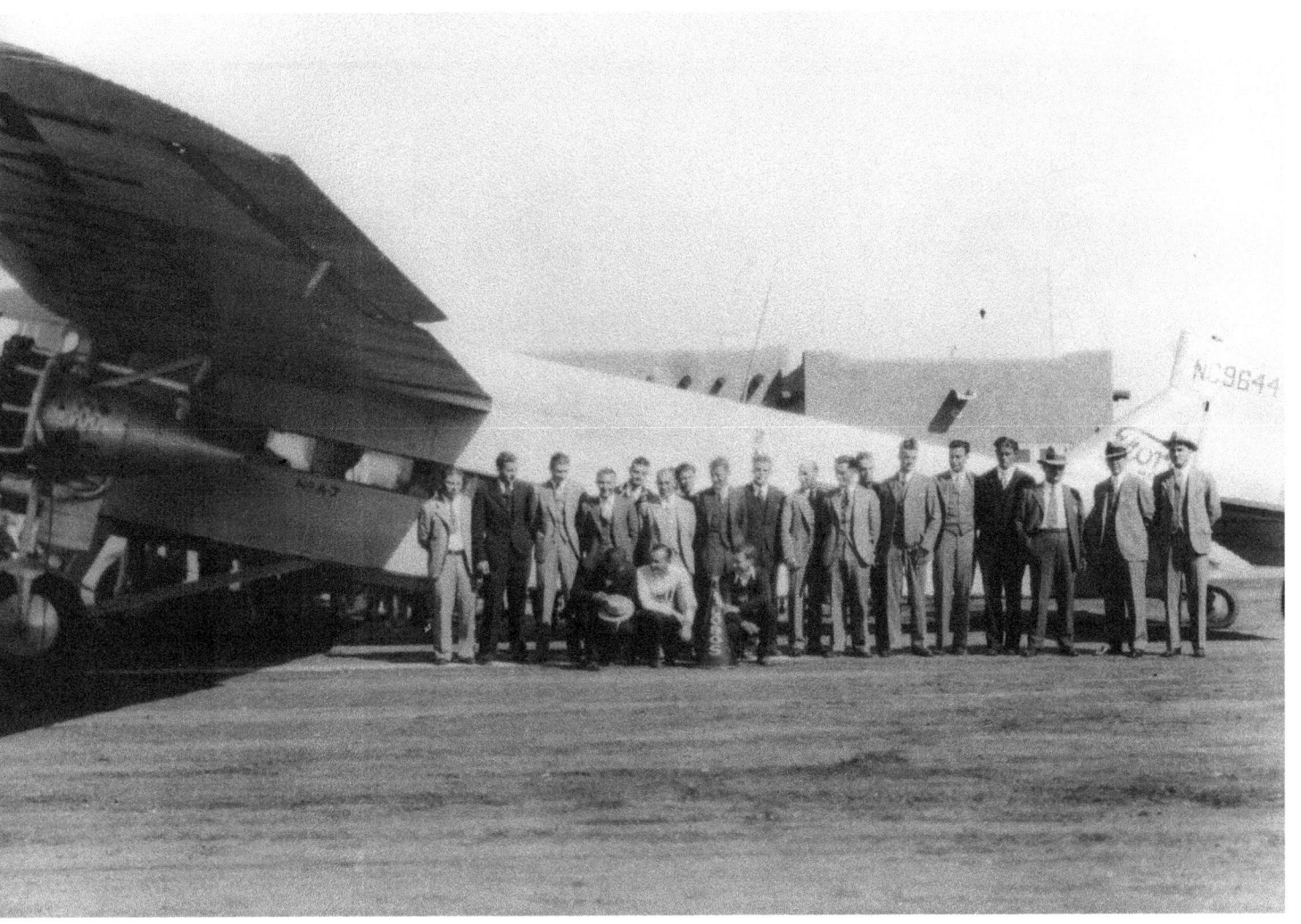

The Fred Harvey Indian Building at the Alvarado Complex was always a busy place and an attraction for people traveling through Albuquerque. The Native American arts sold there were of high quality and were intriguing and exotic to the travelers.

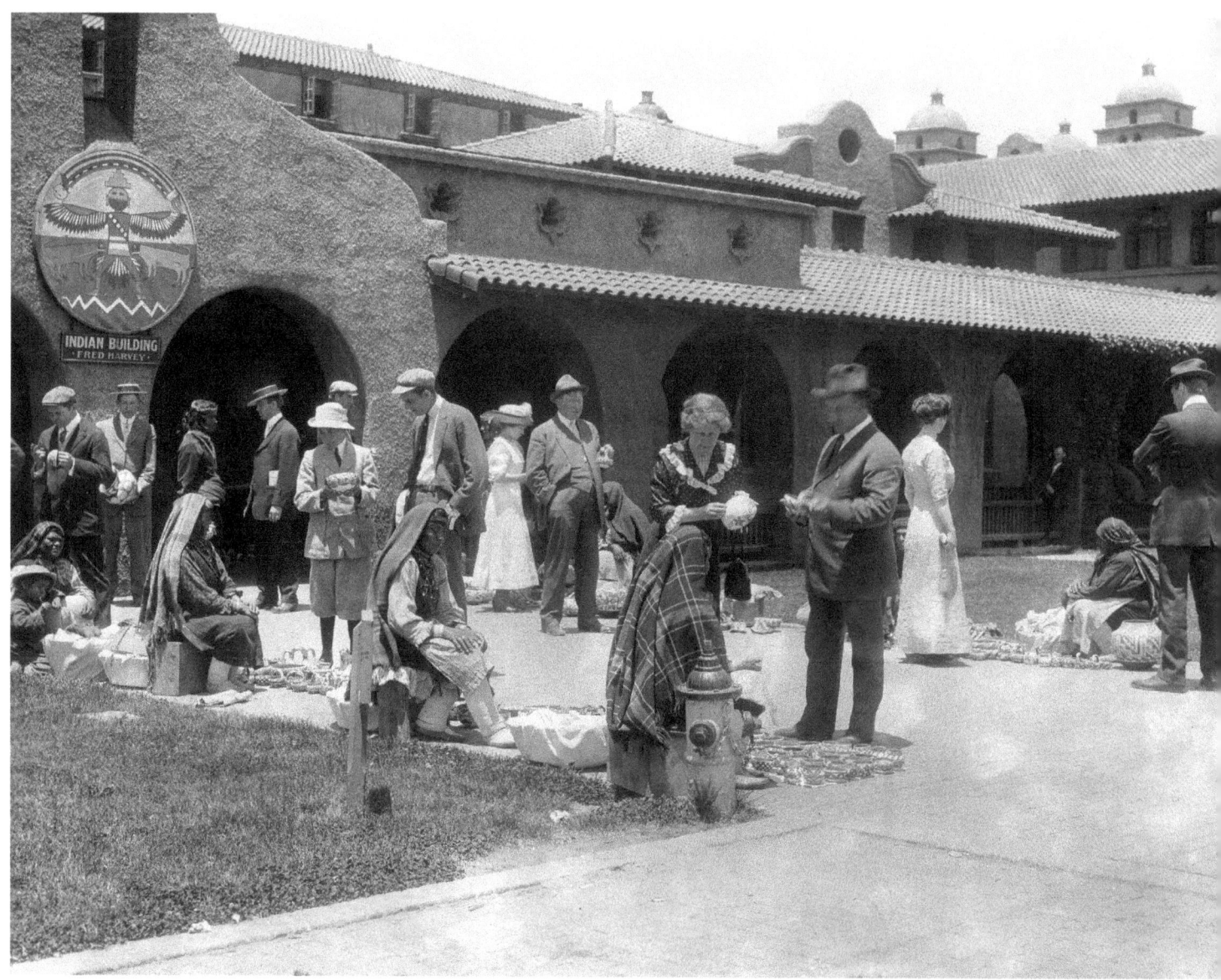

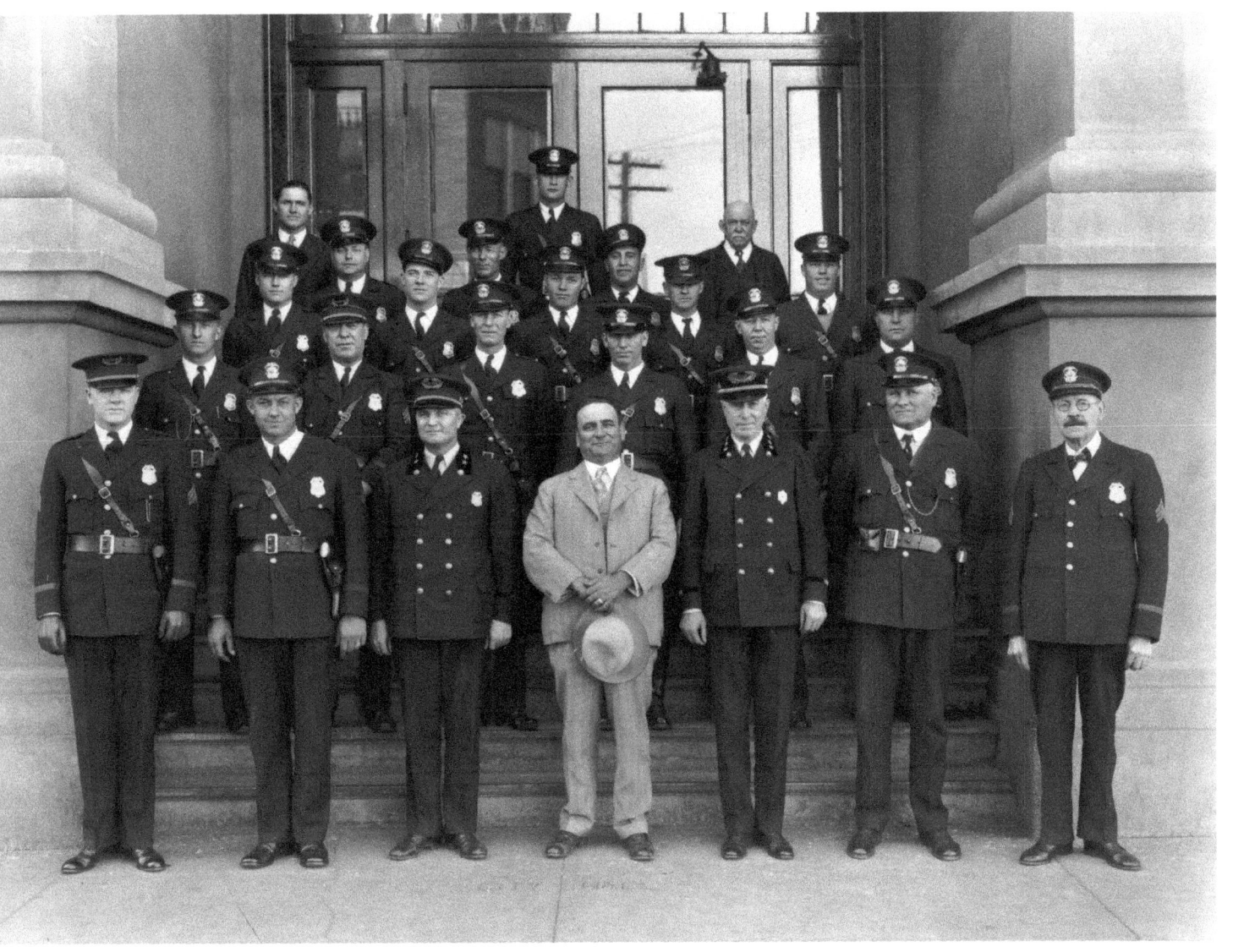

Clyde Tingley, with the Albuquerque Police Force, on the steps of City Hall, at Second Street and Tijeras. City Hall was built about 1914 and was used until a new one was built in the 1970s.

Elfego Baca, left, was a legendary sheriff known for straight, quick shooting, courage, and savvy. He was also a lawyer and private detective who ran for office many times. Walt Disney produced a TV miniseries in 1958 inspired by his exploits. Eddie Mack, right, was a professional boxer from Pojoaque, New Mexico, whose ring name was the Alamosa Flash. He won 74 of his 94 bouts, including 35 by knockout.

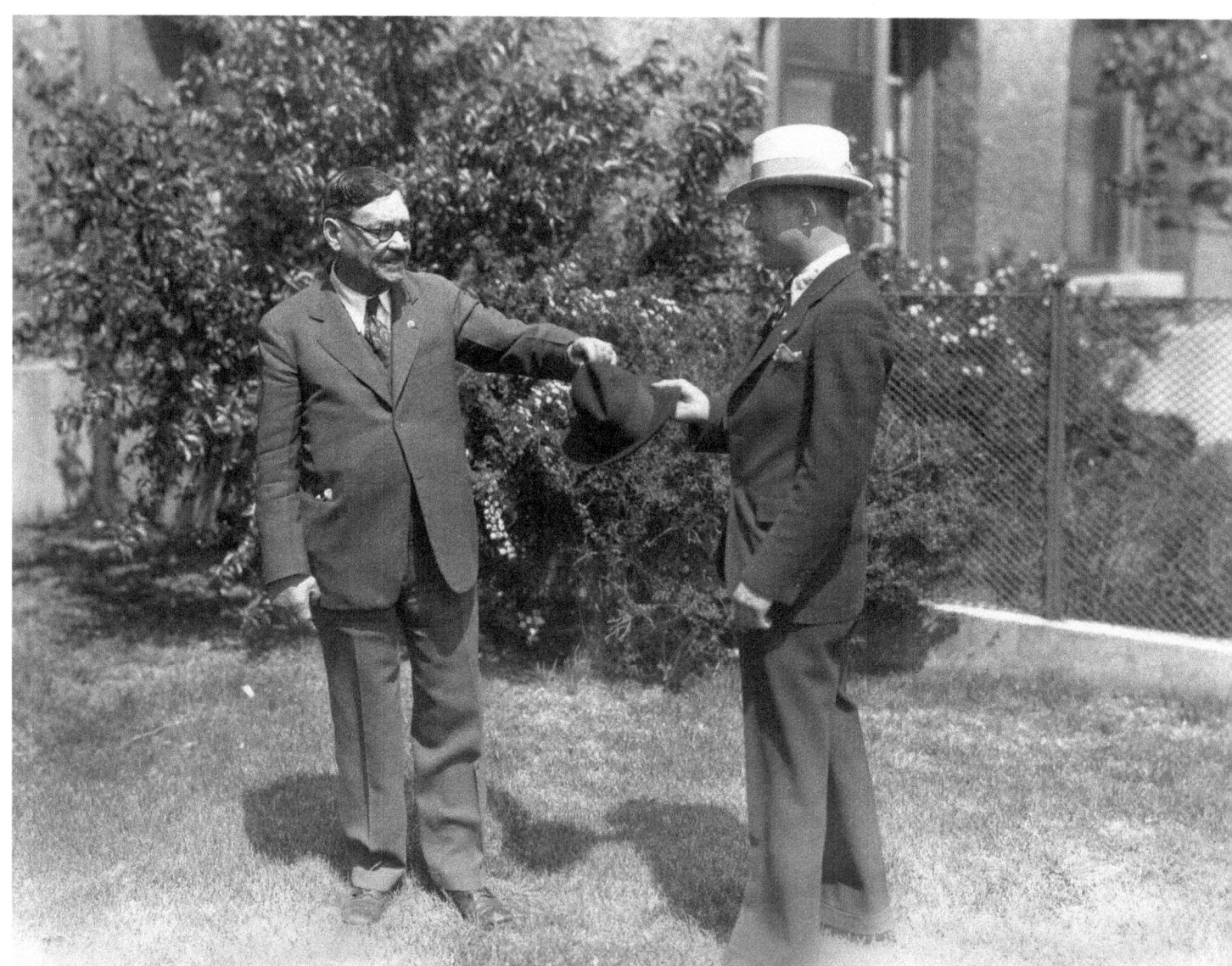

Route 66 went down Fourth Street, before it was realigned. Tourist accommodations and attractions were built along it. The National Old Trails Camp was at 1701 to 1713 N. Fourth Street. The sign near the pump reads "Phillips 66 Gasoline;" the sign on the post, "Red Crown Gasoline;" and the sign to the right, "Free Showers."

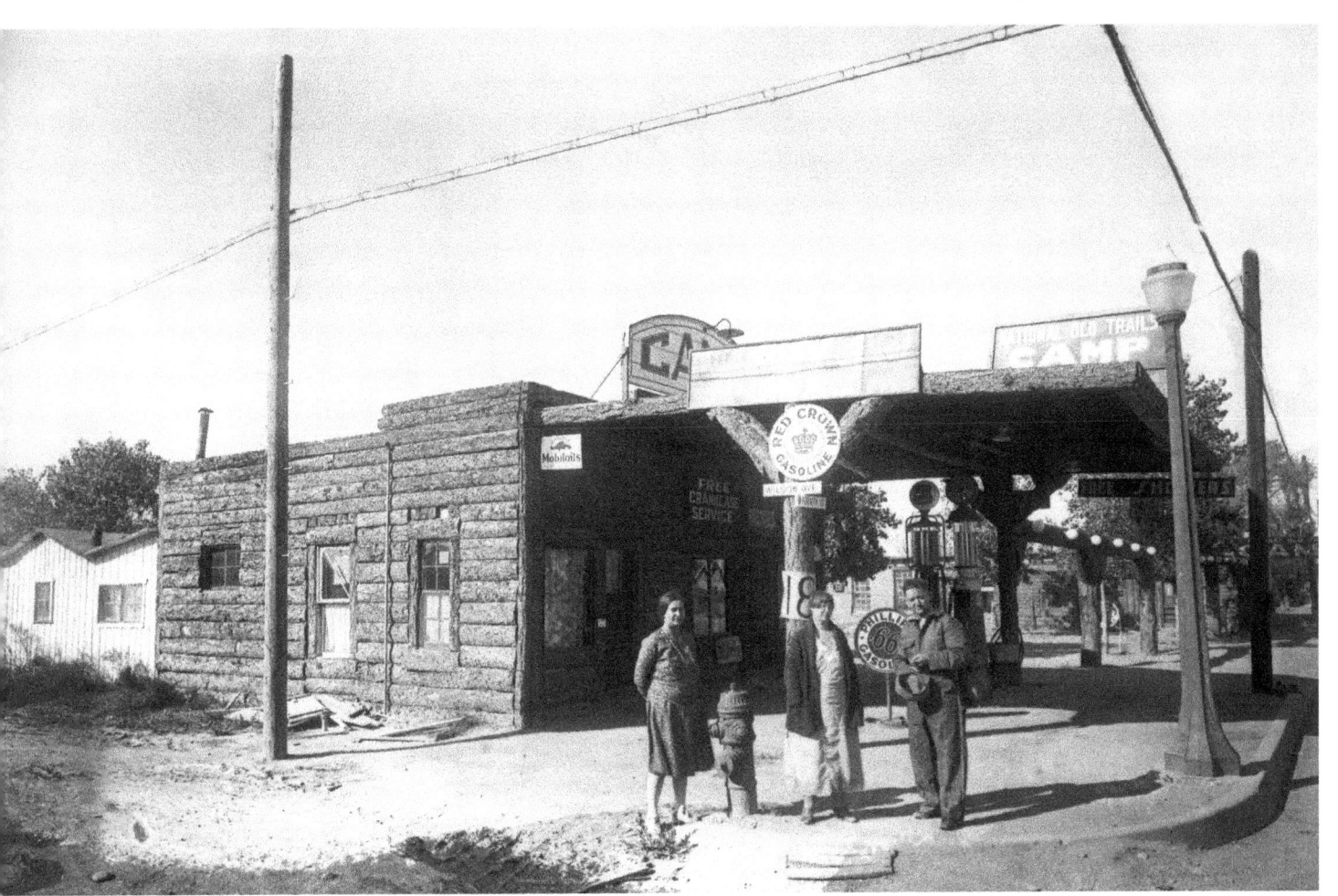

Three barbers, a shoeshine man, and customers at the Craig Brothers Barber Shop, 305 W. Central Avenue. The sale on the cash register is for fifty cents. The Liberty Café calendar on the wall is dated October 18, 1930.

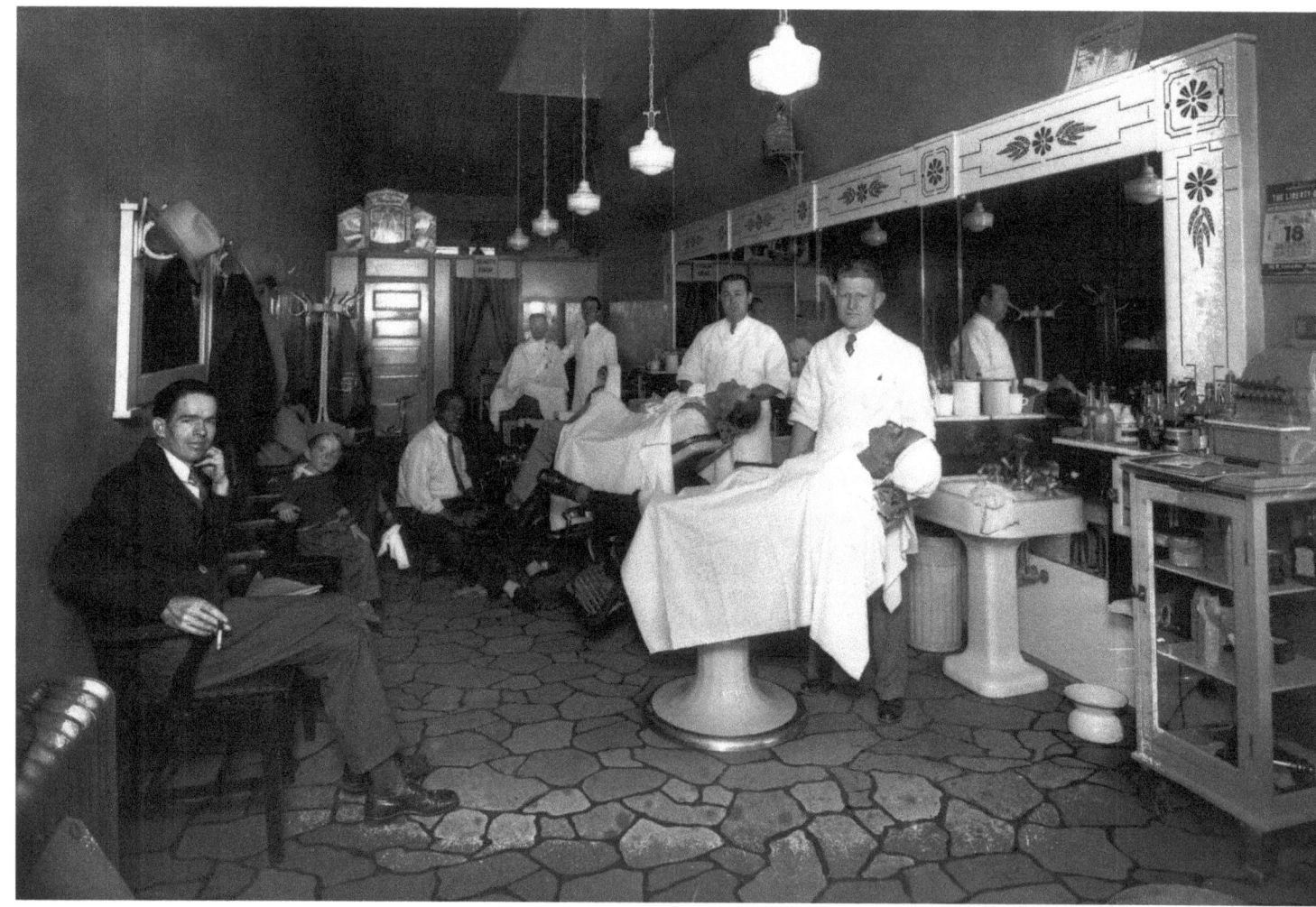

The interior of a curio shop. Many of the Native American crafts that were sold at a modest price at the time are now considered treasures. This is one of a collection of photographs taken by a photographer who was in Albuquerque during the Depression. His name is unknown, but he left Albuquerque a wonderful pictorial history.

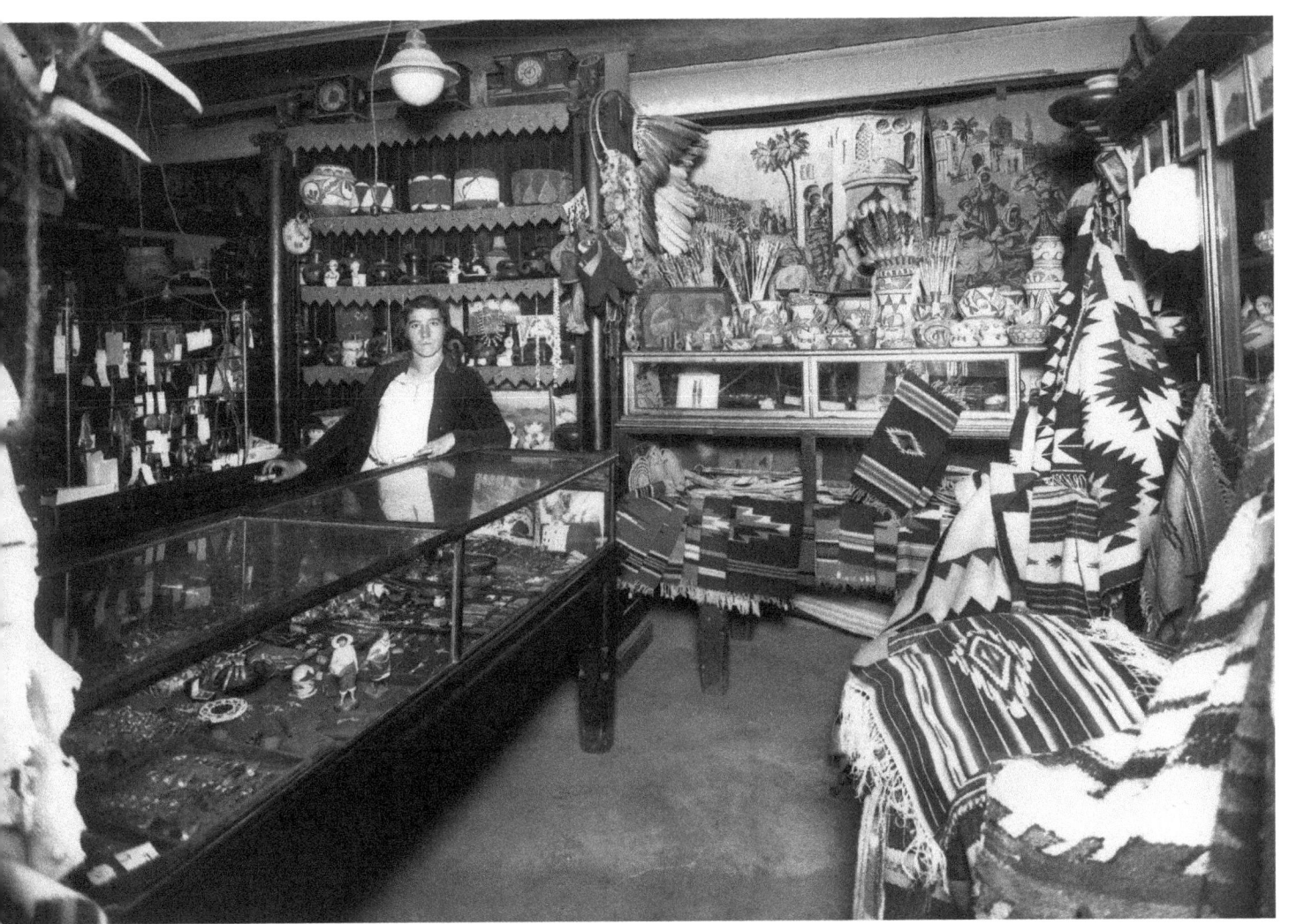

Zamora Saddle Shop at 109-111 W. Copper Avenue, owned by Felipe Zamora. New Mexico had many cattle ranches. The cowboys and *vaqueros* who worked the cattle herds were attracted to fine saddle shops like Zamora's.

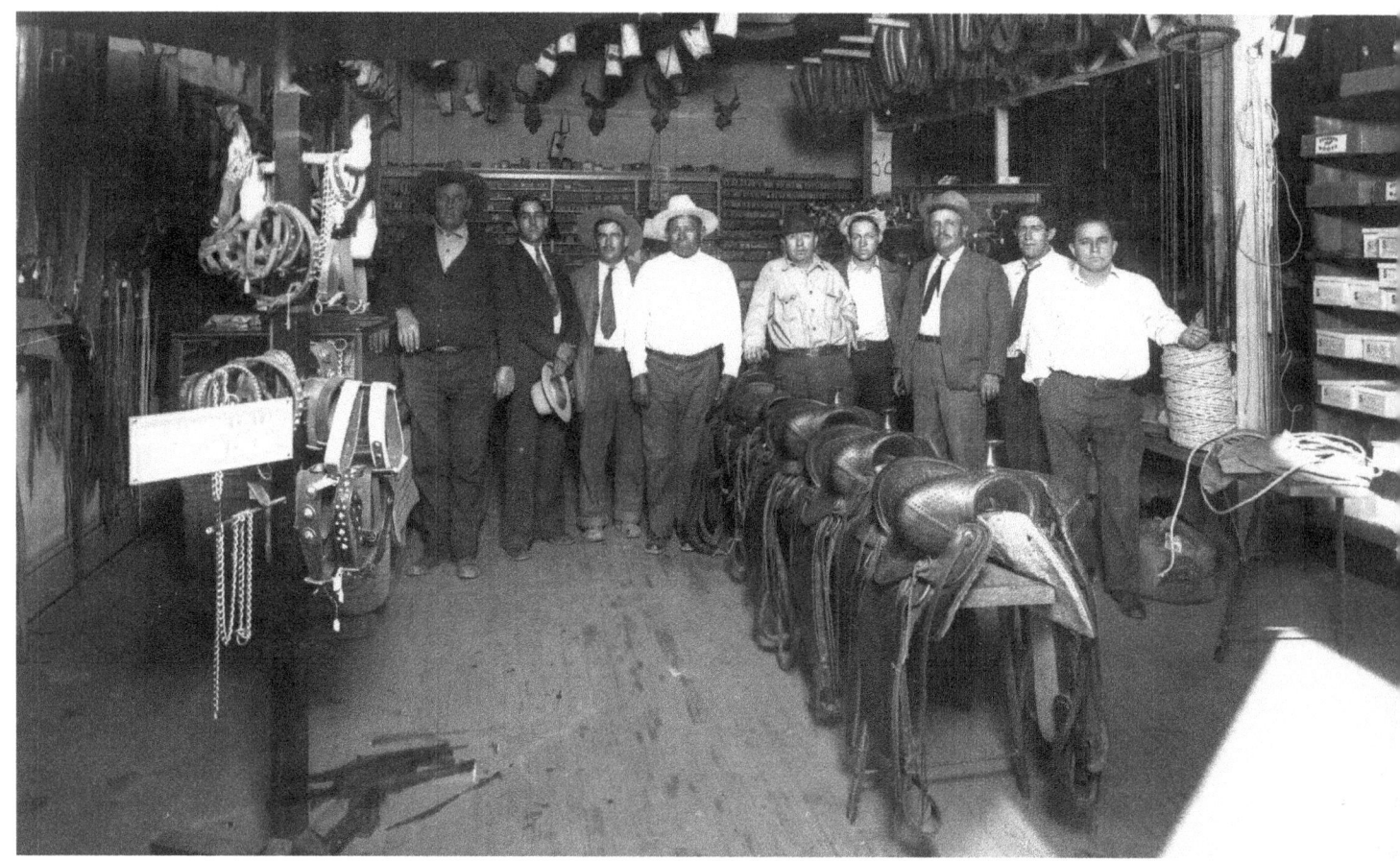

Coney Island Cafeteria opened in 1929 at 500 W. Central Avenue. William Kirkikos and Spiros Ipiotis were the owners. Many children ate hot dogs there while their parents shopped across the street at Sears. The Coney Island was in the Bliss Building, built between 1903 and 1908. There were hotels on the upper floors. Lindy's Coffee Shop is there now and still has the classic diner interior.

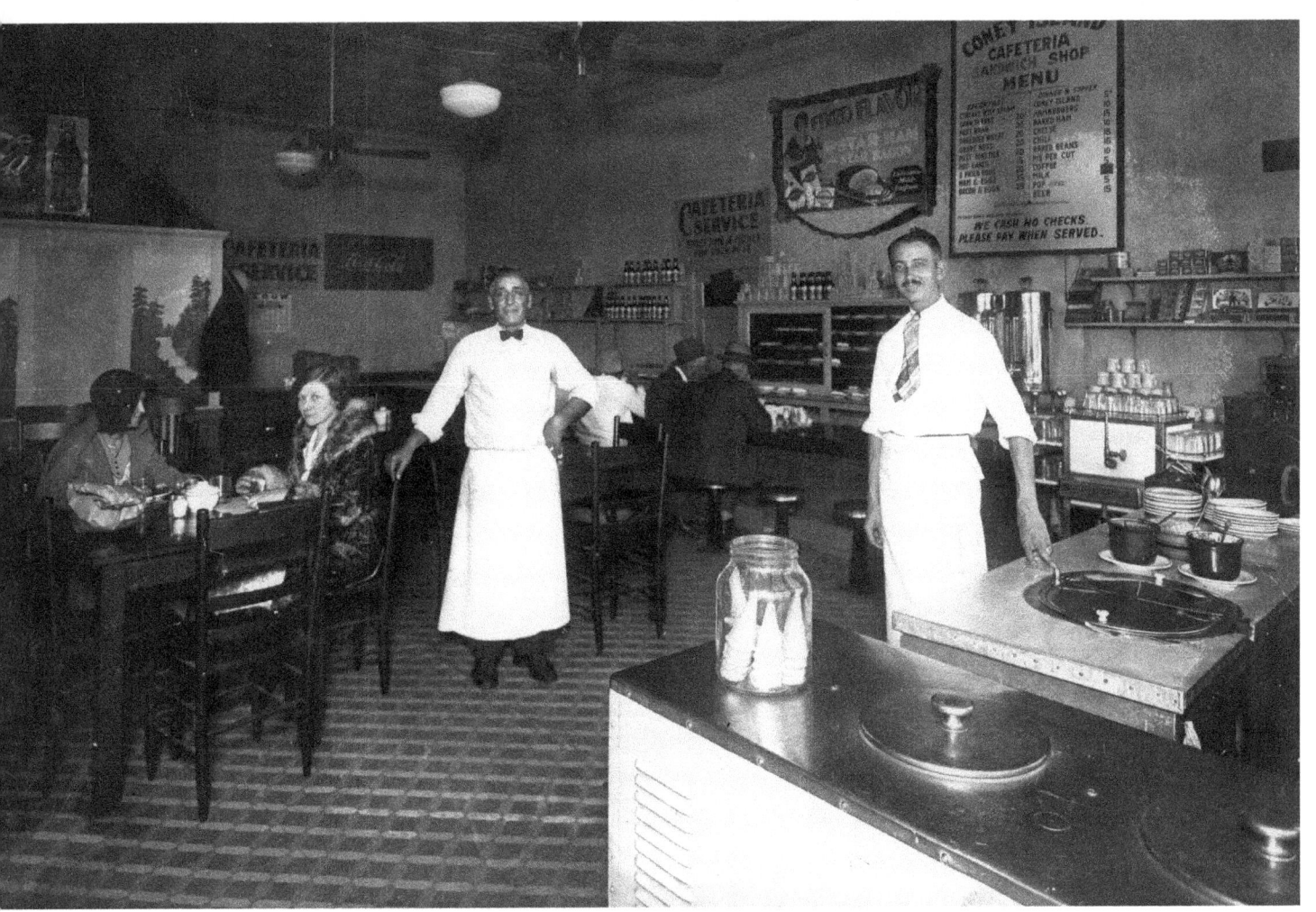

Sugar Bowl Candy, at 524 W. Central Avenue, was a soda fountain and confectionery. The Sugar Bowl was a favorite hangout for the high school and college crowd.

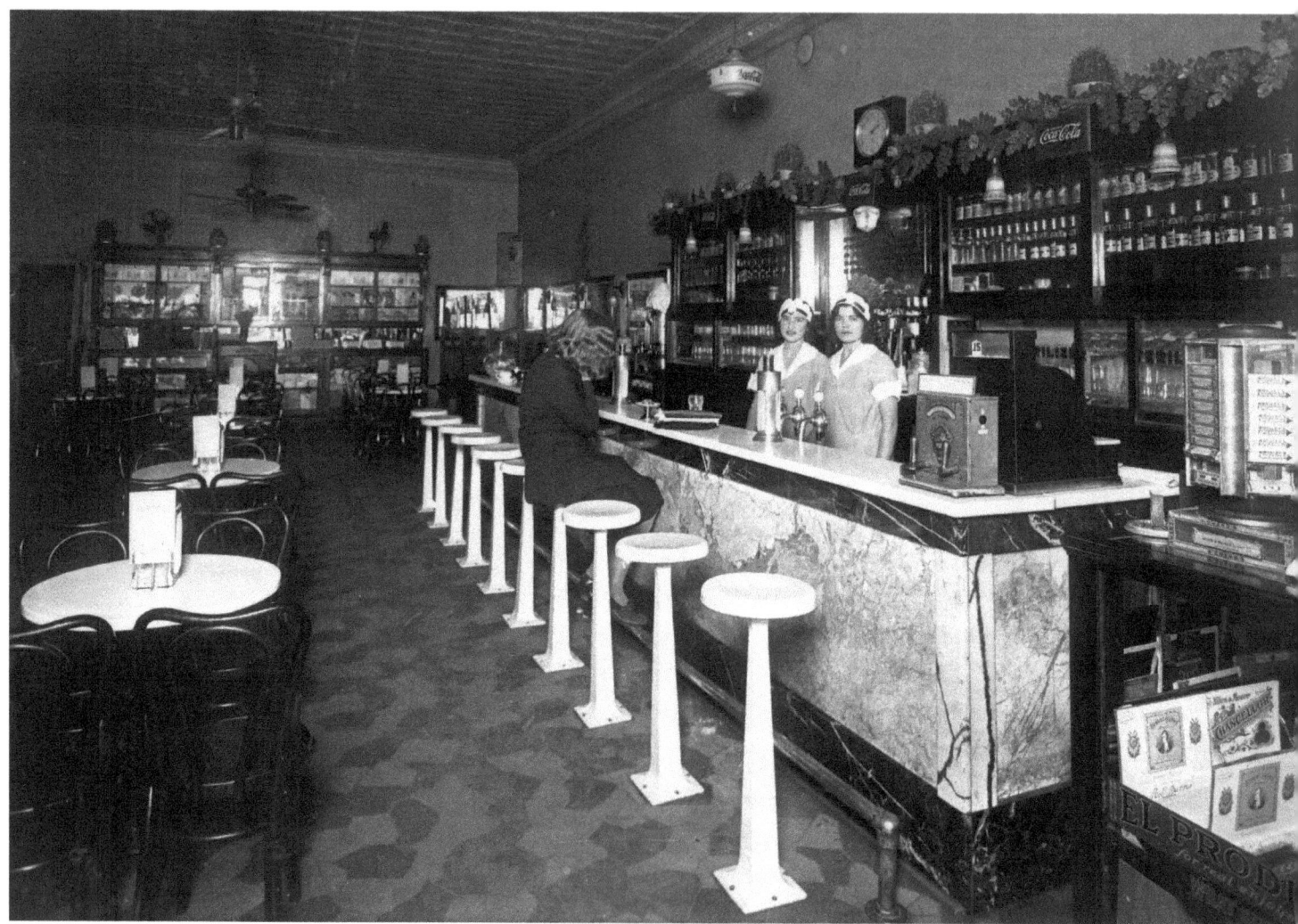

Ed's Barber Shop, at 204 W. Gold Avenue, sold Wildroot Quinine, according to the sign on the mirror. The Wildroot Company also offered hair wash, a dandruff remedy, and hair tonic. No credit was extended at Ed's.

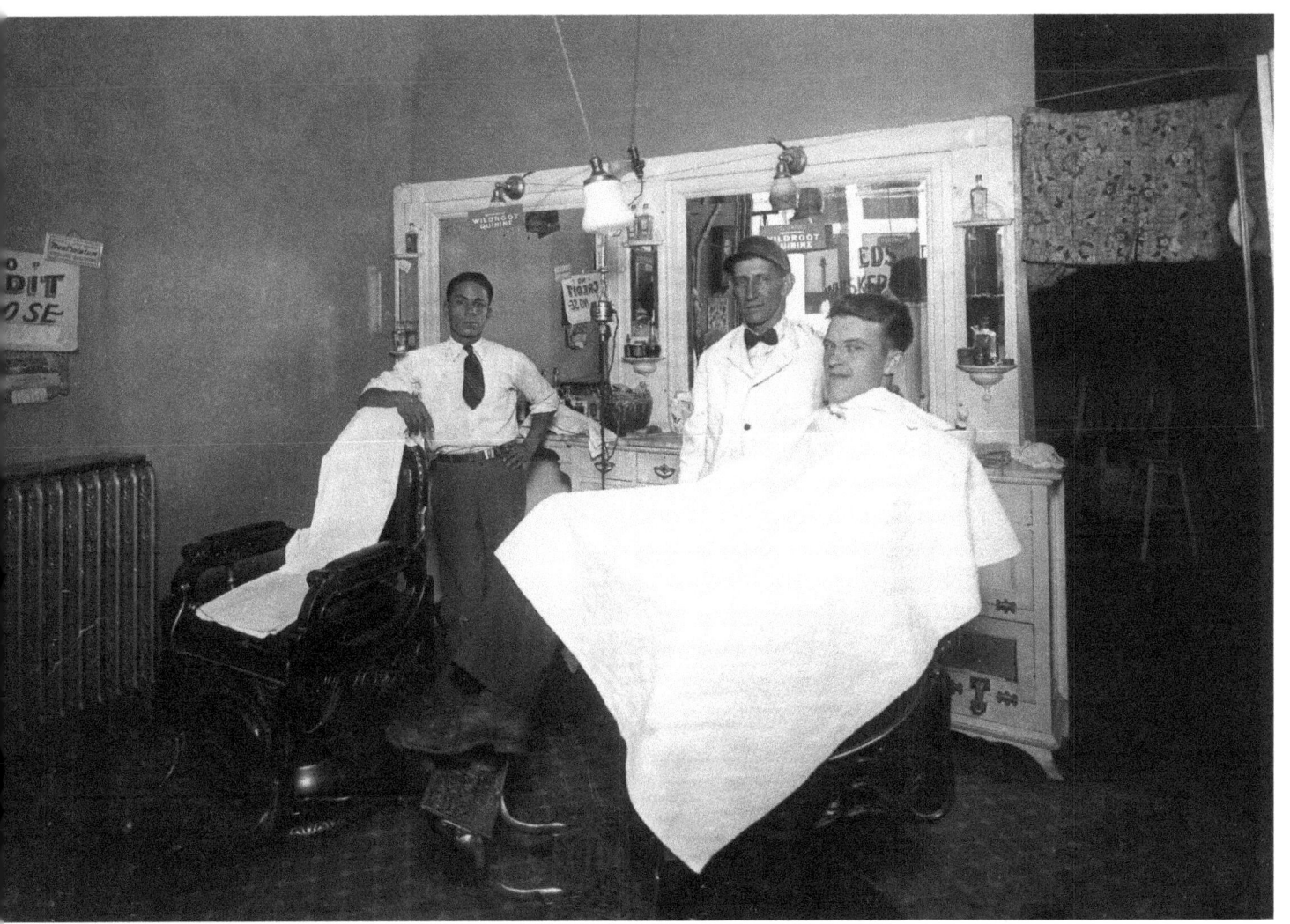

R. L. Harrison Company, Automotive Jobbers and Distributors. The men are putting parts in an airplane for delivery. Caterpillar and heavy equipment dealer R. L. Harrison was one of the first people in Albuquerque to own his own airplane, which he flew to various construction projects.

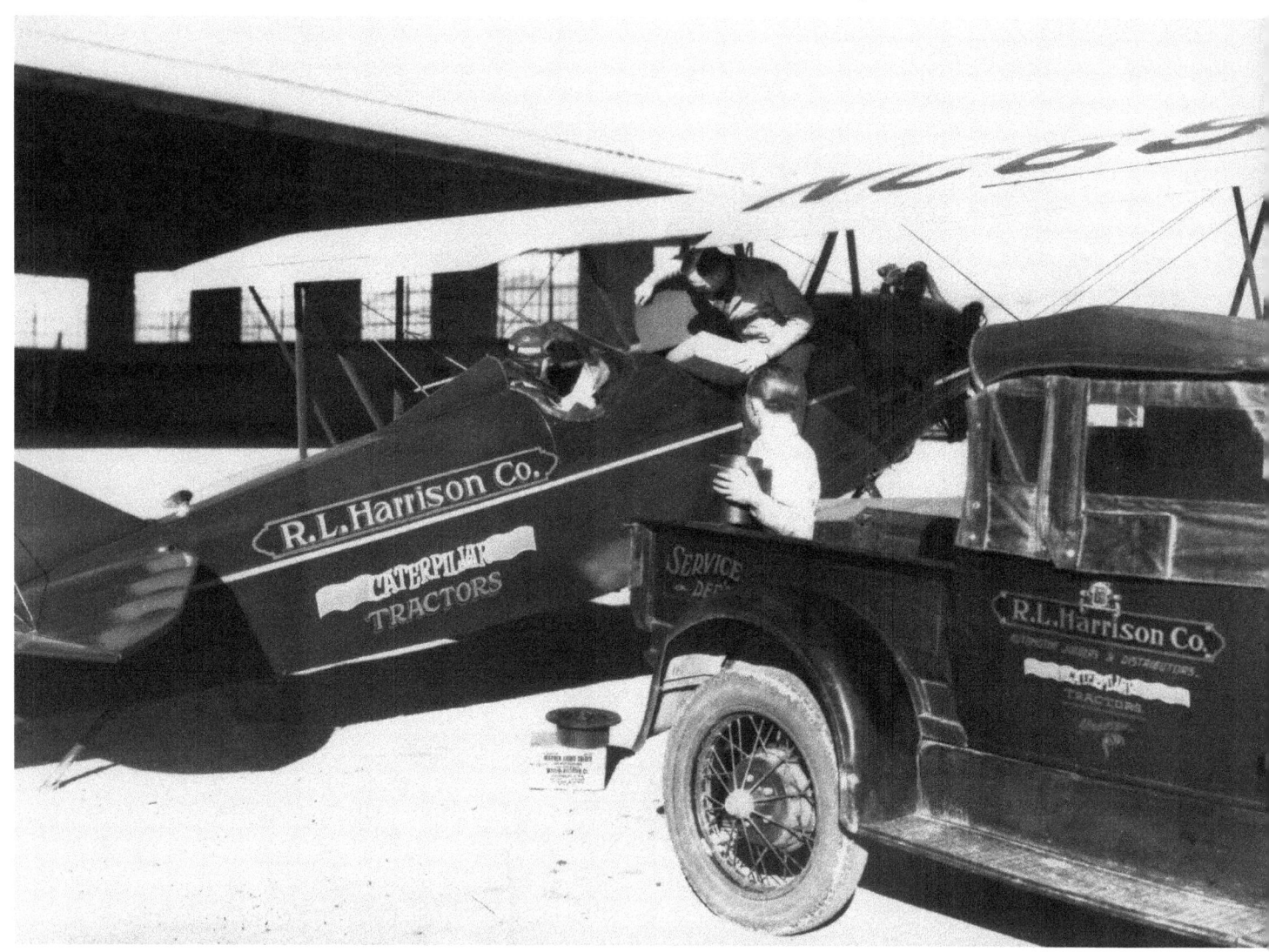

Charles and Anne Morrow Lindbergh are standing in front of a TWA airplane, an all-metal Lockheed Vega. Charles and Anne Morrow were married on May 27, 1929, about a year before this picture was taken.

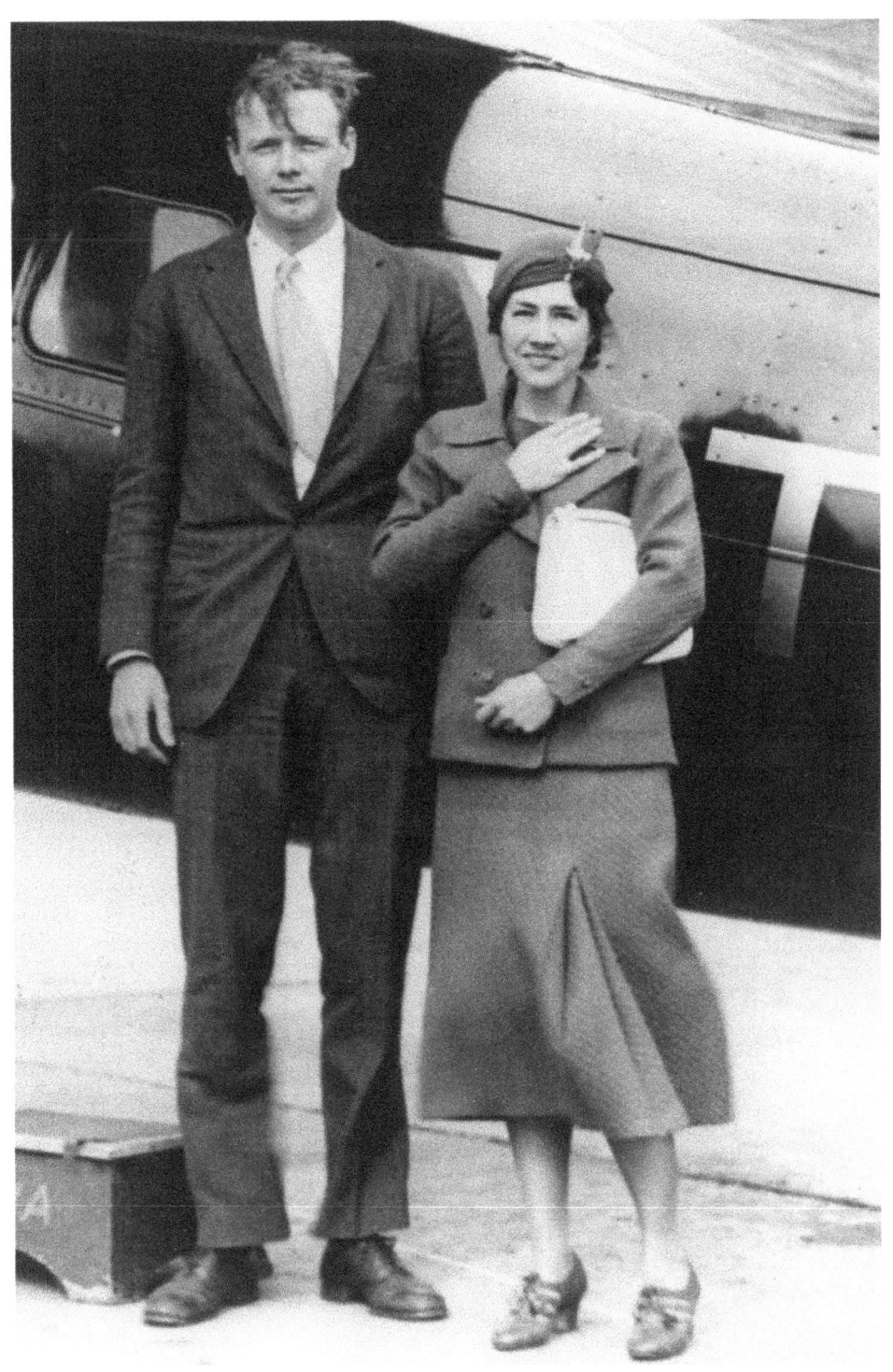

The congregation of Mt. Olive Baptist Church included members of the Austin, Bramlett, Carson, Darrick, Dixon, Eubanks, Faucett, Kidd, McDonald, and Young families. The church was started in Mrs. Tabytha Watson's house in 1898. A brick church was built in 1909, at 510 Lead Avenue. In 1934, a lot at 508 Lead Avenue was purchased and a parsonage was built. The church continues today, at 2401 University Boulevard S.E.

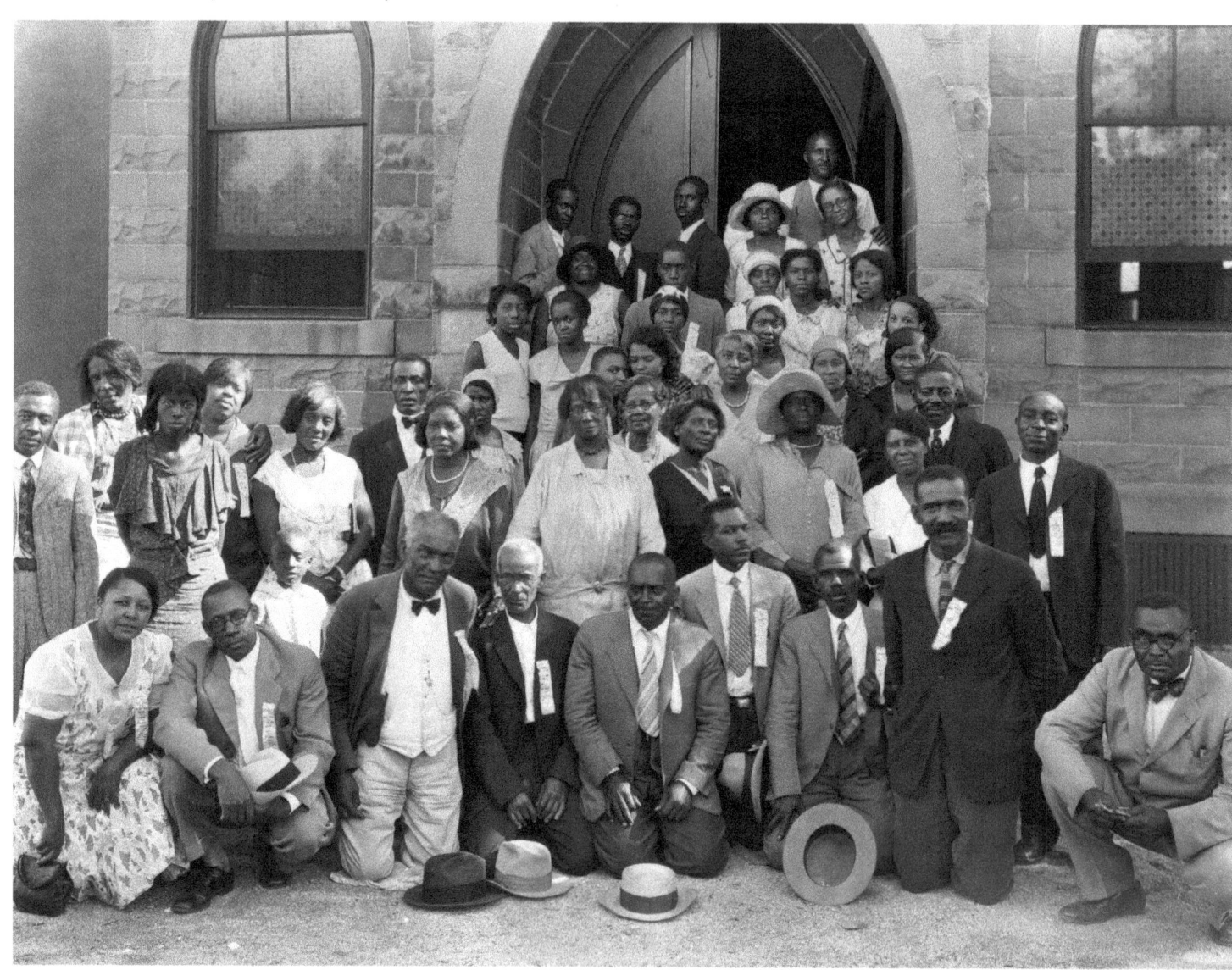

In 1931, Albert Einstein and his family were on their way to see the Grand Canyon and their train made a brief stop in Albuquerque. F. M. Denton, a professor at the University of New Mexico, took his recently written book to the station for Einstein to autograph. Denton's family just recently donated that book and copies of Einstein's correspondence with Denton to the University.

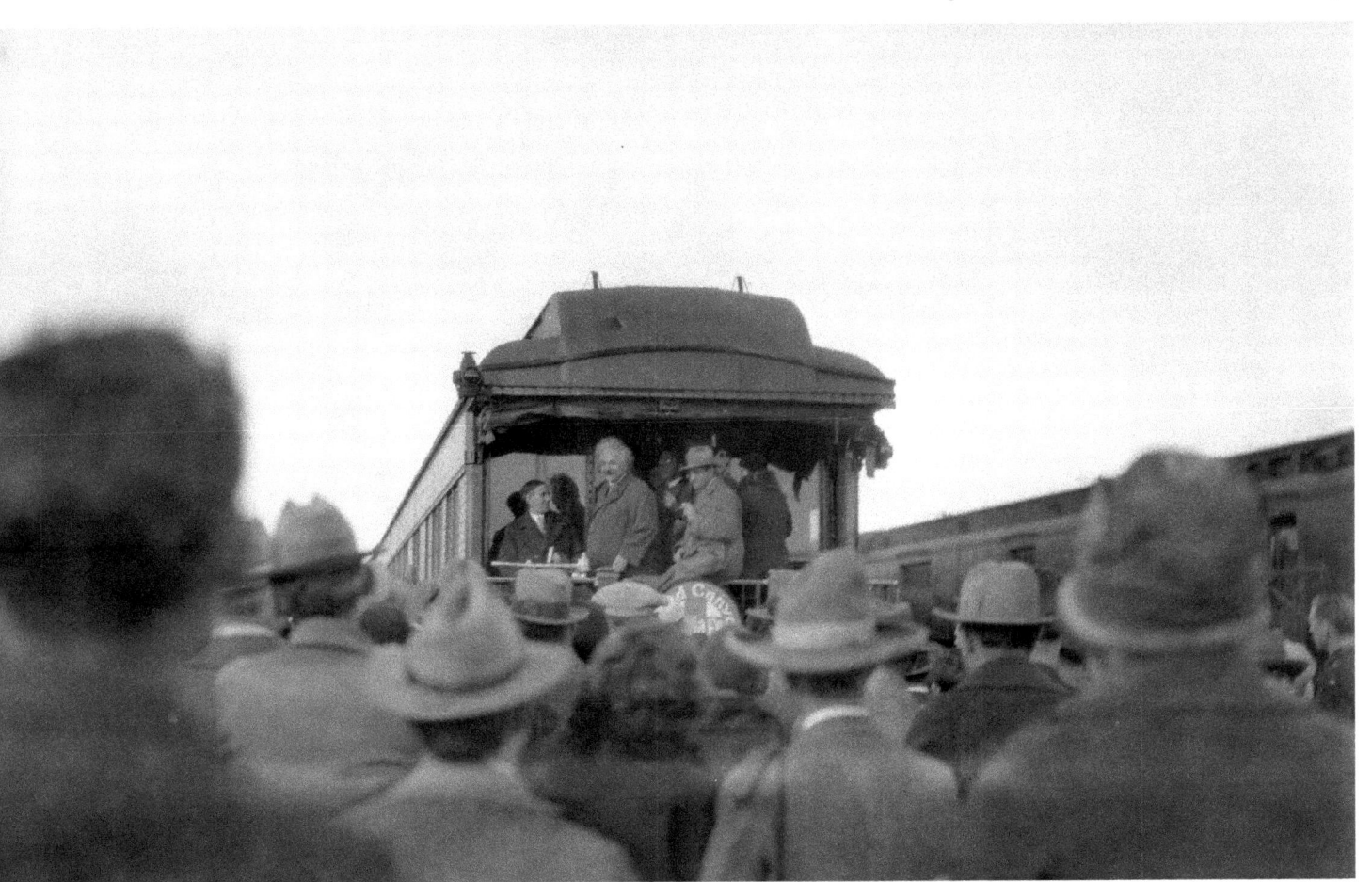

This 1931 aerial photograph is looking across the Rio Grande. The Central Avenue Bridge is shown and on the right is Tingley Drive.

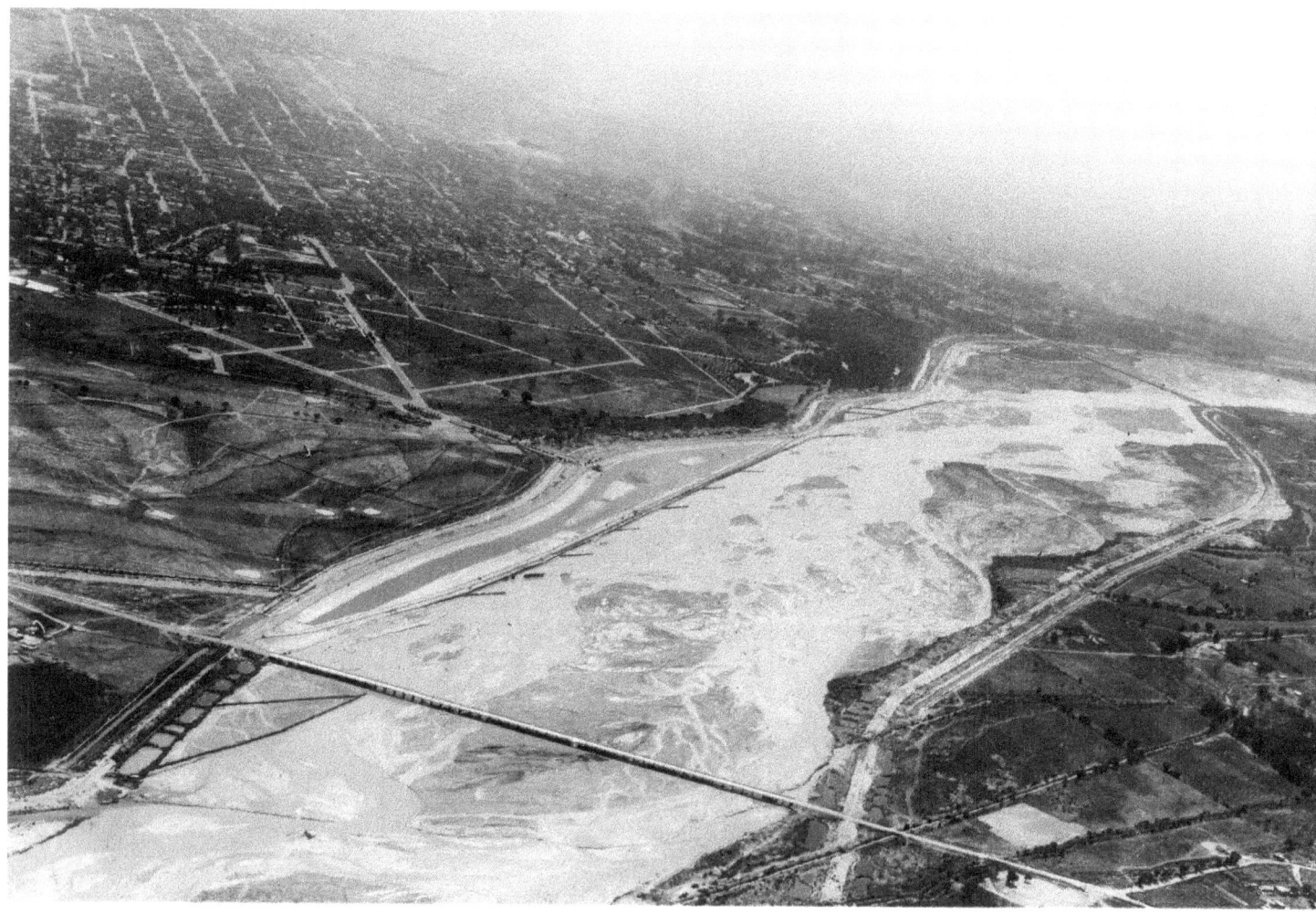

This 1932 aerial is looking east on Central Avenue from Seventh Street, toward the University of New Mexico, the Monte Vista Subdivision, and the Sandias.

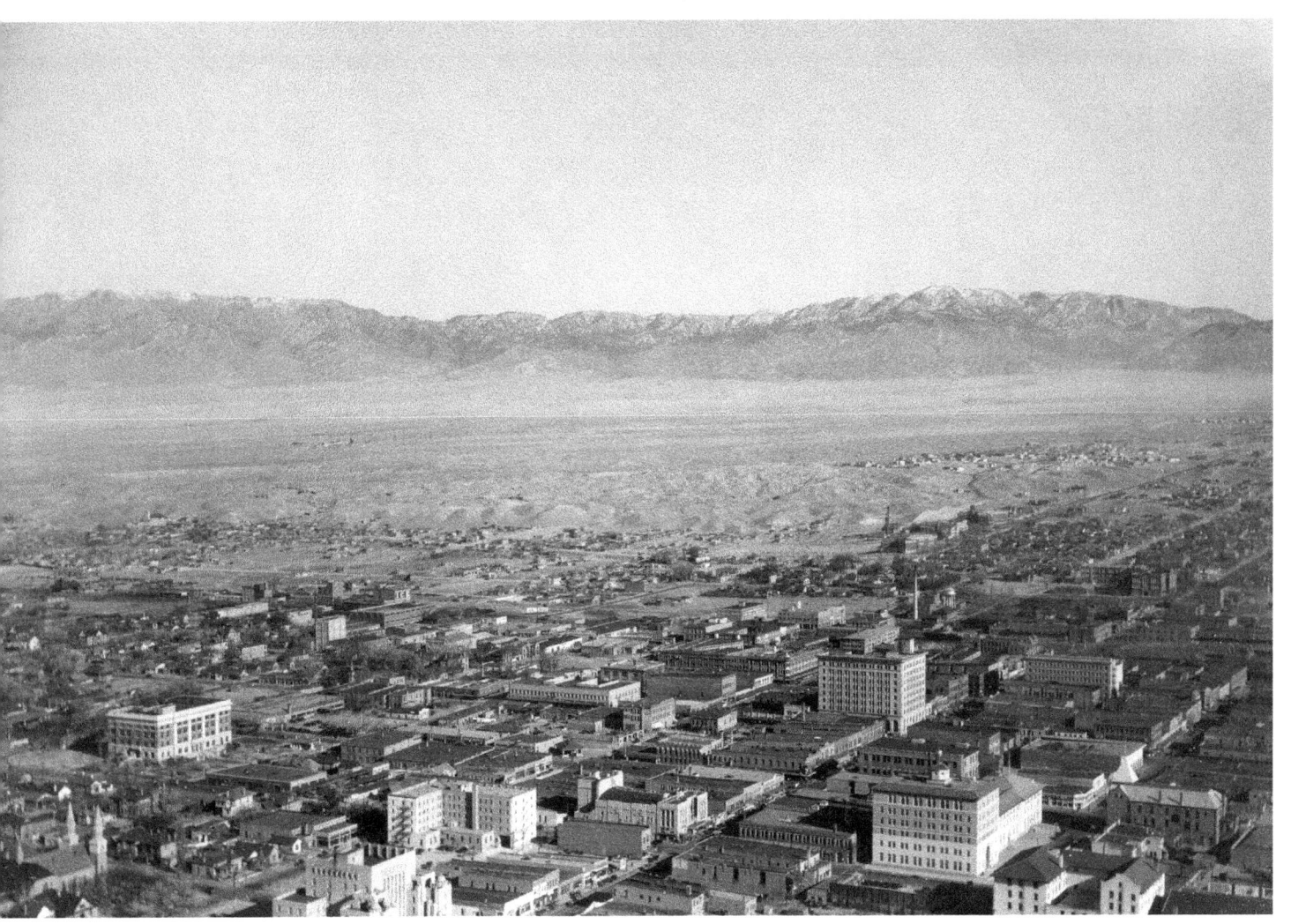

Downtown Albuquerque at First Street and Central Avenue, looking west. The Sturges Hotel was in a central location, near the Sunshine Theatre and the Liberty Cafe. The Sunshine Theatre, owned by Joseph Barnett, opened on May 1, 1924. The Sunshine Building was one of Albuquerque's first skyscrapers. It is still there and the theater is used for live music performances.

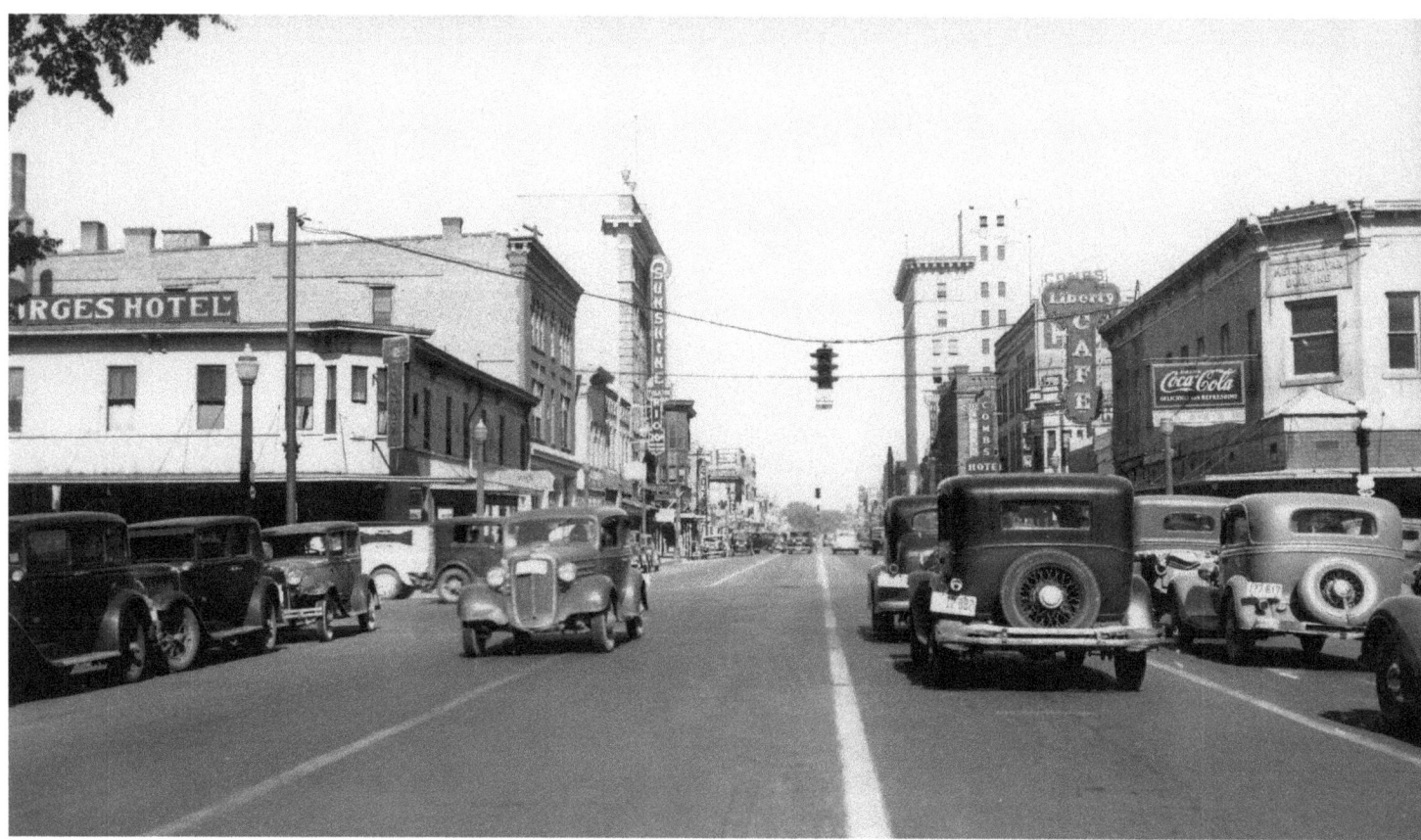

Atchison, Topeka and Santa Fe Railway Fire Station, built in 1920, to protect AT&SF property. Their firemen also helped fight fires in town. The sandstone used for the building is from the Laguna Pueblo quarry and was taken from the demolished 1881 Atlantic and Pacific Railroad roundhouse. The building still stands.

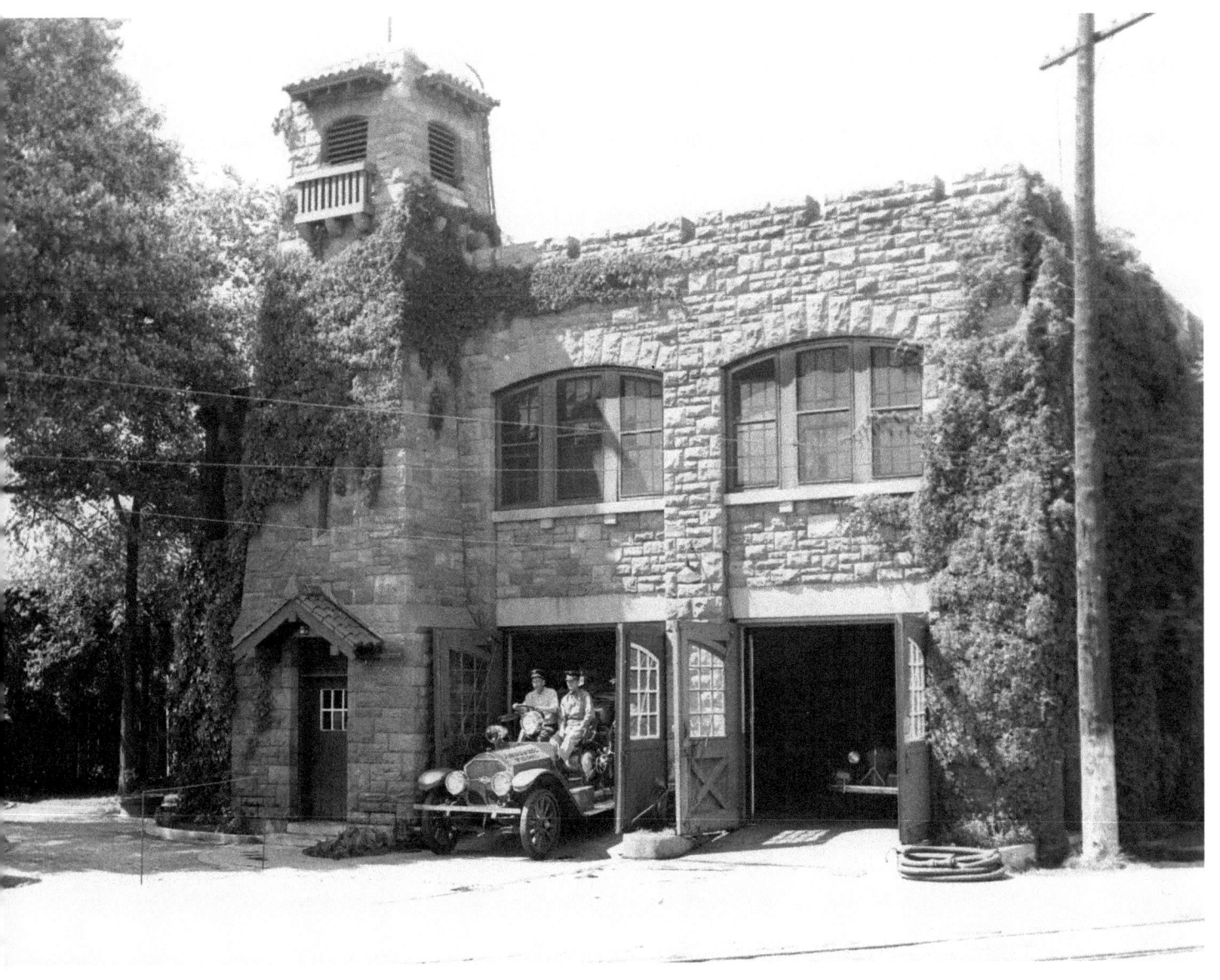

J. C. Penney Company opened in Albuquerque in 1916, in the Melini Building. A fire on June 5, 1933 damaged $100,000 worth of merchandise. On June 11th, Penney's began a huge fire sale in four temporary locations.

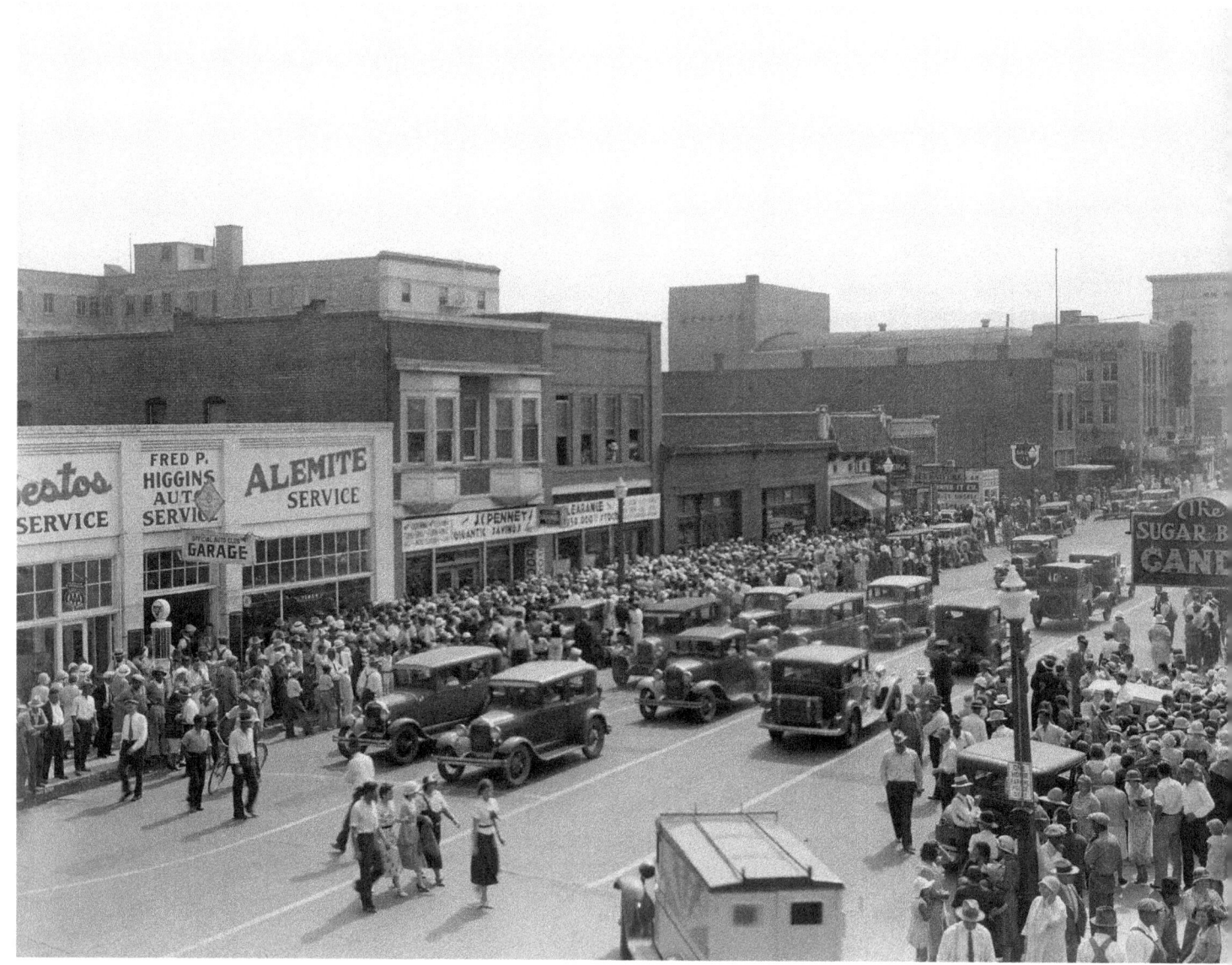

In 1927, the KiMo Theatre opened at 419-423 W. Central Avenue. Oreste and Maria Bachechi's dream was to provide Albuquerque with an opulent movie palace. Carl Boller, of Kansas City, designed the theater. The name KiMo came from Isleta pueblo resident Pablo Abeita. The Pueblo Deco style was restored when the city bought it in 1977 to use as a community arts center.

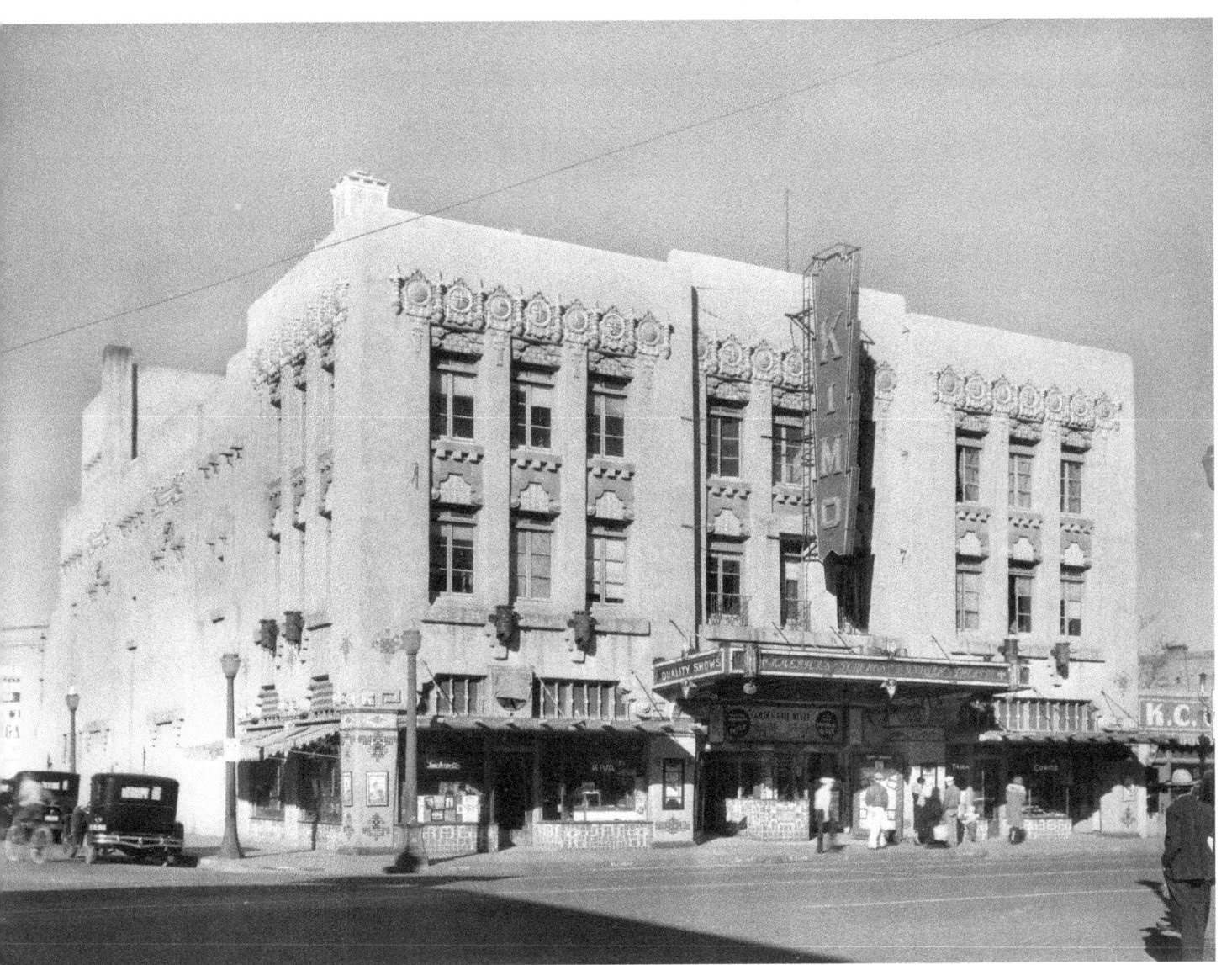

Oden Buick, Inc., 312-324 N. Fourth Street, was on Route 66. "Today's Special " was $85.00 for a used car. The brick building was remodeled with added southwestern touches. Clyde Oden was very civic minded and he and Clyde Tingley often treated children to a show and treats at the KiMo Theatre.

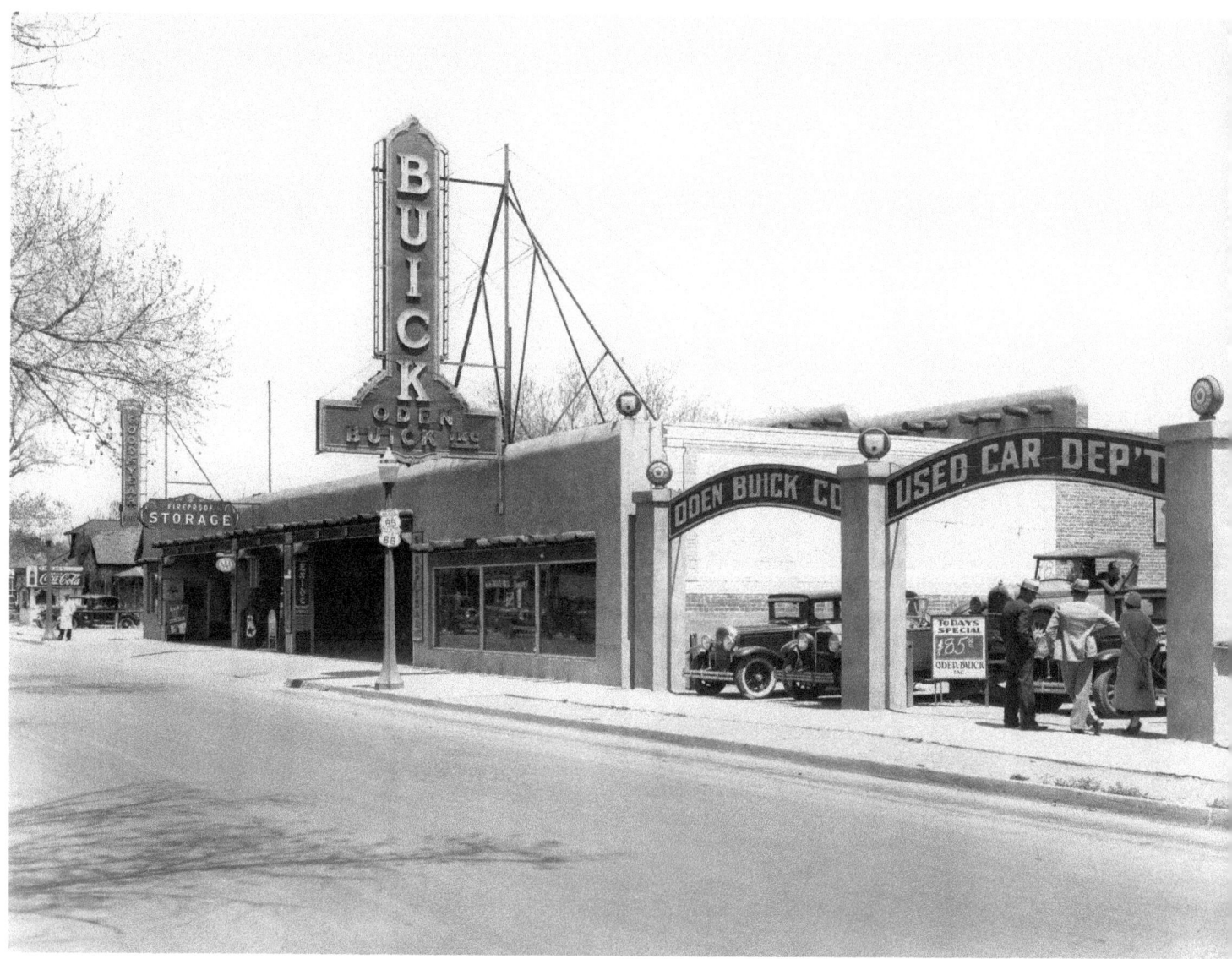

The KGGM radio station studio in the Hotel Franciscan at Sixth Street and Central Avenue. Comedian Ed Wynn, wearing a fireman's hat, is looking over at Albuquerque politician Clyde Tingley. The picture is inscribed "To Mayor Clyde Tingley a Peach of a Chap, Ed Wynn 1933."

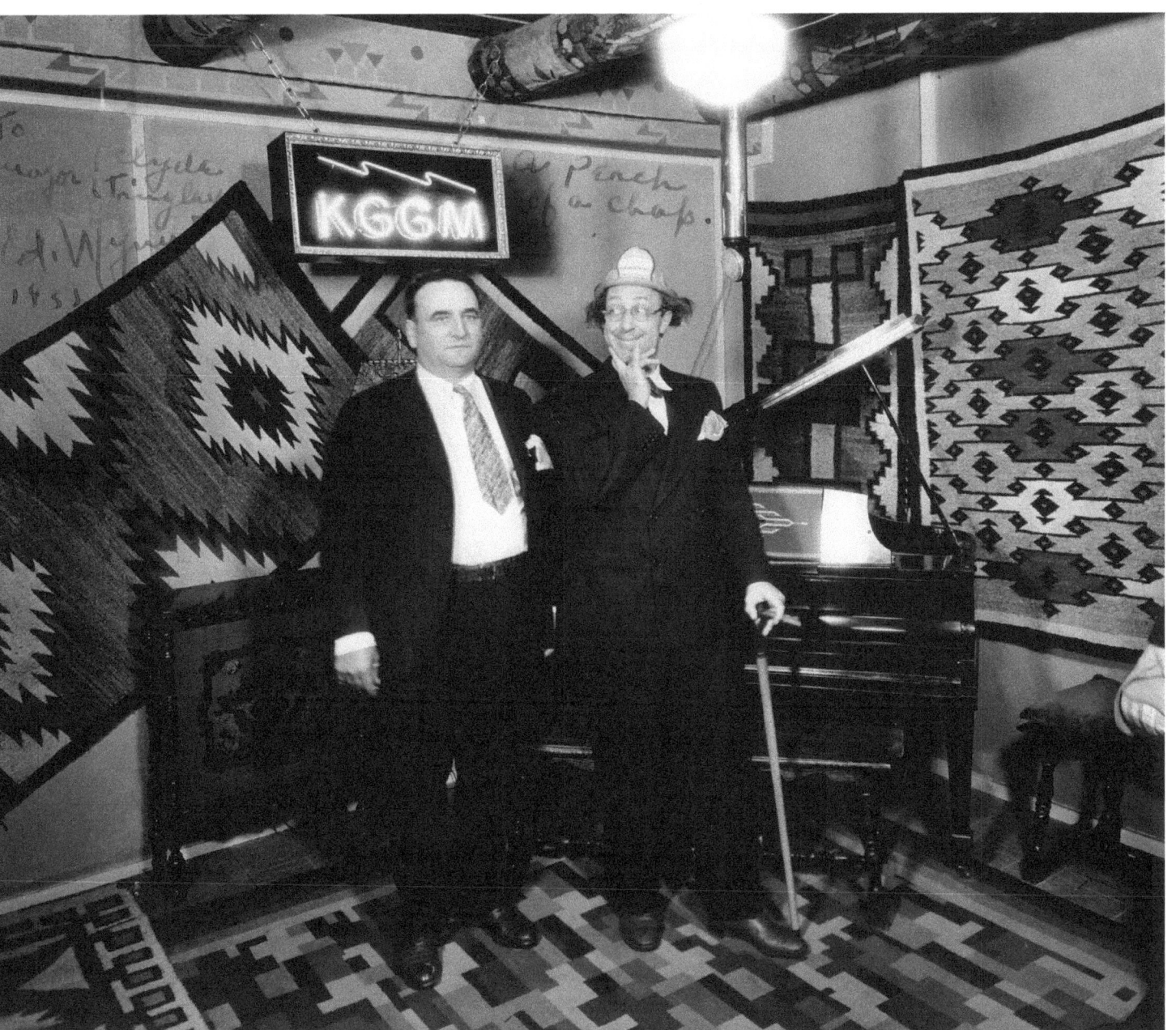

The interior of the Oden Motor Company Lubrication Bay. Two women wait for their car to be serviced. Above their heads the sign reads "Why not watch us lubricate your car." Clyde Oden opened his Buick dealership on Gold Avenue in 1921 and later added Chevrolets and GMC trucks to his line.

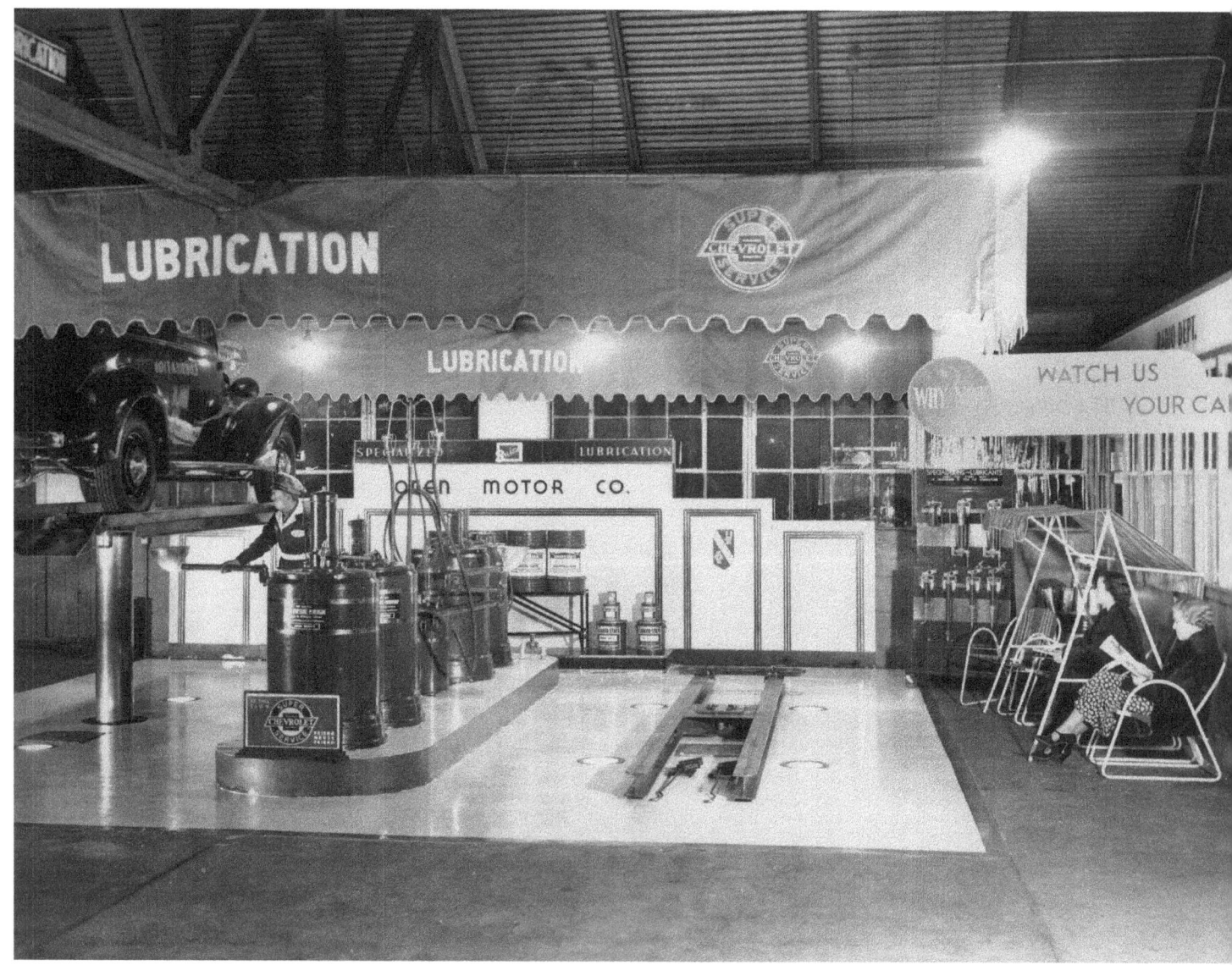

Street scene with El Fidel Hotel, a Standard Oil Station, and Galles Motor Company, at Copper Avenue and Fifth Street. An addition is being constructed behind the hotel. The building is still there, as Copper Square.

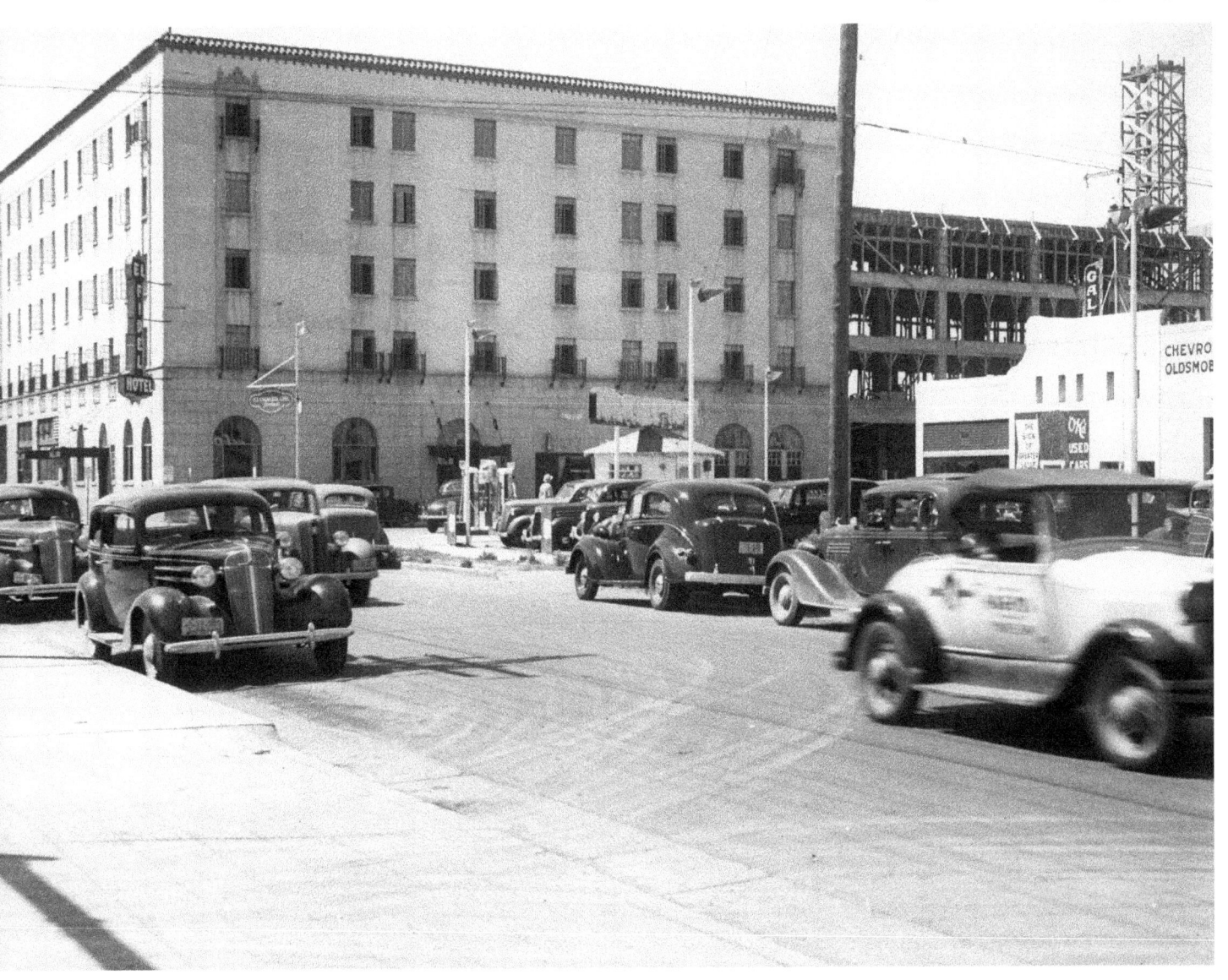

Safeway Store No. 951, 409 W. Central Avenue, which opened in 1930. In 1936 there were five Safeway Stores and a district office in the area. Tomatoes were four cans for 49 cents; soap, ten bars for 39 cents; peas, three cans for 35 cents; and corn, two cans for 35 cents. This store closed in 1934, when stores were moving east of downtown.

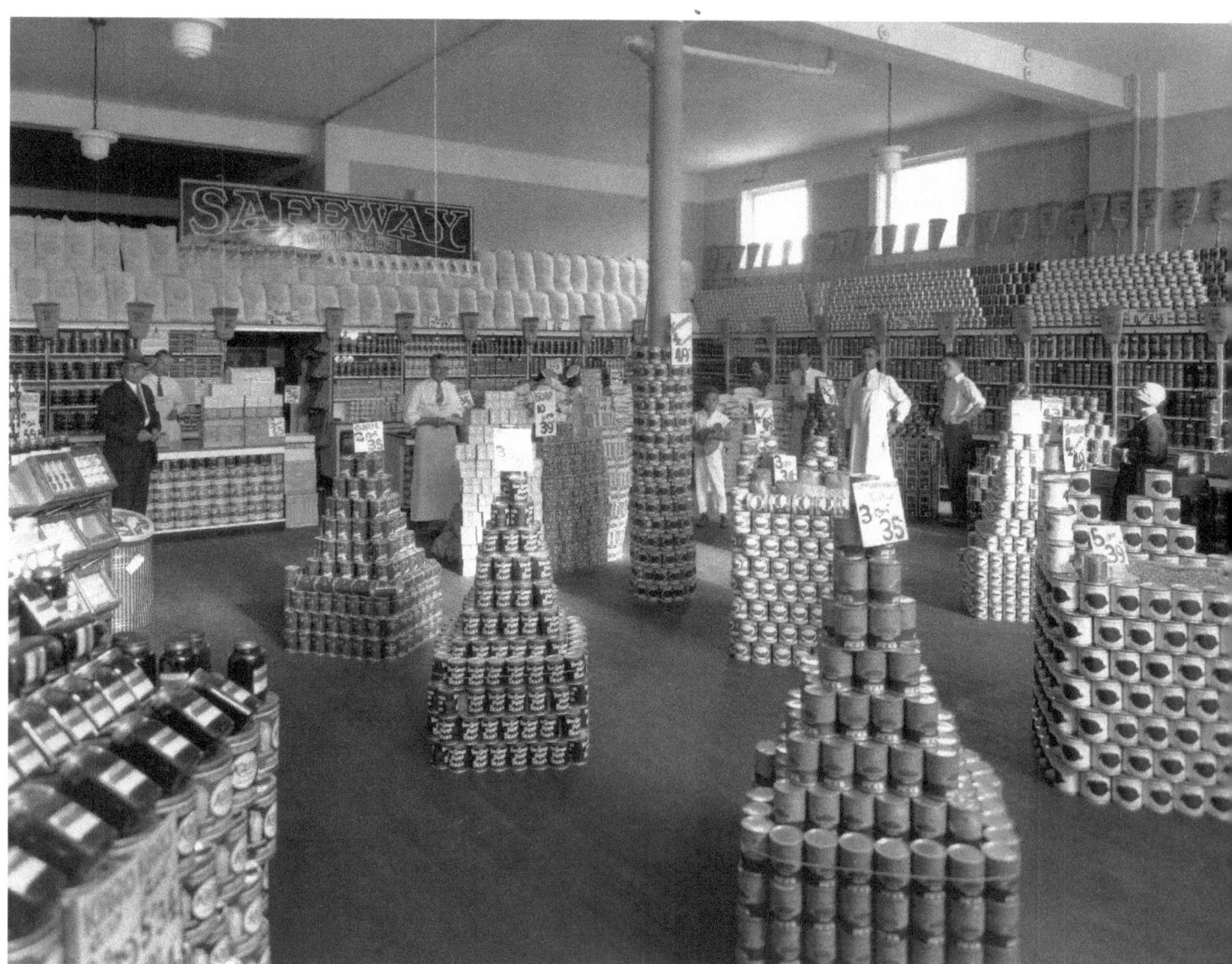

This flagstone wall and gazebo at the Old Town Plaza was a WPA project, constructed about 1936. Many people in town hated it, and Old Town Historical Society's first project was to tear it down. It was razed around 1948. The Old Town Historical Society became inactive in about 1955, but reorganized in 1962 as the Albuquerque Historical Society.

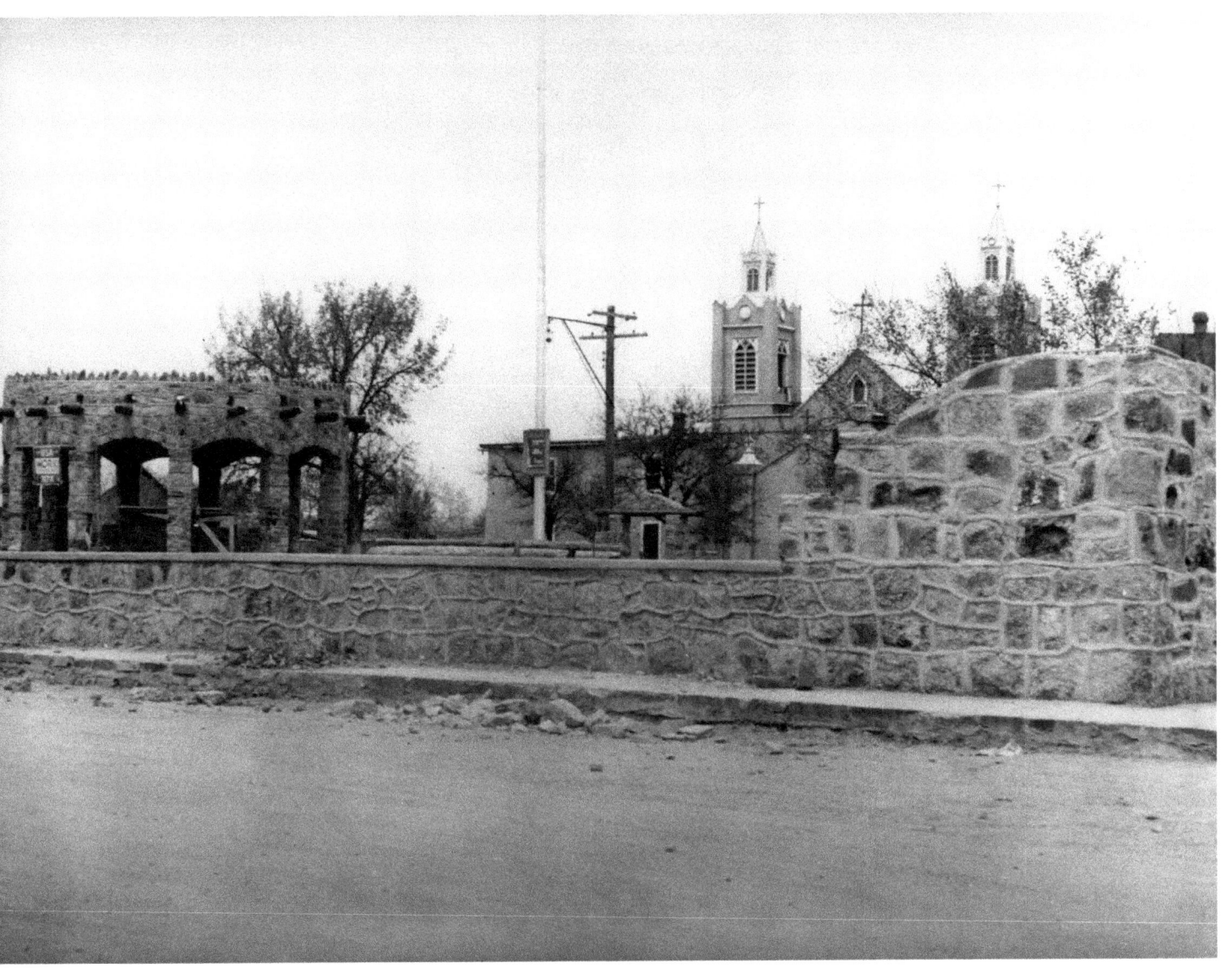

The service station, at the corner of Second and Copper, is dwarfed by the northeast side of the First National Bank. The First National Bank was eight stories high and was very elegant inside, with marble counters. Doctors, lawyers and other professionals had offices upstairs. The N. T. Armijo Building is on the left.

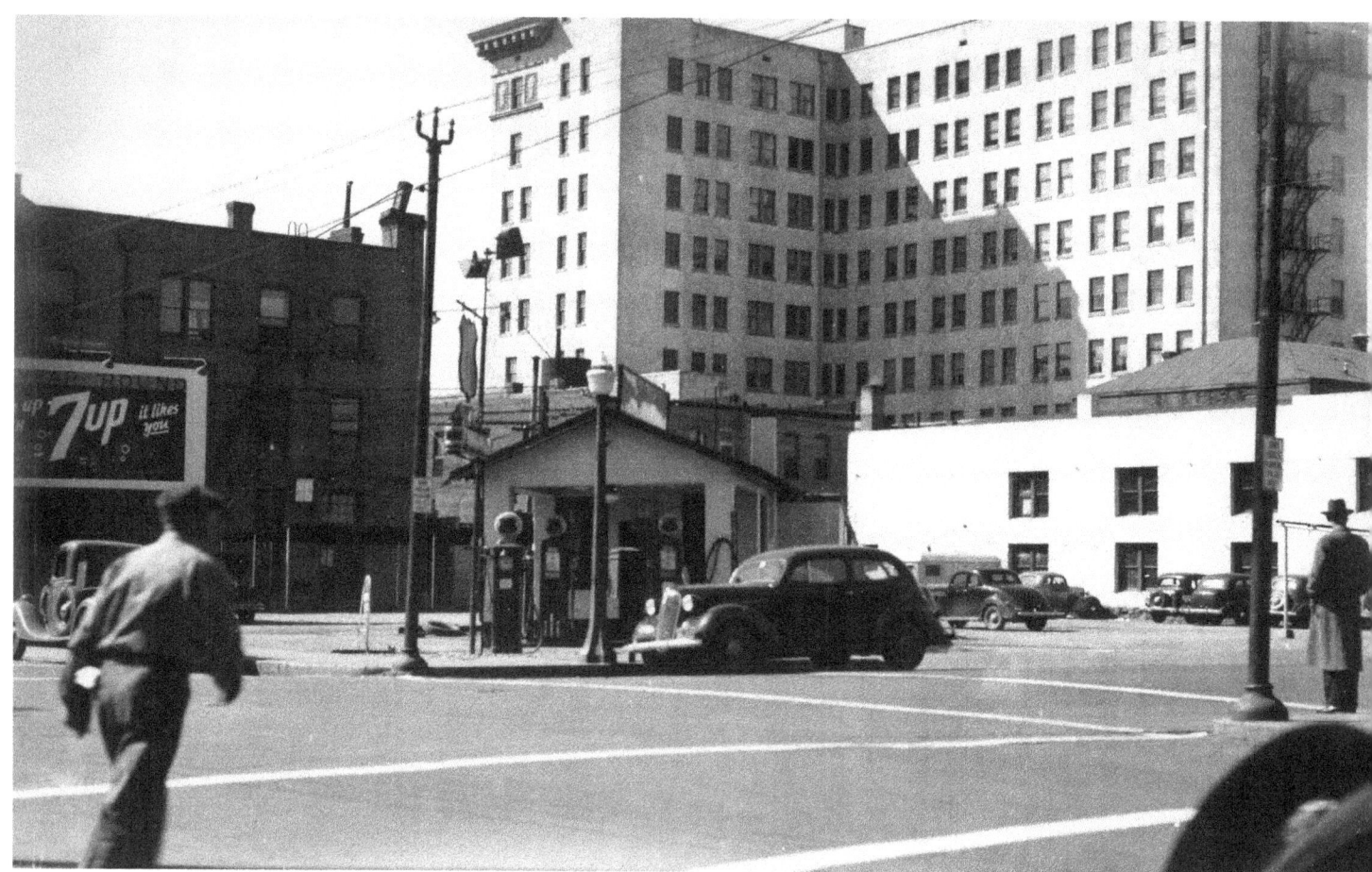

This local restaurant was at 209 W. Central Avenue. It was the privately owned McDonald's Restaurant. Many of the people living in the downtown walk-ups ate most of their meals in restaurants. Miss Alabama Milner, the photographer, documented many of the downtown businesses.

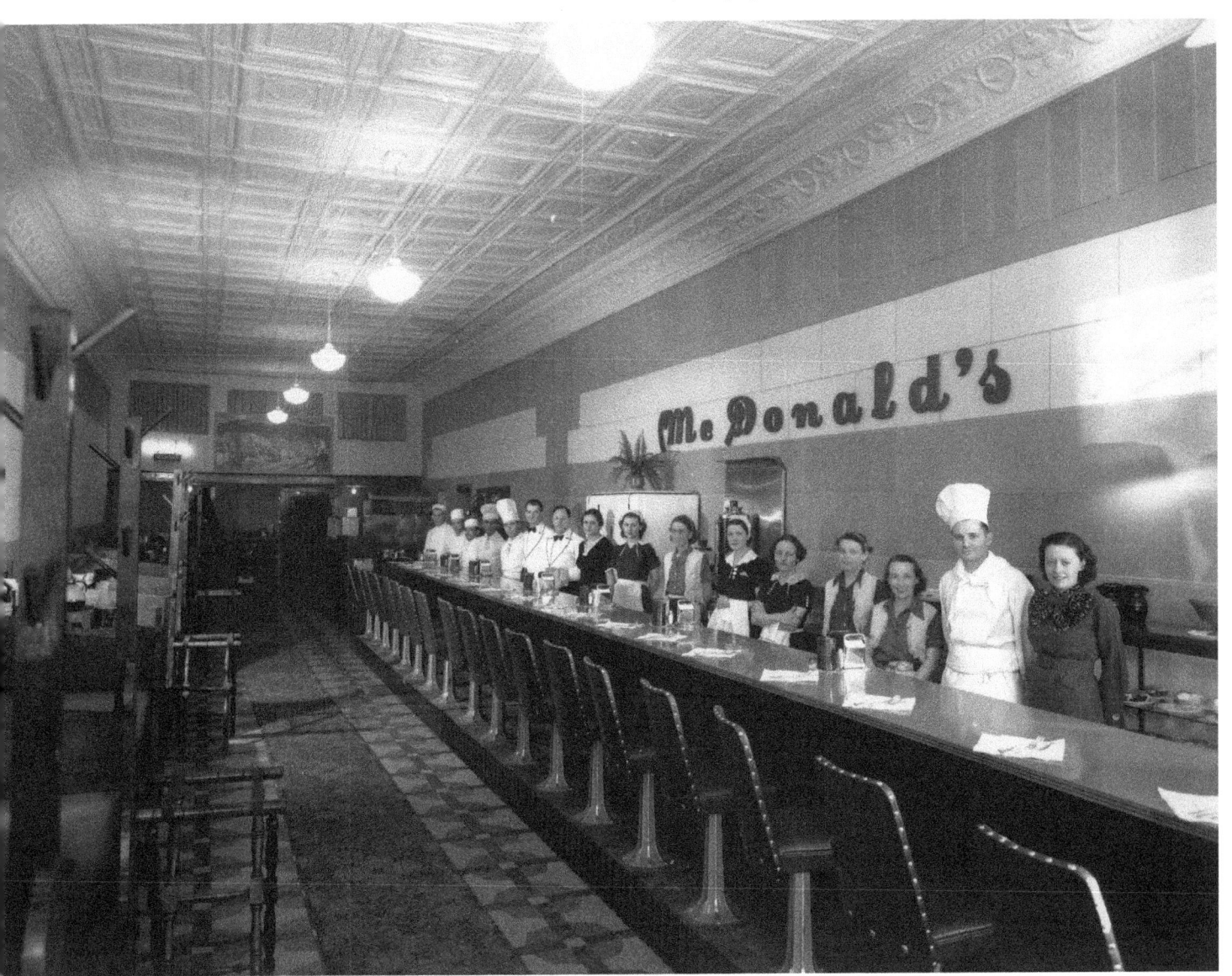

Standard Stations Inc. at 3123 E. Central Avenue, with a Texaco Station next door. The Lobo Theatre was playing "Go Chase Yourself," starring Joe Penner and Lucille Ball. Opened in 1939, the Lobo was the first theater in the Northeast Heights and is still there.

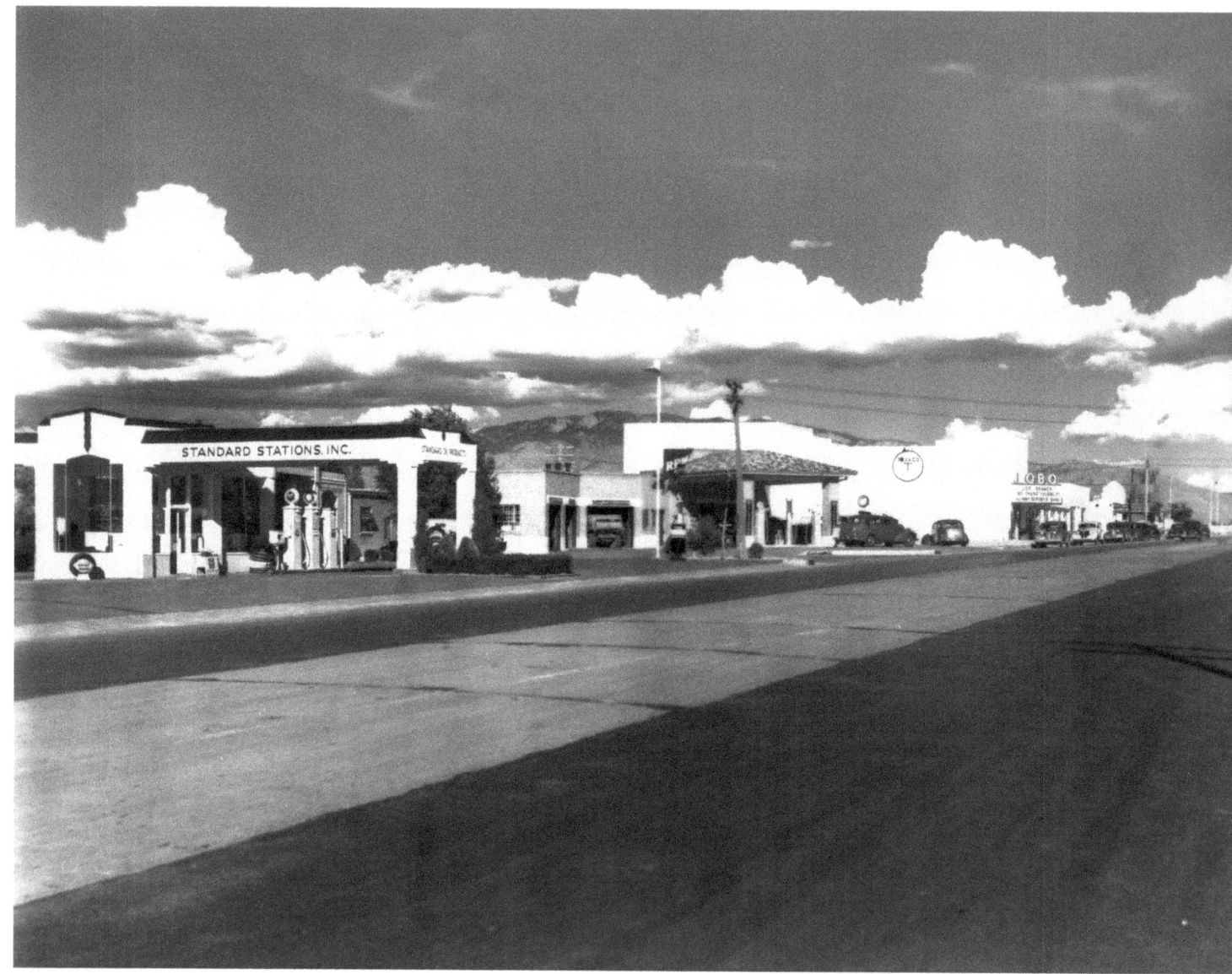

WAR, AIRPLANES, AND ROUTE 66

(1940–1980)

Construction of Albuquerque Municipal Airport, using WPA matching funds, expanded air travel. It featured Southwestern furnishings, nice gift shops and a good restaurant. TWA and Continental airlines, the Weather Bureau and the United States Army Air Corps had operations there. Albuquerque had been trying to attract an air base and, with the help of Major General Henry H. "Hap" Arnold, established a National Guard Aviation unit and an Air Cadet training program. A military delegation came to town in 1940 to survey the proposed site. Albuquerque Army Air Base construction began in January 1941. It was renamed Kirtland Field in 1942, in honor of Col. Roy C. Kirtland, an Army aviation pioneer who had flown with the Wright brothers as a student.

The Bureau of Federal Highways realigned Route 66 to go straight through Albuquerque on Central Avenue. Tourist camps, hotels, curio shops and restaurants stayed busy. Drive-in restaurants opened for the travelers and the locals enjoyed them, too. As more places opened to cater to tourists, roadside architecture was used to beckon them. Gasoline stations became larger, offering repairs, food, and other services. Whiting Brothers Stations popped up all over the Southwest, adding cafes and souvenirs. Old Town was annexed to the City of Albuquerque and regulated to keep its historic character. The San Felipe de Neri Church remained active, serving the community and tourists.

The Army Air Base created a building boom for housing, during the war and afterward. Military men who had come to Albuquerque liked it and stayed or returned after the war. Government contracts awarded to the area brought more people. Kirtland was used to store weapons. Sandia Peak Ski Area and Tramway opened on May 7, 1966. The University of New Mexico brought people to the area as men and a few women used their GI Bill to go to college. The student population more than doubled in 1946 and continued to grow.

The Albuquerque Fire Department chief's car drives past a group of onlookers during a parade. Clyde Tingley is seated in the back, tipping his hat to the crowd.

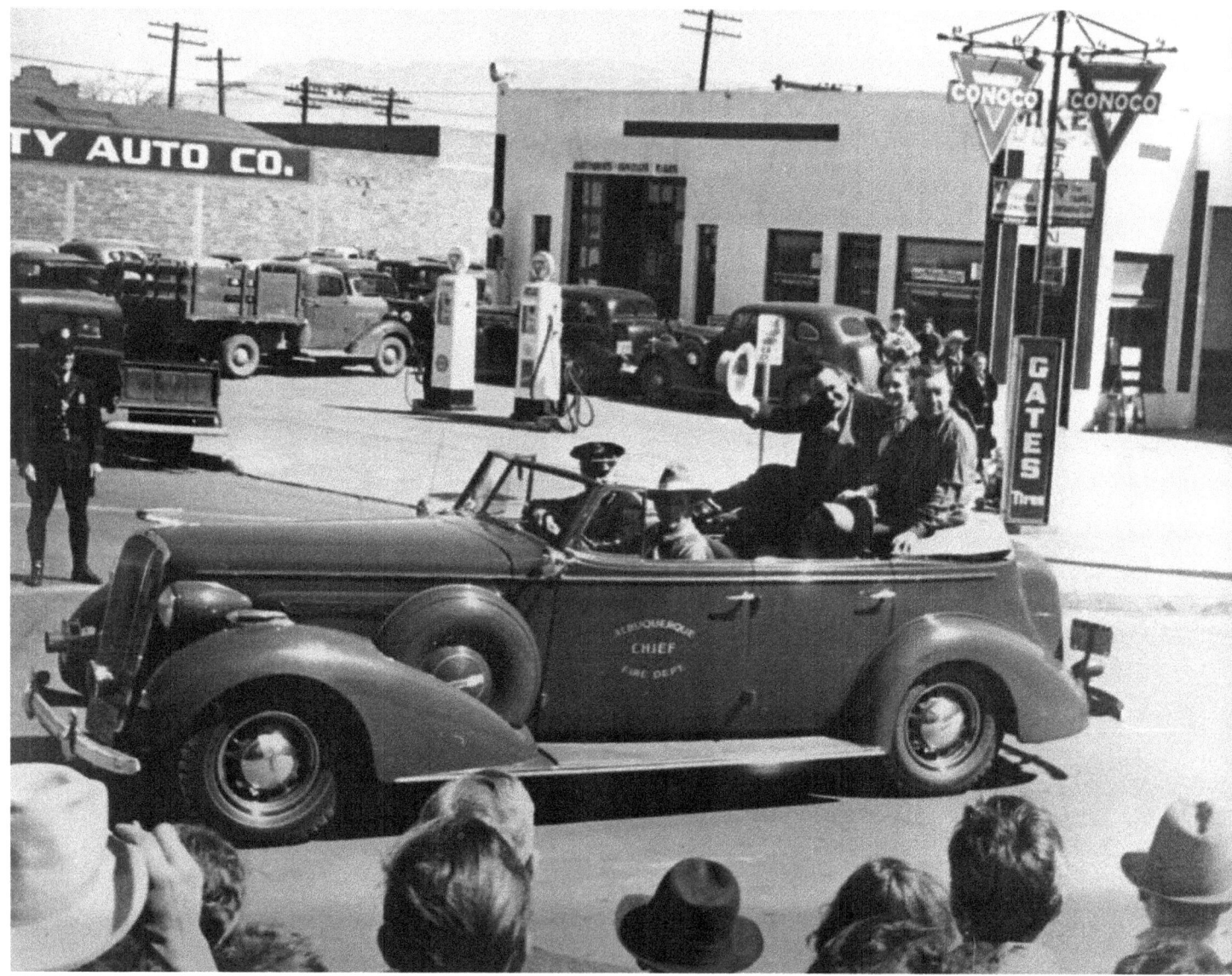

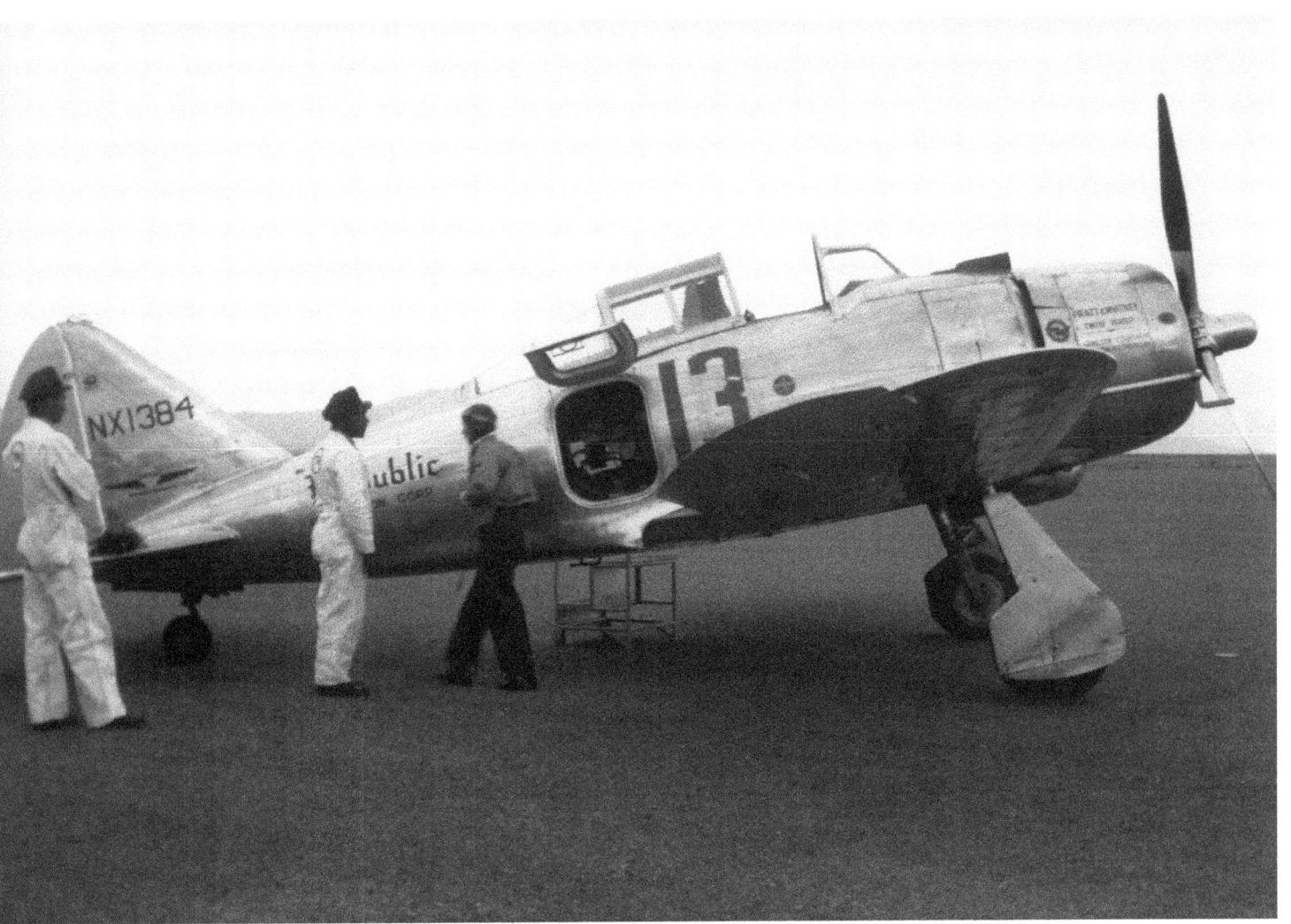

Jacqueline Cochran stopped for refueling at the Albuquerque Airport, in the spring of 1940. Three years prior, the famous aviatrix won the Bendix Air Race. The Republic Aviation Corporation airplane in the picture is a later version of the airplane Jackie won the race with.

On January 7, 1941, construction started on the Albuquerque Army Air Base. The 4th Air Base Group came to operate the base as a training facility. It was finished on August 8, 1941, and the 19th Bombardment Group and the 3rd Air Base Squadron arrived. TWA trained more than 1,100 pilots and crewmen in eight months for the Army Air Corps. Here, B-24 Liberators fly over the mountains.

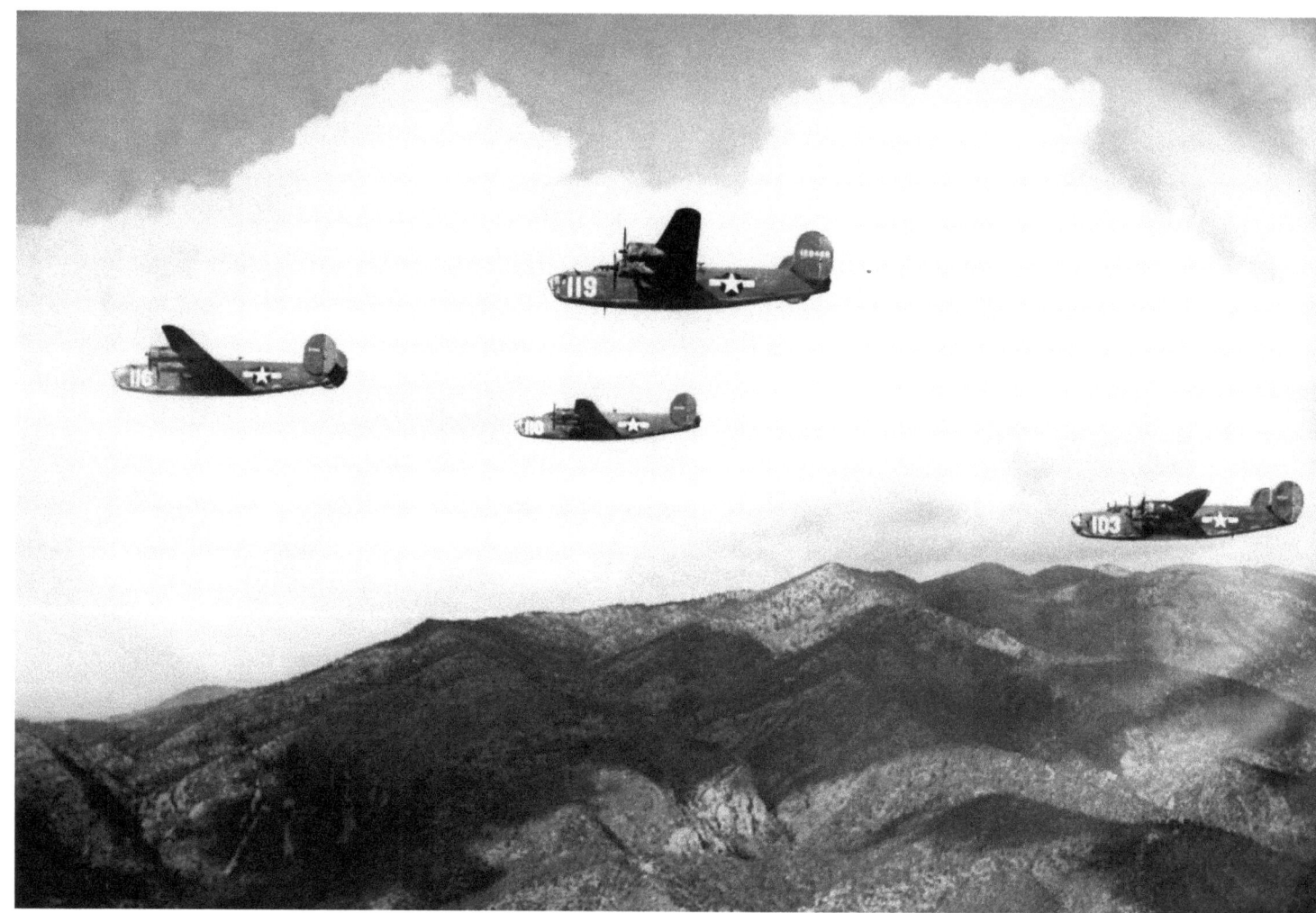

This February 1943 photograph, taken at Fourth and Gold, is the United States Post Office, with the six-story Federal Building behind it. The Amy Biehl School, a charter school, now occupies the Post Office building.

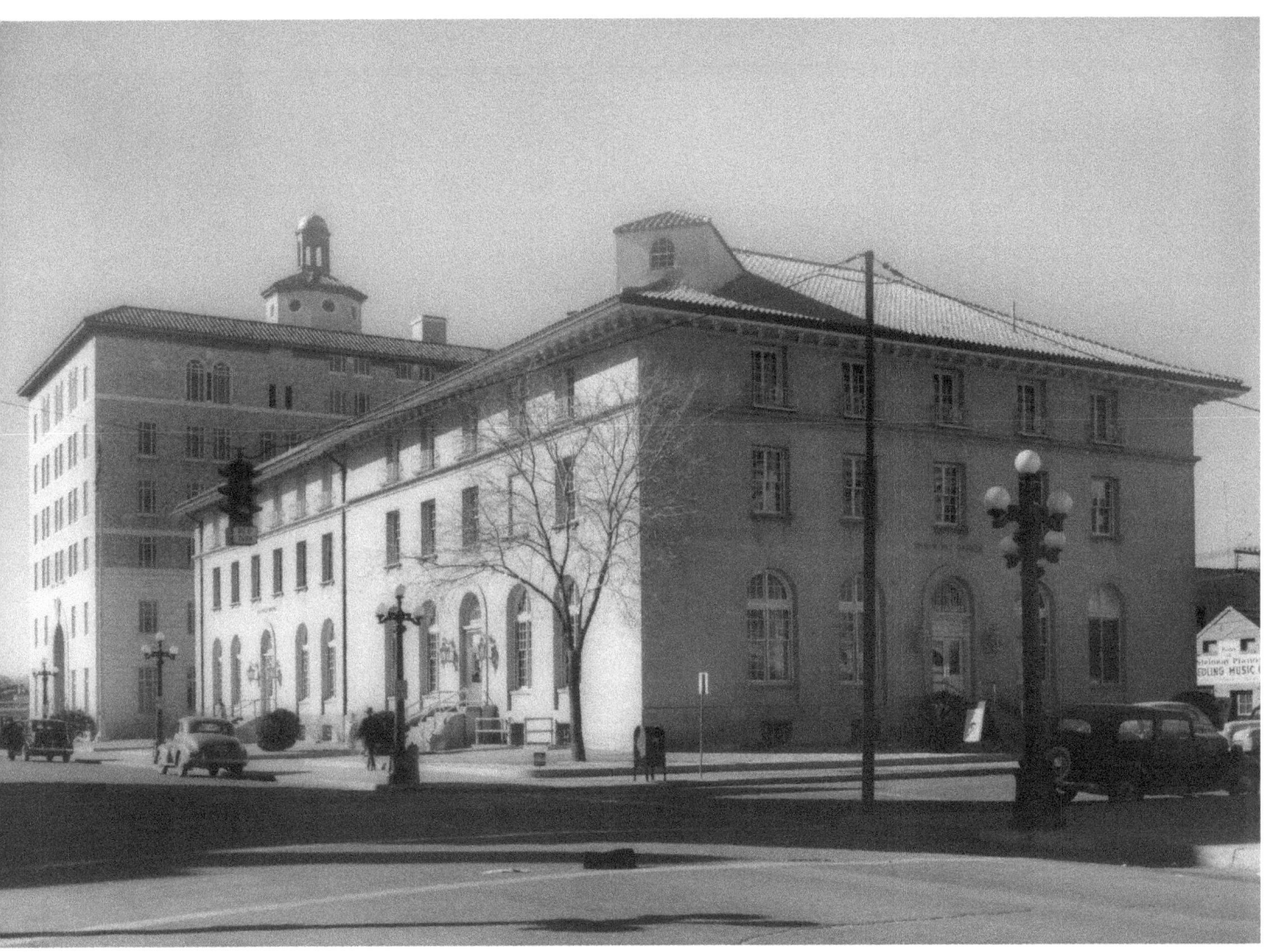

McLellan's Department Store entrance, at Central and Fourth, is next to the stoplight. Sun Drugs and Maisel's Indian Trading Post are behind it. Maurice Maisel was a supervisor for Western Union as a young man. When he opened his store, he employed Native American artisans to design and create jewelry. The business still exists.

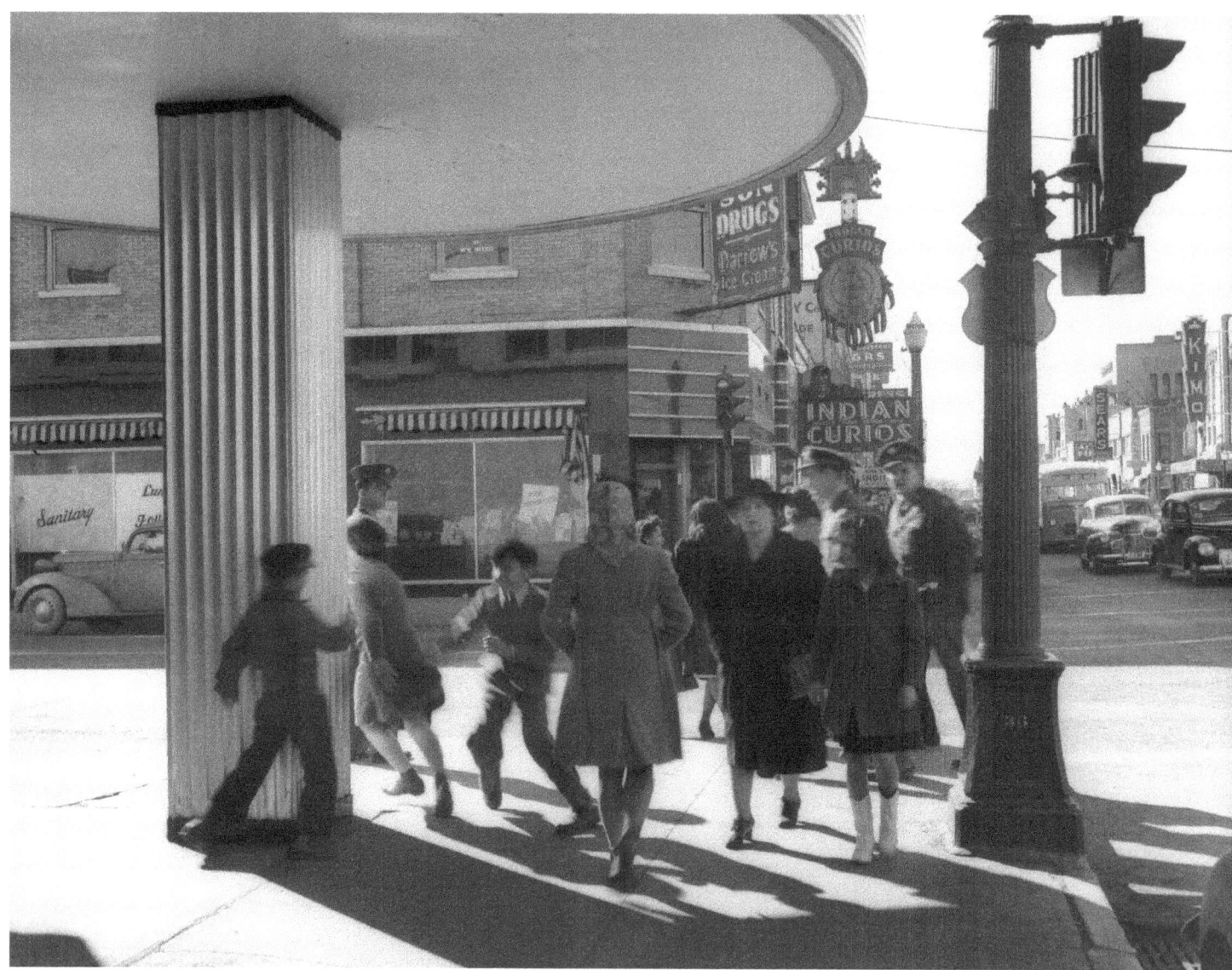

The Hotel Franciscan's pueblo style made it an instant landmark. It was a popular place for weddings, proms, receptions and parties. It was demolished in the 1970s. The Masonic Temple, on the left side of this picture, burned down in the 1960s. This photograph was taken in 1943.

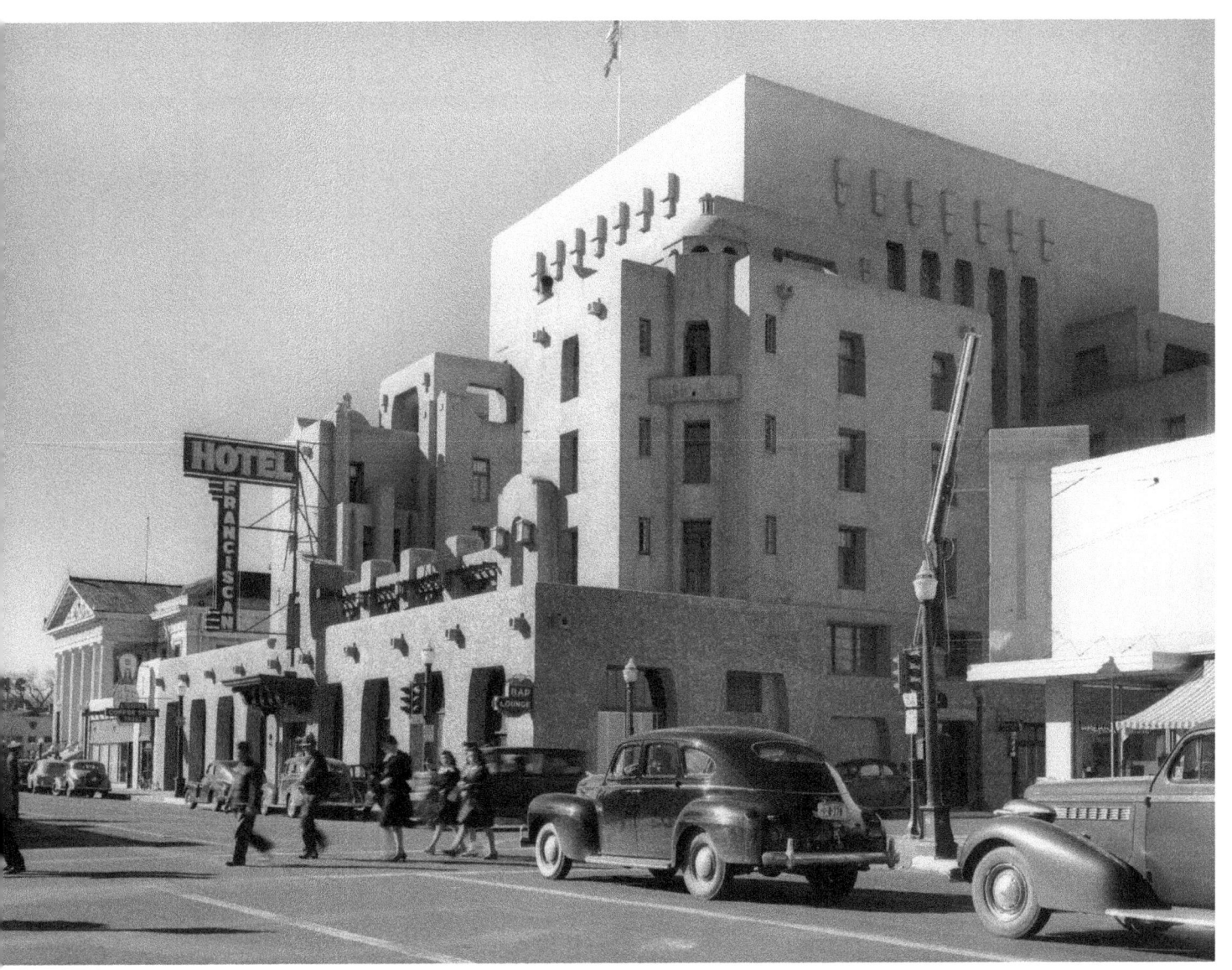

Army Air Force airplane, a Beechcraft AT-11, on a bombing training mission. The bombardiers used planes like these to train over the West Mesa during World War II. They flew from Kirtland Field to the West Mesa to drop dummy bombs, then flew back to the base. Children loved to watch the planes flying over town.

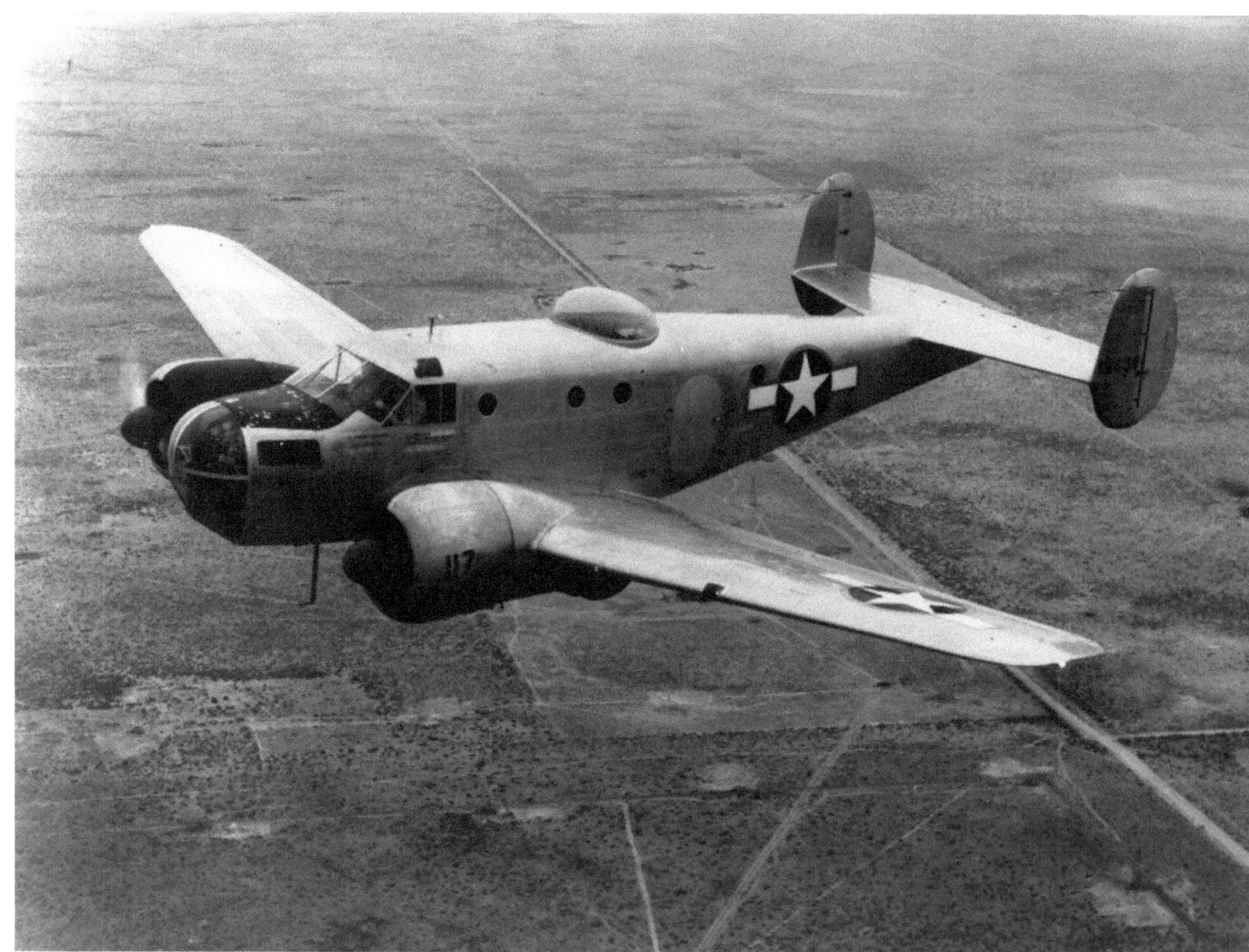

This two-man Japanese submarine is going down Central Avenue. The submarine was used in parades all over the United States and for War Bond drives. The picture was taken from the second-floor window of the Barnett Building. This shows the first Albuquerque Walgreen's Drugs, which was in the N. T. Armijo Building.

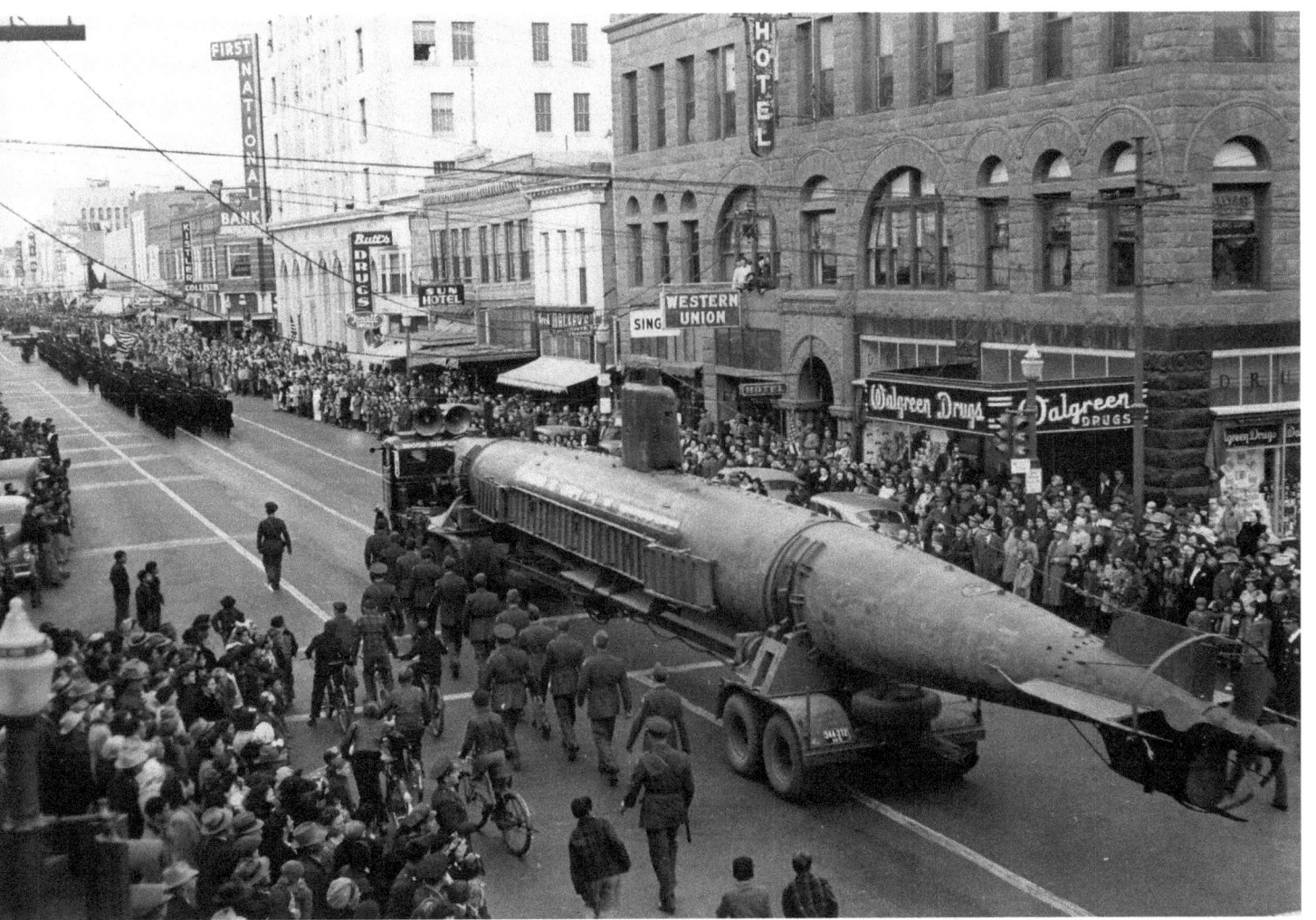

Ernie Pyle was a columnist for Scripps-Howard Newspapers in 1940 when he and his wife Jerry built a house, at 900 S. Girard Boulevard. Pyle won a Pulitzer Prize for his war correspondence in 1942. He was killed by a Japanese sniper on April 18, 1945. His wife died seven months later, and their house was purchased by the city. The Ernie Pyle Library, the city's first branch library, opened in 1948.

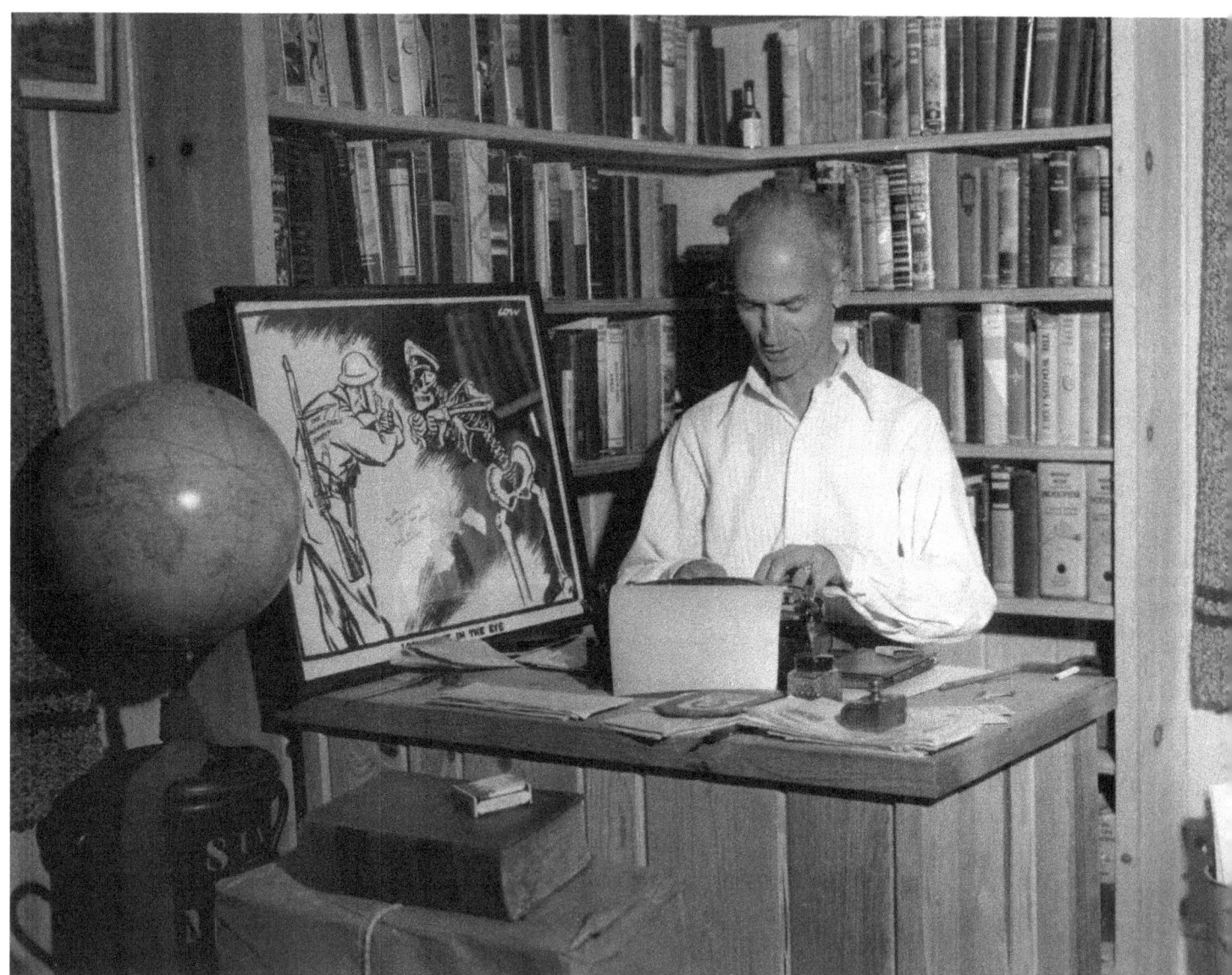

General George Patton and General Jimmy Doolittle, 1943, at the Albuquerque Municipal Airport. The two commanders were admired during the Second World War and were close friends. General Doolittle led the first bombing raid on Tokyo before commanding the Twelfth, Fifteenth, and Eighth Air Forces.

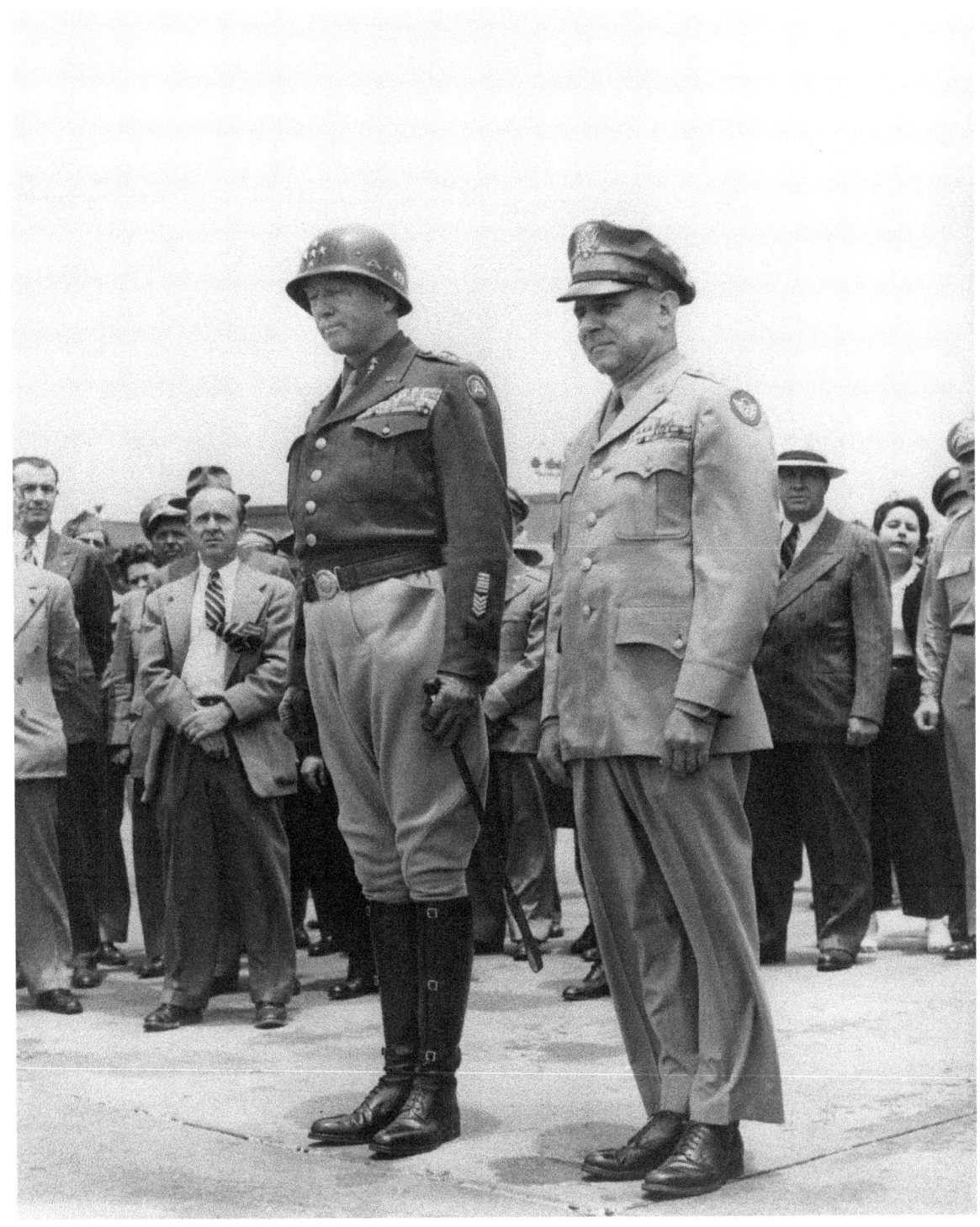

The EMD E-1 Diesel-powered *Super Chief* makes a stop at the Alvarado Complex before continuing its westbound journey. On the next track is the venerable steam *Chief* that will soon be phased out by its faster, more luxurious rival.

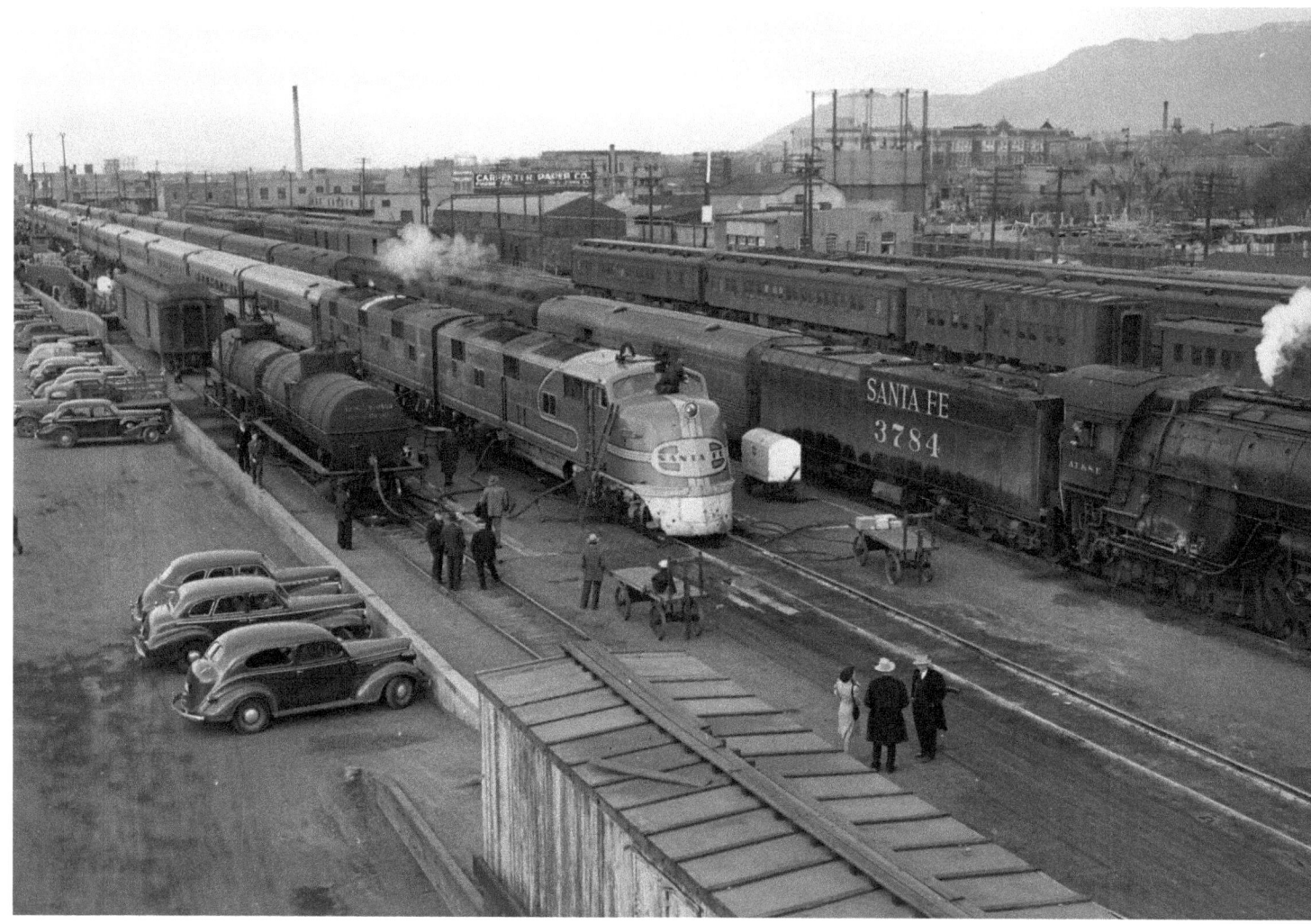

Passengers waiting for the train at the AT&SF depot. The Alvarado Hotel and depot shared California Mission Revival Style, marketed by the Santa Fe Railway. The City of Albuquerque has recreated what the AT&SF bulldozed in 1970 and built the Alvarado Transportation Center.

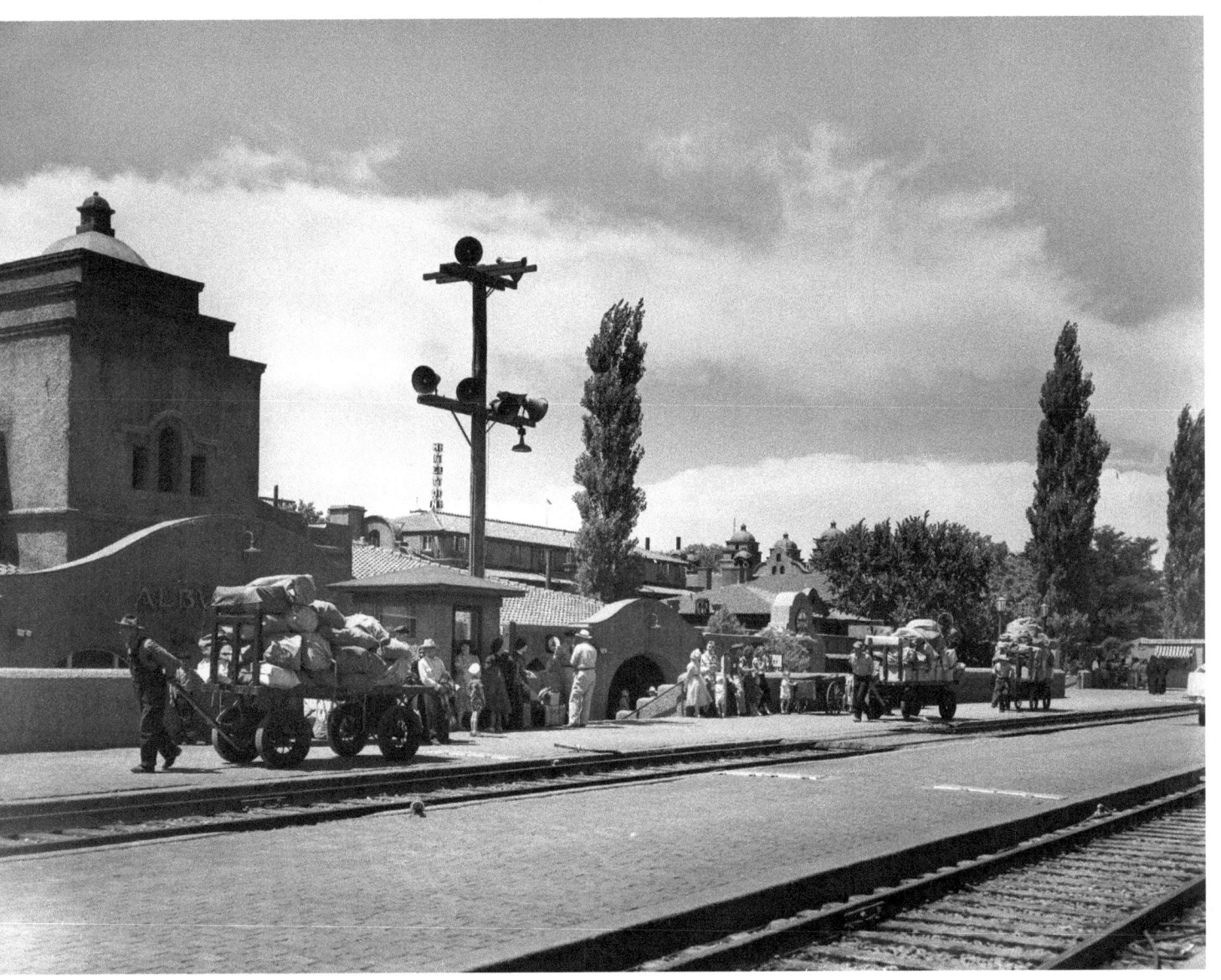

Zia Lodge, along Route 66, 4611 E. Central Avenue. This picture was taken in 1948. The lodge started out with five cabins and carports. The carports were remodeled into rooms, and a swimming pool and sundeck were added.

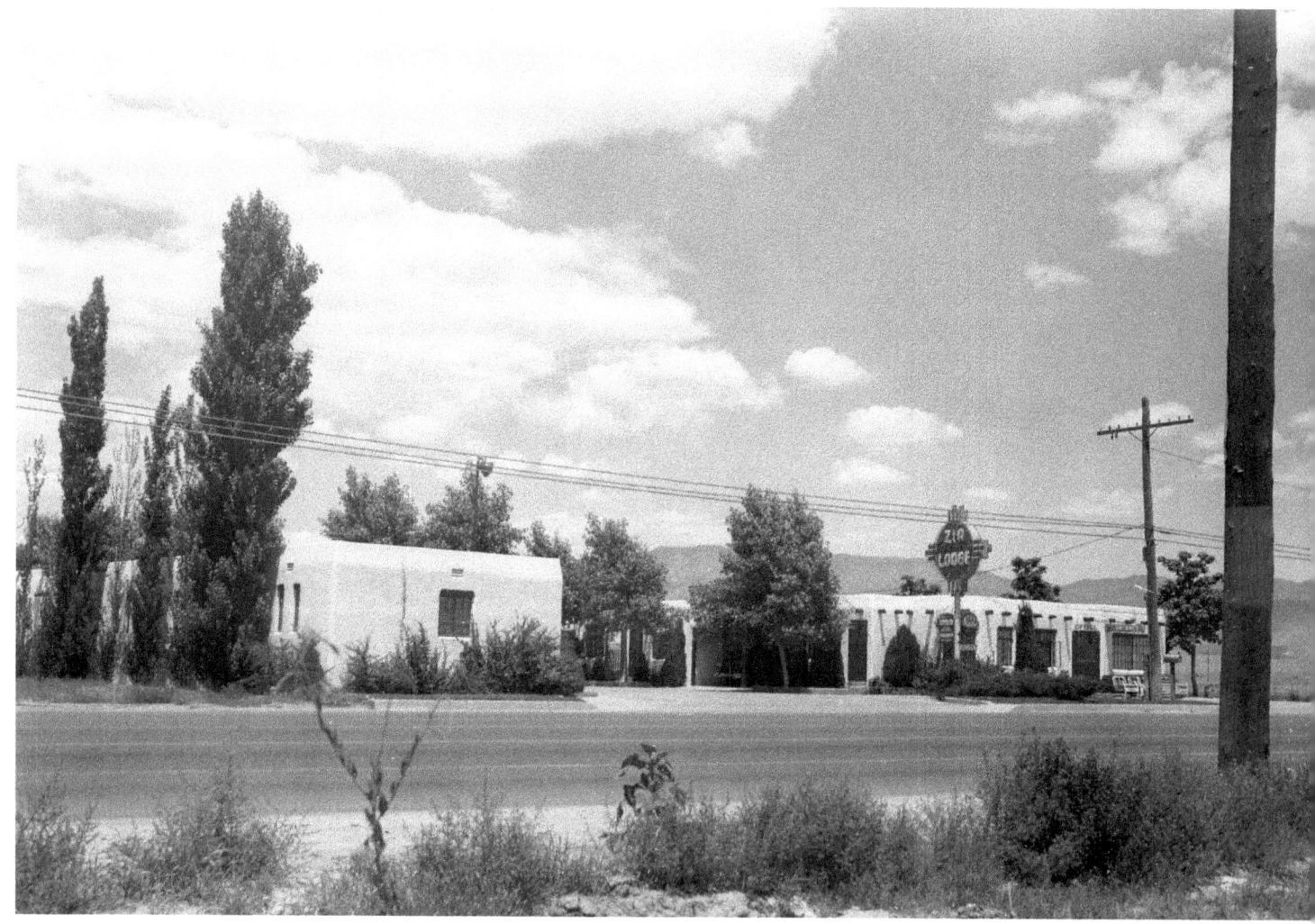

Traffic jam in the 100 block of N. Second Street. Albuquerque National Bank is on the left, the Sunshine Building south of it. Across the street are the Barnett Building and N. T. Armijo Buildings.

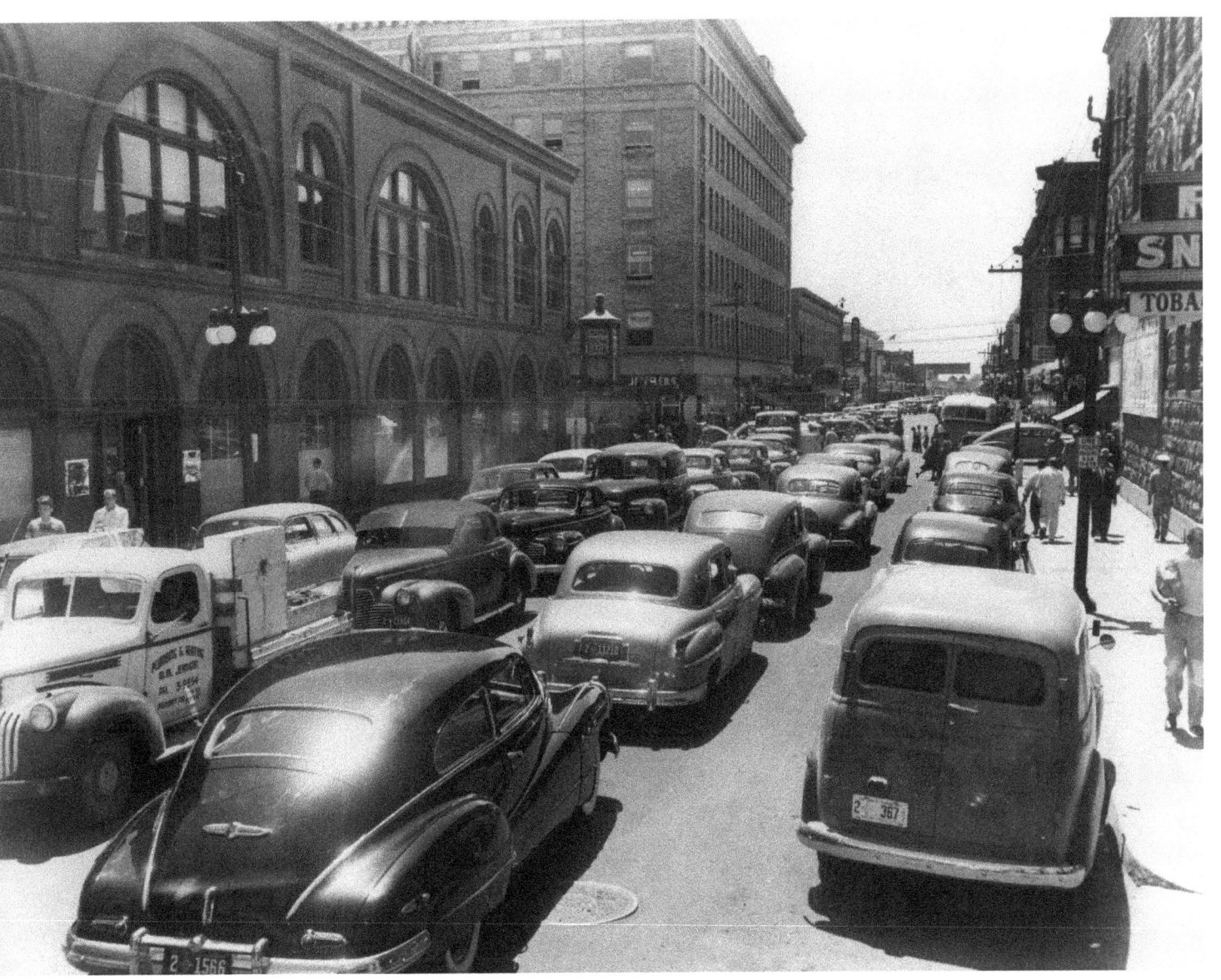

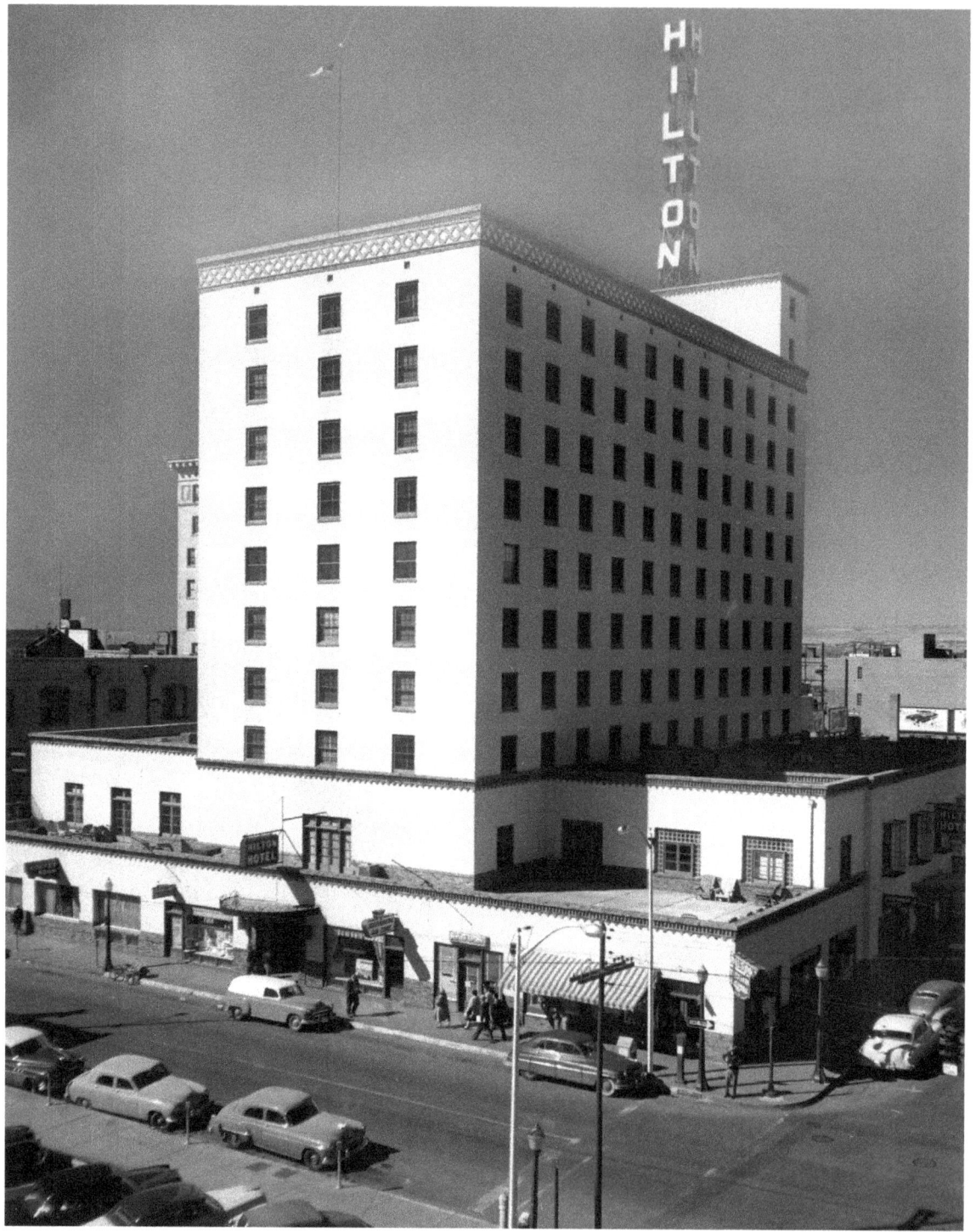

The Hilton Hotel, 125 N. Second Street, was built by Conrad Hilton in 1939. Hilton stayed there with his bride, Zsa Zsa Gabor. It was his fourth hotel. The Hilton Hotel became the La Posada, which is now being restored.

This is a view west on Central Avenue at the Sunshine Theatre, where the first movie shown was *Scaramouche*, starring Ramon Navarro. A live orchestra accompanied the film. Next to the Sunshine was Payless Drugs, in the Barnett Building, where kids all bought school supplies. Across the street are the State Theatre, which opened in 1949; the Grand Central Hotel in the N. T. Armijo Building; Albuquerque National Bank; and Kilroy's Army Surplus Store.

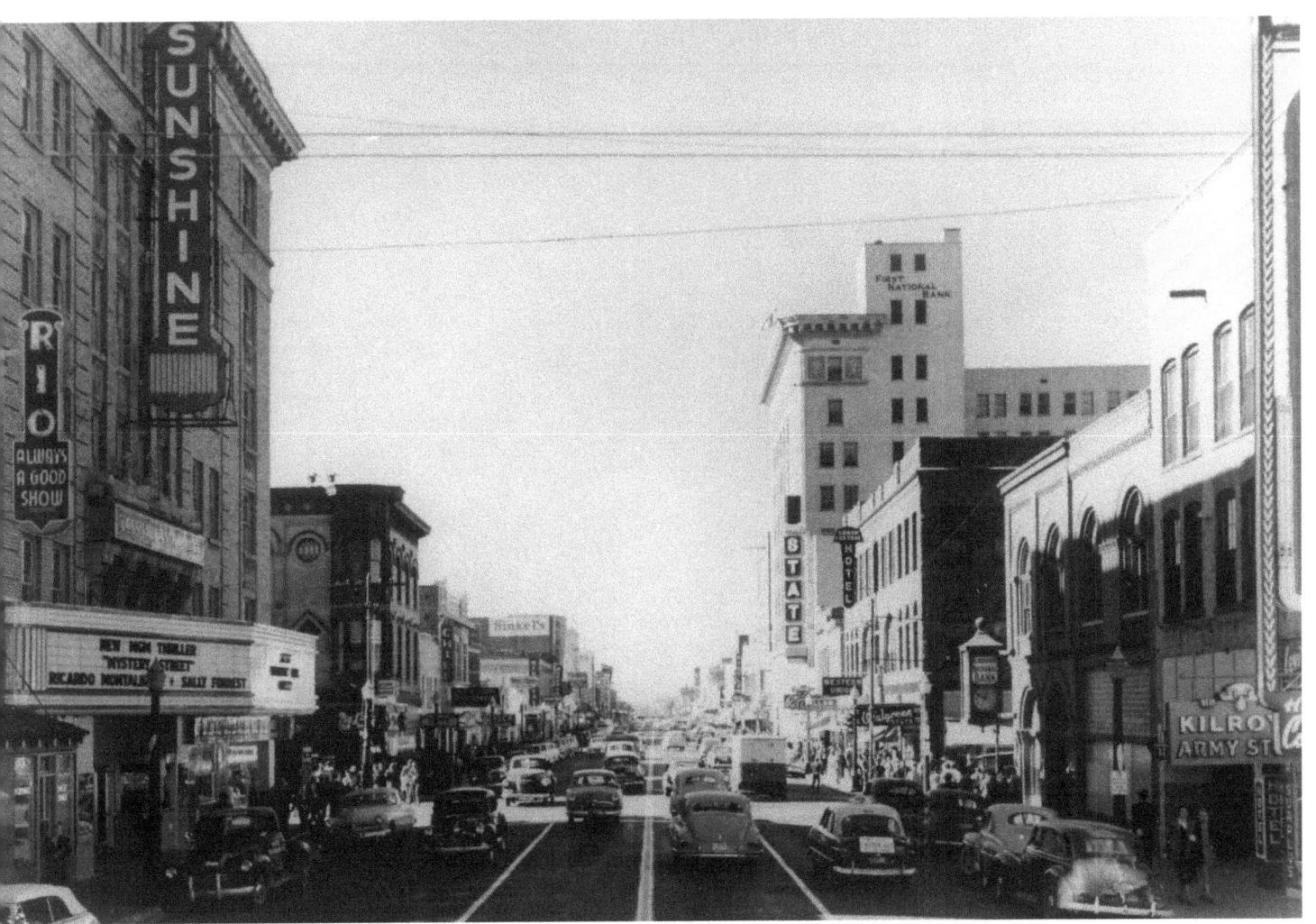

The portal of the Albuquerque Municipal Airport terminal building was a favorite place to watch airplanes land. After the Continental Airliner landed, people could walk right out to it and meet passengers. At this time, going to the airport was a thrill and people dressed up to go there. People went on Sunday drives to the airport, to park and watch the planes come and go.

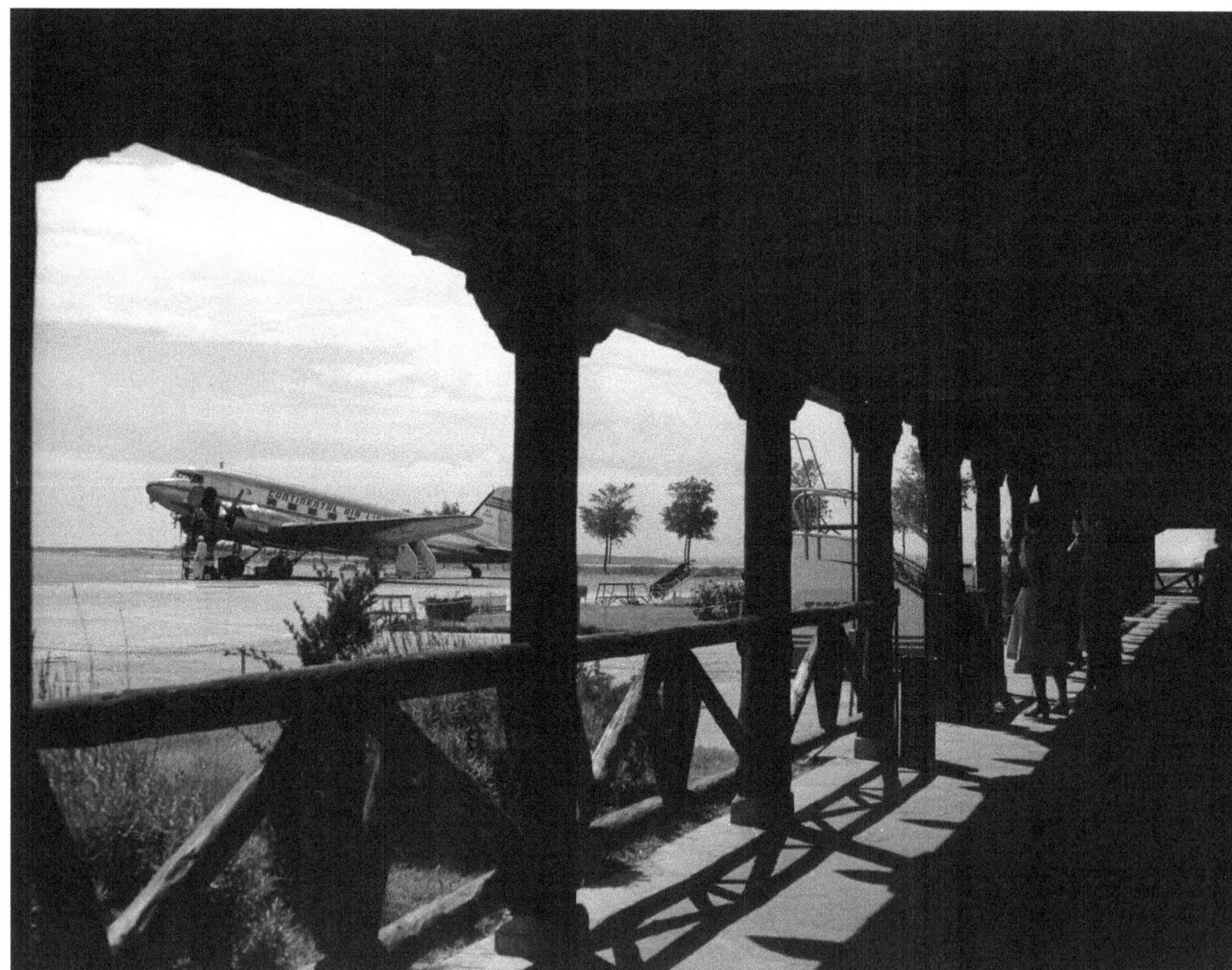

Lucky Boy Hamburgers, 3627 Monte Vista Boulevard, February 1951. Lucky Boy is now Lucky Boy Chinese Food and Hamburgers, on Constitution NE.

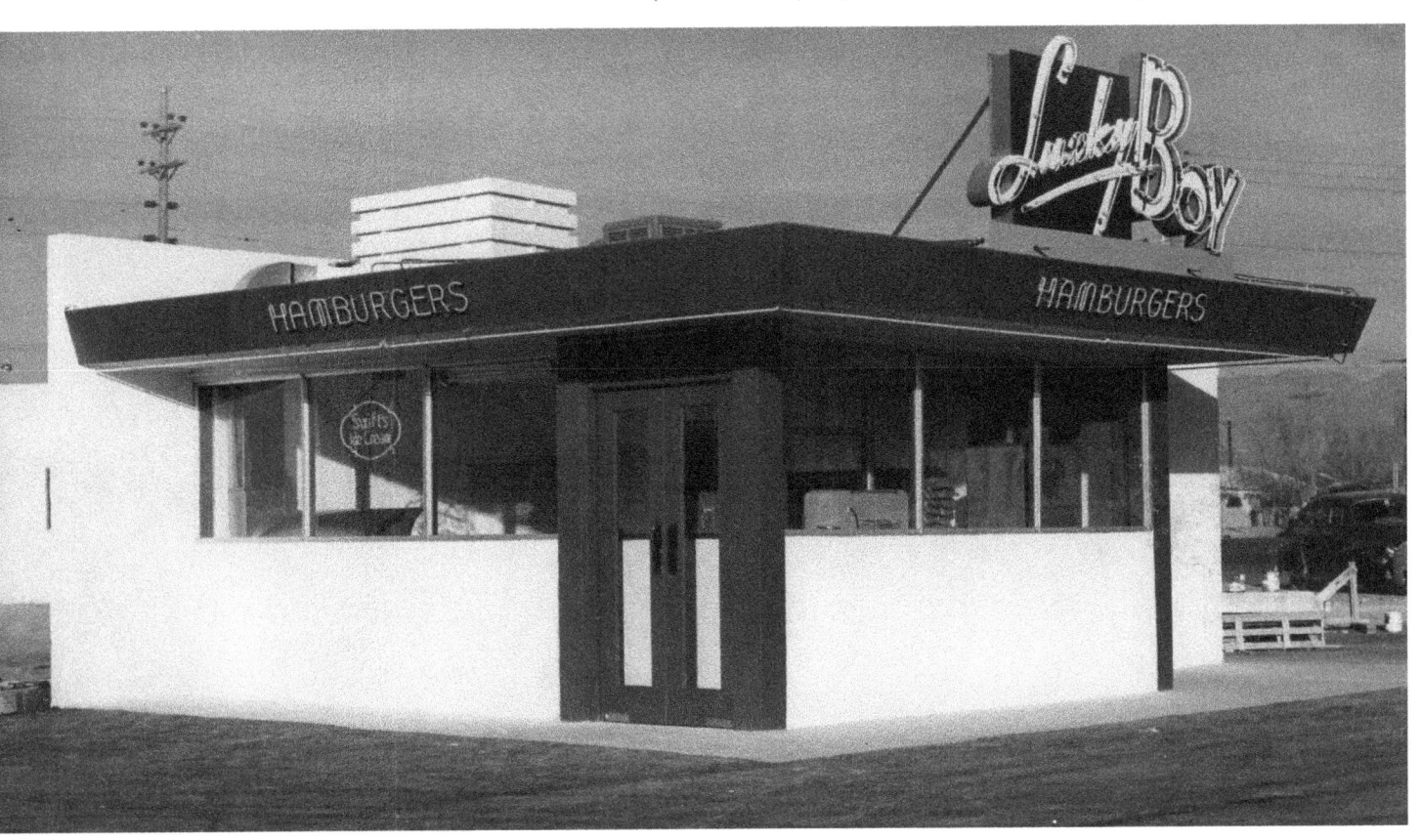

Whiting Bros. Service Station, 10605 E. Central Avenue, February 1951.
Whiting Brothers was founded in 1926 and operated stations all along
Route 66, from Texas to California.

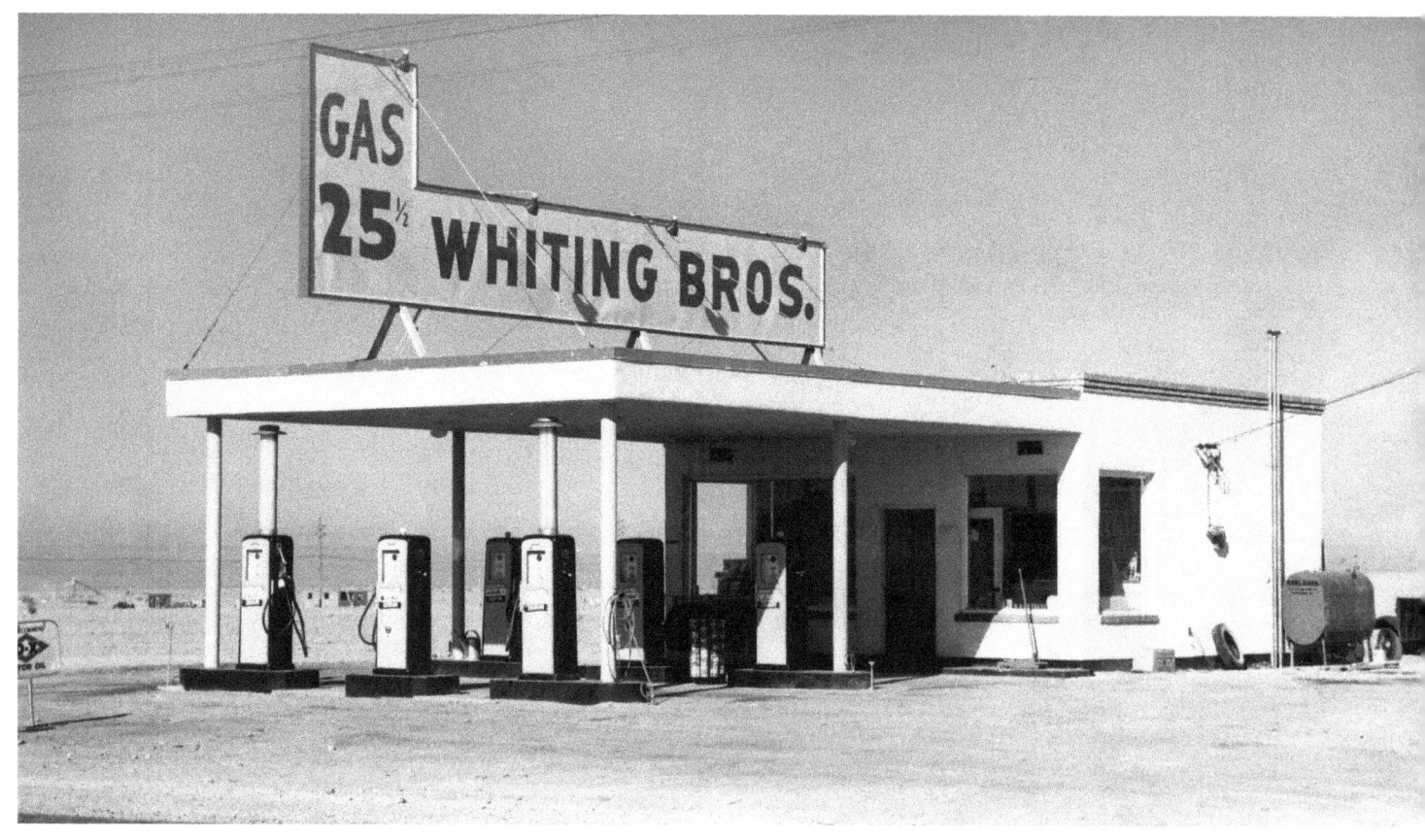

Long distance operators at Mountain States Telephone Company, at Fourth and Copper, November 1953.

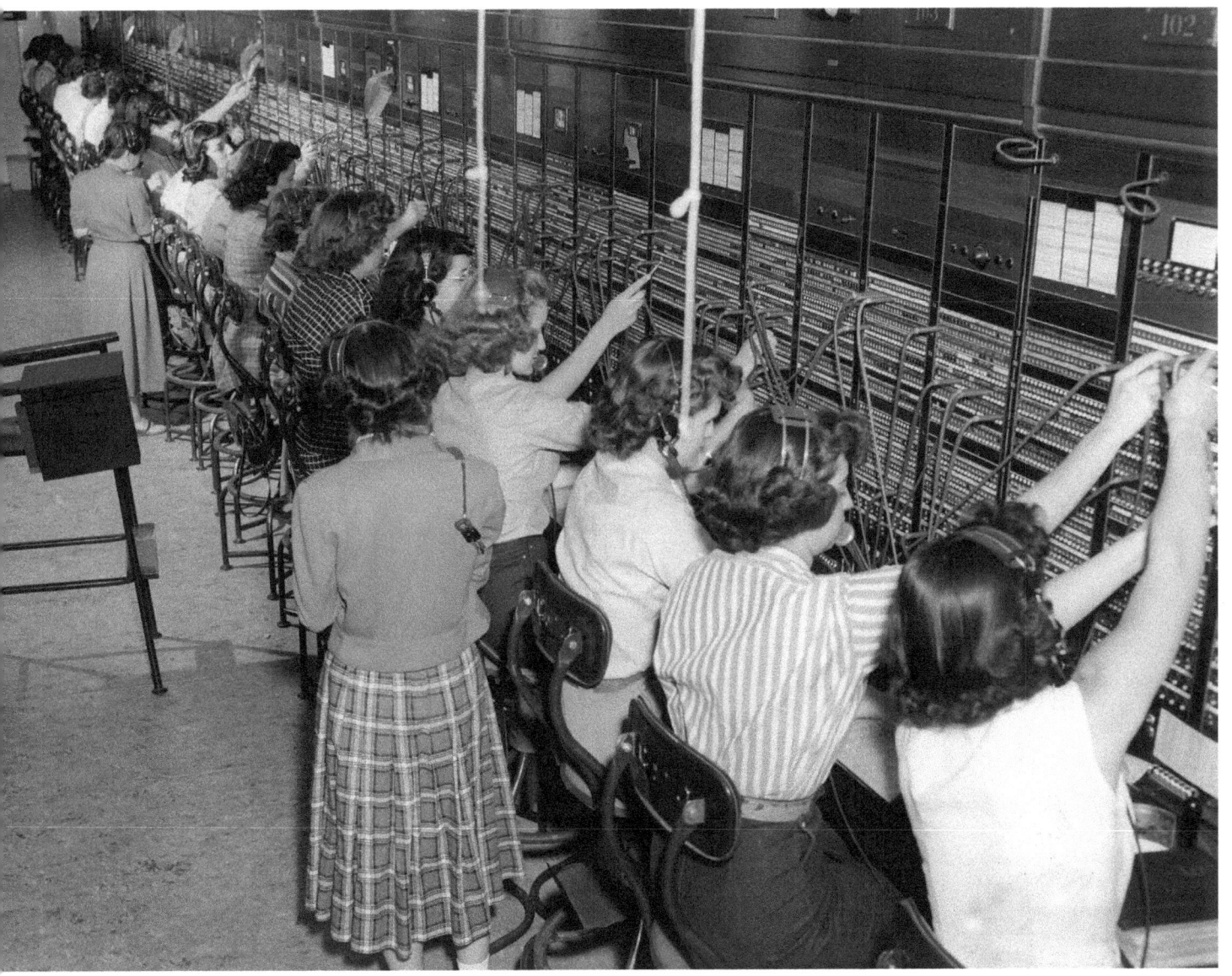

Bernalillo County Courthouse, Fifth and Marquette, opened in 1928. This building replaced the 1886 Bernalillo County Courthouse, in Old Town.

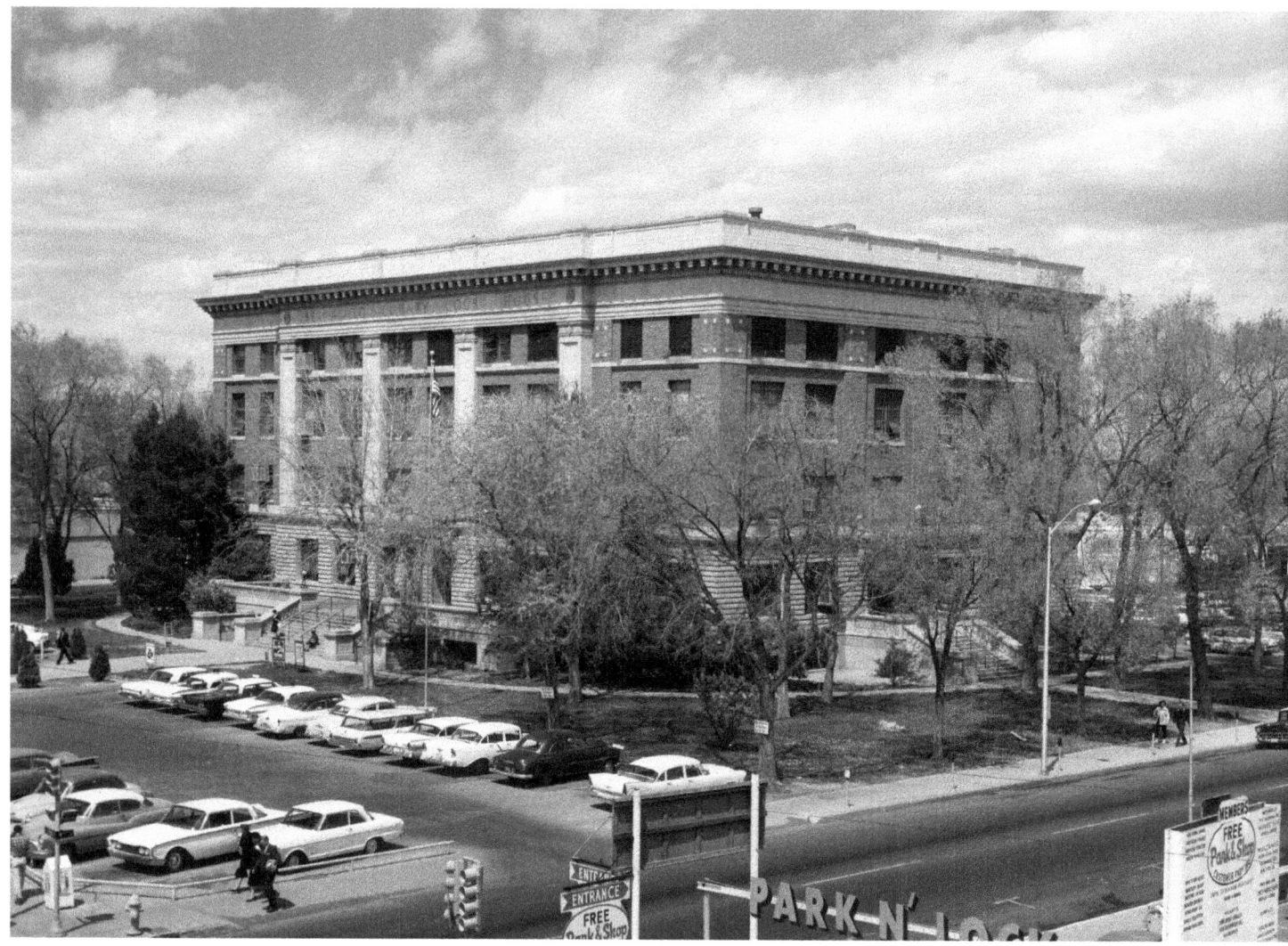

An aerial view of Albuquerque, looking east. The triangular grove of trees is Robinson Park at Eighth and Central. Robinson Park had a bandstand, and people enjoyed concerts there in the late 1800s. Central Avenue extends to the horizon, with Tijeras Canyon beyond. *Tijeras* means "scissors" in Spanish.

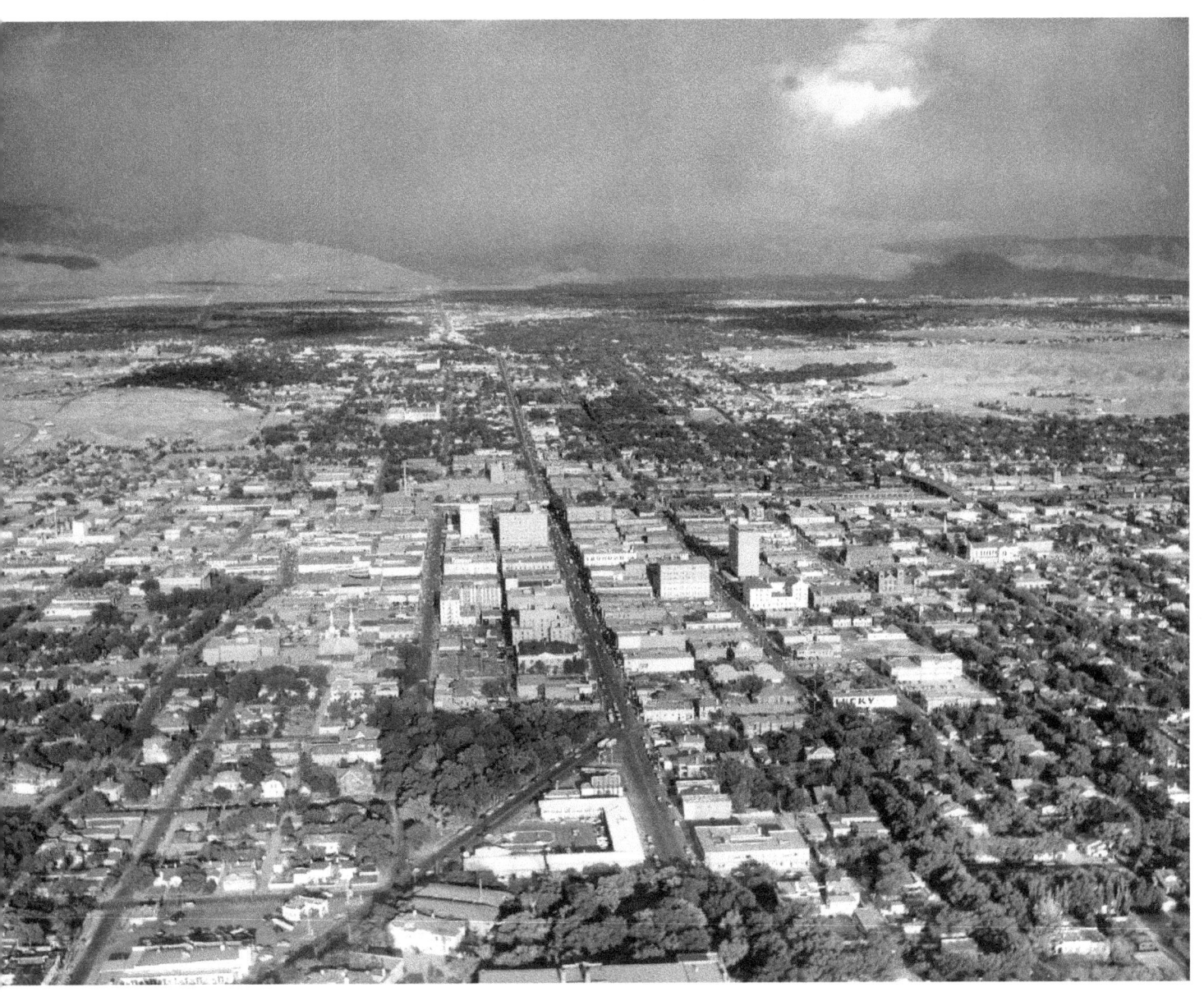

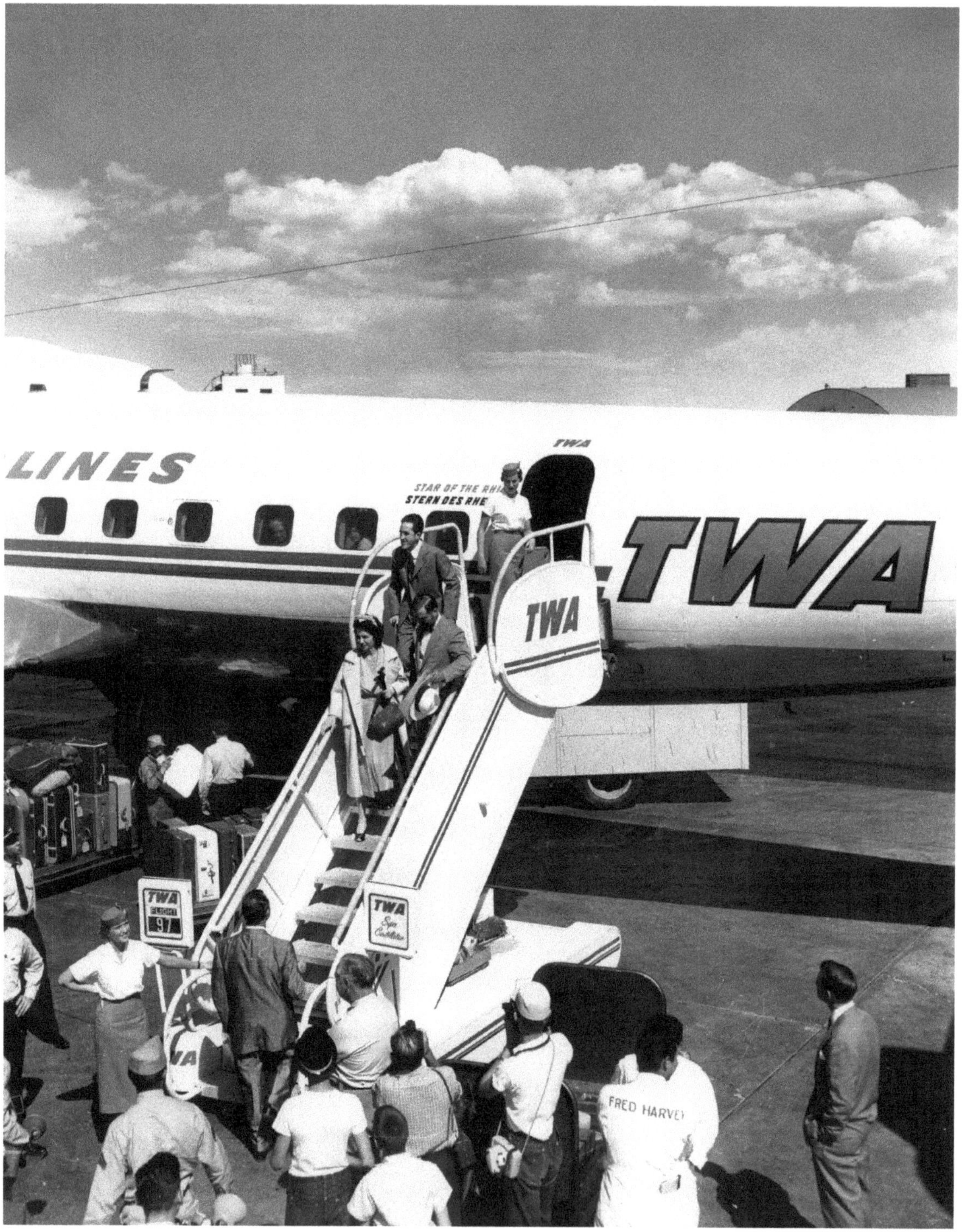

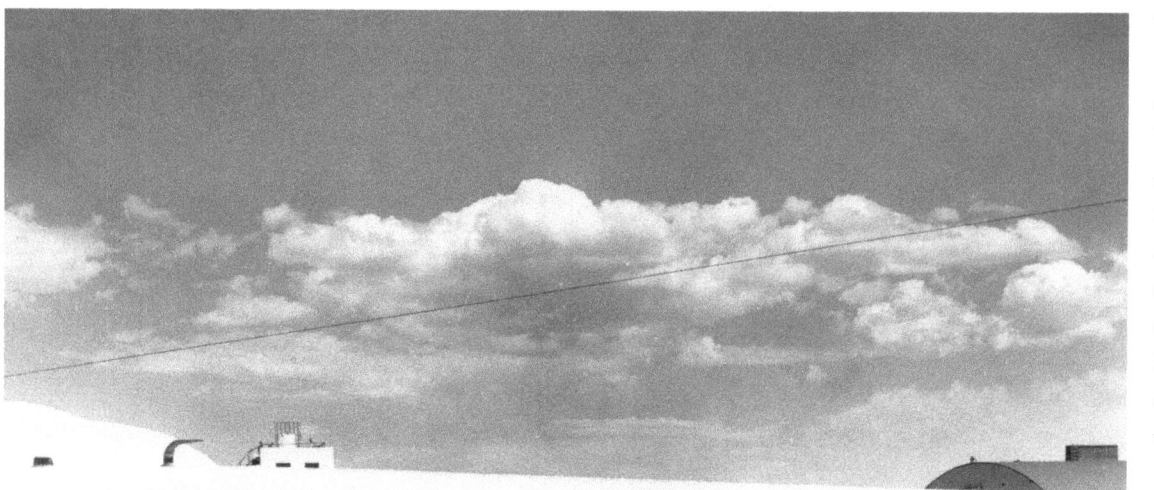

The eighteenth Duke and Duchess of Alburquerque, Spain, getting off a TWA airliner, to help Albuquerque celebrate its 250th Anniversary. Albuquerque, the city, at some point, dropped the extra r from its name. The 250th anniversary of the city, celebrated in July 1956, was called Enchantorama.

Enchantorama, Albuquerque's 250th anniversary. The eighteenth Duke of Alburquerque, Don Beltran Osorio y Diez de Rivera, presented the city with a seventeenth-century *repostero*, an embroidered tapestry, on July 10, 1956. It is on display at the Albuquerque Museum.

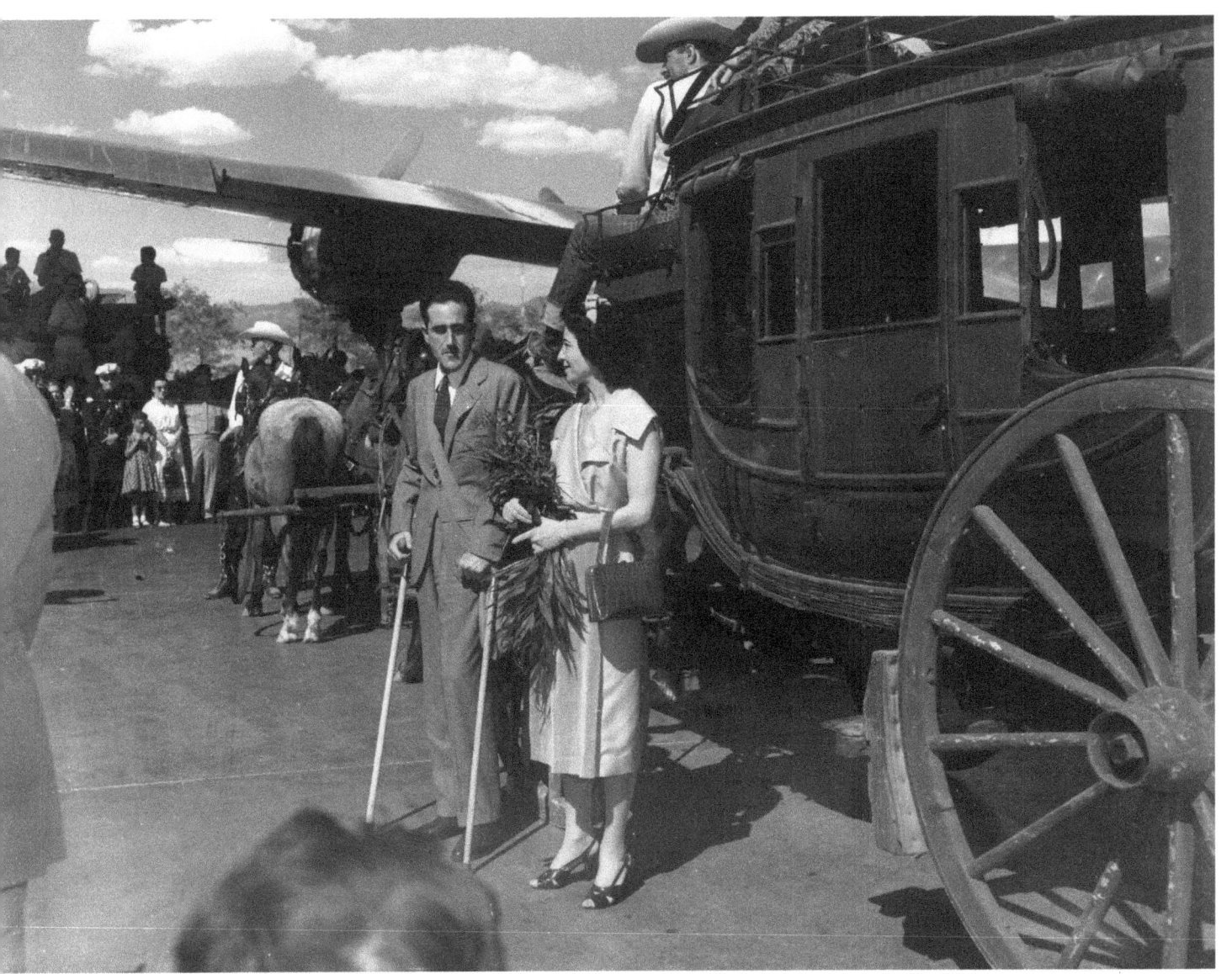

Notes on the Photographs

These notes, listed by page number, attempt to include all aspects known of the photographs. Each of the photographs is identified by the page number, photograph's title or description, photographer and collection, archive, and call or box number when applicable. Although every attempt was made to collect all available data, in some cases complete data was unavailable due to the age and condition of some of the photographs and records.

31 LADDER COMPANY
University of New Mexico
UNM 000-119-0468

32 BASEBALL TEAM
University of New Mexico
UNM 000-119-0437

33 GOLD AVENUE
University of New Mexico
UNM 000-119-0721

34 FAIR PARADE
University of New Mexico
UNM 000-119-0723

35 COMMERCIAL CLUB
University of New Mexico
UNM 000-119-0718

36 DEPOT PARK
University of New Mexico
UNM 000-465

37 ALBUQUERQUE GUARD
University of New Mexico
UNM 000-119-0456

38 ISLETA PUEBLO
Albuquerque Museum
PA 1990.13.126

39 BUILDING CONSTRUCTION
University of New Mexico
UNM 000-119-062

40 BANKER'S CORNER
University of New Mexico
UNM 000-119-0576

41 TRAPEZE ARTIST
Albuquerque Museum
PA 1990.13.160

42 COMMERCIAL CLUB
Albuquerque Museum
PA 1990.13.59

43 BOSS SALOON
University of New Mexico
UNM 000-119-0609

44 HIGHLAND ADDITION
University of New Mexico
UNM 989-024-0001

45 NOVELTY WORKS
Albuquerque Museum
PA 1990.13.77

46 MONTEZUMA SALOON
Albuquerque Museum
PA 1990.13.147

47 GOLD AVENUE
University of New Mexico
UNM 000-119-0591

48 PROGRESS DRY GOODS
Albuquerque Museum
PA 1990.13.75

49 WHOLESALE STORE
Albuquerque Museum
PA 1990.13.48

50 CONGREGATIONAL CHURCH
University of New Mexico
UNM 000-119-0617

51 COLUMBUS HOTEL
Albuquerque Museum
PA 1990.13.22

52 LIVERY STABLE
University of New Mexico
UNM 000-119-0598

53 ADOBE RESIDENCE
Albuquerque Museum
PA 1990.13.228

54 FIRST PRESBYTERIAN
University of New Mexico
UNM 000-119-0616

55 HORSE-DRAWN BUGGY
University of New Mexico
UNM 000-119-0357

56 BLACKSMITH STORE
University of New Mexico
UNM 000-119-0584

57 WASHBURN AND CO.
University of New Mexico
UNM 000-119-0484

58 IMMACULATE CONCEPTION
Albuquerque Museum
PA 1990.13.125

59 DAILY CITIZEN
University of New Mexico
UNM 000-119-0590

60 TRAIN STATION
University of New Mexico
UNM 000-119-0567

61 SECOND STREET
University of New Mexico
UNM 000-119-0578

62 WOMEN'S FOOTBALL TEAM
University of New Mexico
UNM 000-119-0444

63 WHITING BUILDING
University of New Mexico
UNM 000-119-0580

64 GOLD AVENUE
Albuquerque Museum
PA 1990.13.12

65 WHITE ELEPHANT SALOON
University of New Mexico
UNM 000-119-0389

66 YOUTH HOSE CART TEAM
Albuquerque Museum
PA 1990.13.150

68 HOOK AND LADDER CREW
Albuquerque Museum
PA 1990.13.149

69 BEER GARDEN
University of New Mexico
UNM 000-119-0400

70 CACTUS ROADHOUSE
University of New Mexico
UNM 000-119-0483

71 FOOTBALL TEAM
University of New Mexico
UNM 000-119-0443

72 FIRST AUTOMOBILE
University of New Mexico
UNM 000-119-0747

74 BICYCLES
Albuquerque Museum
PA 1990.13.15

75 THIRD STREET
Albuquerque Museum
PA 1973.12.4

76 ED PICKARD
University of New Mexico
UNM 000-119-0702

77 ELKS BURLESQUE PARADE
University of New Mexico
UNM 000-119-0703

78 "MISS ANNIE OAKLEY"
University of New Mexico
UNM 000-119-0701

79 HODGIN HALL
Albuquerque Museum
PA 1978.50.716

80 SANTE FE RAILWAY
STATION
Library of Congress
LC-USZ62-50691

81 BARELAS BRIDGE
Albuquerque Museum
PA 1978.50.65

82 ST. VINCENT'S ACADEMY
Albuquerque Museum
PA 1977.118.2

83 WOMEN'S BASKETBALL
TEAM
University of New Mexico
UNM 2 000-119-0445

84 ARBOR DAY CELEBRATION
University of New Mexico
UNM 000-001

85 PRESIDENT ROOSEVELT
University of New Mexico
UNM 000-119-0724

86 RAILROAD AVENUE
Albuquerque Museum
PA 1990.13.31

87 GIRLS SELLING POTTERY
Albuquerque Museum
PA 1978.50.794

88 STREETCAR PARADE
Albuquerque Museum
PA 1990.13.238

89 HODGIN HALL
University of New Mexico
UMN 0011

90 HODGIN HALL
University of New Mexico
UMN 0011

91 WOMEN'S BASKETBALL
University of New Mexico
UNM 009

92 ALVARADO HOTEL
Albuquerque Museum
PA 1972.31.13

94 HORSELESS CARRIAGE
University of New Mexico
UNM 000-119-0626

95 INDUSTRIAL EXPOSITION
University of New Mexico
UNM 991-030

96 1908 PARADE
University of New Mexico
UNM 0021

97 "ALL THE WAY"
University of New Mexico
UNM 0043

98 EXPOSITION ARCH
University of New Mexico
UNM 0083

99 ARMORY
University of New Mexico
UNM 0024

100 AGRICULTURAL DISPLAY
University of New Mexico
UNM 110 991-030-0057

101 COPPER STREET
Library of Congress
LC-USZ62-50690

102 OLD TOWN PLAZA
Library of Congress
LC-USZ62-50689

103 FIRST STREET
Library of Congress
LC-USZ62-50687

104 BERNALILLO
COURTHOUSE
Library of Congress
LC-USZ62-50688

105 PUEBLO BAND
Albuquerque Museum
PA 1978.50.442

106 TOM INSLEY
Albuquerque Museum
PA 1990-13-241

107 CASTLE HUNING
Albuquerque Museum
PA 1980.154.25

108 LINCOLN BEACHY
Albuquerque Museum
PA 1981.168.27

109 CHARLES F. WALSH
Albuquerque Museum
PA 1978.1.13

110 CHILDREN'S DAY
University of New Mexico
UNM 000-119-0748

111 BARELAS BRIDGE
Albuquerque Museum
PA 1990.13.28

112 BRYANT COMPANY
University of New Mexico
UNM 000-119-0482

113 UNIVERSITY LIBRARY
University of New Mexico
UNM 988-012

114 YMCA GROUNDBREAKING
University of New Mexico
UNM 000-119-0755

115 ALVARADO HOTEL
Albuquerque Museum
PA 1982.180.210

116 INDIAN ROOM
Albuquerque Museum
PA 1982.180.212

118 KORBER BUILDING
Albuquerque Museum
PA 1992.5.14

119 KORBER BLOCK
Albuquerque Museum
PA 1992-5-305

120 COUNTY JAIL
University of New Mexico
UNM GF Small 43

121 NATIONAL GUARD
Albuquerque Museum
PA 1993.004.008

122 MILITARY DRILL
Albuquerque Museum
PA 1993.4.3

123 STREETCAR MOTORETTE
Albuquerque Museum
PA 1992.5.81

124 ARMY TRAINING CORPS
University of New Mexico
UNM 128

126 RIO GRANDE BRIDGES
Albuquerque Museum
PA 1992.5.107

127 HODGIN HALL
Albuquerque Museum
PA 1992.5.615

128 SAN IGNACIO CHURCH
Albuquerque Museum
PA 1994.14.69

129 ELECTRIC STREETCAR
University of New Mexico
UNM 000-119-0692

RESOURCES

Alberts, Don E. *Balloons to Bombers, Aviation in Albuquerque 1882-1945.* The Albuquerque Museum, 1987

Balcomb, Kenneth C. *A Boy's Albuquerque, 1898-1912.* University of New Mexico Press, 1980.

Biebel, Charles D. *Making the Most of It: Public Works in Albuquerque during the Great Depression, 1929-1942.* The Albuquerque Museum, 1986.

Bryan, Howard. *Albuquerque Remembered.* University of New Mexico Press, 2006.

Dewitt, Susan. *Historic Albuquerque Today: an overview survey of historic buildings and districts.* City of Albuquerque, Historic Landmark Survey, 1978.

Fergusson, Erna. *Erna Fergusson's Albuquerque.* Merle Armitage Editions, 1947.

Johnson, Byron A. *Old Town, Albuquerque, New Mexico, A Guide to its History and Architecture.* City of Albuquerque, 1980.

Johnson, Byron A., ed., with Robert K. Dauner. *Early Albuquerque: a Photographic History, 1870-1918.* Albuquerque *Journal* and City of Albuquerque, Albuquerque Museum, 1981.

McIntyre, Wade. *State Fair! the Biggest Show in New Mexico.* McIntyre, 1995.

Palmer, Mo. *Albuquerque Then and Now.* Thunder Bay Press, 2006.

Planning Department, City of Albuquerque. "Albuquerque's Historic Landmarks." 1993.

Rudisill, Richard. *Photographers of the New Mexico Territory, 1854-1912.* Museum of New Mexico, 1973.

Simmons, Marc. *Albuquerque: A Narrative History.* University of New Mexico Press, 1982.

Helen Lowley Emerson and Mike Lowley, Fred Harvey silversmiths, greeting passengers. The airport had a Fred Harvey operated gift shop that showcased many local crafts. Local people even shopped there for presents. The TWA airliner is in front of the terminal building, at the Albuquerque Municipal Airport. The old terminal has been restored.

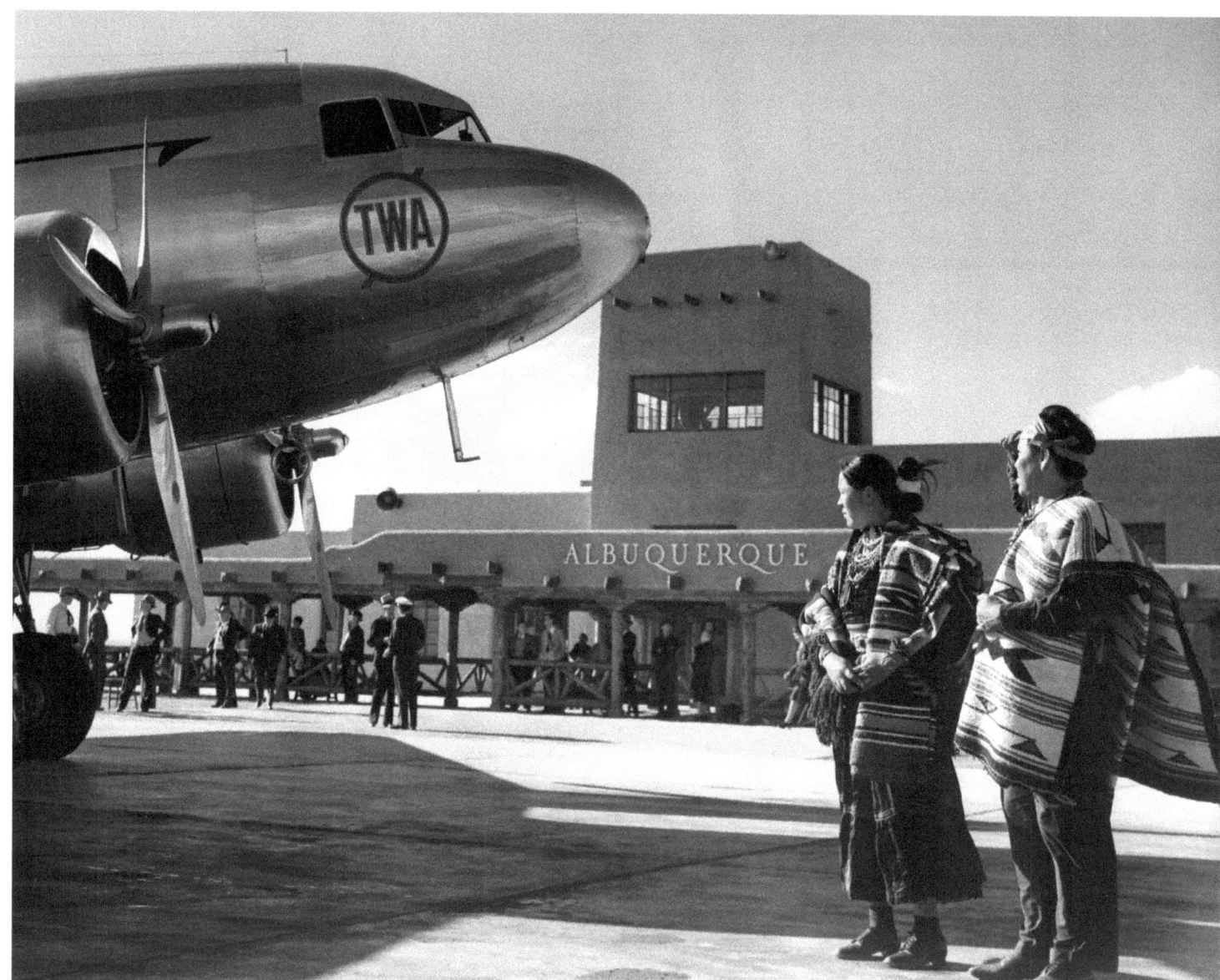

HISTORIC PHOTOS OF
ALBUQUERQUE

Albuquerque is an American city quintessentially founded upon change. From its birth to the present, Albuquerque has consistently built and reshaped its appearance, ideals, and industry. Through changing fortunes, Albuquerque has continued to grow and prosper by overcoming adversity and maintaining the strong, independent culture of its citizens.

Historic Photos of Albuquerque captures this journey through still photography selected from the finest archives. From the arrival of the railroad in 1880 to a population explosion after World War II, *Historic Photos of Albuquerque* follows life, government, education, and events throughout the city's history.

This volume captures unique and rare scenes as depicted in nearly 200 historic photographs. Published in striking black and white, these images communicate historic events and everyday life of two centuries of people building a unique and prosperous city.

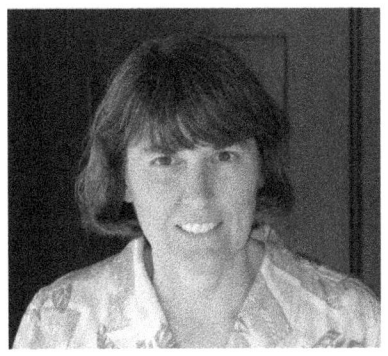

Sandra Fye graduated from the University of New Mexico with a bachelor of arts degree in Geography and an English minor. She is currently the registrar at the National Museum of Nuclear Science and History in Albuquerque.

Sandra has had a long-term interest in photography. She lives in Albuquerque and enjoys the art, history, and geography of New Mexico.

She has written *Historic Photos of El Paso,* also available from Turner Publishing.

WWW.TURNERPUBLISHING.COM

www.ingramcontent.com/pod-product-compliance
Lightning Source LLC
Chambersburg PA
CBHW052134170526
45162CB00003B/14